MONEY TALKS

THE COMPLETE GUIDE TO CREATING A PROFITABLE WORKSHOP OR SEMINAR IN ANY FIELD

Dr. Jeffrey L. Lant

Published by JLA Publications
A Division of Jeffrey Lant Associates, Inc.
50 Follen Street, Suite 507
Cambridge, Massachusetts 02138
Tel: (617) 547-6372

MONEY TALKS

THE COMPLETE GUIDE TO CREATING A PROFITABLE WORKSHOP OR SEMINAR IN ANY FIELD

Dedication:

For Robert Dobson, my friend, who has watched it all happen and gratefully known when to keep quiet.

Copyright Renewed 1988, Jeffrey Lant Associates, Inc.
ISBN 0-940374-08-0

Reproduction of any portion of this book is permitted for individual use if credit is given to Dr. Jeffrey Lant and Jeffrey Lant Associates, Inc. Systematic or multiple reproduction or distribution of any part of this book or inclusion of items in publications for sale is permitted only with prior written permission.

Acknowledgements:

As always, many people have been most generous with their time and information as I've written and produced this book. Two, however, deserve a special mention: Bill Guthy of Cassette Productions, my audio guru, and John Hamwey who has as usual provided his excellent technical assistance in producing this volume.

TABLE OF CONTENTS

SPECIAL PREFACE FOR THE SECOND EDITION		ii
PREFACE		iii
CHAPTER 1	Mental And Technical Prerequisites For Success	1
CHAPTER 2	Creating Programs That Sell	7
CHAPTER 3	Training Yourself: All You Need To Know About Speaking And Presentation	21
CHAPTER 4	Breaking In	37
CHAPTER 5	Successfully Following Up First Engagements	53
CHAPTER 6	Selling Your Participant Prospects: Secrets Of Catalog Copy, Flyers, Brochures, And Paid Advertising	85
CHAPTER 7	Unabashed Promotion	107
CHAPTER 8	Delivering the Successful Program	129
CHAPTER 9	Cashing In I: Profiting On The Spot From Products You Don't Produce And From Those You Do	155
CHAPTER 10	Cashing In II: Producing And Selling Audio Cassettes	171
CHAPTER 11	Cashing In III: Selling And Selling Some More	187
CHAPTER 12	Audio Conferencing & Video Teleconferencing: Your Audience Of Thousands Awaits You	203
CHAPTER 13	Still More Possibilities: The Lecture Circuit And The Talk Conglomerate	217
CHAPTER 14	Taking Care Of Business	235
CHAPTER 15	On Your Own: Succeeding In Self-Sponsored Programs	247
CONCLUSION		262
SAMPLES SECTION		263
ABOUT THE AUTHOR		292
JEFFREY LANT'S SURE-FIRE BUSINESS SUCCESS CATALOG		293

SPECIAL PREFACE FOR THE SECOND EDITION

Dear Friend,

Since I wrote this book — the third volume of my "Get Ahead" Series — it has become generally recognized as perhaps the most thorough and detailed volume ever written on how to make money talking — and more particularly by talking at lectures, workshops and seminars.

This is something I've been doing now for a decade, something I expect to be doing the rest of my life. For good reason:

- I use talk programs to make immediate profit. Handled properly, talk programs are very lucrative, a source of continuing income for you.

- I use talk programs to connect with new clients. I've always gathered a significant fraction of my consulting clients from talk programs, and so will you. And what could be better than having your prospects pay a fee to attend a talk program that convinces them to hire you?

- I use talk programs to get superb publicity, publicity that enhances my professional image and that brings word about my products and services to large numbers of people. The great thing about publicizing talk programs is that you can benefit from the publicity even if people don't attend the program!

- I use talk programs to make friends and influence people, that intoxicating combination. I feel better when members of an audience supercharge me with their enthusiasm and, yes, their gratitude. And, in turn, they are better because they've had the benefit of hearing my ideas about how to improve their lives. Talk programs make this crucial symbiosis possible.

You can get all this — and more — from talk programs. If you'll follow the suggestions of **MONEY TALKS**. Don't just read this book once. Refer to it often — until you feel confident that you are deriving every possible advantage from the talks you're giving.

And stay in touch with me — as thousands of people already do. I like to know what you've done and how I may have helped you. If you didn't get this book directly from me, send me your address, too, so I can send you my Sure-Fire Business Success Catalog and other information I keep developing. **MONEY TALKS** isn't an end; it's a means. And I keep making the means better. As you do, thanks, in part, to this very book!

Very much your get-ahead friend,

Jeffrey

PREFACE

Why I Wrote This Book

Workshops, seminars and lectures are a superb way of making money. I know. I give over 100 presentations annually at colleges and universities, trade associations, events organized by other entrepreneurs and at those I mount myself. If you know something, have the solution to someone else's problem, have the expertise, technical dexterity, information and presentation skills, you ought to consider an occasional seminar or workshop. Even though you do only one or two a month, you can make thousands of dollars of additional income each year. Who couldn't use that?

I say this as straightforwardly as I can: if you have technical proficiency of some kind and cannot make money from this book, it's your own fault. If, however, you follow the many suggestions in these pages, you will succeed and your investment in this book will be returned thousands of times over.

Why MONEY TALKS Is Necessary

The available information on this subject is thin at best. There is little of it and much of what's been written tends to deal with independently-produced programs. I deal with that subject last for a very good reason. Independent programs can produce a terrific return on your investment — can. But they are for those who have extra money to risk and a good deal of experience in all facets of the talk business. I don't advise anyone to start at that level, and I won't advise you to do it either. This book gets as close to guaranteeing your success as any self-help book can. It lays out a comprehensive, comprehensible plan and model for you to follow as you develop your skills and become seasoned in this business. I am not going to ask you to take any risks that I haven't taken myself and don't know about.

I know what I'm talking about. Too many people writing self-help books don't. I read as many volumes of this genre as anyone in the nation, and it's a wonder my blood pressure stays normal. There's no theoretical meandering in this book. Here are the pros and cons of this line of work and of the various techniques to make it pay off for you. I don't want you hanging like so many self-help books make you hang. One story epitomizes all that is wrong with the genre. A mail order self-help I was reading this year suggested that egg carton advertising made sense. What it didn't say was how much it cost, whom to contact, the items that work best in egg cartons and those that don't, in short everything you wanted and needed to know. I find these lapses reprehensible and have worked hard so that you won't find them in my book.

If, however, you're still unsure of a technique, call me. I have a responsibility to my readers and I intend to meet it. My number is liberally sprinkled throughout the text and I answer my own telephone. If you want a clarification, ask me. If I think you need more extensive consulting assistance, I'll tell you. Fair enough?

I consistently hear from those already in continuing education that they are not making enough money. This book is for you. Many people in the continuing education, lecture world make peanuts. Then again either they haven't thought through what they should be offering or they don't have a plan. Often, too, they are exploited by those who hire them. This book will right the situation on all counts. After you've read it, you'll have a plan and a model to follow and ways of increasing your take and entering into juster, fairer relationships with program planners.

I wrote this book because people with technical information and proficiency are becoming smarter about how to capitalize on their skills and on what they know. Developing a workshop/lecture component is yet another way of doing that. It's part of what I call the Mobile Mini Conglomerate. Those of you who have taken my workshop programs are already familiar with this concept. It's a multi-step wealth generating machine, a circuit of possibilities for those with knowledge, information and expertise at their command. It consists of the following parts:

- Selling what you know as a consultant by the hour or day (directly billable time).

- Retainer contracts with those who pay you a fixed, flat fee usually monthly in return for your guarantee that they will have a certain amount of your time.

- Supergroup of Independent Contractors. Here you benefit by taking a percentage of the fees of those professionals you market to your clients in fields other than your own.

Preface

- Supergroup of Products (Cooperative Marketing Agreements, Drop Shipping). You take a percentage of all product sales made to those with whom you do business, but you don't manufacture or warehouse the products, just promote them.

- Writing articles about what you know.

- Producing newsletters about what you know.

- Producing books about what you know.

- Producing audio and video cassettes about what you know.

- Producing workshops and seminars about what you know.

- Producing lectures about what you know.

- Buying and selling related or unrelated properties like any other conglomerate.

I call this the *Mobile* Mini Conglomerate because with it you'll be doing a lot of travelling. I call it *Mini* because you can keep it small and profitable with the least possible expense and the greatest conceivable return. And I call it a *Conglomerate* because as you develop and become more and more profitable you'll be functioning just like any other conglomerate anywhere in the world buying and selling related and unrelated properties.

Remember these words: *Mobile Mini Conglomerate*. You can make a lot of money from them.

MONEY TALKS is designed so that you can launch a profitable side line without leaving your present job. With this book in hand, you can turn a couple of evenings a month and a couple of week-ends into profit centers. Deregulation of the airlines has made this objective all the more possible. If you live in the Eastern United States, two thirds of the population of the country is within easy access of you. It's a little trickier in the West thanks to the greater distances involved and the less dense population, but even so, you can probably leave home on Friday afternoon, deliver a workshop anywhere within a thousand mile radius and be home for a late dinner the next evening — all at a cost you can comfortably assume even if your expenses are not covered by the booking organization as they sometimes will not be. This is a fact of incalculable importance and one that you should be regularly exploiting.

Most of the prevailing literature seems perverse and wrongheaded to me. It shows you how to create and find an audience. That's not at all where I'm coming from. This book will show you effectively how to go after audiences which are already gathered, that is how to minimize your marketing and maximize your return. Only those who are seasoned and are sure of their product should be chasing an audience. I don't do it and neither should you.

This book extends my series of self-help books and I commend them to you. Each has been successful and I anticipate that this one will be no different. My confidence in this matter bothers certain reviewers who feel that authors ought to be humble and perhaps contrite as they launch their books upon the public's consciousness. I am not. I have done my homework. I know that people conscientiously following my advice will do well, often very, very well from it. I have seen the results that my other books have brought to people, and I have a filing cabinet stuffed with unsolicited testimonials. Moreover, I do not choose to regard with much interest the jeremiads of the occasional critic who has spent at most a few hours with my material when I have lived these suggestions for years and years. Let them make what they will of this flourish! The fact remains that this is a book which you will use for the remainder of your professional life and which will pay for itself over and over again from the first day you implement my suggestions. You are getting a disproportionate benefit compared to fee, and I believe myself entitled to feel glowingly about it!

Yet another reason why I have launched this book is to use it as the course text in a new workshop of the same name. If this book appeals to you and you'd like to attend one of these workshops, kindly let me know. You can drop me a line if you'd like to be contacted about such workshops or other books and materials emanating from me.

It goes without saying that I've written this book to make money. As this book goes to press, I can report that **THE CONSULTANT'S KIT**, the first book in this series, has grossed well over a half million dollars and **THE UNABASHED SELF-PROMOTER'S GUIDE** has done over a quarter of a million in gross sales. Moreover, the sales on neither book

Preface

show any signs of diminishing. This book will do well, too. That's as it should be. I remain an unreconstructed believer that we who assist other people, who do good, should do well in the process. Keep this belief as your credo and you, too, will do well. There's nothing wrong with making money; the only ones who will cavil are those who are tinged with jealousy and who would somehow like to gild their own failure to achieve significant results. I have no time for such people.

Many people have told me after reading one or another of my books that they feel as if they know me and call me up or write as if we were old friends, without barrier or initial awkwardness. That's also as it should be. I do look upon my readers as friends and look upon a book as a sustained communication between us. In this connection, it helps to know just a little about me and how I work. Inevitably you will alter the model to suit yourself. Particulars will change. Circumstances will be different. You must be prepared to change with them and make appropriate modifications which will insure and continue your success. Even so, it helps to know with whom you will be spending some time.

I operate a one-man show. I have no clerical staff and no support staff except for a handy-man, delivery boy who also functions as house-cleaner (a necessary luxury). All the others who work with me are independent contractors. I have developed a system, the workshop/seminar/lecture portion of which constitutes the heart of this book, which minimizes expense and ensures profit. I suffer from no false need for protection from the world. My telephone number is on millions of brochures, catalogs, *etc.* But I unhesitatingly answer my own telephone, a trick I learned from one of the richest men in the nation who does the same. If you call or write me with an idea, I'll deal with it myself, and I'll type the letter in which I respond.

As I said in **THE CONSULTANT'S KIT**, I put $100 into my business over 9 years ago and not a cent more. All the money of the firm has been raised by the firm and my activities and products.

I spend part of each day on the creation of new products like this one; I spend another part of each day on marketing and promotion to new clients and through the media. I spend a portion of every day reading new materials which keep me current in selected fields. I also have a bevy of private consulting clients in a variety of states, and I travel a great deal. In any given year I will be in between 30 to 40 states, often several times. The way to make this work is to put packages together; this is partly what this book is about — how to get maximum return from any given connection.

Now that you know this much about why I wrote this book and a little about your author, let me tell you what you'll find in **MONEY TALKS**.

Section I deals with your introduction to the subject, the mental and technical prerequisites for your success. To succeed you must put yourself in the mind for success, and you must simultaneously develop the necessary skills which will bring about and ensure that success. You will learn how to create programs that sell and about the Problem Solving Process Workshop, the key to your success and the heart of your workshop/seminar programs. This is a multi-step process which enables you to structure your presentations whether you are giving a 50-minute lecture or a multi-day institute. It enables you to find the material you need and shows you how to organize it. I find the method invaluable, and I commend it to you.

Once you have psyched yourself up and crafted a saleable product, I want to spend some time on helping you master the essentials of training. Here you'll come to know what to do to deliver a winning presentation.

We then go on to selling. It is a truism, but nonetheless worth stating, that fine programs are created only to die on the vine and that many mediocre ones flourish like weeds. Undoubtedly, part of the reason for this unfortunate disparity is to be found in how both are sold.

You will learn how to break into the world of workshops and seminars, how to take your early success (and indeed any success) and leverage it through The Success Letter and garner further assignments, each more lucrative than the last. I will explore the essentials of the business contracts and relationships you need to develop with your clients.

Selling in this world is, of course, a two-tier process. First, you must sell program sponsors, trade associations, deans and directors of continuing education and in-house planning directors on your services. Then, in all but the last case (where attendance is deemed mandatory), you must sell those who will pay the cost of the program.

You will find a chapter on selling your audience through brochures, direct mail and other means. You will find a chapter on selling your audience through the free media — newsletters, radio, television, magazines and newspapers.

Preface

Thereafter we go on to the day itself: all that needs to happen to make your program a success from the moment you get into the taxi to leave for the program. I include a detailed check list of all that can — and probably will — go wrong and what you can do about it. As you develop your workshop and seminar program, you will want to take this book with you as a helpful guide and quick check (and you'll probably want to sell it, too. Don't worry: I have a mechanism!)

Once you have had a successful program, I'm going to show you how to sell more programs to your original sponsor and cement the link. Success breeds success. Once you've got it, hold on and exploit it! This is the first of three phases of program follow-up which need to be accomplished.

Phase II is leveraging your success and selling the unconverted. You will learn how to get access to new organizations where you can make presentations through networking, through the development of your own catalog with program descriptions and other means.

Phase III involves selling to your audience. One of the several ways you can make money on the workshop/lecture circuit is by getting your audience to become your clients. I'll show you how.

This chapter serves as the introduction to the section of **MONEY TALKS** entitled "Making Real Money." Many people do not do well in the lecture business. By this I mean they make $100 to $300 per day, put in hours of preparation time and leave exhausted, depleted. This isn't at all what I have in mind for you! Or you for yourself! That's where "Making Real Money" comes in.

We begin with a chapter on "Back of the Room" sales, well known to every successful practitioner of the talk trade, that is the sale of topic related products to your audience. Many lecturers actually make more from their product sales than from their workshop fees. I have many days like this myself! You will learn how to increase your profit when you don't have a product and how to develop profitable booklets, books and cassette productions which not only make money for you but act as your advertising agents, keeping your name before your customers and attracting new ones, too.

I will tell you, in another chapter, how to sell newsletters and other publications as sponsors for your programs and how to enter into profitable business relationships with them. We live in the age of vertical media, that is highly specific, focused publications appealing to precise demographic groups with defined interests. This is very good news for you, the workshop entrepreneur, if you have programs that will interest the particular readership of any given publication. The key is to know your market, identify the right publications and master the two-tier sales process: first to the publication executive and then to the ultimate buying audience.

You will learn how to create annual programs and conferences that act as a long-term annuity for you and how to succeed in audio conferencing and video teleconferencing, something new, something very lucrative indeed.

I'll tell you how to master the lecture circuit, and I provide specific methods of selling yourself to a lecture agency and where to find the leads you need.

Finally, in Chapter 15, I present detailed information on how to produce your own independent programs and the necessary preconditions which help insure success in what can be a very profitable venture.

MONEY TALKS is like all my books. It is the product of my extensive experience, and it is packed with letters, contracts, marketing documents, and other materials which you can use and reuse year after year. The way to read this book is pen in hand. Mark it up! As you read, write down your ideas in the margins and keep a running "Task Action List" for yourself. Write down what you want to do and give yourself a deadline for doing it. The methods in this book work! I know! But they will not work, cannot work for the slothful, the disspirited, the timorous, the unprepared and the impatient.

MONEY TALKS is not a get rich quick book. It is, however, a book that will enable you to make money regularly and keep a good percentage of it. You can get rich following my methods but only if you keep working at them. Just as I do, day after day.

Preface

One last word. I have tried whenever possible in this book to delete the much argued-about masculine pronoun. Occasionally it has crept out and may affront those who are on the alert for such evidences of inequality. Don't let it bother you! Don't let a pronoun, written in an attempt to save the endangered English sentence, create a barrier to your understanding and profiting from what I've writing about. If you do, more's the pity, but it's your problem, not mine.

Having offered this caveat, let me offer no more. Profit, fame, new clients, the joy of name recognition, the satisfaction of helping others all this and more lies before you in the pages ahead. It is with a thrill that I offer it all to you.

> J.L.
> Cambridge, MA
> June, 1988

PREPARING TO SUCCEED

Chapter 1

MENTAL AND TECHNICAL PREREQUISITES FOR SUCCESS

You are about to embark on a useful, profitable and extraordinarily enjoyable career whether full or part-time. This chapter will help you prepare yourself for what you'll be doing. To do so, you must be both mentally and technically prepared.

This book is largely about sales: selling to potential program sponsors and selling to prospective program participants. To succeed in sales takes a certain mindset. You must, to begin with, believe in yourself. This is of course easy to do when you're rich, popular, sought after and successful. It's less easy to do, perhaps even onerous, when you're not. Stop right now! Don't get into any sales situation — including those that I shall recommend to you in **MONEY TALKS** — until you've spent a few minutes communing with yourself, being honest about how you feel about yourself and what you are contemplating. Success, as has so often been said, breeds success, but just as surely failure breeds failure.

You must believe in your product, in this case the value of the information you'll be imparting to people. Will it really help them? If not, you may have a bit of transitory success, but it won't last long. People who sell pap don't succeed for very long. Most people don't realize that with more than 230 million people in America this is in fact a small country! I am constantly amazed by how much is known about me by those I deal with and how people talk. They'll talk about you, too. Perhaps only a little at first. Later, more and still more. Word of mouth is a powerful advertising tool and if people have only bad things to say about you, you can rest assured they will say them — to your incalculable detriment. Don't begin to sell yourself until you believe in yourself. Don't sell any product that you don't believe in.

This means, of course, that you must use your own advice and information. Do what you say. It will give you a credibility which can only help you. If you recommend products, use them. If you recommend techniques and services, use them. This authenticity will be of the utmost assistance to you and help build your credibility.

Develop the mindset of a winner. You must start from the first day, from this very minute, believing that you will win. I begin each sales call with the expectation that I will make a sale or that at the very least I will begin to create a relationship that will result in due course in a sale. I am willing to make the investment with that source because of my belief, my vision if you will, that that sale will take place. If you have done your homework, if you have developed a marketable program, if you have identified a real buyer prospect (not just someone who might conceivably be interested), and if you have approached this prospect in the proper fashion, you deserve to feel this confidence, indeed you ought to feel it. Many people wrongly condemn this confidence as unwarranted arrogance. Let them. They are wrong, quite wrong. You are entitled to the feeling of confidence if you are prepared when you begin. You are entitled to the glow that emanates from you when you have this confidence.

Understand that you are not asking for a favor when you approach people with a proposition that is well considered, well thought through and which has benefitted from your careful consideration. You are offering the chance for mutual gain, mutual benefit, and you should not be hesitant about saying so.

I approach prospective seminar and workshop buyers in this way: I have thought long and hard about the substance of this program. I know that it is needed and I have the evidence to support this conclusion. I have thought long and hard about whether to bring it to your attention. I have reasons why I think you'd be interested in what I've got to say. Interested because it will be to your benefit. You'll profit from my idea financially but you'll also know that you've helped others by disseminating useful information they need. Having so considered the matter of the program and your potential benefit, I have nothing to feel ashamed about in approaching you, nothing to fear in what you might say or do. Remember: there's no need for you to feel sheepish about approaching program sponsors. You're not asking for a favor.

Having got this far, expect your prospective client/sponsor to be less certain of his self-interest than you are. Most people, contrary to good nineteenth century liberal theory, are not very clear about what will benefit them. They are muddled, fuzzy, uncertain, incomplete in their knowledge and uncertain in their movements. This is where you come in. You have a vision of a better world for them, a more profitable world, a world which can be born from your well-considered programs. Expect the sponsor prospects to need a little prodding, some persuasion, time to think and consider. Never stop the process moving ahead using all the specific sales strategies I shall be proposing in other chapters. Supersales people understand that it is their responsibility to keep the ball rolling.

Chapter 1

Part of the right mental attitude is your approach to money. It's important not to apologize or get defensive about your fees. Here's the right positioning for yourself, "I state fees. I do not discuss them." If you have made the decision that people will benefit from your workshop (and by people, I mean sponsors as well as participants), you need not apologize for its fee. Mentally this is a very hard position for many people to take; they feel they ought to give away what they know or else they won't be liked. Let me tell you something: you're not running for office. You're not a candidate for homecoming queen. You want people's professional respect. What they think of you personally doesn't much matter so long as they respect you professionally and understand the value of your work.

Collectively too many Americans have a paltry self-image. I see this all the time and have decided in the next year or so to concentrate some of my efforts in trying better to understand why this is so and begin correcting a problem which is titanic. Remember this: no one with a poor self-image can succeed in sales, especially on the talk circuit. I don't care how good your information or your product you have to do your part or else you are courting failure. To succeed in the business of selling your workshops and programs you need to know something about the business of sales. Beyond an acute belief in yourself and a knowledge of what your seminar/service will do for those encountering it, here are a few critical points:

- **Develop selective hearing and selective reading skills.**

I have by inheritance and upbringing a fiery temper. Also, I like setting the record straight when people make mistakes, which they do with infuriating frequency. Over time and with a lot of patient attention, I have minimized both these problems. You must do the same. When you are discussing business with a seminar sponsor prospect, you have in fact a couple of sales to make. The sponsor must first respect you and, if possible, even like you. Moreover, the sponsor must believe that what you are offering will do good both to his program and your program participants.

Thus you must learn the fine art of selective hearing, the fine skill of selective reading. This means knowing when to ignore misstatements of facts, small errors and the irritating idiosyncracies which come with most people. In such circumstances you may feel inclined to set the matter right. This is usually a mistake. You will find, for instance, that program sponsors don't read what you send them and don't hear what you tell them. I find, for instance, that they ask over and over again for materials which I have already sent. Rarely, very rarely, do I tell them this. Why point out their incompetence? Moreover, most are inclined to some particular hobbyhorse which is as irrelevant as it is dull. Your task nonetheless is to indulge these people and ignore all that is not germane to your objective. I find this, as you may find it, difficult to do, and yet I have learned to overcome my natural predisposition to mutter, "Get to the point!" Your objective after all is to schedule a program and begin to develop a lucrative long-term relationship. A soured beginning with a program sponsor may not only cost you a single program; it may cost you a lifetime of earnings from that source and all the networking possibilities that normally spring from a successful relationship. Think about it and cultivate a meaningful smile while developing the facility of daydreaming with an intent look upon your face.

- **Take yourself and your needs out of the sales proposition.**

However badly you need this sale, don't say so! There are, of course, different reasons for needing sales. The most obvious is money, but there are others. For instance, I like to rack up a new sale of some kind every day. Like most winners I have a well developed need to win. So will you. But I never say this to the prospect. What's the point? They can scarcely feel as happy as I do about my next score. Nor will they be happy to look well upon you if you seem to be a charity case desperately needing the work. Instead sell yourself and your seminar proposal exclusively on its merits, on what it will do for those attending and for the putative sponsor. Whatever you are getting out of the deal — money, promotion, leverage for a future program, enhanced credibility on the talk circuit, &c — is of utterly no consequence and you should never mention it. Exult at home, of course, in front of your adoring family but with the sponsor focus entirely on the benefit others will derive.

- **Demonstrate knowledge of the prospect and his needs.**

The more you know about the individual you are approaching the better. Since a workshop/seminar sale to a university or trade association will benefit you greatly in a variety of ways (increasingly evident as you master this book), you can well afford to put in some time towards understanding the prospective client and his needs. You will, after all, be making between $500-$5000 per day (and more as you become a commanding presence on the talk circuit) and this kind of return suggests that you should make a commensurate investment in preparation.

Chapter 1

- **Follow up every contact.**

If alma mater has just turned down your seminar program, fretting about it doesn't do much good. The university will be around long after you've gone, and you had better reconcile yourself to this perhaps irritating fact. Moreover, the individual you have spoken to will probably be in that position for awhile and will most likely be in a similar one thereafter at another place. Thus, you must develop a relationship where you can present your ideas passionately but take any momentary setback philosophically.

After such a setback, write a letter or make a call saying, in effect, that you'll be back with new ideas and that you appreciate the time and consideration you've been given so far. When one is in the talk business, one becomes necessarily an educator attempting to persuade people to see our point of view and the need for the programs we offer. This is difficult to do, and I confess to you it takes practice. I know. I like to win NOW! and I am impatient. But even those of us with these personality traits can learn.

At all times be clear about why you have identified this organization/individual as a prospective client/sponsor and be prepared to say:

- First, send a letter to the prospect and then follow up with a telephone call. When selling over the telephone, work from a check list of objectives. Have all your papers in front of you before you dial.

- Once you've begun a contact, follow it through until you receive a definite answer one way or the other. Never expect anyone to return your calls or answer your letters. When they do, it's a sure sign that you've arrived (or that you've somehow found one of the last surviving courteous people in the nation).

- Ask for the sale. The contract. The date.

- Summon up your enthusiasm. If you cannot be enthusiastic about the proposition you are offering, no one else will be. You can count on that. Program planners regularly say that if you have no enthusiasm about what you are offering, it's a sure sign that it shouldn't be adopted.

Technical Skills You Need

Mental attitude is a precondition of success but it is not a sufficient condition for success. **MONEY TALKS** is testament to that. You will also need to master certain technical skills, many mundane, all necessary, if you are to achieve your objectives on the talk circuit. Here they are:

- **Typing**

Face facts. There is a lot of correspondence and many written documents which you need to prepare for this job. If you can't type, you are adding an unnecessary barrier between yourself and success. Moreover, in the beginning you're probably not going to be generating sufficient income to pay for all you need in promotion as well as a secretary. In this business quick turn around on proposals, letters and applications is most important. No matter how expert you are in your field, you're probably going to need typing skills. These you may consider *infra dig*, beneath the position you've visualized for yourself. You'd better forget your pretensions for the moment and get the skills you need.

- **Telephone communications skills**

Surprisingly, many people are terrified of the telephone and most use it ineffectively. If this is a problem for you (and you'll have a clear conception if it is at the end of this book), practice. Role play sales calls on the telephone. Write down all the remarks you must make. Stay tuned; I've got some more specific tips for you later.

- **Good basic English language skills**

You are now in the communications business, and you'll need the best language skills you can get. This means mastering the simplest and most lucid of language. Too many people inflate their language. They do this because they think it makes them sound more erudite, because they don't really know the right word, because they are more interested in

Chapter 1

sounding smart than being understood, and for other self-interested reasons. Don't you do it! Use simple language simply and powerfully. And practice. Learn to get your message across in the most powerful way most quickly. There is a skill. Make no mistake about it! It's a skill you can practice and which you must have to succeed.

- **Good written communications skills**

Same as above. I receive thousands of letters in a single year, and I can attest that I rate the intelligence, creativity and preparation of the individual by just a few lines. Program planners do the same. Since a written document is usually the first impression you make, learn how to make it effective.

- **Good follow-up system**

It doesn't so much matter what kind of system you use, so long as it works. I use shoe boxes: "pending media," "pending speaking engagements," &c. You can have a system this simple or something more complicated. It doesn't really matter. The fact remains you are going to be following up a good many initial contacts which can take as long as a year or even more to come to fruition. Get used to it! Prepare thorough systems that work for you.

In this connection try hard to answer your mail promptly. This sounds too elementary even to mention, but it's not. While the program sponsors can perhaps afford to be negligent about such mundane matters, you cannot. This is, after all, a business where telltale signs can work to your benefit. Particularly when you are unknown, cultivate all the good habits that we tell our children they should have. A swift reply to a letter will indicate your enthusiasm and your keenness for consideration. That works to your advantage.

Yet Another Note on Follow-Through

Here's a critical point that deserves being made over and over again. If you are not prepared to entirely follow through on a contact after you have sent your initial letter or gotten a lead, don't even begin. The pay-offs in this world can be very substantial. A contact with a university, for instance, can result in an annual increase in your income year after year so long as the program is offered. This kind of pay-off on your initial investment of time and professional care means that you should follow through on everything you start. If you don't, you'll damage yourself and your reputation by appearing disorganized and unprofessional. Such people do not get the jobs whatever the value of their information.

- **Develop patience**

Unfortunately, I personally was born without patience, and it's been a long time coming. Some modicum now exists perforce. The talk circuit is a slow moving universe. While the rest of the world is sweltering in 90 degree heat and unbearable humidity you'll be working on your winter programs and when the snow is ledge high, you'll be quilting a summer schedule. Major conventions take even longer to arrange, sometimes being organized up to two years in advance.

Many people get involved in speaker decisions and there are as many opportunities for things to go wrong, for the slender thread that connects you to your objective to be snapped. Your job is to oversee the long, often tedious process and insure that all that needs to be done is done and that you have placed the responsibility for success squarely on the right person: yourself!

Three More Items Which Enhance Your Preparedness

- Establish at once a beneficial relationship with an illustrator/designer, someone who can help you lay out your flyers, spec the type, and (if a printing jobber) find the best printing establishments and prices. You will need, as I do, a regular flow of what I term "leave behinds," as you'll see when you read Chapter 6 on the promotion and development of your own catalog of courses. Very often, as in my own case, the designer can double as the printing jobber. This person works for you as an independent contractor which is a necessary precondition not merely for success but for peace of mind.

- If you don't have a jobber, you must establish the necessary relationship with a printer directly. Printing charges vary wildly for the same job. Shop around. And never stop shopping. Always ask people where they get their printing done. Occasionally do small jobs elsewhere to check quality and efficiency as well as prices.

Chapter 1

- You'll need, too, a good relationship with a travel agency. Like printers, travel agencies are good and not so good. They make their money off the commissions they earn. They are thus eager to keep your travel costs high. Keep pressing for better rates, for off-peak fares, &c. The groups you address will always be grateful to have you keep your prices low and on those occasions when you are paying your own traveling costs, so will you!

One Final Point

Practice visualizing your success. I am a dreamspinner, someone who helps people create visions for themselves. These visions are an indispensable ingredient of success.

There will be days as you work with me on the tasks set by this book you'll be tired and frustrated; you'll wonder, as I do, if the world is administered by idiots whose single pressing necessity is to create obstacles for you. At such a moment, pause and rekindle your visions of success. This is perhaps the most important prerequisite to advancement that there is. Then, having again been seized by this vision, begin again to move ahead. Try to achieve some immediate success no matter how small to start things moving.

No one in this world cares if you succeed. No one is prepared to give you much assistance. That is why achieving success is at root the most personal of journeys. Fortunately, it's a journey I want to take with you and that I have carefully plotted.

Chapter 2

CREATING PROGRAMS THAT SELL

The biggest mistake you can make is simply to assume that there is a market for your program. Perhaps there is. I believe that entrepreneurs can sniff out a market and develop a sense of timing for a developing trend. I have been the beneficiary of such olfactory precision myself. But it's risky. Far, far better is to do some testing to see what people want. That's the thrust of this entire business: giving people what they want.

Now perhaps you are one of those people, who seem to come to my workshops with regularity, who want to give people what you think they need, whether they know they need it or not. Here, then, is your problem.

Effective sales on the talk circuit consists of identifying sponsors and selling them on their ability to benefit from your program and then selling the ultimate consumer who pays the bills. If you add to this a grand educational component, the need to instruct your buyers on their need for what you've got to offer, you have saddled yourself with a significant problem which will retard the development of your practice and result in a delay in your income. Can you subsidize this problem? The delay? If so, you can afford to add this educational module to your work. If not, you had better stick with problems that are already perceived to be problems to which you have the undeniable solutions.

Remember: particularly in the beginning of your speaking career you should be dealing with the problems people already know they have and should be creating solutions to them through your workshops and seminars. You are not, after all, a missionary, not a zealot out to convert. You are a consultant out to dispense the best possible information in a way that can easily be understood and as easily applied by the program participants and which will lead to the solution of their problems if conscientiously followed. That's quite enough. While you may wish to use the lecture/workshop lectern as your personal pulpit, in most cases — and certainly for beginners — this is hardly recommended.

Having thus contained your zealotry (at least for the moment), the question becomes: how can you discover what it is people need and already want? Here are some suggestions:

- If you work with clients regularly in any field, you see the kinds of problems they bring to you on a continuing basis. Your workshop should deal with the top two or three problems that constitute the bulk of your practice.

- Ask your clients what they think they need. Develop a questionnaire to determine what your client's current interests are. Questionnaires, let's face it, are usually dull. However, they can provide you with essential information. Don't forget, too, that in your first workshop productions, you'll be expanding on this questionnaire and refining it and the information you need. After all, you are still developing your product (workshop) before taking it on the road. The questionnaire can be helpful in refining what you're offering.

Here are the kinds of things you need your prospective clients to tell you:

- What are problems that inhibit your success?

- Name the single most significant problem you have in your professional life just now.

- What do you wish you could do better?

- What problems are costing you money?

- How much?

- In what areas do you see growth next year? (Be specific!)

- In the next three years?

- If you've attended a professional development program in the last year, what was good about it?

- What could have been improved? In content? In arrangement?

Chapter 2

- What book or materials have you consulted recently which has helped solve your problems?
- Whom do you admire who is working in this area?
- What's your own advice for solving your problem?
- What problem would you first pay to solve?
- How much would you pay for the information if it were available?

The purpose of this questionnaire is to:

- Find out what those you deal with like/don't like about others working in the field.
- Find out if there are anxieties you can address in your program which are not otherwise being dealt with.
- Learn what aspirations people have and whether they are currently being addressed elsewhere.
- Find out whether clients are losing money and if so how much?
- Discover whether a prospective workshop participant would spend money to gain a solution to a perceived problem.

Handling The Questionnaire

Whenever possible (and it always isn't), go over the questionnaire in person with the individual filling it out. The best sequence is to get the person to fill it out privately and then for you to go over it together. I have done many questionnaires, and I know this isn't always possible. People, however, will often write tantalizingly, infuriatingly brief answers which need to be developed. This is less likely to happen in a conversation, even if you have to do it over the telephone.

Remember: you are trying to discover what will cause people to invest their money in your program. They are investing because they have an anxiety they wish to allay or an aspiration they wish to realize. You are the solution vehicle. People enroll in seminars less because of the speaker's credentials (which are, however, marginally helpful and the more so as you get better known) and more because they want to master the solution and achieve their ultimate result. As you emerge as a successful and known speaker that surely will help you, but it helps because it assures participants that the workshops will be well organized and the material will be current. People enroll in programs because you are offering them what they need to succeed. Success in this context means that you offer the prospect of reduced pain or enhanced gain.

This process of learning from your workshop participants does not stop. Once, for instance, that you are on the workshop/lecture circuit, ask people what *other* subjects they would like to know about. Develop your programs accordingly. The basic point is this: don't just trust your own instincts, however well developed. The program you think people need may be all well and good, timely, well developed, &c. It can still fail miserably. For when did people ever do exactly and in all circumstances that which was absolutely certain to benefit them? No! Give the people what they want. The more of them you benefit, the more benefitted you yourself will be.

Seek Out Your Competitors And Observe Them

Attend workshops, seminars and lectures by competitors. Do so with notepad in hand. Jot down comments to yourself from the look of the program's promotional materials, to the signs in the lobby, placement of coffee, arrangement of rooms, all through the content of the course. When you attend programs from now on, even if it only be a PTA meeting, become a constructive critic, an involved observer. It is in your interest to do so. No more can you take a passive role in any program. For you are not just appraising the program you are witnessing, but insuring that you will not make the same mistakes.

While I think it is a wise idea to have a general folder on workshops where you can keep flyers, brochures, ads, catalogs, &c., of programs that look successful to you, I think it is far more important to seek out your competition. Do this before you get to be known, for then it gets more and more difficult to remain unobtrusive. I once stopped a very well

Chapter 2

known competitor of mine from attending one of my programs when I saw his name on the attendance list, simply because I didn't particularly want to have him reviewing my program and perhaps usurping my ideas. A simple letter asking him to withdraw was sufficient to achieve his absence.

It may help you to take along a check list which you can annotate as you go. In point of fact, of course, this entire book is a check list of how to do things properly, but there are critical points which you should be observing and this list should help.

Once you're at a program, mix. You're not just there to observe the program itself; you are there to do some audience surveying and you need information from participants.

Find out:

- why they came
- whether they are enjoying themselves
- what is being left out
- what is out of date
- what problems they themselves are having and what material/techniques/information would be helpful in solving them
- whether they have been to other programs and if so the names, places, and prices
- whether they felt the price was fair, too high or possibly too low
- whether the materials are adequate
- what they think of the speaker
- how they evaluate the room set up
- whether they might advocate a different kind of place, different space, &c.

Talking To The Speaker

Do not indicate that you are thinking of launching a program. I'll never forget the man in San Francisco who barged into one of my programs (didn't even pay the gate!) and told me in no uncertain terms that he was launching a rival program. I was polite, but I told him nothing. I don't want you to be deceptive (heaven forbid!), but I think you should exercise a little basic discretion. *N.B.* I have heard nothing more of the brash gatecrasher.

Ask the leader/speaker how the program is going. Ask whether the current audience is typical in size, age, sex, and their level of involvement. Find out whether other programs are scheduled and, if so, where. What kind of return does he get from direct mail or from a space ad. What percentage of the program's success comes through back of the room sales and what percentage from the gate price itself?

There are more such questions you can ask, too, but you will be allowed no more than 5-10 minutes to query during the course of the day and you will have to continue at breaks and at lunch. Under the circumstances, then, make sure you sit next to the leader during the meal. Be forceful. If the speaker stays behind to answer questions, linger. Other people will dash into the dining room. Don't be so quick about that yourself.

While you are talking to the leader, don't write the information down as you are listening. You'll have to remember the key points and write them down afterwards. It looks a little too contrived for my tastes to sit there writing eagerly. The conversation should look like Assertive Courtesy, your eager interest in the speaker rather than an investigative mission. Given people's overweening interest in talking about themselves, you will ordinarily experience no difficulty about getting at least some sense of this individual and the market.

If you can't accomplish all this at lunch, do invite the person for a drink or coffee after the program. At that time the speaker is depleted, either depressed because the day was not quite the success he wanted, or elated because it was. In either case the speaker needs some human contact. That's you, the investigator. Use this time carefully. Get the answers you need but don't be too probing. That will defeat the purpose.

Chapter 2

Surveying The Field

Write to your competitors or anyone offering programs in your field even though the topics may be different. Ask to be put on their mailing lists. As you get to be better known, use your spouse or significant other to receive mail. You should know that most people doing mailings will send things to you once or twice on speculation. If you don't buy something, you are then weeded out. So consider buying a book, newsletter, or, finally, attending a workshop program. That will insure that you'll remain on the mailing list much longer.

Here's the proper way to consider these expenditures. Remember: when you begin speaking for money, you are in business, and there are expenditures you must make. Wisely handled these are investments. You will be able to discern a profile of your competitors and ascertain what areas they cover both in terms of subject/content and geography/marketing territory. Both are significant. Having gathered the answers to these questions, you can determine how much of a competitor the individual is. Occasionally you will be able to approach this individual and suggest joint programs, dual appearances. This can be productive. Also, as you develop programs, you can put together distribution agreements whereby you can benefit through the sale of each other's products to the other's workshop participants. This makes a lot of sense. Moreover, and this is a key point: remember that where you are offering the solution to workshop participant problems (and this is the purpose for your being in business in the first place) people who continue to have this problem, or who want to refine their problem solving techniques, will probably be open to taking more than one program in the field. Why not? People recognize that one person rarely if ever has a monopoly on the truth and good ideas and realize that so long as they are seeking a solution to their problem they must search out those who have developed such solutions and are offering them through a workshop format.

The process of assaying your competition will continue so long as you are in business. Remember too: as you develop your speaker conglomerate (to be discussed later), so long as the individual is not in direct competition with you, you can offer this "competitor" through your conglomerate to others who may have booked you and so continue to work your connection.

Developing The Participant Profile

Once you have researched the competition and done your initial market surveying, it is time to make the first important decision: what problem(s) are you going to solve? Answer these questions:

- What problem(s) am I going to solve in my program?

- How do I know this is a problem (specific proof)?

- How many people have it?

- What are the characteristics of the people who have it? Age? Sex? Geographical distribution? Income? Educational level? Other pertinent demographic information?

- How many of these do I want to attend my program?

- Do I want a general audience, or will I develop specific programs that attend to the needs of each specific subgroup?

- Do I have a sense of what percentage of the market is being served by my competitors?

- Will people attend more than one program on this topic?

- How often will they attend?

- Would they attend a series of programs on this topic?

- Will they pay for this program themselves (is it of personal benefit)?

- Or will the program need to be paid for by employers who will more greatly benefit from the participants' participation?

Chapter 2

You must know to whom you are marketing, what they know and want or need to know, how much they'll pay, how far they'll come for the information, whether your competitor gets to them, if so whether they'll buy yet another program on the same or related topic, &c.

This Participant Profile is most important. It is the basis for successful marketing. From it you can advise contracting organizations that must themselves market for participants about how to position your program in the market place, how to promote it, what mailing lists to buy, where to hold the program, and generally how to arrange it. Without such a profile you will undoubtedly attempt to be too many things to too many people. This is a mistake. Your program can be a rousing and continuing success by focusing on precise groups so long as there is a sufficient number of people within your marketing territories.

Moreover, once you have developed a Participant Profile, you are poised for diversification and intensification. One of my general programs, for instance, is designed for consultants but from this program spring many very detailed programs. I can tell you very specifically in either instance about the people who take the program. This description holds true across the country.

- Age: 28-65, the large majority being 35-48

- Income: Above $25,000 annually

- Education: All college-educated, a large majority with graduate degrees

- Dress: Conservative, standard corporate costume

- Place of residence: Affluent surburbs of major cities

- Reading matter: Major business publications

- Sex: 60% male, 40% female

- Occupational level: predominantly midlevel management

- Career experience: Minimum of 10 years in their respective fields

This pattern shows up repeatedly wherever I am in the nation — Portland, Maine to San Diego. It doesn't matter. Very rarely does the audience for the particular program deviate from this profile and the deviation is statistically insignificant. The minute someone who does deviate from this profile enters the room, he knows it as much as I do. I remember, for instance, doing a program in Pittsburgh last year. As people went around the room introducing themselves, one man in his twenties announced he was a bricklayer. I knew this program wasn't for him and by the end of the introductions (just a few minutes) he knew it wasn't for him either. He left at the end of the first hour and neither of us was at all surprised!

A general program like this one can be segmented into very precise demographic and professional foci: consulting for financial planners, consulting for accountants, consulting for lawyers, &c. The trick here is to diversify and intensify to develop new audiences.

Starting From The General Audience, Working To The Specific — Or The Reverse? Which is better?

It is usually better and smarter to begin with the most specific audience that you can and create a highly focused program. It will be easier to get information/questionnaire specifics from them and easier to market through a professional association or even occasionally from a general marketing effort. It will certainly be easier to do direct mail marketing, although it is not advisable for the novice to begin with that expensive form of promotion.

Once you have a clear perception of your audience (and it's best to write this down in a narrative form or at least as answers to a questionnaire), you must be able to visualize the individual participant and must understand what makes this individual take action. I have a clearer understanding about my consulting audience because these people are most like me: affluent, upwardly mobile, well educated, &c.

Chapter 2

The Anxiety-Aspiration Axis

Once you have this clear perception, you must master the Problem Solving Process which will give you the structure for your workshop.

Remember this: you are officially in the workshop/seminar business to solve someone else's problem, to allay an anxiety (or cluster of anxieties) and to assist them to realize an aspiration. I call this the Anxiety-Aspiration Axis. In my consulting program, for example, here are some of the anxieties that the participants have: they feel that time is passing them by, that they are not moving ahead quickly enough, that they are becalmed on the job, that their progress while perhaps real is not as great as they have a right to expect. They feel, in short, that their progress is insufficient, even insignificant, and that they are failing themselves and their great expectations. This is their anxiety. Their aspiration is the flip side of all this: to succeed according to their own ample desires. My job is to be the facilitator, the information dispenser, the individual who, while playing on their anxieties, assists them to realize their aspirations.

The Problem Solving Process allows you to realize the aspirations of your audience and to deliver the information they want which will calm their considerable anxieties.

The Problem Solving Process

The Problem Solving Process is the backbone of any workshop or seminar program that disseminates information with a view to assisting participants achieve a desired result. Here are its significant parts:

Step 1. Are you (the participant) mentally prepared to do what needs to be done to realize success?

All seminar leaders are to a certain extent in the motivation business. We have to let our participants know that to achieve the success they want — whether it's achieving financial prosperity or a thinner waistline — they must be mentally ready to do what it takes to achieve that success.

You must tell them what mental attitude to adopt and how to sustain it during difficult moments. This is the beginning of your program. Never begin without it. It is a great, great mistake simply to begin by launching into factual information. People can be factually potent and prepared while mentally unready to begin their trek to success.

Step 2. Are you (participant) technically ready? Do you know whatever you need to know to achieve success from a technical perspective? Are there things you must know how to do before you can achieve success and on mastering which success is contingent?

To achieve success means not only to be mentally ready but to be technically prepared. Perhaps you need to take classes, perhaps to master skills in other ways. Whatever it is, you, the expert, must know. You've obviously had to master these skills yourself and it is your job to level with your workshop participants and tell them what they must master, too. Americans, of course, are notoriously gullible and want to believe that it is possible to achieve results quickly, painlessly, effortlessly, without their earnest involvement, their blood, tears and sweat. This is fatuous. Anyone who has achieved any measure of success knows that. To retain a shred of moral responsibility and self-respect as well as to boost your reputation with your workshop participants, level with them. Tell them exactly what skills they must master to achieve even a modest result and what skills to truly reach their most lofty goals.

Don't be afraid about this. What I have discovered in giving workshops around the nation is that people really want to know what it takes to succeed. There will, it's true, always be those who look for the easy way out. It's part of our national tradition after all. There will consequently always be those who will prey on the credulous. Don't be one of these vulpine creatures. People will respect you if you tell them the truth. And perhaps more importantly, you'll continue to respect yourself.

Be prepared, however, to justify your reasons if you specify, as you should, detailed courses of action that people should take. Also be prepared to provide exact information about just where to take courses, get the needed preparation, which books to read, the licenses to take, &c.

Under Step 2 of the Problem Solving Process format, it is your responsibility to set out in clear, specific detail exactly what technical preparation is necessary to achieve success and exactly where and how participants can go about mastering these processes.

Chapter 2

This technical readiness item actually breaks down into two parts:

- Either you will train yourself to be technically ready to do what needs to be done, or

- You will have to recruit other individuals to do the service for you.

It is your responsibility as workshop leader both to tell participants how to become technically ready themselves (if this is feasible and a realistic alternative for them), or how to go about finding technically prepared assistance.

On both points seminar/workshop trainers can be maddeningly imprecise. I offer a workshop on fund raising for non-profit organizations. I begin with a section on becoming mentally prepared for fund raising, how to get yourself in the right frame of mind, so to speak, for what can be a very aggravating business.

The second section, following this problem solving format, deals with technical preparation. I list the skills that participants need to become successful at fund raising. I also let them know that there are individuals at hand who already have these skills and can help them: professional fund raising counselors.

Now at this point I am not coy. The participants know (through pass-outs which will be discussed later) and the catalog description that I am myself such an animal. I don't say, and neither should you, "You don't need to know anything more about these consultants since I am available." While few might be as bold as this in their speech, many workshop leaders effectively do leave this exact impression. This is in fact damaging to their credibility. Besides, there's no way as a consultant or service provider that you can accommodate all the people in every room at every program, particularly when you are in another city.

Thus you must instruct participants specifically how to locate the service they want and need. Be precise. Tell them each thing to do, in this case how to locate professional fund raising counselors in the telephone book, which professional society to call for recommendations or a book of members, how to handle the initial telephone call, what kind of information to ask for from a counselor, how to evaluate it when it comes, who should attend an initial interview, how long it should take, whether the counselor should be paid for this time at this meeting, what a reasonable fee might be, what kind of follow up to expect from the counselor, how to evaluate it, what kind of references to ask for, and so on. Give it all!

The idea is that at no point should your audience, people with a defined problem to solve (in this case the need to raise funds for their organization) be left without a means of action. Granted, in the event what they do might change with circumstances, but your job as the seminar leader is to outline a reasonable course of action and to provide specific information so that the participants can expeditiously reach their goals.

Don't Oversell Yourself!

Many workshop leaders make the mistake at this point of overselling themselves and their services. There is no need to and it's a great psychological error, damaging to your own objectives. You are present as a facilitator, as a credible, knowledgeable, helpful expert. Don't withhold information. Provide an overabundance of it in the most useable formats conceivable.

People always leave my seminars remarking on the avalanche of specific information. If this is a "complaint," it's one that makes me proud, because they are getting as much as anyone might reasonably expect. I hold nothing back, not failures and certainly not successes. I detail each step they need to take whether in becoming trained in specific skills and what it takes to succeed or in retaining other professional or technical help and what it takes to find the right person for the job.

Don't stint on either.

Your goal is to get people to trust you and believe in you. Selling is a two-tier process. People must buy you before they buy your product, service and way of solving problems. Since most people who offer workshops and seminars are selling other products and services, too, (if they're smart!), this selling the audience on you is critical.

Note: It is perfectly permissible to change the order of this last point and put it towards the close of your program. In other words, your entire program acts as the lure to the participant to purchase further goods and services. By the end of the program, they may be weary with knowing all that they need to do to achieve success. At that point you step

Chapter 2

forward with specific information on how to find knowledgeable professional or technical help. In the process intimate that, of course, this is what you do. At whatever point in the program you place this information, however, don't oversell either it or yourself.

Further note: Of course, it may be that the organization/participant would not need to hire a consultant but rather take on full-time staff. In this case, it is your responsibility to outline just what this staff person should do and what skills and technical expertise he should have. For instance, in my fund raising workshop, there are things the executive director needs to know about raising money (one component of the workshop). In a small agency, the executive director will also do other functions which in a larger agency will be handled by additional paid staff. Finding these staff and outlining their duties constitutes another portion of the workshop. Personnel recruitment techniques thus logically find themselves a part of most Problem Solving Process programs.

Step 3. Success demands the proper mental attitude and the right technical skills, but it also needs a plan. The third component of your workshop under the Problem Solving Process is to inform participants how they can develop their Success Plan. Call it that.

Success cannot be achieved overnight and demands continual thoughtful consideration. It is your job as the workshop leader to instruct workshop participants in how to find the information they need (research) and how to structure their Success Plan.

Let's take my fund raising workshop as a good example of what I have in mind. Participating individuals represent organizations which need money. They think they know how much they need, but they usually haven't researched their needs or researched the funding market. Thus they have some real research to do before launching any fund raising activities. They need a Success Plan. So the first thing that I tell participants is how to do the necessary research:

- when to begin (calendar considerations)
- whom to involve
- what kinds of meetings to have
- how to structure them
- what the outcomes should be
- how to develop a budget for planning
- how to evaluate selected items for possible funding, &c.

In short, I advise on activities which will help the organization determine its priorities as against the amount of available funds.

Having once done this research (and instructed the audience how to do it for themselves), the next task is to assist them in developing their plans.

I am a believer in written plans. I think that people should write down their goals and develop specific strategies that will help them achieve them. Your job as seminar leader is to help people develop written Success Plans for themselves to which they can refer at regular intervals and so gauge their progress. These plans should not come out of the blue. They need to be realistic so that people don't get discouraged and so that real progress can continually be demonstrated.

Chapter 2

The plan should have short-term, intermediate, and long-term goals. I prefer to write plans for a year at a time. Short-term in such circumstances is 3 months; intermediate, 6 months, and long-term is the full year.

As you do your workshop more and more, you'll come to have a very clear sense of what a good plan would be for the participants. It's your responsibility as the expert, right from the start, to lay down some guidelines for them, guidelines which you think are realistic given certain commitments of time and resources which it is also your responsibility to detail. From this develop a Success Plan matrix which you can distribute to participants and which they can fill in for themselves later. Go through each point of the plan step by step and explain why you included it and what it's intended to do.

Step 4. Help your participants develop the documents they need.

In my workshops we rely on many different kinds of written materials and documents. In the fund raising workshop, for instance, we need:

- development proposals
- direct mail letters
- précis
- brochures
- solicitation letters
- volunteer training guidelines, &c.

In the consulting workshop:

- brochures
- direct marketing letters
- contracts
- retainer agreements
- letters of intent
- corporate by-laws, &c.

Most workshops have the need for explicitly developed materials which participants can master and so realize their Success Plan. Yours will probably be no exception.

You need first to draw up a *complete* list of every document that those taking your workshop need to achieve success. List them. Then begin sifting through your files to come up with pertinent examples of each document. From these you will develop your pattern materials. It goes without saying that you should consult other relevant repositories, books, and materials to see what they recommend.

If you want to copy a document from another book, &c., you must write to the publisher for written permission and you must credit the source. It may be that the publisher will not give you permission. I usually don't, for instance, the reason being that if people want my materials they can buy them, so why should I let someone else use them in a program without cost when they are probably deriving benefit? Nonetheless you can try.

Chapter 2

As you develop these documents, consider a format I have developed. On the left hand side of the page, I write the "essentials" of the document and explain the sequencing of paragraphs and points and what they are intended to accomplish and why. This page is in bullet format just like the samples section of this book. On the right hand side, I include the actual document. Many people have told me they find this arrangement helpful.

Without having a list of these documents and complete samples of them, you condemn your audience to a lot of writing. They can't listen effectively to you and take detailed notes simultaneously; you will be fueling their resentment and frustration.

It should be clear that in producing these documents you have the germ of a book and at the very least your documents and supporting materials should be incorporated into a pamphlet or loose-leaf binder. Make sure that any pamphlet/binder has an introduction by you which acts as a continuing sales piece.

Your documents may include samples of:

- letters

- memoranda

- letters of intent

- contracts

- minutes

- by-laws

- proposals

- reports, &c.

Note: the value of your workshop increases substantially as soon as you put these documents into an attractive binding and distribute it as part of the program. Moreover, you can charge the materials as an expense against the gross proceeds of the program. As we will later discuss in the publications chapter, there are two ways of pricing this material.

The mainstream publisher's rule of thumb for price is about 5 times production costs. In this instance, that would probably mean a price of about $5-$7.50 per item. You should also consider Lant's Disproportionate Benefit Compared To Cost Rule. How much time, energy, and money would it cost the participant to get this information working alone? How much benefit are they deriving from it? Charge accordingly. That, by the way, is the rule behind the pricing of this book. Given that you will make tens of thousands of dollars from following this advice, I think I should derive some trifling benefit. Don't you agree?

This point about documents seems obvious to me, but it isn't to many workshop leaders. I have attended several programs in the last year where no documents were handed out and discussed. One of these programs happened to be on publishing and the speaker was billed as a leading expert in the field. That turned out to be a lot of rot! The bill of fare should have included:

- initial letter to publisher

- initial letter to literary agent

- sample contracts with both, explained

- publisher's publicity questionnaire

- subsidiary rights contract possibilities, &c.

Chapter 2

There were no examples of any of these materials. Honestly, how can such an incomplete program conceivably be thought to be of any value to participants, who are left to wonder about all the critical essentials under discussion?

Step 5. (As needed) Sometimes those in your audience will not be the decision makers, the people who can order the implementation of your program. You must act to train the audience so that they can sell their superiors on the need of the Problem Solving Process you are proposing and so move matters to a solution.

For instance, I often lecture to executive directors of agencies about fund raising for nonprofit organizations. They must report to their boards of directors, and it is the board that actually retains me as a consultant. So I have added an additional step in the Problem Solving Process which details how those in the audience can sell the ultimate decision makers on the need for doing whatever it is that will assure success and bring about the result they desire. This includes specific guidelines, suggestions and recommendations about:

- how to make a presentation at a board meeting (sales information)
- what papers to bring, what back up materials
- what specifics to discuss and how
- how to present a fund raising plan to a board of directors
- how to deal with recalcitrant members of the board (the wheedling factor)
- how to motivate and persuade board members to tackle appropriate tasks, &c.

Remember: you will not always be dealing with the ultimate decision makers in your workshops. Even if you are, in their own individual professional careers *they* may not be dealing with the decision makers and will need to know this kind of information. For instance, in my consulting program I have the actual consultants and consultant prospects in the workshop. But they must often have to brief individuals on how to sell superiors on the need for their services. Hence the need for this module.

Step 6: Implementation Strategy

You now have your workshop participants well positioned for success. They are:

- mentally prepared
- technically prepared individually or knowledgeable about how to find and retain technically prepared full-time or part-time help
- they have researched the problem and developed a Success Plan
- they know which documents they need to develop, why they need them and how to develop them, and
- they have persuasion and motivation strategies which will assist them in moving the ultimate decision maker to buy into the plan.

Now you need an Implementation Strategy, that is to say a precise method through which workshop participants will work to get the success they are now positioned to achieve.

What does this mean?

An Implementation Strategy shows workshop participants exactly what they must do, when, and in what way to achieve success. Of course, one could say that the entire Problem Solving Process is itself an Implementation Strategy, and one would be right! But the Implementation Strategy is the heart of achieving success for with it one moves bit by bit, inexorably towards success. The strategy deals with such matters as:

Chapter 2

- whether meetings must be held. How often? Including what people?

- whether telephone conferences should be held? If so, how often? Who calls whom?

- whether peer counseling takes place. If so, who assembles the group and acts as leader and organizer?

- what self-paced workshop participants need to do, by when, in what ways to achieve success.

In short, the Implementation Strategy is something set down by the workshop leader (you!) to help participants achieve success in a reasonable amount of time. The entire thrust of the workshop, the entire reason for having the workshop is to help participants achieve some tangible (or indeed, intangible) goal. You will succeed and become more prosperous yourself as those taking your workshop meet their objectives and recommend others to take your program and so meet their objectives, too. This cannot, cannot be sufficiently stressed!

It is unfair to workshop participants and ultimately unwise for your own professional status and success merely to impart information. You must give them all the tools they need for success and a method of reaching that success, a specific step-by-step method that you continually check and know to be useful in achieving the objectives which members of your audience have a reasonable expectation of reaching.

The Implementation Strategy must address all the preparatory items which have gone before. It should include a time schedule for:

- becoming technically prepared (assuming that your own workshop does not provide all that is necessary)

- for finding and training outside staff and consultants

- for doing the research and developing the complete Success Plan

- for developing the necessary documents and written materials, and

- for selling the ultimate decision maker.

The key word to describe the previous five steps is: Preparation. Preparation for success. The right descriptive phrase for this item is Success Achievement. What must be done, by when, by whom, in what order and in what way to bring about the success which both you and your participants should equally desire?

Step 7. Part of the Implementation Strategy but justifying separate treatment because of its importance is the Reporting of Success and the Foreshadowing of Potential Failure.

Success demands review. Each workshop participant must either:

- self-evaluate his success (how's it going?), or

- evaluate it for the benefit of superiors in an organization.

If a person is achieving the desired success, well and good. But if the individual is not, these frequent review steps enable the individual to find out what is going wrong and to make suitable mid-course corrections to go back, in short, to the plan you have so carefully thought through and presented at your program.

Understand this: a sizeable percentage of people who take workshops fail to achieve the desired objective. They don't lose weight. They don't make money. They don't get real estate with nothing down. They don't achieve career success. They don't learn how to become published writers or experts in mail order. In sum, they waste their time and money.

That may not bother some workshop presenters, but it disturbs me a good deal. In part, this is because I cannot abide waste of any kind; in part it's for very selfish reasons. If people fail to achieve the results they set out to achieve by enrolling in one of my programs, then I cannot expect further benefit from them. I cannot expect them to refer individuals

Chapter 2

to my programs, buy my books, &c. I thus derive an insufficient benefit from my involvement with them. Think about it! You, therefore, need to structure the entire day for success. This, of course, is exactly what the Problem Solving Process enables you to do. The Review Step is a most significant part of this process.

I suggest people review progress weekly in some way. At the very least, monthly. That is before the realization of their goals is overborn by despair, lethargy or sloth. As the workshop expert, you need to tell participants how to handle these review sessions:

- when to hold them

- where

- who should participate

- what criteria for success should be evaluated

- who should keep records (for records there must be)

- what carrots (or sticks) can there be to motivate success and disturb the calm composure of the sluggards.

Step 8. "The Clinic"

It would by nice if all problem solving workshops automatically included a follow-up program six months after the conclusion of the original program. If not six months, then a year, or at least at some reasonable time. This would make a lot of sense, but it's rarely done. People come in for a short time (a couple of hours to a couple of days), are crammed full of ideas which may be wonderful, timely and beneficial but are not followed up. I have not myself entirely managed to solve this problem by any means, but I am very well aware that for education to be effective this format alone doesn't do very well. People need regular follow-up, a "clinic" if you will. And you need a way of getting back in the minds of your audience after some period of time has elapsed and they have been able to try out your methods independently. I will be suggesting in a later chapter some ways of dealing with this problem. Just keep in mind that it will be mutually beneficial to have another period of some sustained contact with those who have taken your workshop in order to reinforce the success methods you are teaching.

Benefits Of The Problem Solving Process

The Problem Solving Process offers you as workshop and seminar trainer a world of benefits:

- It provides a complete framework for a program that lasts for an hour to several weeks.

- It enables you to thoughtfully approach a subject with the best hopes for your participants' getting the success they want.

- All material can easily be organized into sensible units.

- All common questions about the subject in question will be answered.

- Materials are provided to participants that will enable them to work on their own.

- It provides you the workshop leader with the germ of a book which will in due course enable you to make additional profit from this same audience.

- It enables you to state in a perfectly professional legitimate way any consulting or professional services you offer independently and let them be seen as what they are: a follow-up service to workshop participants.

- It leads naturally to future contact with workshop participants through follow-up clinics and additional training sessions.

Chapter 2

- It provides participants a solid means of achieving success if they want it and are willing to work at it. Thus the burden of success is transferred from you to the participants, which is just where it ought to be.

- It provides a structure for articles and promotional materials, for catalogs and direct mail. It provides the backbone for audio cassettes dealing with your subject.

- It enables you to break out individual modules which themselves can be the subject of presentations. In other words, each block of the Problem Solving Process can itself be broken down into an individual and complete Problem Solving Process with continually more detailed information being imparted.

- It does not leave participants hanging at a critical point. You have outlined their options, what they must do to achieve success, and how to review their progress.

As you can see, the Problem Solving Process is replete with advantages to you and to your workshop participants. If you are interested in disseminating information in a way that will be of the utmost benefit to the participants and channel them towards success, this is the way to do it!

Now that you know this process, you simply need to know how to deliver it and you're really in business.

Chapter 3

TRAINING YOURSELF: ALL YOU NEED TO KNOW ABOUT SPEAKING AND PRESENTATION

Most people no matter how well they know their subjects are poor speakers. Indeed survey after survey discloses that Americans' first fear is public speaking. This, as you might expect, causes me to doubt the priorities of my countrymen, but it is nonetheless an indication of how you probably feel, too.

Even people with top notch assistance flub speeches with regularity. You may remember Nancy Reagan's speech to the 1984 Republican National Convention. Mrs. Reagan went on without notes. Asked by reporters what she intended to do, she said she'd "wing it." The result was lackluster to say the least, an opportunity lost, although the wildly partisan crowd cheered lustily notwithstanding. You, friends, will seldom if ever have such an uncritical audience, and you'd better prepare accordingly.

The significant point about this chapter is to persuade you that success as a speaker comes not merely from what you say but how you say it and from the entire ambiance that surrounds you as the speaker. Indeed as Mrs. Reagan's remarks prove, your speech can be a success given the right crowd despite substance which is embarrassingly inadequate. However, you should understand that people will be coming to your workshops not just to hear some charming words from you but to learn something. The substance, in short, must be there.

Having said that, let's begin at the beginning.

Fashioning A Quintessential American Success Image

Too many people have become very, very good at not paying attention. We are continually distracted in our lives by a multiplicity of competing aural and visual images; we have become adept at ignoring most of them. In this day and age, you are always running the risk that people will see you without perceiving you and hear you without listening to you. Frankly, this is a ghastly thought for any professional speaker who aims both to disseminate information and turn his audience into a marketing department.

Much time has been spent in the previous chapter helping you think through who your audience will be. It goes without saying that for each of your programs your targeted audience may and probably will be distinctly different. The kinds of people who attend my nonprofit fund raising program, for instance, are different from those who enroll in my consulting and public relations courses, and it's up to me to be cognizant of these differences and factor them into my reckoning. This is where image enters the picture.

The image you adopt is designed to reinforce the thrust of your language and your impact on your audience. It must heighten and substantiate that impact and project your message in both visual and nonvisual, suggestive ways. It must therefore not jar or contrast with the message of your presentation, the kind of language you use or the ambiance in which it is given. To be successful as a persuader (for that is the business you are in), means to offer a consistent picture, each portion of which reinforces the whole.

Adopting An Image

There are now several prominent books about corporate images but relatively little has been written about other kinds of success images. In my book **THE UNABASHED SELF-PROMOTER'S GUIDE**, I presented a series of what I term Quintessential American Success Images. If you are interested in the subject, I refer you to that discussion. However, most people presenting information, disseminating useful how-to Problem Solving Process material will simply need to consider the following:

Chapter 3

- **The Accessible Expert**

This is a superb image for the workshop lecturer. People come to your programs after all to find an expert, someone who either knows all there is to know on any given subject or who knows where to find critical information. But they do not want to be put off by either the mannerisms of the presenter or by inappropriate language (jargon) or style. They want you to be, in short, accessible. The Accessible Expert can be either a man or woman, one of its great advantages, and can be comfortably used by all us Info-Technocrats, people who know something which is useful to others.

- **The In-Command Technocrat**

Related to the Accessible Expert but different in its nuances, the In-Command Technocrat is the individual who provides all the answers to participant problems. He or she (for this, too, is an image that is open to both men and women) offers a comfortable matrix. "I know," The In-Command Technocrat seems to say, "what ought to be done, the questions you should ask and their correct answers. You are in good hands with me." Whereas the Accessible Expert is a more congenial role model, empathetic, humanistic, the In-Command Technocrat is rather a brisk problem solver. The Accessible Expert is warmer and, perhaps, more likeable as a person; the In-Command Technocrat may lack humor but is unrelentingly professional and straightforward in the solution of problems.

- **The Entrepreneur**

Again, this is an image which now can comfortably be worn by both men and women. The Entrepreneur is a risk-taker uncomfortable with the status quo and interested in shaping a better world in which his/her talents will get full play. Often intolerant and critical of the way things have been done in the past, The Entrepreneur is brimming with key ideas about how to do things better. Enthusiasm is the leitmotif of The Entrepreneur.

- **The Problem Solver**

Related to all three of the above images, The Problem Solver can again be either a man or woman. This person bridges the discernible gap between the In-Command Technocrat and the Accessible Expert, taking on shades of each depending on the nature of the audience. Alternately brisk and empathetic, concerned and as detached as a cool consultant, the Problem Solver exists solely to help participants get solutions to their difficulties.

The key to all these images is that they involve leadership. They provide a structure for the participants, a structure in which participants can expect to be lead, propelled, impelled, stimulated and moved to solutions. Sometimes they will be shown the way, sometimes they will themselves show the way, but there will always be movement. That, that is the critical constituent of the successful workshop leader's image. You are in command; you are the one regulating the environment, creating the milieu and assisting in the movement of your participants to success. Now I know that there are workshops that take place without any ostensible leader, but even in these circumstances, oh-so-reminiscent of the fading decade of the '60's, I have observed that usually there is a leader apparent usually being The Accessible Expert.

You must recall that any workshop or seminar to be successful must be a highly structured experience in which you, the leader, have thought through all the variables in advance of the program. You do not want your image to obstruct the flow of information to the participants. You want it to reinforce your purpose and the ultimate impression you leave with participants.

It is important for you to understand that all the variables in this situation must be consistent and articulate right from the moment the first brochure or promotional material hits your prospects.

Stitching Together The Right Image: Your Clothes

Clothes do not necessary make the man (or the woman) but they can certainly unmake you! They are perhaps the first things that both women and men increasingly look to to give the right impression. Here, then, some do's and don't's!

- **Colors**

Blue is always a safe color, a power color in the new yuppie vernacular. But while yuppies feel they discovered this color (as they feel proprietary about so many things), they are quite, quite mistaken. Blue for hundreds of years has

Chapter 3

represented prestige, power and authority. It is still the color used in the sash of England's most prestigious chivalric order, the Garter, and was equally used by the old Bourbon kings of France. Moreover, it is the especial color of the Virgin Mary. Hence it is equally suitable for men and women and for virtually any gathering.

White. To set off the blue, white is an especially good choice. Blue and white do not distract your listeners from your message but do reinforce you as an individual of power and distinction.

Red. Most outfits benefit from a dash of red, either as a tie (for men) or as an accessory for women. Red indicates energy and is a powerful attractant.

Colors to avoid. Don't use orange (perhaps the worst possible color), magenta, bright green (unless, of course, it's St. Patrick's Day in South Boston), and hot pink (unless you are addressing, Barbara Cartland like, a convention of romance fiction writers). Colors, after all, send a powerful message to your audience. Select those that reinforce you as an authority.

- **Fibres**

Always dress in natural fibres whenever possible. Polyesters look cheap and detract from your perceived status as an individual of consequence. The advice your mother always gave you is accurate: it is better to buy one decent wool suit (for both men and women) than to purchase a dozen polyester or other synthetic creations no matter how trendy they look. Unless you are speaking on fashion subjects, avoid the ultra chic. People will be concentrating on the way you look (and commenting cattily, perhaps) rather than on what you have to say.

- **Jewelry**

Play this down. Make it expensive. Again, the image you wish to impart is powerful, prestigious. Men should not dress like a gigolo on a night on the town. Off with the gold chains; they may look sexy on you but unless you are working for Chippendale's it's the wrong look. And cut the rings, bangles, bracelets, and the heavy gold watches. Understated and assured is the look you want to achieve. Women, the same. You should wear the minimum amount of jewelry and nothing ostentatious. Beware of costume jewelry which makes you look tacky.

- **Shoes**

Personally, I always look at a person's shoes first. They usually betray an individual's social status quicker than anything else because people give them inadequate attention. Here are a few hints for men. Black shoes never, never take bows. There is no such thing as a black loafer that can take a bow and while loafers are perfectly appropriate for speaking in, black loafers are not and never will be. You want something solid, moderately dressy with a dull shine. Patent leather with a high shine is inappropriate. For women stiletto heels are verboten. You want what your mother always called "sensible shoes." It is unbecoming to your image to take mincing steps running down a corridor because your shoes are too tight and too high for easy ambulation. A woman candidate for the New York State Assembly I was advising before the last election saw her standing undercut because she failed the shoe test. Don't make this mistake!

The objective of dress is to project an image of calm control, authority, quiet affluence and assurance. You do not want your program participants to comment on the way you look for this detracts from what you have to say. Nor do you want them so interested in your glad rags that they fail to pay any attention to you or, worse, indulge, in critical nit picking about your costume. This effectively destroys any chance you have to be persuasive. Your clothes must assist to deliver the message that you are worth attending to.

A Few More Things About Dress

Never appear to be more casually dressed than your participants. This will effectively undercut your standing. If your audience is in shirt sleeves, you can be in shirt sleeves, too, so long as you have a tie on (men). Women, I'm afraid have considerably less leeway in this regard.

Always begin your program fully dressed! Men, you can simulate intimacy with an audience by removing your jacket and encouraging others to do the same. This is a signal that you mean to get down to business. But don't approach the audience without a jacket even on the most sweltering of days. Otherwise you appear to have little respect for the participants and you lose the impact of welcoming intimacy with them.

Chapter 3

With clothes you must remember never to underdress, never to dress so that you distract the participants causing them to neglect the substance for the interesting shadow. Use clothes to reinforce your status as the leader and your power and authority with your listeners.

Final rule: break these rules when necessary to achieve a calculated effect.

On Language

I am a connoisseur of language. I love the way English feels on the tongue, the power and thrust of the language, its ability to move, to persuade, to incite and its high poetry and raw power. I am, I'm afraid, in a distinct minority of people.

Americans of this generation have a distinct love-hate relationship with language and all too often their conflicting feelings about their own language seep out when they have a presentation to make. Don't be one of these people for the effects are serious if often shockingly funny.

One of my more curious avocations is to go to workshops and speeches and note the ways in which the speaker destroys confidence in himself through the language he uses or more often misuses. Over the course of many years of this peculiar hobby, I have formulated the following rules which I trust will be helpful to you:

- The simplest language is the best. You are not on the workshop platform to dazzle your audience, at least not with the dazzle of verbal agility. Instead, you are there to disseminate information, problem solving information which will enable them to do something better, to achieve a desired success. That's the reason for your program and the reason for your presence. Never forget it! Your language must therefore be suitable for your participants to understand and for them easily to grasp both the problem (which, after all, they may understand as well as you) and the solution, which they must be able to work towards when you are no longer present. Verbal pyrotechnics and flashes of brilliant language are not appropriate in these circumstances. Plain workmanlike speech is for you.

Do, then, the following:

Eschew obfuscation. Don't use complicated words merely for the sake of demonstrating your knowledge. People are not interested in how knowledgeable you are. They rather want to know how your knowledge can be harnessed to their benefit.

Unfortunately this kind of simple, precise, clear language does not come naturally to us. There is a general feeling in this country, emanating from the highest quarters of obscurantist academe, government, and literature, that the more highfalutin' the language the more penetrating the thought. Of course, this is consummate rubbish and ought to be exposed as such.

Again, I must say: at your workshops and lectures the participants cannot be expected to care much about you and your knowledge. Breathtaking though that must be it is only important insofar as it assists in the realization of the participants' aspirations. This humbling thought is consistently forgotten or disregarded by all too many platform speakers who have decided to enjoy themselves and display the full panoply of their intellect at the expense of those paying the freight. They, of course, usually don't get invited back. And getting invited back is one of the several objectives of the successful workshop entrepreneur.

Here are some things to avoid:

- Pompous phraseology. If you are subject to inflated diction, start writing your glittering phrases down and rendering them in the simplest English equivalent. Rid yourself of pompous phrasing. Although our age is only deceptively casual, it prides itself on the grace of simplicity.

- Aim for conversational speech patterns. Since your objective is conveniently to disseminate useful information to your participants, aim for the kind of speech which will provide what they seek. This tends to be done best in a conversational way. Talk as you would to any good friend. You may not be able to master this easy informality right away and if you can't you must practice. The more platform appearances you make, the less forced and convoluted your presentations ought to be as you become not merely the expert on your subject but an expert on the business of persuasive presentations.

Chapter 3

- Banish jargon. On very, very few occasions is a presentation carried on the cloven hooves of jargon acceptable. Even if 90% of your audience understands you, a significant fraction will not and they will resent your inconsideration. If you are going to use words which are in common use only in a certain area or which have a special definition to a particular crowd, do define them. There's nothing wrong in that. It's courteous in fact. Don't make assumptions. After all, you are now in the communications business.

- Assumptions again. No matter how simple and straightforward you may think you've been, simply by asking your audience to rephrase some of your key points you'll learn you have a lot farther to go. I learned a significant part of this lesson early on in my speaking career. In my senior year of undergraduate school, I used to help grade papers for an instructor at Santa Barbara City College (as it then was). He asked me to prepare a lecture on my germinating specialty, 19th century England.

I worked on this presentation for weeks, brightly polishing witty phrases and burnishing the language till it sparkled. It was entitled "England In The Victorian Age", and I thought it, without great difficulty, scintillating.

The audience was quiet during the lecture, but I thought that was due in large part to natural deference. Only afterwards in the question period did I get my inevitable comeuppance. Having discoursed on industrialism, the rise of the middle class, the great age of empire and imperialism and all the other superb themes of the period, imagine my chagrin when one lounging student said, "Was there some dude called Victor they named it after?" I was predictably crushed, but I learned: make no assumptions.

- Avoid passive language. Throughout this book I will stress and stress again that it is your responsibility to stimulate enthusiasm in your lectures and workshops. People learn better, feel more interested in what they learn and more excited about what they learn if they are enthused by it. From the platform whether you are giving a one day speech or a multi-day institute, you should take on the better characteristics of the cheerleader. I used to distrust their enthusiasm while I was in school. Now I find I have so absorbed it as to be a role model for the young and energetic. I am ordinarily rather bearish in the mornings, but while lecturing matutinally I radiate a certain mad intensity. At all times the language of your presentation should be short, simple, exciting. You must, after all, excite people with the potential of what you're saying.

- Avoid the imprecise. Beware of adverbs and adjectives. Get used to speaking precisely and to providing illustrations of what you're saying. Have the facts and figures at your command so that you can avoid imprecise language configurations which always necessarily mean different things to your listeners instead of leaving them with the precise information they have a right to demand of you.

- Avoid the colloquial. Disdain the colloquial, the casual, slang and excessive informality. Remember that you are a leader and of leaders much is expected. Again and again I shall remind you that your language must be simple, precise, enthusiastic, direct and clear.

Invent Your Own Language

As you progress more and more on the workshop and lecture circuits, you'll develop your own problem solving words, ideas, concepts and phrases. That's as it should be. If you are familiar with my other books, you know that in each I take words and give them a new spin. This book, too, is no exception, and there's very good reason for doing this.

You want people to talk in your language and you want your language to become marketing tools for you. Is this a contradiction to speaking simply and in language that people understand? No, it isn't! Or at least, it isn't necessarily so. Take the phrase "Problem Solving Process." It has been used before no doubt, but it has never been used in connection with creating the backbone for a workshop or lecture presentation. Now it will enter the language. You will use it. You will tell your friends. More importantly, you will define it for your friends and tell them where you learned of it. They will want to buy this book. You will become my advertising and marketing department. I take my hat off to you for the kind assistance.

The trick here is to invent words and phrases, or to give common words and phrases a new spin, so that people will carry them elsewhere and with them your name and expanding fame. Still, the language itself should be clipped, crisp and immediately understandable.

Chapter 3

This concept of inventing your own phrases is not, so far as I can tell, one which appears elsewhere, and yet it is pivotal. It takes the knack of identifying a concept or idea and marking it with your own word, with a title or a phrase so catchy that others will include it in their permanent repertoire. Of course, like all inventions, some phrases will not work. Don't worry about it. Just keep trying. Soon you will enjoy the phenomenon of the world talking like you; very, very like you.

Ultimately, of course, these words and phrases, each associated with some particular part of your Problem Solving Process, will find themselves a permanent home in your books and materials. And you will find yourself quite happily being discussed by the media who are quite properly to be regarded as your most potent marketing force. How else should we regard them?

Organizing Your Material

The Problem Solving Process is the backbone which will help your organize your material. That's already clear. But I also want to address the filing and storage of your information, too, since this can become a significant problem for anyone on the lecture circuit.

To begin with, some of the most popular and lucrative programs deal with subjects which have significant blocks of changing information. Tax regulations change, current licensing and regulatory laws change, depreciation schedules change, new theories evolve, old one are discarded. This is all part of the fast-changing workshop business, and it's up to you to stay absolutely current and hence continually desirable.

Here's some advice. In these circumstances, you will need to read specialized information on a regular basis. Part of being an expert is staying one half step ahead of everyone else. You therefore need information before it becomes current, and you need to know about pending changes before they are in place. Newsletters are your answer in many cases. Therefore anyone on the lecture circuit needs to know about these two crucial resources:

- *Oxbridge Directory Of Newsletters*
  Oxbridge Communications, Inc.
  150 Fifth Ave.
  New York, New York 10011

It's billed as the most comprehensive guide to newsletters and I think it lives up to this self-evaluation.

- *Hudson's Newsletter Directory*
  Newsletter Clearinghouse
  P.O. Box 311
  Rhinebeck, New York 12572
  (914) 876-2081

This organization, organized and managed by Howard Penn Hudson, arguably the eminence griese of the newsletter world, should not be overlooked by any aspiring speaker. The members of the Clearinghouse, the publications indexed by the Directory contain critical information we all need. Tell Mr. Hudson I said so!

So subscribe to the publications you need. When material comes out that is pertinent or when issues are discussed which you can use, contact the information source. Tell this source that you are giving seminars on the topic, that you'd like whatever material is available and that you'll pass both the information and source material on to your participants. Most such letters get prompt, courteous responses and as a result you are in direct contact with another information source, thereby reinforcing your image as the in-command expert.

Information Storage

Information storage is a problem for all those in the workshop business as anyone can testify who has fallen into the paper trap I call my office. One easy way of solving it is to keep a file folder for each part of your Problem Solving Process and sort your materials accordingly.

Unfortunately, you usually cannot trek these file folders around the nation as you travel and deliver your program, so you have to decide what to take and what to leave behind. Here are some suggestions:

Chapter 3

Key points should be written on index cards (the larger size is usually better). It should include the facts you need and a complete reference in case people want more information. You should mention at the commencement of your talk, however, that while you have references for people who are interested, you will not be giving them in all cases. It would make your presentation far too choppy. If there is general interest, of course, in a given matter, you can write the information on the flip chart; if not you can pass it along to the questioner at a break.

It is extremely important that all your points be supported by specific information. Where a fact is likely to be questioned or where the information has significant impact on your audience, you will want to have this supporting material close at hand. However, you will not be able always or even usually to travel with the complete book, article, legislative documents, &c. Expect this and prepare accordingly.

Another way of organizing your information is in a three-ring binder divided into sections. This format is very commonly used on the lecture circuit and includes the information you need, indexed, usually in the order in which you need it, and the complete citation. Occasionally you can include a copy of an article or photocopied section of a book, too, if these are not too long. This binder is called a "swiss cheese" book, the idea being that like a mouse confronting the luxury of an especially large meal, you can finish it off expeditiously one bite at a time. It goes without saying that this arrangement of material lends itself nicely to the Problem Solving Process and to the functional arrangement of all your information.

On Memory

What is in your three-ring binder must be well know to you, be in fact the very fibre of your being. It would be fatal to you to stand before a group and read from a three-ring binder. You are not Joan Kennedy and the performance is not "Peter And The Wolf." Such a display would lack spontaneity and rightly be thought insufferably dull and inappropriate and would lead to questioning your status as the expert and trainer par excellence.

To get around this problem draw up a complete outline of key words and phrases in the order in which you want to approach the topic. This table of contents should appear first in your binder. Each particular section/topic should follow directly from the outline and should be tabulated for easy access.

Now it goes without saying that this book may end up being quite large, 200 or even 300 pages, or more. Also, that it has a very high value which means that it should never be put in your luggage but always hand-carried by you.

I learned this lesson the hard way in Hartford, Connecticut, when one of my critical outlines was stolen from a car while I was having dinner. While I capitalized on this tragedy by releasing the story to the *Hartford Courant* ("Author Robbed!"), I suggest you look for other means of getting publicity. Further (and I speak heartfully) you ought always to have a photocopy of your complete swiss cheese book.

In your swiss cheese book also allow adequate space for notes and comments at the end of each "chapter." Add the questions that were raised to which you did not feel your answers were sufficiently thorough and precise, citations you were not able to give, a new thought which occurred to you for the first time while addressing the audience, a book which you need to reread for clarification, and spontaneous comments which produced a good audience response.

After each program you need to be sufficiently self-critical to renew and revise your programs. The format of the three-ring binder Problem Solving Process book is perfect for this since you can add and delete items with ease.

A necessary note: Your name and address should be placed right at the front with a short note indicating that you'll give a reward if returned, no questions asked. A sad commentary on our times, but necessary for you and perhaps your salvation if this important resource is lost or stolen.

One of the difficulties of the workshop and lecture circuit is maintaining an appearance of spontaneity and excitement after you have given the same program over and over again. This is a more difficult problem than might at first appear. You must remember that each audience you face is entitled to the best of you, and you must do whatever it takes to bring yourself to the highest pitch of performance.

Chapter 3

A final note: It goes virtually without saying that in due course your three-ring binder becomes the basis for a published Problem Solving Process book which you will write on the same topic and which you will sell to enhance your profits. Thus your workshops and programs should be regarded as laboratories where you can test comments, materials, questions and language against the needs and responses of your audiences. A workshop is never, never an end in itself. It is part of a great chain of opportunities, and you must regard it as such.

More On Memory

No one can memorize an entire three ring binder nor should you even try. The material you deliver needs to breathe spontaneity and excitement even if you have given the program over and over. Moreover, memory is a tricky thing and the slightest distraction can throw you off causing acute embarrassment and awkwardness. Instead, strive to develop a mastery of the material and of the three-ring binder itself so that if you do momentarily falter you have a place to refer to immediately.

There are, fortunately, ways to hide temporary faltering. Always make sure that there is water and a glass ready for you. As you are reaching for the mot juste or just wondering where you are in your material, pause for a drink. Make sure that there is no water in your glass when you begin. Take a moment to pour some. Drink slowly and at the same time peruse your three-ring binder. Under no circumstances, apologize to the audience and don't panic. I have come to understand, as all professional speakers must, that most audiences are remarkably tolerant of their speakers, oftentimes too much so as the abundant numbers of boors and bores on the circuit attest. You are, after all, doing something which most of your audience cannot conceive of doing and which grips them with palpable anxiety. You are allowing yourself to be examined minutely and judged. Under the circumstances, they genuinely want you to succeed. Thus, take the time you need to get back on track and then proceed with as few comments as possible about your failing memory and your lost place. People are not interested in your problem; they are rather concerned by the deft way you mastered it, and the less said about that, the better.

Humor

Every good book on speaking, though there are few, will advise you to use humor in your presentations. Each of these books will also advise you to be wary of humor. These observations are of course true. Without humor I could not possibly give programs which are ordinarily seven or eight hours long. Humor for me is not a luxury; it's an absolute necessity.

But is is also necessary to know which kinds to avoid. It ought to go without saying (but probably doesn't) that racial, sexual, political, religious or other ideological or touchy forms of humor are not acceptable. Antagonizing any portion of your audience makes no sense.

Instead, learn the delights and benefits of mildly self-deprecating humor. You will be in a leadership position on the platform. People are willing to accord you this temporary elevation, but they don't want you to gain any semblance of swelled head. If you can make some mildly deprecatory remark which at once indicates your fellow feeling with the audience and compliments them, so much the better! But don't go overboard. You are after all still the leader.

I find that the best kind of humor is spontaneous and situational. I use this kind in my programs regularly. Sadly, it is difficult to advise you about this variety except that audiences will take you to their hearts if you are able to respond deftly, humorously, charmingly to points raised during their program.

Some of these spontaneous remarks are worth repeating, and you ought to write them down. Controlled though it is, I have jokes and lightening remarks which I plug into the same space in the same program time after time. Time after time, they work their well-worn magic. Those that fail are ruthlessly discarded.

You should do the same. Put your jokes and humorous remarks in the relevant portion of your three-ring binder. Humor is so important to the success of your programs that it, of all things, cannot be left to chance although those of you who are quick on your feet will reap an extra benefit by being able to use spontaneous humor which emerges from the program and its participants.

Chapter 3

On Physical Presentation

Like most people, you will probably be nervous when you move to the front of your first groups. Let me assure you, I still have an element of nervousness now after I've addressed hundreds of audiences. Sometimes it's a fierce stab of nerves, sometimes just general butterflies. I regard this as part of the job and by no means all bad. Nervousness is a sign that something important, significant and even risky is about to happen where the outcome is by no means certain. Such is surely the case in the speaking business. That's as it should be. You must be alert to the fact that you are being presented with an opportunity when you are the speaker, an opportunity to win over new converts, disseminate useful information and be thought a generally intelligent and useful member of the community. Or that you are being given an equal, and perhaps more frightening, opportunity to fail and present yourself before a throng of ready witnesses as a living parable of what can and often does go wrong at the lectern. Take heed.

Still, you can use nervousness to your advantage, and you must not let it cripple you. To begin your day or your performance, do a couple of quick stretching exercizes. Go to a stall in the lavatory and do toe touches or whatever you feel comfortable doing to relieve the constrictions of your anxious muscles and tense nerves. Do this as close as you can before going on stage. Often, of course, this loosening up process will be impossible; either the lavatory is not close at hand, or you must sit still in a prominent place before going on. If this is the case, you can always take a couple of good deep breaths before advancing to the podium.

This approach to the podium is itself significant and deserves your careful consideration. Every mother's wish for her adored child is true here: your shoulders should be back, your head high and you should move with what I call power strides to the podium, quick, brisk movements indicating professional mastery and surety. This is not easy when dozens of pairs of appraising eyes are unrelentingly fixed upon you.

Your Introduction

The introduction is important. Not only does it present you properly to the group, but it allows you just a moment to gain your absolute composure. Because this introduction is so important, it cannot and must not be left to chance. Thus you should get used to writing your own. This is, in fact, mandatory. You should write up a spiffy introduction especially for the individual program, and you should also always have a stock introduction handy which you can amend as necessary. Your introduction will vary according to the group as the importance of your various credentials changes. This is important to keep in mind. You need what I call Contextual Credentials for facts about you which are meaningful in one place but will not be at all significant in another.

Here is an alarming fact to keep in mind: people never read introductions the way they should be read. Most people are, of course, inept speakers to be sure. They are, however, even worse public readers. That is why I encourage the individual introducing me to read over the introduction I have prepared and rather than recite it (sure to fail) do the best he can from memory. It's more spontaneous and hence better, even if it's almost always replete with errors. Better a spontaneous error full of human interest than a fact dully recited.

Always make sure you have mastered the name of your presenter. You will want to thank this individual personally from the podium. Also, if there is something that you can do more tangibly to thank this person, do. For instance, continuing educators at college (and nowadays more and more at associations, too) are pushing other programs. Make sure that you point out that there are other courses of interest and that this individual is the person to contact. I encourage continuing educators (in case they need it!) to leave copies of their course catalogs and other promotional materials in the room along with my pass outs. This seems, of course, like Assertive Courtesy, but in fact I want them to distribute information about me and my programs to the other courses that they sponsor.

Your contact with the person introducing you is critical. It gives you not merely the chance to thank your introducer but to transform him into a friend. Perhaps more importantly it should establish you to the audience as a person of warmth and congeniality for now they will be able to draw the conclusion that you are truly pleasant based on how you have treated the person delivering the introduction.

Chapter 3

You, Alone

Often you will not have someone to introduce you. This happens particularly in adult education settings where you will be an instructor rather than an honored guest. You must in this situation demonstrate right from the start that you are in charge and give some ideas of why you are the right person to be teaching the program. Don't rest on the assumption that you are. Give the group a few friendly but firm sentences of introduction focusing specifically on why you are where you are.

Also let people know how often you have given this program and how the format will work best for them. Provide them with the following information in your opening:

- your name and how you want to be called for the remainder of the program
- your basic qualifications for this job
- how often you've given the program before, if applicable
- how the program will be run
- how many breaks there will be, at what intervals
- where the restrooms are
- when lunch (or other meals) will be.

Then go through the order of the day. Tell what will be covered, in what order. This is also the moment to pass out an outline if you intend to do this or to unveil one if you are using a flip chart. Adult learners crave structure. Give it to them! I break down my days by topic and by hour so that there is a clear progression. And, of course, I use the Problem Solving Process format as the backbone of the day.

The Ambulatory Speaker

Just how ambulatory you are going to be is determined by the kind of room, its set up and whether you are going to be using any voice amplification devices like microphones. On the whole I advise you to avoid microphones until you absolutely must have one. The natural voice is by far preferable to that amplified in any way. You can address up to 50 people without a microphone, and on occasions I have comfortably spoken to 100 without one. This is far, far from the oratorial feats of the great Victorians who addressed thousands for hours without electronic assistance (they, instead, were fortified by beaten egg in sherry wine). Here as in so many things we have declined from our forefathers.

Now, if you are making a speech (as opposed to delivering a workshop) your opening will be different, more formal. I advise you to know it pat. It should be in fact practiced and practiced again. The best way is by reciting your words aloud. You need to feel as well as experience the pacing and hear the sound of the words. There is no way around this, and you'll be making a great error if you, like Mrs. Reagan, "wing it." You'll either sound dull, boring, contrived, flat, rampant with clichés or just plain foolish. Remember the last time you tried!

A workshop opening can be more conversational, more plainspoken, more humdrum if you prefer. You'll be with your audience, after all, a long time and the important thing is to indicate who you are, why you are addressing this group, and what comfort considerations have been conceived for the audience as well as the information that will be imparted during the course of your time together. With a lecture audience you have less time to make the impression that you must make. This being the case you must work harder so that in the brief time that is available, the result is all that it can be.

Making Love To Your Audience

To succeed on the talk circuit whether you are giving after dinner speeches or five day institutes, you've got to make love to your audience. People who know me may be surprised to learn that this mild mannered gentleman considers himself a great lover in the Valentino tradition. Only I exert myself on the lecture platform to make my audiences feel special and loved.

Chapter 3

Both men and women speakers have to make love to the entire group. Women will probably have less trouble with this than men who in my opinion often hold themselves back from their audiences and are in consequence much too strict and straitlaced. If I use the word flirtatious it may be misunderstood and yet, properly received, being flirtatious with your audience is exactly what I have in mind. Men, too, though it flies in the face of our absurd machismo, like being flirted with by other men — if it's in public and from a discrete distance!

The fact remains that you have a two-tier sale to make. First you must sell the audience on you and then they will be more likely to buy what you have to tell (as well as to sell) them. People, after all, have relatively little problem dismissing from their minds information and material, even if it's to their direct benefit, if they don't like the messenger.

Why bring this up now? Because to achieve this two-tier sale, you need to go into your audience and move about or at the very least achieve the semblance of intimacy.

Picture me last year when I spoke to a group of candidates for the New York State Assembly. A series of photographs was taken and kindly sent me after the program. There I am speaking without a microphone, sitting on a table with my legs crossed, bending into the crowd. What's interesting is that these photographs show not only my unorthodox approach to the speaking circuit (nothing at all formal here) but also the attentive posture of the audience, quite rapt. I am most pleased by those photographs for the expressions of my audience is transfigured in the way I picture Valentino achieving.

Most speech books advise you to stand straight behind a microphone and podium and get on with your remarks. But they are quite, quite wrong. You must be free whenever possible to move in and out of your audience. Granted a workshop gives you more freedom to do this than a speech, and this is why workshops are my preferred medium. I get more participant contact, more intimacy, as you will.

A podium microphone limits your access to your audience. A hand held microphone looks, I feel, contrived. You are not some swish Las Vegas night club singer crooning a little ditty. This hand held mike is all too reminiscent of spoonerville. If you must have a mike, use the lavaliere which allows you to move freely, and which we'll discuss later.

Also, understand that being in the theatre business, you need a full set of props. I prefer a stand up or at the very least a table top podium, a table and a chair. Move about from one to the other as you feel comfortable. Move into the audience. Move around the room. Don't just stay in one position. Your workshop is your ship and you are the captain. Feel free to go wither thou wouldst.

I liken a workshop to a symphony and you the lecturer to the conductor. This is an apt representation. Thus it perfect apposite to speak in terms of the tempo of your performance.

When you consider tempo you need to know just a bit about people's most beneficial learning periods. Even though you may not be a so-called "morning person," you will be able to disseminate more hard information faster in the mornings than after a meal. Adults slow down after lunch and afternoons need to be marked *adagio ma non troppo,* movement but not too much. If your program is carried on into the evening, then you need a different kind of approach altogether, one less packed with information and more humorous and motivational.

As I hope is now perfectly clear, the Problem Solving Process format enables you to divide your program, be it one hour or several days, into bite-sized nuggets. Each hour consists of 55 minutes of participant contact time and 5 minutes of break. People consistently wonder as I describe my own lecture process which involves no audio visual aides, no film strips, no slides, just hour after hour of talk and audience questions, how such a strenuous program can work. Here's the answer:

- The adult participants must be convinced, must heartfully believe, that they are getting information they need in a form that they cannot get readily elsewhere.

- They must be touched by my excruciatingly intense enthusiasm which must not wane.

- The tempi must vary to respond to their peaks and valleys of energy and collapse.

Chapter 3

Questions

This intense experience is partly successful because of the use of participant questions. Here's the way to regard the seminar/workshop that you are giving: you are a vessel filled to the brim with useable information. The participants need to get this information. It is your responsibility to:

- Provide a structure that allows you to disseminate what you know, and

- To create an atmosphere that makes participants feel comfortable about asking follow-up queries or questions on any other matters that you have not dealt with.

In this connection there are three types of questions:

- Those which are of general interest to the group

- Those which are solely of personal interest to the questioner

- Those which are overtly hostile.

It goes almost without saying that to succeed on the workshop circuit you must become adept at dealing with questions. You can never be a complete success if you merely impart your information even though you do so with consummate enthusiasm and élan. You must deal with the questions put to you by your audience.

Indicating Your Receptivity To Questions

Say right from the start that you are there to provide as much information as you can both through your Problem Solving Process and through the questions asked of you by the audience. When you have reached the natural ending of any given topic, give a brief summary of what you have said and then request questions. You must continually indicate your receptivity to questions. I, for instance, get very few in my first hour. That is because people as yet do not feel entirely comfortable in their surroundings, probably haven't had much opportunity to interact with their fellow participants and may feel shy; moreover, they don't have the necessary context in which questions would be profitable. So don't worry about the seeming taciturnity of participants at the beginning of a program.

If you find that questions still don't come during the day, look for the puzzled or questioning expressions on people's faces. "You look puzzled. Is there a question I can try to answer for you that would make what I'm saying seem clearer?" Many times that puzzled expression is simply habitual to a listener, but at least you have demonstrated your willingness to be receptive.

When A Question Is Out Of Place

Although you have provided people with an outline of your program and have verbally recited this outline at the commencement of your presentation, people will ask questions out of the proper time. That's all right. The best way to handle this is to ask the person to hold his question until the right moment arrives. Ask him to write it down so he won't forget it, or if you care to do this and it doesn't interfere with your presentation and train of thought either jot it in your notebook for handling later or write it on your flip chart. Again, continue to indicate your receptivity to your audience but don't let yourself lose your place.

When A Question Is Personal To The Questioner

If the question asked is of particular interest only to the questioner, ask the person making the query to hold it until the next break when you'll deal with it personally. Ask the questioner to be sure to come up to the front of the room and remind you about it then. It is very easy to be distracted in a workshop where there are many demands on your time and attention, and you must be gently persistent about asking people to step forward and seek you out.

Chapter 3

Questions Asked Privately Which Are In Fact General

Frequently the best questions are asked of you privately during a break. These are questions the answers to which need to be shared with the group. I usually ask the questioner to ask the query at the beginning of the next section of the program so that all participants can hear the answer.

When A Questioner Keeps Asking Questions Or Interjecting Comments

Most groups have one or two people, blessedly not more!, who enjoy hearing themselves talk and who enjoy interjecting questions, comments, and commentary on your remarks. This can be most distracting and occasionally disagreeable. Often, however, these people are authorities in their own right with something valuable to say. How you handle each of these types is rather different.

- **The Mere Interjector**

If a person keeps interjecting with questions that are not of general interest and that after a bit seem to be wearing on the group, simply say, "I'm enjoying your questions, but I'd like to hear from others in the group, too. Let's take a couple of minutes at the break, and I'll see what I can do about answering your points."

What you'll find in group dynamics is that if you give the frequent questioner enough rope he'll hang himself and that you'll have the group on your side. I remember on one occasion in Pittsburgh where a very windy member of the City Council took one of my programs. Accustomed to orating and displays of histrionics, she did the same in my workshop. During the first two hours, I took the questions and unsolicited commentary as I would anyone else's, although people began to seek me out during the breaks to complain about the interruptions. Then I used the words above. She remained comparatively mute for the duration of the day.

You need to grasp the right psychological moment to drop this boom so that you are not seen as prematurely limiting discussion. Of course if the problem continues you'll have to ask individuals for a private word during the next break and ask them to keep their comments to themselves for the duration. You must remember that while you are trying to keep the minority happy, you are the creature of the majority of paying participants. Your principal allegiance is to them and their needs.

- **The Knowledgeable Interjector**

Often interjections and comments are made by someone who is as knowledgeable about the subject as you are. The best way to deal with this individual, often forceful, articulate and persistent, is to coopt him into your program. You must continue to be seen as the leader or the group's attention will drift to the other "expert"; it is always wise to coopt a potential disruptant.

I allow for half an hour at the termination of my program for general questions. This is a good device in general. If you have such time available, allow the general knowledgeable interjector to have some of it to make a presentation on points he wishes to cover. In other words draw on his resources. Note: Don't just use interjectors in this way, either. I'm quite willing to have all participants bring materials they wish to share with me and the group. I'm a student, too, after all and like to learn new things; I don't find this threatening as many of my insecure peers on the talk circuit do. You must be the facilitator, the individual who understands that your adult learners have experience, ideas, and pertinent information and materials to share, and you must, as the conductor, enable them to do so without at any time losing your primacy and your ability to direct proceedings.

More Tips For A More Persuasive You

Too many speakers look in corners, at the ceiling, at their hands or anything in fact but the people in their audience. Don't make this mistake! If possible meet a couple of people before you begin speaking. Look at these people. Smile at them. If parts of what you are saying are of particular applicability to them (you have found out in speaking with them, of course, why they've come, haven't you?), direct a pertinent direct comment to them, "You know, Mrs. Smith, this ought to be most beneficial for you."

Chapter 3

A note on names: Perhaps because I did my first book on Victorian protocol and ceremonies, I am acutely conscious of grades of social intercourse and direct address. I wince when people I have never met call me "Jeff," a name no friend ever calls me (Jeffrey, please!) You must make a decision about what to do and this partly involves the kind of program you have. Announce what you'd like to be called at the beginning of your presentation. "My name is Jeffrey Lant. Please call me Jeffrey." As people introduce themselves (if there is time you definitely want them to do this), ask what they'd like to be called. And as people ask questions during the first hour or two, ask people to give their names so that the other participants get the chance to know them better.

But don't presume. Presumption about names is left to secretaries with bad manners (an engorged group) and U.S. customs officials who are on the whole graced with the most shocking manners imaginable.

As you speak, designate two people to be what I call weathervanes. One of these should have a scowling face and one should be of a blither disposition. Use them to determine whether your program is succeeding, whether your points are getting across and whether your humorous sallies are in fact winning over the sullen crowd. Interestingly enough I have learned that very often the individual who has the scowling face turns into one of my best listeners, perhaps because I direct a little more attention his way. I often tell these individuals at the end of the day that I have used them as measuring devices. I have come to know that they enjoy this special attention which they find flattering. So be it.

Body Parts: What To Do With Them

Most people have trouble knowing what to do with their hands. Hence a few do's and dont's.

Gentlemen: Don't put your hands in your pockets. Models in Bloomingdale ads can do it, but the reason your mother told you to desist from this habit still applies.

Ladies and Gentlemen: Keep something near by to grasp in case you feel like biting your nails, twirling your hair, &c. Use your spectacles as a prop and to emphasize your points. Use your notes. A pencil or pen is also quite good.

Best body language: Lean into your audience when you want to stress a point. Just as you would into a passionate embrace. This gets across the message that what you're saying is important and that you particularly want your audience to pay attention. It's hard to be blasé when you are the object of such concentrated attention.

If two people are talking or whispering together, walk to their vicinity. Stand right beside them if you can and while taking no official notice of what they are doing, just stand there for a moment. They will stop what they are doing, but you won't have to stop what you're doing!

On standing. All books say that you should speak from a standing or even striding position. This is good enough except that being on my feet for 7 or 8 hours or more is tiring. Thus don't hesitate when necessary to sit on a table top and practice leaning into your audience. So long as you are touching your audience, making them feel the electric spark of your presence and the importance of your material and its benefit to them, it frankly doesn't seem to matter much whether you are seated or standing. However for most people this effect only comes when they are on their feet.

Now that you are trained, now that you know how to disseminate your information and handle an audience to best effect, the question becomes: where do you find the audience to dazzle? Read on.

THE MONEY BEGINS

Chapter 4

BREAKING IN

You are now ready to go!

The question is where.

The critical mistake most people make is that they aim for solo, unsponsored presentations before they are ready thinking, in the best American tradition, that to share the financial return from their program as well as the information they have is excessive. I recall in this connection a man I advised last year, a Ph.D. psychologist from New Hampshire. He called me in for counsel because a program he was having on sexual dysfunctions was not going well. He wanted to hold a press conference and promote the program exclusively from the free media. The media, predictably, were not responding and the date was fast approaching.

My first response was to tell him to postpone the program and follow the steps in this chapter, but he, obdurate, wanted to proceed. The result was standard: unmitigated failure and needless further expense.

The Key Rule Of Success

The key rule of success in the workshop/seminar/lecture business is to go where your audience is already assembled or to work with people who can assemble your audience for you. The most expensive programs and the most frustrating for you are those where you have to find the audience yourself spending time and money in developing direct mail lists, newspaper ads, brochures, &c. This doesn't mean that such self-sponsored programs can't and shouldn't be done — there is a chapter of this book that will help you succeed there when you're ready. But it does mean that you have to work up to this level of proficiency, and the way to do it is on other people's money.

Where to Start

Without a doubt the best places to begin are your local community college or noncredit adult continuing education facility. Why? Because people there will be less critical of you (they are paying less money), the costs of producing and promoting your program will be less, you'll get city-wide or more exposure and the chance (if you work with their public relations departments) for learning the media ropes, too. Moreover with both these sources you don't have to worry about framing the budget, finding the space, creating and distributing the catalog or brochures, handling registrations, and all the other administrative tasks that necessary come with program promotion. You can focus on what you like best and know best: the substance itself.

Finding Prospects

There are several ways to find prospects where you can offer your workshops. Note that I say "workshops," for if you have more than one idea this is a good way to test them out. Perhaps this is the best way to regard these places, as institutions where you can test your programs, find out whether anyone is really interested, enable you to get media exposure, refine your Problem Solving Process format and gather useful participant data which will help you when you decide to take your program on the road.

You'll notice that I'm stressing community colleges and adult education centers. Of these I prefer the latter. That is because many community college courses (but by no means all) are offered for credit and on the whole you want to avoid offering for credit courses. Why?

- You'll be tied down to giving a course regularly over an extended period of time.

- Payment is worse in the credit than the noncredit area.

- The application procedures are stricter. You'll have to turn in college transcripts, letters of recommendation, &c., all of which takes time.

- You'll have to spend extra time grading papers, meeting with students and generally doing the academic fox trot.

Chapter 4

- Institutions may cavil at your offering your product (even if it is the relevant book on the subject) to your students suggesting that such a practice smacks of commercialism (heaven forbid!)

All of these are good reasons to avoid giving credit courses and to slant your presentations and applications to administrators of noncredit courses where these serious drawbacks do not apply.

Sources of Prospects

Begin with the telephone directory. Check under "schools." Any programs that look applicable such as community colleges or adult noncredit continuing education facilities you should contact requesting a catalog. They'll be only too happy to send it out.

Remember: you are looking for institutions that have catalogs. Why? To begin with because they get the broadest possible outreach at the least expense and with the least effort on your part. Also, until you have a track record of success, it is unlikely (though by no means impossible) that an institution will invest the time and effort it takes to develop an extraordinary brochure, purchase mailing lists and do all the other developmental and promotional tasks that go into a successful program. You are untried, and the untried have a harder time competing for these scarce investment dollars.

Catalog note: Make sure, as you begin prospecting, that you request the catalogs of two of the most superb noncredit programs available in the nation, The New School for Social Research and the Extension Division of the University of California, Los Angeles. These are places to check and see whether your program is being offered, how it is written up and how promoted. These two institutions probably have the largest program development staffs in the country and you'll get the flavor of what's new and the ins and outs of the business by perusing their fine publications. Read them, too, for good, solid and often very promotional catalog descriptions. Here's where inspiration begins:

- The New School for Social Research, 66 West 12th Street, New York, New York 10011 ATTN Adult Division (212-741-5600)

- UCLA Extension, Department K, P.O. Box 24901, Los Angeles, CA 90024 (213-825-8895)

Check offerings in your field as promoted by these two programs against those of institutions in your area. You will discover that other places are generally behind the times. Such a lag can obviously be used to your benefit by proposing a course to local administrators that they haven't yet decided to add to their curriculum. There are after all only a few ways of your getting to give courses: obviously you have either to displace a sitting instructor (very often quite difficult), fill in for one upon death or retirement, or you have to sell a new course. These are, of course, in inverse ease.

Join The Learning Resources Network

LERN is a national organization. As a member you'll get a list of the adult (primarily noncredit) continuing educational facilities nationwide. You will also get access to their professional development publications (several of which are cited in this book) as well as their newsletters which are chock full of promotional and development advice rendered by such well-known columnists as—me! They have useful conferences, too, on subjects of interest to you, and the price of membership is reasonable.

Learning Resources Network
1554 Hayes Drive
Manhattan, KS 66502

(913) 539-5376

Chapter 4

When In Boston

In Boston, always distinctive, check with The Educational Exchange of Greater Boston. The Exchange is the brainchild of Miss Zelda Lions who has for more than 60 years prepared a fairly complete précis of most of the adult educational classes and sponsors in the Boston area. It's still most reasonably priced at $7.50. (For the rest of you this little book will suggest course possibilities.)

Educational Opportunities Of Greater Boston For Adults
The Educational Exchange of Greater Boston
430 Massachusetts Ave.
Cambridge, MA 02138

(617) 876-3080

After You've Got The Catalog

You have to review these catalogs term after term. If the course you wish to teach is being offered it is unfortunate, but there is something you can do. Although people in a winning seminar tend to repeat it for years and regard it as their own fief, they do eventually die, retire or become worn out, thus opening the position for you. Also, continuing educators are only human and they like back-ups since people do become ill or incapacitated. The stock *42nd Street* format.

To get your name into consideration for such a vacancy, call the college or noncredit adult continuing education center and request the name of the individual planning programs. Get his/her proper title and mailing address and send correspondence asking to be kept in mind if a vacancy for this course develops. (See samples, page 264.) Cite your credentials just as you would when applying for an actual position. The only thing you probably don't need to do is request an interview, although if you do have occasion to get acquainted, proceed. You will probably not be as nervous under these circumstances since you are applying for a contingency and not an actual position.

Be prepared to drop everything and fill the position if it is offered to you. People get sick at the last minute; you must be prepared to fill in as needed. Once in the position, make sure you structure the course around the Problem Solving Process and proceed as if it were your own. However, always make sure you announce to participants that you are a last-minute replacement for the actual instructor. You will not be so harshly evaluated for any mistakes or false starts you happen to make!

Note: wherever you want to teach (and I hope you are targeting the prestigious places!), update your folder from time to time with news and feature articles about you and your courses elsewhere, catalogs, brochures, and participant evaluations. Send these using Assertive Courtesy. Presume that the program planner maintains an interest in you; don't worry if it is only embryonic or worse. Your task is to groom yourself as the inevitable successor and as an individual offering a successful program. This will definitely pay off for you. Someday you'll warm the spot yourself! Someone else having benefitted from this book will begin to look forward to the day when you won't. . .

If There Is No Course

Here's the problem if your course doesn't exist: either the program planner or institution has offered it in the past and the course has failed because of insufficient enrollment, or they haven't yet thought of it. In either case you have a sales task confronting you.

Your first job, then, is to produce a compelling sales letter. As you contemplate doing so, remember that continuing educators are by their very nature experimenters. Trends don't last forever; program planners know this and are continually on the alert for new ways of making money from courses. They are also aware that just because a course doesn't succeed the first or second or even third time it's offered that doesn't mean they'll never offer it again. Perennial optimists, they want to find the way that will insure its success. You have to be the one who helps convince them that this time — for sure! — the course will succeed.

Here's what that winning sales letter should contain:

- benefits to the program planner in sponsoring the program

Chapter 4

- your introduction
- a sense of your credentials
- why the market is primed for this course now
- sample catalog copy
- sample media release
- suggested target groups and why they'd be interested
- whether you have the names of possible participants
- when you'd like to offer the program and why. (See samples, page 266.)

Sending The Letter To The Right Person

Send this compelling letter only to the program planner. This is the person you need to contact and remain in contact with. This contact need not be direct, person to person, although that helps. After all, the longer you work in this business, the more selling you'll do by telephone or simple letter.

Networking

If you know someone who has taught at the institution you've targeted (a successful instructor, please!), ask that person to recommend you. While continuing educators are perfectly happy to take proposals from people they don't know, it certainly is advisable to use a connection if you have one. Note: I have networked several of my former workshop participants into positions at universities and speaking engagements at trade associations. Usually they write charming letters of recommendation for me to selected associations with which they are connected, and I return the favor. Interested? Give me a call.

The networking letter should be timed to precede your letter of application/introduction by about 3 to 5 days, not longer. The problem in most instances is that people (you!) don't follow up the initial networking letter quickly enough. This reflects poorly on them and irritates the person to whom the letter was sent.

Many Courses Look Alike

If there is something in the catalog similar to what you're proposing, point out the difference in what you're going to do vis á vis the other course. How do you know? Telephone the instructor and find out what he's doing. You'll get the number by calling the program planner directly and asking for it; most offices will give out instructor telephone numbers if asked. If this fails, write the instructor a letter care of the program planner. This should get forwarded.

You are clearly in a stronger position with the program planner if you know that your program will not interfere with an existing one. Moreover from the institution's standpoint if the two programs can be seen to be distinct yet related, those enrolling in the one may be induced to enroll in the other. The advantages of doing so can be pointed out in the catalog and may well work to your advantage by indicating that a repeat sale to a single customer is possible. Definitely go for this leverage.

Initial Follow-Up

Nowadays I am hired sight unseen over the telephone by people I often don't meet for months or even years (since they may not work on Saturdays when I offer many of my programs). This happens because my courses are well known not simply for their content but their profitability to sponsors. In the beginning, however, this won't always happen with you! Thus it is a good idea for you to meet with continuing educators whenever possible. For one thing it's easier to come to an arrangement with people when you are physically present. You have taken up a slice of their life and rather than

Chapter 4

admit they've made a mistake (certain anathema), they'd rather proceed to give your course a try. Maybe, they reason, it will work! You need to be present not only to sell yourself and your programs and make an ongoing, useful contact. You also need to know as much as possible about how this individual program planner thinks and what his prejudices are, for make no mistake about it this is a very idiosyncratic group of people.

Telephoning

Follow up your initial letter with a telephone call. This call should be placed early in the day. It is always best to place calls where you are seeking something early. That gives the program planner the entire day to call you back. (By the same token, return unpleasant calls, if at all, at their lunch hour or at the very end of their day!)

If the person you are seeking is not available, leave a detailed message not just your name. Say to the secretary, "Please tell Ms. Smith that Dr. Jeffrey Lant called and that I'm following up my recent letter. I'll be available at 617-547-6372 the remainder of the day."

Unless you have called during registration week (find out when it is and avoid it) or during their holidays (too numerous to mention), expect the program planner to call you back. You have after all written a sparkling sales letter designed to appeal to their desire for another successful program. You have in this letter indicated that you are the consummate professional, the kind of person, in short, they really ought to be doing business with.

If the program planner fails to call you back in two days, call again. Then call once more. Then write and indicate that you want to get in touch and would be grateful for the consideration of a return call. If at this point the planner still isn't getting back to you, it does not necessarily indicate a lack of interest. It does, of course, prove a decided lack of organization. Wait a bit, perhaps a month, and try again. Or wait until you have secured an engagement elsewhere. Again use Assertive Courtesy. Send the catalog for your new program and send other appropriate materials, too. Say that you still are looking forward to establishing a productive relationship with this organization. Moreover as you have successes elsewhere, as you prove your ability to bring in participants and dollars, use the Success Letter format, discussed shortly, to get back in touch with this recalcitrant, disorganized, downright rude but indispensable administrator. Remember: this person can afford to be all these disagreeable things. You cannot. In this game with very tangible, very valuable prizes you must remain persistent until you snag the berth you want.

When You Connect

The program planner may not want a meeting. In this case your selling must be done over the telephone. This puts you at a relative disadvantage because you don't know the quirks and objectives of the person with whom you're dealing. In this instance, therefore, you need to be quite clear about the reasons you feel your suggestion would be a popular one and you must have these reasons right at your finger tips. Reasons may include:

- a rash of articles on the subject in major publications. Cite these articles. Have them available for review. Don't hesitate to send one or more of them along with your initial letter even though you didn't write them yourself. If you did write these articles, use them to your advantage. After all now you are the perceived expert and should derive a little beneficial homage.

- other, noncompetitive institutions offering a similar program. I say "noncompetitive" advisedly. If the institution is local and competitive the program planner may pass on the course not wishing to go head to head with another institution. Yet by the same token, if no one local is offering the course, the administrator may also pass since the course is clearly speculative. A typical continuing education Catch 22.

- a popular new book on the subject.

- a defined marketplace with a clear set of problems that you can solve.

Chapter 4

Don't stint on your reasons. You may find it tedious to trot them out. Don't. Remember what you are getting out of this contact:

- the money

- an annuity if the course is successful, that is money for this course term after term with minimal preparation

- a networking connection with the administrator you are now dealing with

- a Success Letter to other organizations based on your record with this course

- a basis for sustained media attention

- access to further market data on the participants, the kind of people who will swell your later programs

- catalog copy and other validating documentation to convince others of your safety and value

- the possibility of attending a course or two for free and so enhance your own skills, make another instructor contact, and evaluate someone else's training and teaching skills to your own benefit.

Oh, yes, it can be irritating and tedious, but it is worth it!

Objections You Are Likely To Encounter In This Conversation

Continuing educators are experimenters to be sure. But they also fall prey to carping criticism which can dishearten you. Don't let it. Get used to the string of negatives they may unleash at you and prepare your responses based on the following:

"We tried that once before and it didn't work." How aggravating! Don't get flustered, however. What you are likely to suggest may very well have been tried before. There is probably nothing new under the sun!

In this case ask when the program was tried. If it has not been tried within the last year, then give your professional opinion about why you think it would be more likely to succeed now. It's a given that the continuing educator doesn't know anything about your field or its substance, the ebb and flow about which you are the expert. Stand on your position as the expert. Ask what the format was. If the course met week nights, perhaps it should be tried as an all-day Saturday program. If on a Sunday, then during the week, &c. Don't be afraid to suggest a change of format and time to benefit the course. Continuing educators don't always (or even usually) know why certain days work for a given program, but if you have a sense of your participants, you can suggest confidently what times and dates make more sense for them and why.

Ask how near the course came to succeeding. How many registrants did it have? Ask whether the names and addresses of these people still exist. Perhaps they can be recontacted and so form a core group of pre-registrants. Ask, too, whether there are related courses; (you should, of course, know this from the catalog). If so, perhaps a special letter could be sent to them. You can write it yourself and have the institution mail it. Remember: the more work you are willing to do, the better. Indicate your willingness to help.

Ask for the instructor's name and telephone number. Perhaps he can give you a sense of why the course didn't previously succeed. Perhaps it was administratively botched. Find out whether the sponsoring organization is now sending out more brochures and catalogs.

Indicate that you are willing to bring the course to the attention of your friends, professional associates and colleagues. Indicate that you'd be willing to send a special letter to them along with marked copies of the catalog. This is especially appealing since it provides the institution with new names, new prospects, something they quite like and which turns you into part of their marketing effort.

Chapter 4

Tell the program planner that you are willing to appear on media shows promoting the course (to your advantage in any case) and that you are willing to work with their public relations department to achieve a beneficial result. Moreover, say that you are willing to schedule your own interviews. This is another plus.

In short, overcome this objection.

"There is no one to assist you with public relations." Again, let them know you can do it yourself. (If you've mastered **THE UNABASHED SELF-PROMOTER'S GUIDE**, of course you'll have no problem.)

"We're short handed this term. We'd need marketing assistance in bringing the program to the attention of people who might be interested." You have friends, colleagues, business associates and others who are interested. You can be helpful.

"Not now. We've fully booked for the next session. Call me back." Don't leave this conversation until you find out when you can call again. Get a specific date. Mark it on your calendar and call back promptly.

"We've just hired an instructor to teach a course like that." Find out whether the courses really are the same. Ask to chat with the instructor. If they are, then ask the program planner to keep your name on file as a substitute. Keep in touch as I've indicated above.

As you see, there is a Pyramid of Possibilities here. Of course you want to be told that you're hired sight unseen because of your reputation. It's gratifying and it frees up a lot of time. But remember: I've been working in the continuing education business for 15 years now and if I've reached this eminence it's because I've worked to reach it. So will you. But you must be persistent. You must use Assertive Courtesy. And you must keep bringing your ability to offer successful, financially lucrative programs to the attention of those program planners you want to influence. In due course, you'll be the sought after speaker you want to be.

The Meeting

As I've said all this is difficult to do on the telephone. Whenever possible, then, try to meet your contact. This will make it easier to get the agreement you want.

At this meeting take notes. Also, aim to make a friend. You need a two-tier sale here: to sell yourself as an amiable, personable, knowledgeable authority and as someone who'll be easy to work with and will take part of the unbearable burden of the administrator's job onto yourself. The administrator has two occasionally contradictory interests. Administrators want to put on profitable programs. They are also overworked themselves (or consider themselves to be, a very different thing of course) and want instructors who will take onto themselves as much work for their own programs as possible.

Thus in any meeting you have indicate that you know what needs to take place (reread this book!) and indicate that you'll do what it takes (be specific) to insure the success of your program. Here are the tasks:

- writing catalog copy

- designing brochures and other promotional materials

- suggesting new target populations and suggesting means of access to them

- marketing via the free media.

These tasks never change. Just who does them does. Indicate your willingness to take on reasonable assignments in each area and so improve the chances of success for your course and for your longterm relationship with the institution.

Chapter 4

Taking Notes

You need to get much specific information during this meeting. Find out:

- When catalog copy is due and if what you may already have submitted is acceptable.

- When catalogs will be available and how many you'll take (100 is a reasonable number).

- Whether these can be mailed to you or whether you have to pick them up.

- Whether you can submit a list of names of individuals to mail to.

- Whether a letter from the administrator (or from you) can be inserted into this mailing (an important point).

- Who the public relations person is and whether a meeting can be arranged.

- Whether a class list can be made available to you.

- What institutional facilities are available to you. If, for instance, you are offering your class on Saturday, you may find that you'll have to do without photocopying machines, &c. Find out.

If all is going well in this meeting, suggest future course possibilities. If they are not in the catalog, this is a good time to begin planning for the *next* available term. I cannot stress this planning function sufficiently. Even with universities which know me well, we plan at least six months in advance. Administrators need time to consider new courses and to make an informed decision.

This meeting need not be longer than 30 minutes and should not be longer than an hour. You have other things to do; so does the administrator. But before you leave, ask to see the director of public relations.

One More Thing: If The Administrator Still Isn't Convinced

If at the end of the meeting, the program planner still isn't convinced don't necessarily give up. Ordinarily the planner will ask for time to "think it over." This may mean that he has to check with others about the advisability of offering your course; it may also mean, of course, that he wishes you'd just go away and is too courteous to say so.

If there is an opening, make sure you follow it up. Find out when you can call back and attempt to move matters along. If the administrator is not receptive, then use Assertive Courtesy. As you succeed at other places, send him the brochures, catalogs and promotional materials that will induce him to proceed. Even if the personal chemistry was not good, don't worry. I told you that to succeed in sales you'd have to have selective perception. This is a case where it's probably necessary.

Whatever you do, don't forget this: listen to what the administrator says to you. Perhaps you were told that your program wasn't well developed or timely. Even though you have thought through your program and have seriously considered it, these are professionals and occasionally you ought to consider they may be right. You have to balance what you know about the field and what's happening in it and any objections the administrator may have made. Then make your decision. When you approach another administrator with the idea, see whether you can't bolster your case by dealing with the previous arguments in your new application. This will strengthen your presentation.

Working With Continuing Educators

You'll probably be working with two people in planning and marketing your programs: the program planner and the public relations officer. In smaller institutions the former may also be the director. In larger institutions not. If not, you'll want to meet this person at some point and begin a relationship.

Chapter 4

You already know how to handle the program planner. Now it's time to get on to the public relations officer. I have sadly found that the people who handle public relations in continuing education are not very knowledgeable. Knowledgeable or not, however, they are certainly not at all aggressive or imaginative. They suffer from a manifestly inadequate belief that public relations involves no more than writing a media release, mailing it out to a calendar section of a newspaper and hoping for the best. This isn't public relations, of course; it's paper shuffling and nothing more. The chapter on unabashed promotion will help you out in working with these people and in realizing your objectives, but here are some guidelines to help you with them.

The Public Relation Officer's Point of View

Here are some of the things these creatures are likely to tell you:

"Your course is only one of dozens. To be fair we can't treat you any differently than anyone else."

"I'm the only person in public relations, and I'm swamped. I don't have time to write a media release right now, and I certainly don't have time to make follow-up telephone calls for media sources about your program."

"The media publish quite enough about us and regularly publicize our programs. We don't need any more and asking them will interfere with the publicity we get."

Your Point of View

Here are some helpful lines you can offer:

"This is the first time I've offered this program here, and it would be mutually benefical to launch it properly."

"This is the second (third, &c) time I've done this program here. We've got a winner! Promoting it will help increase your profit!"

"I'll write all the media materials myself. You can duplicate them on your stationery and if you give me envelopes, I'll mail them out to the right places. Perhaps you can give me some tips."

"I'll make the necessary follow-up telephone calls."

Remember: while all this indicates that you know what you're doing (you do, don't you?) and that you are willing to be helpful, you may still encounter a certain amount of opposition because by being this helpful you are not following the desultory way things are "usually done." Continuing education Catch 22 again.

Be patient. Unfortunately, as you already know, I was myself born without patience and have a limited amount of tolerance for the stupid, misguided, obstructionist and constrained. Don't, please, follow my example but try harder to be better. Note: even I, I'd like to tell you, have improved in the patience department. No continuing educator has yet suffered bodily injury on my account.

Developing Sizzling Catalog Copy And An Alluring Title

It goes without saying that your course title is important. If it's successful it will not only induce the interest of program planners but participants and the media, too. It will become the title of your book on the same subject, your audio and video cassettes and, if you're lucky enough, a newsletter. This book is a perfect illustration of a title that does most of this if not quite all. (No newsletter yet.)

Frankly, there's a gift to creating catchy titles. Titles ought to be in two parts like good book titles with a grabber **(MONEY TALKS)** and a descriptor **(THE COMPLETE GUIDE TO PRODUCING A PROFITABLE WORKSHOP OR SEMINAR IN ANY FIELD)**. The descriptor will ordinarily occur to you first; the grabber comes later and is the more difficult to conceive.

Chapter 4

People are always asking me where the titles to my programs come from. That's both easy and not so easy to say. The descriptor comes straight from the Problem Solving Process. It should indicate to the prospective buyer exactly what he's getting. It should in a single phrase and just a few words summarize the program exactly. The matter of the grabber is more complicated. Try using a common phrase, song title, expression, &c., and giving it a new spin just like I've done with **MONEY TALKS**. Everyone in the country already knows the name of the book; my task is to get them to associate it with these pages.

When dealing with the media both the grabber and the descriptor are important. Grabbers make nifty headlines but the descriptor is the backbone of the coverage you'll get.

Remember: clever titles can occasionally be *too* clever. If your program isn't drawing it just might be the title's fault. The best way to discover whether the title is the problem is to ask participants what they think of the title and try some alternatives with them. There's nothing wrong with running the same program with several different titles and attempting to find out whether that is the significant variable

Catalog Copy

Use the existing catalog of the program hiring you as a guide for copy length. Unfortunately the more catalogs you read the more you'll see that while many instructors spend a considerable amount of time preparing their courses, many fewer devote any attention to the title and catalog copy. This is of course, a mistake. Catalog copy needs to do the following things:

- Snag a prospect's interest.

- Differentiate itself from the mass of other courses both at that institution and at other, competing institutions.

- Establish immediately that there is a substantial benefit for the reader.

- Not overwhelm the potential participant with the difficulty of the subject matter.

- Make it easy for the participant to enroll.

Mind you, all this needs to be done in between 75-150 words. This is not, I hasten to remind you, an easy assignment.

Aim for copy which is at once sleek, brisk, lean and substantial. Aim for action words, energized adjectives and adverbs, withhold the passive voice, pack the copy with benefits for the buyers, outcomes that they can use and an urgency which propels them to buy now.

As you draft your copy don't forget your Participant Profile. You know the kinds of words which should appeal to your prospective audience and which motivate them to action. My audience, as I've said, is professional, well educated, upwardly mobile, past its first youth, relatively affluent and desirous of more, and feeling that the best things in life are eluding them. They want movement, demonstrated progress, hard-hitting, fact-filled techniques. They need to know what you're going to do and whether the program has been validated by others

Suggested Course Copy for "Money Talks", A One Day Workshop

"Professionals today understand that what they know is worth a lot. They are not always sure, however, how to get the most benefit from their knowledge. This one-day fast-paced intensive workshop under the direction of nationally known author and lecturer Dr. Jeffrey Lant will answer the question of how you can turn your expertise into extra money on a regular basis. You'll learn the ins and outs of paying talk markets, of trade and professional associations and continuing education. Find out how to launch a national full-or part-time practice that will result in thousands of new dollars of income annually. Learn how to cash in on 'back of the room' sales, how to promote yourself, master the lecture circuit and do lucrative national programs with video teleconferencing."

Once you've written the first draft of such copy, edit it by deleting all the slow language, all that focuses on you (except some quick indication of your expertise) rather than on client related benefits. Your copy must surge and sing and make the prospect want to take action right now.

Chapter 4

In writing this copy it's important to keep in mind that there are basically two kinds of talk audiences: upscale and downscale. The approach to them will vary.

Upscale Participants

These are people like me and most of my readers and workshop participants. We suffer from a peculiar urgency and anxiety that is very much a characteristic of our times. We are afraid that the good things will be gone before we get them or that they will remain tantalizingly out of reach forever. We have good reason for thinking this.

Smart advertisers make use of our fear, anxiety and this urgency to get us to take immediate action. When you write catalog copy for this group, which is after all only another form of advertising, you must impart the need to take action now. Fortunately this group needs only a dollop of urgency in the copy to become motivated. It already understands that it is in a race for a dwindling stock of glittering prizes and has made the commitment prior to contact with you to do what it takes to win. The fact that this commitment to winning has already been made is important to you since now you simply must convince them that what you've got is a key constituent of the goal they wish to achieve. That's the trick of advertising to the upscale.

This group of buyers, which has much of the discretionary income in this country and a disproportionate share of the motivation, is very susceptible to advertising. Your task is to impart as quickly as you can a sense of urgency and a clear picture of the desired outcomes

Downscale Participants

Downscale buyers are also aware that life is a race. Only these poor people have the definite feeling that it is a race which has already passed them by and left them in the dust. The anxiety that must be used on them is different from that used with the upscale. Here you must convince the downscale, those with limited resources and dwindling options, that if they don't take action now — the kind of action you are recommending — what freedom of action they now have will be further curtailed and they'll be worse off than before. You must convince them, in short, that a failure to act today is in fact a choice and that this choice will have dramatic consequences in their lives.

As I said, most of my workshop participants are upscale, subject to upscale anxieties. The high ticket courses nationwide are all populated by upscale people while most of the lower priced are populated by the downscale. Let me say this as straightforwardly as I can: it is the downscale buyer who is the more difficult. This individual, with very limited options and resources, does not understand that the achievement of success demands sustained work and regular outlays of cash. He wishes to achieve miracles for trifling sums and is petulant and critical when he doesn't. These are the people who nickle and dime you to death and in the seminar business they are poison.

I had a vivid illustration of this last summer. During a single three day period I offered a one-day consulting seminar in a large city where the price was $40 for the day as set by the sponsor. For this princely price, the participants expected much and were most demanding about all aspects of the course. **THE CONSULTANT'S KIT**, the course text, was not of course built into the program at that fee and fully half of the people did not buy it despite the fact that it contains all the contract forms and other business documents that each would need to launch a practice.

The next day I began a two-day version of the same course with a major university that was charging $400 for the program, exactly ten times as much. **THE CONSULTANT'S KIT** was built into the price as were two pleasant lunches, but there were no further amenities. Still, there were more people in the $400 course than in the $40 and half the participants, the usual number, made additional purchases of my books. Having invested $400 an additional $30 or so was a trifling expense.

What a difference and what it taught me. I severed my connection with the first organization and vowed never to do a cut rate program again. They really are no bargains!

Your Financial Arrangements With The Sponsoring Organization

Face it, you're not going to get rich from what noncredit continuing education pays you at the level of local noncredit centers and community colleges. That's why I don't offer programs at such institutions any more and why you are going

Chapter 4

to have a directed relationship with them. Resolve from the start to take your programs to such places only to perfect them and get a clear understanding of the audience. Then remove your program and yourself from them as soon as you can since a longterm relationship will be detrimental to your success on the talk circuit. This universe is for training, for perfecting your lecture skills, your program content, your knowledge of your audience. Unlike other training programs, however, in this one you will be paid to learn even if the money is decidedly limited.

Stipends And Profit

For a one-day program of 7 or 8 hours duration you can expect to be paid between $90 and about $300 with the lower stipends coming from the noncredit continuing education facilities. This is, of course, subject to negotiation. The operative factor, however, is how much the institution is charging for the program and how many people they expect to draw. Expect their calculations to be conservative. So long as you regard this fee as paying for being trained for better assignments elsewhere, you can bear it. The problem arises when you decide to remain in this universe and fail to realize that real profit within it is nugatory.

There is an exception, however, and that comes about when you have books and other materials to sell. This entire subject will be discussed in another chapter. In such circumstances the fee will be incidental to the money you can make selling products. However you must understand that the lower the entry fee the less likely people are to buy products.

In this connection, I have tried offering workshops through the burgeoning number of noncredit adult education facilities. Some of these programs are offered over coffee and dessert; others take place in a single evening or on the weekend. All charge under $50 for the course and those over coffee are often just $15.

The plain truth about these programs is that many people use them as alternatives to dating bars. They are there to learn a little and to meet as many people as possible. They are not there to buy your products. In such circumstances, then, you should offer your programs at such places only to learn the trade. As soon as you are comfortable not only with what you know but how you present it, genteelly sever your connection.

Contracts And Problems

The sponsoring organization will in most cases have standard contracts. I advise you to sign it and not worry about it unless there are clauses relating to the following:

- Taping: Don't sign a contract that prevents you from taping the course and offering it for sale to participants on the spot.

- Books and materials: Don't sign a contract that prevents you from selling your books and materials at a workshop or that forces you to share the proceeds with the sponsor. In this universe, if there is any money to be made it's from sale of products to participants. You need this money to make the experiments profitable.

Let's be very clear about this community college and adult noncredit continuing education universe. Many people in it have peculiar notions about education and the role of instructors. They seem often to feel that the job of the instructor is to remain simon pure, disseminate information for a pittance, and be grateful for the opportunity. These people are dangerous, of course, and misguided.

Those of us in the workshop business are clear that information is valuable to the extent that it solves people's problems and helps them reach their ultimate objectives. If it does and if these objectives are important to the buyers, the instructor (the problem solver) should be compensated accordingly. If the instructor cannot be compensated through direct stipend from the sponsor, he should profit from the sale of related products. If the sponsoring organization wishes to pass judgment on the value of the product that may be acceptable, always presuming that they have the competence to render a thoughtful evaluation. The instructor, however, must be allowed to profit from delivering problem solving information.

I am often told by certain ill-favored program planners that this vigorous attitude smacks of commercialism. Of course it does and it's nothing to be ashamed of! You see, program planners are badly paid and for whatever reasons (usually gross feelings of inadequacy and insecurity about their ability to compete in the real world) have selected a career pathway that offers minimal monetary rewards and psychic ones that seem thin at best. Consumed with bubbling jealousies

Chapter 4

and anger about their own constricted lives, they often are inclined to use what little power they have to bedevil the lives of creative entrepreneurs who have thought through the needs of a given market and realize that they have information at their disposal which people need and will pay for. Because they do not intend to give away this information they are deemed philistines and pilloried by those *soi-disant* humanists who run the programs.

Sadly, you will regularly encounter these people but as you move up on the talk circuit their numbers diminish. When you do meet them, however, bear with their pronounced inadequacies and smile inwardly at their petty travails. Remember: you're there to learn and having learned sufficiently, you'll be on your way. They will remain behind and seethe at your ascension. Isn't that a pretty thought?

Ascertainment From Participants

Make your workshop as similar as you can to the program you'll offer later. Even though your audience is likely to be somewhat different (less upscale since your price is lower), you need to function in the same way that you will later. You need to know as much as you can about the participants and shape your program accordingly. Your questionaire will help you ascertain the attitudes, needs and objectives of your audience and help you sharpen your substance and offer more of what your buyers want.

Your Workshop Questionnaire

Make the name, address and telephone number optional. The only question where this is useful is individuals to whom the participant would recommend the program and if you choose you can have this information on a separate piece of paper. The other questions concern:

- participant's age
- educational level
- level of employment
- income
- zip code
- professional associations you belong to
- number of programs you take in a year
- number of miles you traveled to this program
- your opinion of the price of this program: About right? A little low? Higher than it needed to be?
- the most valuable thing you learned today
- the least
- what related courses you might consider taking (be specific)
- how you heard about the program
- how you'd rate the course content
- the instructor

Chapter 4

- was the time the time the course was held adequate

- was the number of contact hours sufficient

- what about the place

- would you recommend this program to others

- if so, could you give their complete names and addresses for follow-up?

Finally, ask whether the individual has a comment which could be used in promoting future programs and ask whether you can use his name.

Some Do's And Don't's

- It goes without saying that the format you select for your program, all-day Saturday, two nights at three hours each evening, &c., should be identical to the one you wish to develop. This means that in all probability you should be offering an all-day Saturday program since this is the one most frequently used when people pay for their own continuing education. If the program is being paid for by someone else like an employer use an all-day mid-week (Tuesday, Wednesday, or Thursday) program since this will be your most preferred format.

  - Anything you pass out should be developed by you. It's infinitely better that the materials, even a potpourri of assembled articles, should have the look of being crafted by you, as if you were the guide. Such pass outs as you have should be placed on your stationery with the complete citation as well as your name, address and telephone for ease of follow-up. Many people make the mistake of photocopying documents on plain white paper. This is absurb! Each thing you hand out should function as an advertising and marketing agent for you. Each piece must be complete in itself and offer the means of getting back to you. By the same token, if the materials you want to make available don't fit neatly on to one or two pages, then place them in a manila folder with your name, address and telephone number. Your participants will retain these materials for their own libraries and the more useful they are the more they'll thank you and refer others to you. For this, they'll need follow-up information. Note: if you are using other people's materials, then write the publisher for permission.

On Student Evaluations

Make sure your program gets evaluated. All continuing educators make much of participant evaluations. This makes sense, of course, since the participants do pay their salaries. However it seems to me that nowadays the presumption exists that whatever a participant says has validity. This does not sit well with me. Nonetheless, evaluations have their place and are most useful to you in indicating the success of your program.

Thus, make sure that before the day has ended you distribute the evaluations along with your own questionnaire. They will overlap in certain particulars but that's to be expected.

Curiously, many program planners don't share the evaluations with the instructors nor do they use them to plan for future programs. On both counts this is in error. You as the instructor need to see what the participants are saying. As you review them here's what you may find:

- Comments about the substance of your course. People will recommend your program for two reasons: because of the value and utility of the information you dispense and because of your own enthusiasm and instructional ability. If you are being faulted about the substance of your course try to understand why. Is your information up to date? Do you really know what you're talking about? Or is there some problem with the audience? I have discovered for example that many professionals are averse to marketing information because they don't like to do it. Negative comments about this subject may then have more to do with the resistance of the listener than any lapse in your training techniques. Still, be honest with yourself. We can all do better.

Chapter 4

- Don't worry if you do not get "excellents" for every response on an evaluation. As I have learned, even after I've given a superb program that I know has been well worth the participants' time and money, about 20% of the audience will still select the category of response immediately beneath the top one. Expect this!

- Comments about your delivery. Were you speaking too fast? Too slow? Too many pauses? Was the program too unstructured? Or far too structured? Listen to your participants. You need to heed them.

You need, too, to learn when to dismiss them. Ultimately you will develop your own clear standards and you will be your own best critic, your own fairest critic. I have to tell you that I treat with a grain of salt many of the comments an audience gives me. Many people are too apt to bubble over with infectious enthusiasm. You can predict this response and you can benefit from it by getting the evaluations completed promptly upon the completion of your program. Other people are notoriously niggardly about giving good marks. This is just the way they are.

You must learn, then, to evaluate yourself. I know when I've been good, and I know when I'm having a day that is less than exemplary. The trick is to take what is germane and useful from the evaluations and leave the rest behind without a feeling of remorse.

Called To Account By The Program Planner

Most times the evaluations will be completed by the participants, lightly reviewed by the program planner and occasionally sent on to you for your own information. If the comments are commendatory this will be the rule. Sometimes, however, you may receive so many mixed comments that the program planner feels compelled to bring the situation to your attention for a response. If this happens to you remember these two things:

- It's the program planner's job but one that the planner does not especially like doing.

- The program planner does not wish to get rid of you, particularly if the program made money. Remember: it's costly to replace an instructor.

The program planner wants to keep you and will probably be looking for reasons to do so. Make it easy.

The best way to approach such a meeting or conversation is humbly. Admit that you have things to learn. Don't rush to defend yourself. Listen. This is, of course, easy advice to give and damned difficult to follow. I know. Follow it you must though. Allow the continuing educator to dish out a homily (they like doing that). Promise that you'll try harder and that you're grateful for the professional attention. Be soft. Be yielding. Be malleable. Take it and forget it. Besides, it might actually help. At the very least it has humanized you in the eyes of the administrator on whose good side it pays to remain.

It goes without saying, of course, that if something pejorative or downright false has been said, take the opportunity to correct the misimpression. And if there's been a disruptive, unresponsive element in your class, get the jump on them by writing a short note to the program planner suggesting that there was a problem.

Stroking The Program Planner

Always send a thank you note to the program planner who has hired you, especially the one who can help you on your way. You want a record of your gratitude. Moreover, if this individual has done more for you than called for, gone beyond the call of duty, then write the planner's supervisor and say so. This isn't bad policy in any case, since it will allow you to network up. Program planners rarely if ever get thanked. I know. When I worked at Boston College after graduate school in their continuing education program, not one of the instructors I hired ever sent a thank you note. They seemed to feel that they got the jobs because of divine right. That's not true. They got them as you will get them because someone saw the spark of genius in you and you ought to say "thank you" to that person, not once but often.

Chapter 4

Contemplate Your Success

If you have given a successful program, pause a moment upon its completion and contemplate it. Consider the following:

- You have made it through the first of hundreds of programs and are now on the way to becoming a seasoned performer.

- If the program broke even (or perhaps lost just a bit of money), you're going to be able to do it again. Properly handled this will become an annuity for you, a way of making perhaps a couple of thousand dollars annually with minimum work and preparation. Courses become staples in catalogs. Some continuing educators call them "cash cows" and that's just what they are: vehicles which term after term produce much-needed operating revenues for the home office. These revenues allow them to speculate on new courses such as the course you've just given!

- If you've handled the course properly, you've received media attention and a good catalog write-up. These can be leveraged to secure new assignments and work your way up in this marketing territory to a better, more profitable sponsor.

- You've got a clearer sense of your market and its needs. Moreover, with the questionnaire results you've got a sense of links to professional and trade associations through the participants who now know about you and your abilities.

- You have a sense, too, of your materials and their value. This is the germ of your Problem Solving Process book.

- If you've made any money at all for the sponsor, you have a confirmed success which you can leverage to future assignments. Everybody loves a winner and when you can come in with the promise of success you'll find that you are a most desirable person indeed.

Thus it may be that the chief benefit of even a single success, so long as you have made more dollars than it cost to produce the program, is that you have the basis for a Success Letter, a letter that is that will bring you to the attention of other program planners in other cities and marketing areas who will want to replicate your success for comparable audiences. You are now ready to hit the road, to truly distinguish yourself from the vast majority of those in the continuing education business who stay small and at home. Not you! Not now! For you like Daisy Buchanan have money in your smile and as such the world looks forward to the pleasure of your company.

Chapter 5

SUCCESSFULLY FOLLOWING UP FIRST ENGAGEMENTS

Many people in continuing education make no money. Instructors regularly tell me they are working for $10 an hour or less, well under $100 per day and that they are not reaping the benefits of their knowledge. In part this is because they stay too long in the low paying sphere, in part because they don't extend their workshop and seminar business to its furthest extent, in part because they don't develop profit making products and services to sell their workshop participants, in part because they don't adequately follow up their participants by offering the professional services they need. Under these circumstances how do they expect to make any money?

Yet as I pointed out earlier, these are superb times for the entrepreneurial info-technocrats who use talk programs as one of many means to disseminate information. Airfares are still generally reasonable (although new restrictive policies do bedevil our flexibility in ways that were not the case when I first wrote this book). Despite these restrictions, you can still take your program to new markets with the reasonable expectation of making a profit even if your expenses are not paid. To be sure, this can happen in selected situations even with noncredit adult education centers, but more usually your prospects are better with the nation's colleges and universities. So it is that the entire nation must become your marketing territory and all those colleges and universities with noncredit programs your possible clients.

Psyching Yourself

You now have a series of important decisions to make. Having launched a program in your immediate neighborhood that was successful, you can sit back on your laurels offering the same program again and again. Understand, however, that you will deplete the supply of available workshop prospects and in time, no matter how useful the program, you'll have to rest until the market is again ready for you. This is what most instructors do; it's a very slothful and uncreative way of doing business. Not very profitable either.

Determine, then, that you won't simply offer one program in a single marketing area. Instead, assign a weight to the program you have already offered and set an income objective for it. Decide, for instance, that you will offer it twice each year while looking both for new assignments elsewhere and perhaps a more prestigious and more profitable connection closer to home. Of course, in the beginning of your career you may feel it rather audacious to make this determination. Who, after all, are you, the Caterpillar might say? This is where your vision of yourself and your longterm objectives come in. You must understand that your neighborhood program is only one of many that you'll be offering. You can wax nostalgic about it after a second martini, but you need to remain hard headed about its place in your plans at all other times.

Assuming you have made the right decision, the decision that is to branch out and extend your program to other marketing territories, you need to ask yourself how far you can go if you get no expenses. Make no mistake about it: many college, university and other adult noncredit programs will pay no expenses to you, but they are nonetheless worth doing and can be most profitable. It all depends on the following variables:

- ease of access (is the city, for instance, on a discount airline route?)

- number of participants

- possibility of follow-up consulting or other service sale

- availablility of product to enhance revenues

- amount of preparation needed from you

- stipend sponsor is prepared to pay you

- cost at which they can offer the program

- possibility of offering other programs back-to-back with original offering.

Chapter 5

Branching Out

Now that you are on the talk circuit, you must approach these United States like a checker board. Given your particular subject area and participant groups, you need to consider whether each city or each metropolitan area could in fact become a profit center for you. This is a different approach to life than most of your friends have and so you must learn not to look to them for inspiration and sound advice.

The key to your success on the talk circuit, at least insofar as you are offering one-day workshops and seminars, is to conceive of each major city as a market and begin to solidify relationships with sponsoring colleges and universities in each one. Understand this: once you have a relationship with an individual institution in any given city, that institution will expect an exclusive arrangement. That's all right for any single program. So long as you only have one program, you won't have any problem. The difficulties begin when you have developed, as I have, a number of programs and one institution in a single marketing area wants one but not the other. Institutions these days are all fighting for the relatively scarce discretionary dollars of adult learners. Moreover, they like sending clean, crisp signals to their buyers. If you are being marketed simultaneously by one institution for one program and for another within the same area for a second program, the sponsors get quivery. In this situation, my advice to you is to work out a package arrangement with a single institution so that it markets all your programs. If it won't, you have to decide whether you want to risk a certain relationship with one sponsor while securing a relationship with a second. This is always a tricky business.

Note: The presumption here is that the institutions are marketing to similar groups. If you can assure that program planner that the marketing arrangements will in fact be markedly different, then there should be no problem, although you may as well expect a perhaps muted outburst of anxiety notwithstanding.

Selecting Sponsors

Now that you're looking around the nation (or at least your region) for new sponsors, two publications are of value to you. I've already mentioned the member directory published by the Learning Resources Network. Remember, however, in using this directory that many of the nation's adult noncredit continuing education centers are LERN members and that these on the whole offer the lowest priced programs. They will therefore find it most difficult to accommodate the enhanced fee and payment for expenses which will make your program possible in many areas.

That being the case you need the National Center for Education Statistics' *Education Directory, Colleges And Universities*. (Order from the Superintendent of Documents, U.S. Government Printing Office, Washington, D.C. 20402 for $15. Cite stock number 065-000-00268-0. Updated every other year.)

This book is a pivotal one. It usually gives the names and addresses of all the deans and directors of continuing education at the university level nationwide along with those of other senior administrators. Using this book you can zero in on the cities where you'd like to offer programs and begin assembling catalogs from those institutions with programs thereafter following up with the kinds of sales materials we've already discussed. While you're selling your original, proven program, there is now much more for you to do: diversify.

Diversification

You should now be doing the following: cementing your relationship with your original sponsor to re-offer your successful program in your primary marketing area. Alternatively in your primary marketing area (that is, your home area) you should be seeking a more prestigious, more profitable sponsoring organization. At the same time, you should be selecting those other marketing areas in which you'd like to present your proven money-making program and begin the sales process with them we've already discussed.

While these activities are taking place (and remember, you are ordinarily working at least 6 months ahead), you should also be giving your attention to diversifying your repertoire, that is adding new formats and subjects to your original offering. The successful speaker, after all, maintains a list of programs which can be tailored both to fit different time slots and different participant groups. The reason for this is obvious: the more speaking you want to do, the more you must be able to shape your material to the needs of specific audiences, both in terms of time and approach.

Chapter 5

Developing Time Modules

Each program that you offer should be developed into the following specific time lengths or formats:

- the 50 minute speech
- the 90 minute workshop
- the 2½ hour (half-day) workshop
- the 7-8 hour (full-day) workshop
- the 14-16 hour (two-day) workshop
- the five-day institute (35-40 contact hours)

These are the program lengths most commonly found, and you must develop and shape your material so that you can use each one. Fortunately the Problem Solving Process format is ideally suited for use in this way. While each of the significant areas of the process is touched upon in each module, it is only in the longer time periods when the points can be significantly discussed.

Here is what happens in each of the formats:

50 Minute Speech

This is straight talk from you, the problem solving expert. You as the featured speaker disseminate your information with a minimum of direct audience interaction. (There will, of course, still be a high level of nonverbal communication.) If your speech is to be followed by a hands-on workshop (an increasingly popular format and one which you'll use when you are a convention keynoter), there will be no questions immediately following your speech, just applause. In this speech the emphasis should be on entertainment, inspiration, motivation, persuasion as well as hard information. This speech can be given at any time.

90 Minute Workshop

This is a shortened workshop program. It's often used for showcasing talent for those who might later retain you as a speaker for their association. This often follows a speech. This format, particularly when it's used as an audition, demands that you be at your most energetic and winning. Strive for some audience interaction.

2½ hour (Half-Day) Workshop

This is standard convention fare nowadays. Generally workshops of this length are held either in the morning or afternoon at conventions. Where the schedule is particularly packed such programs may also precede the main offering or be held over into the evenings; (try to avoid either unless you get special billing in the program). This program format allows for more audience participation and the opportunity for you to get across some problem solving information and the strong impression that you yourself are a superb problem solver and hence worth keeping in touch with.

7-8 Hour (Full-Day) Workshop

This format is occasionally used to introduce a convention or held after the main convention offerings are completed. It is held by universities during the week (better if someone else is paying the bill for the participant) or on Saturdays (the best day if the participants are paying for themselves). Now some are being tried on Sundays (more often in a four hour version from 12:30 to 4:30 p.m.) This is really the first of the workshop formats that allows for a substantial amount of audience involvement. The other formats are simply too short for more than questions. In a full-day program, you can devise audience participation devices. (In this connection see *The Encyclopedia Of Icebreakers: Structured Activities That Warm-Up, Motivate, Challenge, Acquaint, And Energize* by Sue Forbess-Greene. Distributed by University Associates, 8517 Production Avenue, San Diego, CA 92121. 417 pages, $54.95)

Chapter 5

14-16 Hour (Two-Day) Workshop

This is an elaboration and extension of the full day program. In this model, you can even begin to assign homework and so mold the habits of the participants so as better to insure the successful realization of their objectives. In a two-day program you need to devise more audience participation vehicles and if possible review the attempts of the participants to implement your success techniques.

Five Day Institute (35-40 Contact Hours)

This format allows for extensive interaction between the participants and you and for a series of homework assignments and assigned readings. This is a very intensive format and perhaps the most draining of them all! But as you'll see when we discuss this format later, it has some real advantages.

Here is an illustration of how a single Problem Solving Process program can be spun off and be appropriate for each format. It's based on an actual course I give entitled "Fund Raising Essentials: Raising Money From Corporations, Foundations, And Individuals."

- 50 Minute Speech: "Development Today: The Fund Raising Situation And You" (the title ties in to my book **DEVELOPMENT TODAY**)

- 90 Minute Workshop. This workshop touches on all the major points of the Problem Solving Process format and allows for limited questions on how the participants (representing in this case nonprofit organizations) can apply my methods to their situations.

- 2½ Hour (Half-Day) Workshop. The greater time available allows for the development of specific methodologies designed to assist the participants to raise money from corporations, foundations and individuals.

- 7-8 Hour (Full-Day) Workshop. One hour each on the different steps of the Problem Solving Process and how it relates to fund raising and to the specific situations of the audience.

- 14-16 (Two-Day) Workshop. Assigned reading from **DEVELOPMENT TODAY** and specific homework and groupwork assignments. More detailed information presented on not just the essentials of fund raising from corporations, foundations, and individuals but how the participants can solve common, difficult problems that will inevitably arise as they begin to implement the methodology.

- Five Day Institute. Allows for the invitation and participation of major philanthropists from corporations and foundations, bank trustees, foundation officers and corporate giving specialists as well as much specific attention to the individual problems of participating agencies.

The Right Approach To Potential New Sponsors

Even before you have actually offered your first program you can make use of your connection to the sponsoring organization. At the most elementary level you'll want to make sure you have several copies of the catalog and other promotional and advertising materials. As soon as you have an indication that your program is going to be successful (and this will, of course, ordinarily be before you step up to the podium to give it), then is the time to launch your assault on new prospective sponsors. At the very least, before your program takes place, identify these sponsors and begin to get the packets and letters together with which you'll approach them. This means writing a cogent, compelling Success Letter, a key document which you will use over and over again so long as you remain on the talk circuit.

The Success Letter

I cannot stress the importance of the Success Letter sufficiently. What this critical document says in effect is this: I have already offered this successful program elsewhere. I understand what you, the program planner, need and must have: a reasonable assurance of program content and a strong suggestion that the program will be profitable. I am ready, willing, and able to bring this documented success story to you and replicate it under your sponsorship.

Chapter 5

Let's be very clear about something. At a stroke this most important letter obviates the need for a resume. A resume is for people who are seeking. The Success Letter is used by people who know themselves to be sought. Ultimately, this means that you are not selling a doctorate. Or your years of experience on the job. Or your degree work however impressive. You are selling problem solving information that works and you are selling a profitable program. In such circumstances you are irresistible.

No resume? I can hear you sputtering now. Get over it! Resumes are used by those breaking into employment, by middle management drones without a future and by all others who misunderstand the fundamental nature of the job market. In this world, people who have a successful track record get the best of everything. The rest use resumes and hope for a consideration they rarely get.

Again, you need to know something about the program planners you'll be dealing with. You will succeed in getting yourself hired to the extent that you offer the likelihood of solving two problems they have: their own continuing need to make a profit and their oh-so-human frailty for wanting to avoid work and find others to do things for them. Here are the constituents of their world:

- They work with the knowledge that as many as a quarter of their courses will fail because of insufficient enrollments. If you are targeting a prospective sponsor that can offer you access to a similar market whence you have just drawn success, you've sliced the likelihood of failure dramatically.

- Program planners are likely to feel more comfortable with instructors who are tried and true and know the ropes, that is what program planners themselves need. Through your Success Letter and supporting materials you exude an air of confident assuredness and a quality of the heaven sent.

- Program planners like to take the recommendations of their peers. By using the sponsor of your last program for networking purposes, you'll come in as an old friend whether or not the two program planners even know each other. You'll remember I previously mentioned that one of the things you are getting from any continuing education assignment is a networking connection from the program planner. Now is the moment to use it. You are desirable because you come highly recommended from an individual with whom the new program planner can easily identify. (See samples, page 268).

Getting This Necessary Recommendation

Let me say this: even if you have only offered a single workshop, you can be the beneficiary of a superb letter of introduction. This is something most poor creatures in the regular work force will never understand. It is not, remember, the number of hours that you have spent on the project that matters; it is the degree of success that the program has brought to the sponsor and the degree to which you have succeeded in reducing the lamentably considerable workload of the program planner. These two necessary conditions, once met, ensure the right degree of enthusiasm for your recommendation. And if the participant evaluations are excellent, too, why you're a shoo-in for further consideration.

To get the letter you want, schedule a meeting with the program planner. Say that you are taking your successful program to other marketing areas. You must let the planner know that you are not planning anything competitive! Say that you'd appreciate a letter which discusses the following points:

- number of participants

- their characteristic evaluative comments

- profit from the program to the sponsor

- ease of working with you, the instructor

- plans for rescheduling the program at the original sponsor.

Add, too, any marketing and promotional materials (catalogs, brochures, &c) which may be available.

Chapter 5

Ask the program planner for the names of peers in other cities who might be interested in scheduling this program. Remember: all decision makers have certain contacts which are useful. Your task is to find out who they are. This is called networking, that much discussed and little implemented activity.

Program planners in continuing education situations are part of what I term the Next Check Network. That is they have the capacity to produce money for you. This is where the Pyramid of Contacts comes in.

The Pyramid of Contacts allows you to plot your next steps, quickly efficiently. Here's what it looks like:

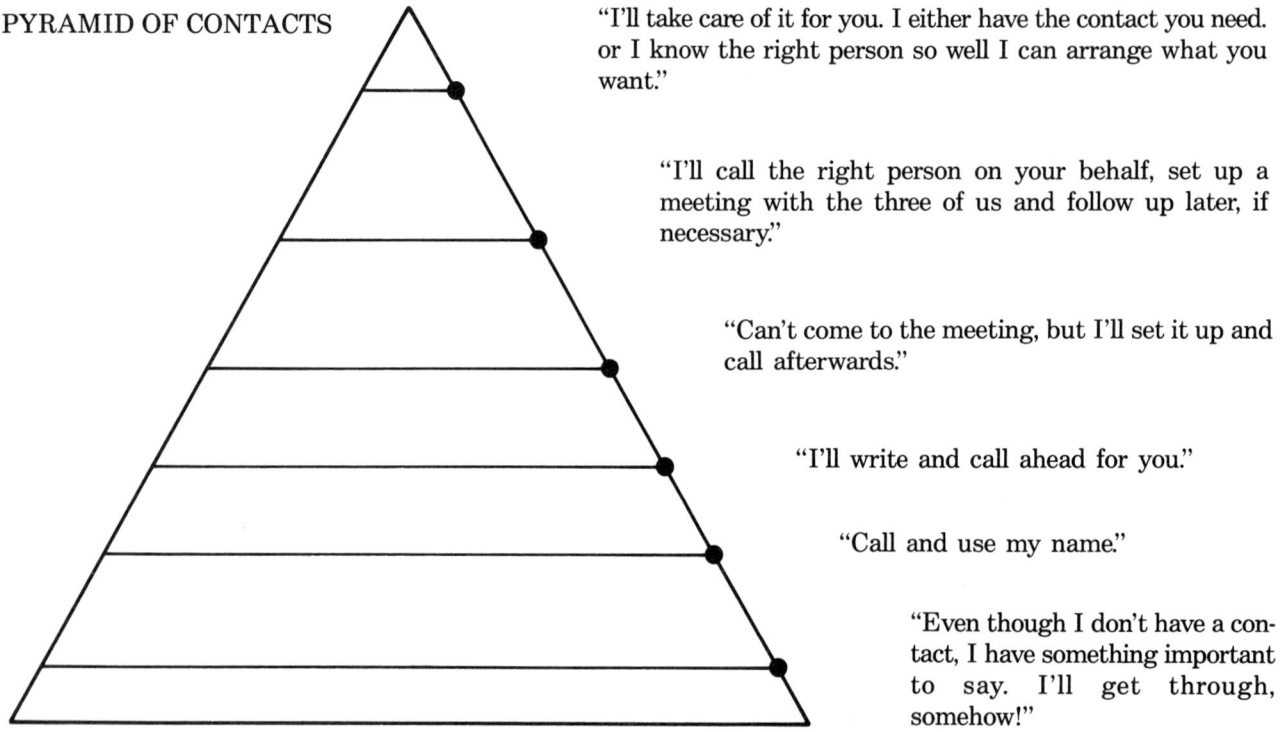

- You are looking for a program planner who has a friend who is a program planner who'll say "I'll take care of it for you." The planner knows another comparably placed decision maker and will do what is necessary to move you to a profitable new connection. This is networking. Get used to it, because you'll find yourself using it over and over again.

Even where there is no such personal connection, don't worry unduly. A letter of recommendation properly framed along the lines I've just given you will also work for you.

The Success Letter, Continued

What you want in this letter is approximately the same information that you want the program planner to include in his letter of recommendation:

- a clear indication of the prior success of your program in a marketing area you regard as comparable

- dollar gross

- profit

- number of participants

You also want to suggest a time when the program should be offered and a possible fee.

Chapter 5

Make sure, too, that there is an element of urgency in this letter: the need to make a decision quickly. Even though I have been in this business for some time, I still make use of this urgent element regularly. There's nothing false about it either. Part of the problem is that program planners often move very slowly; another and more significant part of the problem is that there are only so many days of the year when you can offer programs and if you're like me you want to be using as many of them profitably as you can. As you know, I do many of my programs on Saturday. Given the nature of the calendar, there are only some 33 to 36 Saturdays annually on which programs can be given: the last two of September, four in October (with Yom Kippur being out for many areas), 4 in November (not Thanksgiving, of course), and the first two or maybe three in December. Then the last one or two week-ends in January, 4 in February, a maximum of 4 in March (unless Easter is early), the same for April, 4 in May (but not Memorial Day week-end) and 4 in June. July is problematic depending on your program and August is probably the worst week-end month of all.

Time is, therefore, important. You have to convince a program planner not only that your program is important and timely now but that a decision must be made promptly.

Note: even now when most of my Saturdays are booked, I still use the urgent element profitably. If I find at the end of November that I still have any week-ends left from January to July of the next year, I either send out a letter to selected universities or get on the telephone and press home the need for a decision. Inevitably at this courteous push, laggards book. It will be always thus.

Success Letter Attachments

Generally the Success Letter can be sent alone to open a connection with a prospective sponsor. But you will want to have available certain other, corroborating materials. These include:

- the catalog from your successful program
- catalog copy if different from this
- media release
- printed media stories
- participant evaluations (including significant comments from your own ascertainment questionnaire)
- participant testimonials and complimentary letters (yes, they do come in! And if you don't get them voluntarily, request them from your adoring participants.)
- program planner letter of recommendation.

What you'll find the longer you're in this business is that the continuing education universe nationwide is very small and very gossippy. The more programs you do, the more successful they are, the more you'll be talked about. Moreover, continuing educators are often on each other's mailing lists. Thus, they may well be aware of your programs and contact you directly. This, of course, is a nice development but not one you can count on just at the beginning. Until you have reached this eminence, have all the supporting materials you can and have them immediately ready to be dispatched. Nowadays my filing cabinets are stuffed with these things, and I'm very rarely asked for them. In the end, what they care about having from me is just what they'll want from you: the secrets of how your programs make money and anything you've got which will help realize that objective. In short, with fitting irony, all this material is most important when you have least of it and when you could fill a boxcar with the detritus of a hundred programs, no one shows the slightest interest in the reams of dazzling material you've accumulated. Of course.

Benefits Of The Success Letter

The Success Letter offers you many benefits:

- It establishes you as the complete professional.
- Using it, you will be often, even regularly, hired sight unseen over the telephone as I am.

Chapter 5

- It establishes the kind of relationship you want with most sponsors. You come in, deliver the program, collect your check and go home only to return when you're delivering the next program.

Have I, perhaps, made all this sound just a shade too easy? If it were, why then do so many otherwise intelligent people rusticate at the local noncredit adult education center wondering, as they do, why they get no recognition and less money? Perhaps under the circumstances, I should offer you another possibility so that you can ease into your stride gradually.

An Intermediate Step

Perhaps before you make a full-fledged assault on sponsors nationwide, you'd prefer to establish a stronger record nearer home. That's all right so long as you realize that you are building this strong record so as to sell yourself and your program elsewhere and are not just indulging yourself in comfortable obscurity. In these circumstances, continue with your initial sponsor until you have a track record of two or three successful programs. Then move laterally to other similar adult noncredit continuing education centers and begin to rack up a comparable record. Working with moderate intensity over the course of a year, for it will take at least that long, you can establish an enviable record of success which you should be able to use in gaining profitable assignments with larger sponsoring institutions.

The Intermediate Or Long Jump? Which Step Is For You?

Which of these options should you adopt? It depends on certain professional and personal factors which you must consider.

To begin with, what kind of success have you had? What were the gross proceeds of your program? The profits? How many people participated? What had to be done to get them? If you have just had a marginal success, it will be more difficult to launch the program elsewhere. Perhaps you'd better strengthen your record before trying.

Beyond these professional considerations, there are personal factors, too, which need your attention. What kinds of objectives do you have for your speaking career? Do you just like to hear yourself talk? If this is the case, your local connection will probably suit you well enough just as it does most people. Or is your objective to make money and become celebrated like mine is? If this is your objective then as soon as you have a profitable program, you should begin to leverage it. You must use each successful experience as the means of getting new and more profitable assignments.

You must also consider, before considering the long jump, whether you are willing to make the personal sacrifices that even a limited speaking schedule entails. Even if you simply give Saturday workshops once or twice a month, you'll find that your available free time is severely reduced if you maintain a full-time job. And if you offer the occasional midweek program, you're going to have to give up vacation time to do so. There's no way around it: success means sacrifice and the more success you have, the more you'll want and the greater the sacrifices you'll have to make. Think about it and be sure this is what you want for yourself.

Perhaps this last point is, in the end, the most significant. Perhaps their unwillingness to make the necessary sacrifice (while continuing to mouth the shibboleths of success) is what keeps most people in the talk business offering little programs to limited groups of people. They don't press to develop all the necessary program modules they need. They fail to extend their marketing territories and take their programs into new areas. They don't make the necessary commitment to produce the books and other profitable materials that they need to make the talk circuit truly profitable. Instead they stay at home and grumble while their glorious expectations recede.

I assume you are different. If so, whether you use the intermediate or the long jump you must now begin to develop three distinct sets of program prospects:

- the college continuing education market
- trade and professional associations, and
- corporations for inhouse workshops and training programs.

The world of talk is a multi-billion dollar universe. In so far as you succeed in mastering these three parts of it, you will get more than your share.

Chapter 5

Profiting From The College Market

This is a universe in which I do a lot of my work, and I know its value. Colleges and universities offering noncredit programs, and there are at least 2000 of them across the nation, are most willing to enter into relationships with info-technocrats like us so long as there is a likelihood of a profit at the end of the day. Once you have demonstrated you can produce that profit, these programs will want you back, again and again. Why not? So long as they can benefit, there is every reason to do business with you. The trick is knowing how to approach them and what they need from you to make an informed decision. In reaching these goals, it helps to know as much about this world as you can and the following resources will help you do so.

The two leading professional associations in the university continuing education market are:

- American Association for Adult and Continuing Education (AAACE)
  1112 16th St., N.W., Suite 420
  Washington, D.C. 20036
  (202) 463-6333

- National University Continuing Education Association (NUCEA)
  One Dupont Circle, Suite 420
  Washington, D.C. 20036
  (202) 659-3130

Both these associations stage conventions, maintain publications that have information you'll want to follow, and offer other services speakers within this universe should be cognizant of. Membership fees for those without an institutional affiliation are not excessive.

In addition to the publications of these associations, there are three other newsletters produced by independent entrepreneurs which are of interest to you:

- *Dean And Director,* published by The Bureau of Business & Technology, Inc., 2472 Fox Ave., Baldwin, NY 11510 (516) 868-5757.

Try to get yourself mentioned in this publication; it's read by just the people you want to get to. Even if you can't, at $60 a year you'll want to subscribe!

- *Meeting Marketer Quarterly,* published by The Marketing Federation, 7141 Gulf Blvd., St. Petersburg Beach, FL 33706 (813-367-4934) $5 a year. Published by Anver Suleiman, one of the best known seminar promoters in the nation.

- *The Professional Consultant & Seminar Business Report,* published by Howard L. Shenson, Inc., 20750 Ventura Blvd., Suite 206, Woodland Hills, CA 91364 (818-703-1415). Howard Shenson is one of the most successful entrepreneurs in the country of self-sponsored programs promoted via newspaper ads. His newsletter is packed with useful information that will pay back your $96 annual investment many times over. You'll also find his book *How To Create & Market A Successful Seminar Or Workshop* useful, particularly its contract information.

Using these resources along with the *Education Directory Of Colleges And Universities,* you are well positioned to identify the prospects and keep abreast of this world's current concerns.

Identifying Prospects

It should already be clear to you that you'll want to keep collecting the continuing education catalogs of every institution in which you are interested. This remains your least expensive way of discovering what is going on in the market and whether any given continuing education program could benefit from a program like yours.

To get access to these people, there are really just four ways:

- networking

Chapter 5

- personalized direct mail

- general direct mail

- unabashed promotion.

Networking

Always ask people you have worked for to give you referrals to potential new clients. So long as the markets are not competitive expect the person you've asked to be helpful. You will find that although you are marketing yourself nationally, it won't take too long until you are a known entity to the decision makers. This can, of course, both help and hurt you; the latter is the case if your programs are ill-conceived or you become known for being "difficult."

Aside from the obvious networking that you can do through deans and directors of continuing educations, here are a few other suggestions:

- Get your friends who are alumni of various institutions in which you are interested to write letters to the deans of continuing education at their schools. It doesn't matter whether they are known or not. Alumni correspondence gets treated with respect. This will at least open the door for you.

- Use, too, the college affiliations of those individuals taking your workshops. They can also recommend you. It goes without saying that you'll have to draft the letter for them (it's better that way) and secure the appropriate name and address.

Personalized Direct Mail

The way to handle your dealings with the collegiate market is to begin with an objective for how many programs you want to offer in a given year. How much revenue do you want to earn? If you decide on a goal of $10,000, for instance, and you are currently charging $500 per day plus expenses you'll have to produce 20 programs. If you are offering these programs on Saturdays, you'll have to have a very aggressive marketing plan in place because of the limited number of dates you have to work with. Given the difficulty of securing this many dates when you are a relative unknown, you may decide to raise your rates to, say, $750 a day, which would be a perfectly reasonable decision if your target audience will make up the difference in fees.

Once you have decided how many dates you must do, then you have to begin to identify your target sponsors. Let's say that you want to do 10 programs in a year. Say that this would involve a spring and fall program in each of 5 major markets. Now you must identify all the likely institutions within the five markets you've selected and begin the process of selling them on you and your program. Here is the proper sequence:

- Identify your prospects from the *Education Directory*. They should include all the four year colleges and universities within the metropolitan area you have selected.

- Write for their continuing education catalogs. If you are told that there is a continuing education program but no catalog, assign this prospect a lower priority unless your program has previously been successfully marketed using individual brochures. For most people, it is better to have their programs in a general catalog where they will be seen by more people. Particularly for those who do not have a strong marketing track record, sponsoring institutions will be less likely to invest the money it takes in brochures and other promotion until shown that such an investment makes sense. Thus, institutions without catalogs should be assigned a lower priority particularly for the untried.

- Review the catalog to see whether your program exists. If it does you may wish to write a note offering yourself as a substitute if needed.

- If your program doesn't exist, then you'll want to send a strong sales letter to the dean or director although it is perfectly acceptable to telephone the institution and ask the name of the program planner and deal with that person directly. The sales letter should have all the parts we've previously discussed and should make a strong case why the institution will benefit from the program by demonstrating how a prior sponsor has done so.

Chapter 5

Before you send these letters (for you'll no doubt be sending several to a single marketing area) you'll want to consider the question of your fee. As should by now be abundantly clear, when you work for adult noncredit continuing education centers, community colleges, &c., your fees will be low. As you branch out beyond these places, you should raise your fees. To raise your fees, however, you have to have a clear sense of what price your workshop participants will pay for your program. There are several ways of getting this information.

- Check the prices of similar programs sponsored by various institutions.

- Seek out workshop leaders who are self-sponsoring programs in your field and see what they charge.

- Ask your participants how much they'd be willing to pay for the information you've got and how desperately they are seeking to solve the problems you're addressing.

Fee is not something that can be determined independently of the market. You must consider, too, whether the individual is paying for this course himself or whether his employer or other organization is paying for it. Usually fees for the former are lower than those for the latter.

Once you've made a decision about what the market will bear both because of the existence of competitors and the perceived value of the information, then you can begin to artfully craft your own fee. Understand this, too: one is never entirely free of one's history. That is, prospective sponsors will probably ask you how much you've been paid for previous programs and will shape their offer to you accordingly. By the same token, you must focus the program planner on the likely gross proceeds for the program and not on your own remuneration which should appear to the planner to be incidental.

The question immediately arises about when these letters should be sent. Within this universe all decisions regarding programs beginning in February are made by the middle of November. Thus for winter-spring programs, you must begin the sales process about Labor Day. For programs beginning in September, you need to be in touch with program planners in March or even a little before.

- Once this letter has been sent, a friendly, personal letter, mind you, wait 10 business days (two weeks) to follow it up with a telephone call. Understand this: your proposal will be only one of many on the planner's desk. You can feel confident if you have followed my format that it is one of if not the strongest proposal he has received, but you should nonetheless follow it up personally along the lines previously suggested. There is a certain tempo in the continuing education world. The four weeks beginning October 15 are when most decisions for winter-spring are made and most of those for the fall take place in March or early April. That is when you must be most visible, most active.

General Direct Mail

Most readers of this book at least initially will be best off simply using networking and personalized direct mail. It is inexpensive and cost effective. The sum total of your investment is limited to a series of targeted letters which can be produced by word processor and by follow up telephone calls. Considering the return on investment you can get if you've targeted the right market and really thought through your program, this is a very lucrative way of doing business.

When you begin diversifying, however, you may wish to consider what I do. Twice each year, once in September and once again in January I mail out a catalog of available workshops to all the nation's four year colleges and universities. This catalog not only contains the workshops I offer myself but also some offered by other info-technocrats whom I market under my Mobile University. This is sent primarily to the university market but also to selected trade and professional associations. (See samples, page 270.)

You are ready for a catalog like this when:

- You have multiple programs to offer.

- You have a strong track record in the continuing education market.

- You have other speakers to market.

Chapter 5

- You have products available (books in my case) which can be bought by continuing educators themselves and so help offset the cost of the mailing.

These points are in decending order of importance. The first two are by far the most important.

Having done this mailing many times, I can give you some idea of the return you'd get on it. The "rules" of direct mail suggest that with a 1% response you would get about 40 replies. I've never got close to this and it's never bothered me. Here's why. The total cost of a mailing of 2000 pieces, which is about the number of four year colleges and universities there are in this country, including bulk rate (third class) postage, printing, envelopes and labels (which I rent from a list broker) is about $1200-$1500. My minimum fee for a single program is $1250 plus expenses. Thus this mailing will break even with a single positive response. I offset the difference between cost and my minimum program fee by offering copies for sale of **THE UNABASHED SELF-PROMOTER'S GUIDE**, a book that has always sold well to continuing educators who need to master its promotional techniques. I rate as successful a mailing that brings me just 4 new clients, for remember: this is not just four one-time-only gigs. It's four continuing programs probably twice each year until the market is exhausted. By which time, of course, I shall have sold them other, newer, trendier programs. Profitable though this mailing is, however, I would not advise you to undertake it until you have met the conditions above.

Unabashed Promotions: Associations & Publications

One of the several things I like about the continuing education universe in this country is that it is small and if you play your cards properly, you can become a known quantity within it in a short time, say three to four years. The techniques of unabashed promotion will help you do so expeditiously. There is, of course, an entire chapter of this book on unabashed promotion, but here I should simply like to expand on the delights of public relations directed to a vertical universe. What this means is simply that you can use the several publications within this universe to get your message across and become a known entity. Such publicity will help reinforce the message of your networking, your letters and other sales materials and so establish you as an individual worth considering and worth doing business with.

In general there are two ways of getting the right kind of publicity within this universe. The first is to promote your successful programs to the attention of program planners by using the association and other publications previously cited. The ways you can do so are explored in chapter 7. The second and arguably shrewder way is to promote yourself as an individual who has problem solving information of personal and professional relevance to continuing educators. In this connection, I have a regular column in one of the newsletters published by the Learning Resources Network in which I dispense career advice to continuing educators.

Anyone who can help solve the personal or professional problems of continuing educators thus has a perfect opportunity to promote himself using the very publications which these people, your future clients, read regularly. This is a very, very smart thing to do. (If you have something that would interest continuing educators and would like to write a column about it contact William Draves, LERN's Executive Director at the address previously given. Tell him I sent you!)

Promotion Through The Three Major Adult Education Associations

If you find that you have something that the continuing education associations want to hear about through their publications, then you should also consider making a presentation at one of their regional or national meetings. Let me say right from the start that you'll not be compensated for most of these presentations, although there are exceptions when both honoraria and travel expenses are met. Even without these emoluments, however, it may be to your advantage to make the investment and appear.

The reason I make usually unpaid presentations before continuing education groups is clear: the people in the audience are client prospects and if the experience is properly handled I am properly promoted to my future buyers both before and after my presentation. Here is the proper sequence of events:

- If you offer a program which is of professional or personal interest to continuing educators, which will improve the quality of their lives or their professional success, then write LERN, AAACHE, or NUCEA and request information about their next national and regional meetings. While the application procedures vary with each association, each accepts proposals for workshop and lecture programs usually in the spirit of the theme of the forthcoming meeting.

Chapter 5

- Complete the request for proposals or call for papers applications.

- If you are accepted, work with the organization to achieve results which will benefit both of you. Here are some suggestions: since you're probably not being paid you want to make sure that you get the utmost in promotional and professional benefits. Thus work with the organization to insure that you receive proper recognition in advance of the program in announcements sent out about it and in the appropriate publications. Find out, too, whether your literature can be placed in all registration packets or otherwise distributed to participants. Make sure you have some agreement about how your speech will be covered by their publications after the fact. Try and establish a marketing agreement relating to the tape of your speech. Would the association consider marketing and selling it to members in return for a percentage of the price? The same holds true if you have written a book which is of interest to continuing educators. In short, use your creativity and intelligence to make this a rewarding and profitable experience for yourself. At the very least get a list of the participants, so you can follow up selected prospects in person.

- Once you arrive at the convention, you have to work it. If your literature has not been placed in the registration packets, make sure to keep it available throughout the convention. Hint: don't place all your materials in one place. Keep small piles available in various locations. Be assertive. One good way to do so and still appear polite is by hosting your own reception during the convention. Simply use your hotel room for the affair. Bring the invitations with you (for continuing educators a photocopied invitation on colored paper is quite adequate) and distribute them at the convention. Invite the people in your workshop session to come. Also send this invitation with a little hand lettered plea for attendance to those people you really want to attend. The hotel will get it to them. I had such a party at the last year's NUCEA meeting in Atlanta where I was a featured speaker and it worked quite well and at surprisingly low cost. These days party fare is inferior chablis and hard tack cheese. You really needn't splurge. The key is to getting the people to come and meeting them all once they arrive. Since these are your future prospects, I suggest you make yourself very congenial.

All this is very well and good but what if your proposal is not accepted and you are not selected to be a featured speaker? What then? You have a couple courses of action. If the meeting is being held near you, you can simply register as a participant and go and mingle. There's nothing wrong with this. You'll have opportunities for networking at the set meals, cocktail parties and the various meetings. If you do this, however, make sure you go with an objective, that is a set number of people you will make contact with and follow-up. Ten a day is a good number. Again, take your literature and display it prominently. I often get up early and leaflet all the seminar rooms in the hotel so that those attending the programs will get some dose of me whether I'm speaking or not. I challenge you to be as brazen.

Booths are also available, but should you bother with one? I think not. I attend many, many conventions during the course of the year, and I've come to the sad conclusion that the life of the exhibitor is an unhappy one. Booths are quite costly and people are often reluctant to approach them. Moreover exhibitors don't mix with participants at most functions and thus end up being second class citizens. On the whole, if you can only go as an exhibitor I advise you to sit out the dance.

Whatever you decide to do, to be the speaker or just a participant, the most important work for you will take place after you return. All the people you've met will need follow-up letters; most will need telephone calls, too. Everyone exchanges cards at these meetings, but very few people make good use of them. You be different. Even in this way you can indicate that you are the kind of crisp, efficient professional that the program planner really ought to be doing business with. And if you secure even a single contract from the experience, take a moment and congratulate yourself. You deserve it! But don't let this revelry go to your head. You've got a contract to negotiate.

Contract Considerations

Perhaps it's a benefit that contractual arrangements within the continuing education world tend to be minimal. There is still the remnant of "shake hands and agree" that supposedly characterized the Wilder West. In any event, contracts are quite simply arranged and are often no more than the barest exchange of letters.

In such a situation, there is not great uniformity between institutions. Nonetheless, you can usually expect the following items to be addressed. As there are really two groups of items, I've divided my list into distinct parts. The first consists of the mundane matters that usually cause no problems; the second can.

Chapter 5

List I

What follows is a series of items that will ordinarily be addressed in a contract between you and a continuing education facility. If they are self-evident, I have added no commentary. In the one or two cases where they are not quite so obvious I've added a word.

- names of contracting parties
- their addresses
- your telephone number and whether it can be given out to prospects. (Yes, give out both a day and night number. Remember: people will not always call you during the day.)
- course title
- outline or description of course
- materials needed
- how you'll be compensated for them
- time, day, date and place of course
- cost of course
- payment to you
- your social security or federal identification number.

List II

- number of half-price or free admissions from sponsor
- cancellation policy
- compensation to you if program is cancelled
- compensation to institution if you cancel
- when you'll actually receive your check
- rescheduling
- noncompetitive clause
- admission of media.

These items need discussion.

- **Number Of Half-Price Or Free Admissions From Sponsor**

I have found that institutions generally like to enroll their own people at a special half-price discount or occasionally for free. This is a perquisite that in part makes up for the poor pay that distinguishes most universities. In point of fact, there's relatively little you can do about this. So long as you are not suffering economically, don't complain. However, when you have products to sell, half-price or free admission participants must pay for these. The institution will usually insist on this since the participants are already getting a benefit. Don't give way on this count. You must under no circumstances give away your materials. If the institution is reducing or giving away seats, you might want the same

Chapter 5

privilege. The institution may wish to dispute you, but consider: perhaps you may wish to trade an admission to your workshop for someone else's service. Or you might like an association program planner to come and audition you for a future assignment. Fair's fair.

- **Cancellation & Compensation Policies**

Within the continuing education world, there is a distinct cancellation policy and it may not be to your liking. It does, however, make sense once you know the business. If a course is cancelled due to insufficient enrollment, do not expect to derive any fee from the program. Also, if enrollment is low you can expect the continuing educator to wait to the last possible minute before making a decision about whether the course will take place or not. You must therefore remain flexible in what is a very fluid business. When you are hired by a continuing education institution you enter into a pact either written or tacit. The institution agrees to spend its time, money and other resources to promote and sponsor your course. If their efforts do not succeed in drawing sufficient participants, the course may be cancelled by them without penalty. Remember: possibly as many as a quarter of the noncredit continuing education courses nationwide are cancelled in any given term. Institutions could not possibly afford to pay cancellation fees in all these cases, and it is unlikely they will agree to pay one to you.

By the same token, the institution will probably be as forgiving to you if you have to cancel the program for some valid reason. Personally I have never cancelled a program and unless the circumstances were truly out of my control (bad weather forcing cancellation of all planes) I'd never do it. Even if I were ill (unless infectious), I'd still give the program. In fact, I'd especially give it if I were ill because I could count on the audience's support and even admiration right from the start. I've often said I intend to die on the lecture platform, and I advise you to do the same. It'll be a great finale to a wonderful run.

If, however, you must cancel, let the sponsoring organization know in as much time as possible. Before you cancel, however, line up a replacement. Or at least reschedule the program so that those enrolled (and found at great expense!) can be saved and still produce benefits for you and the sponsor. Don't lose these people. Keep in mind that some organizations require that if you cancel fewer than 48 hours before an engagement without cause (as defined in the contract) you are liable to a penalty. Personally, though, I have never had this clause in my contract; it will be rare that you will find it, too. In part, this is because there is still a gentlemen's aspect to this business. As such I try to respond in kind. So should you.

- **Receiving Your Check**

Continuing education facilities are slow to pay. It is nothing to wait 90 days for payment. This, of course, is an outrage. If one of the continuing educators had himself to wait three months for a pay check, he'd strike. Insist on prompt payment. Sadly, this is about all you can do. No continuing educator will agree to a penalty clause. They'll always claim circumstances are out of their hands when the sad fact is that their financial systems are poor.

- **Rescheduling Program**

This is a key clause. Once you have created a succesful program with a university, you want to be assured that so long as the program is profitable and you wish to offer it, you will be allowed to do so. Universities are subject to some unusual pressures in regard to their continuing education programs and these can often affect you, a noncredit instructor. Universities which are unable to reward their regular faculty with raises may yet offer them berths in the continuing education program as alternative compensation. This compensation may be at your expense. This happened to me once with a very reputable university which behaved in this instance with despicable mendacity. Learn from my experience. Get an agreement from the institution that you will have first choice in offering the program again so long as the circumstances which create profit continue to exist and the participants regard your presentation as acceptable.

- **Noncompetitive Clause**

Just as you want some assurance that the university will respect your interest to be able to offer the program again, so the sponsoring institution will want to know that within their marketing area you will not contract with another organization to offer the same program to the same prospective participants. Just as you must insist on the foregoing clause, so the institution will insist upon a noncompetitive agreement. You will fatally undermine your relationship with the institution if you don't agree to this provision.

Chapter 5

As previously discussed, the only problem that arises is when you are offering several different workshops and an institution wishes to book only one. In this case, you can only agree to give the first institution an exclusive with the program it has bought and with no other. It was their decision not to book other programs, but they have no right to an exclusive relationship with you covering all your offerings. That is beyond the scope of your agreement. Understand, however, that even though the institution has no right to limit your access to other organizations, it may well feel itself aggrieved if you enter into relationships with others within the same marketing territory even for noncompetitive courses. If possible, therefore, try to stay with a single institution within a single marketing territory and work with them to have offered as many of your courses as you'd like to have promoted.

- **Admission Of Media**

Whenever possible it is to your advantage to get media to attend your classes, the more so of course when you have products to promote. The more unusual your class, the more hard information of a problem solving kind you're offering that would be useful to the media's audience, the more likely you are to get superb coverage. This coverage is very useful the next time the program is offered because snippets of print coverage and on-the-air remarks can be quoted in the brochure or other advertising.

Unfortunately, all too often universities are most shortsighted about the free admission of media people. They often make it as difficult as possible to admit them without paying a fee and are reluctant to provide them with the day's amenities. I remember on one occasion when the program coordinator at a major university told a media representative he couldn't eat with the group because the state wouldn't pay for his meal. When he said he'd pay for it himself and would like to stay, she said "No!" because it would foul up the accounting. She thus dismissed him to have lunch on his own! When I found out about this treatment my usual equanimity deserted me. What boorishness! To say nothing of the outright stupidity! Remember this: nothing that happens to an on-site media person is off the record, and it's damned fortunate no mention of this contretemps ended up in the eventual story. If you are fortunate enough to snag media people for your program, make sure they'll be properly treated.

Final Thoughts On Continuing Education Contracts

As you do more and more work with continuing education programs nationwide, you'll find yourself developing long-standing, productive relationships, and you'll come to know the strengths and weaknesses of the people you're dealing with. If, for instance, you know that a given program planner is weak in public relations (a very general fault) no paragraph explicitly defining what the institution will do in public relations will assist you even though you might want to include it as I so often do. This is just plain realistic. Let's say, after all, that you did get the public relations paragraph you wanted and that the institution did not meet its obligations. What would you do realistically? Sue? Lose the contract and all your advantages? Not bloody likely! You'd grin and bear it, urging them along with a little bit of the carrot ("You'll make money from this!") and less of the stick ("I'll switch schools on you!"), just like we do in real life.

Remember: you are dealing with casual people who are not often very businesslike. While this has its infuriating dimension (those late checks, you know), it is also not without its benefits. Contractual relationships are most informal. The program planners expect you to show up and do your job. They'll do what they can depending on their available resources to make your program a success but no more than they generally do. This casual approach, which is shot through continuing education nationwide, is infuriating, but it is also reminiscent of a perhaps better period now gone forever from most other areas of American life (and sure to pass away here, too). We might as well enjoy it while we can.

The Trade And Professional Association Market

Speaking to associations is big, big business. You need to get into this lucrative market. Just how many associations there are seems a rather elusive figure. The Gale Research Company in its *Encyclopedia Of Associations* (citation below) indexes approximately 20,000 of the largest. In fact the number is easily twice or even more than this across the nation. Still, it's more than you could do in a lifetime even if you did one a day. Moreover I'm pleased to tell you the number is growing all the time. As Alexis de Tocqueville, that sage aristocrat, pointed out early in the nineteenth century, Americans are a very joining people. No more so than now, either!

Chapter 5

Virtually without exception these associations use speakers of one kind and another at their meetings. Many of these associations try to get their speakers without cost; at many others the remuneration is truly princely, considerably better than in the continuing education market. The drawback, however, is that it is difficult to establish an ongoing relationship with a trade or professional association since they crave novelty. As I'm about to show you, however, this is by no means an insurmountable difficulty although the solution of the problem demands your persistent and creative effort.

Breaking In

Following my suggestions earlier in this chapter, the time to begin looking at the association market is after you have established a solid if not spectacular record of success working in local continuing education programs. What is important is that you can provide evidence the information you have is valuable, timely and that the audience response to you is good. Associations, after all, usually sell their programs to membership by saying that they constitute the state-of-the-art information in the field and that they are also entertaining and pleasurable. It cannot be stressed too often that when you go into the speaking business, whether you are addressing the annual meeting of General Motors or the smallest class at the smallest continuing education facility in the nation, you are in show business and the entertainment factor is important. Thus your tested ability to entertain people while enlightening them is pivotal to your success.

Assembling Your Association Persuasion Packet

As in continuing education, you need to assemble all your significant persuasion materials in advance of any approach to an association. Here's what you need:

- program description(s)

- media packet including sample release, press clippings, articles by and about you on the topic, newsletter comments from organizations booking you, &c.

- audio cassette(s) of past speaking engagements

- video cassette(s), if available

- testimonials from recent speaking engagements

- audience response indicators

- types of presentations you give

- fee requirements.

All this must be thought out and assembled in advance of any approach to any association so that you will be able to respond quickly to expressions of interest.

Program Description(s)

I use a single packet for both continuing education and association program planners. You can, too. If you prefer, you can simply use your continuing education program descriptions with a special letter addressed to association program planners. This letter should be used to point out the effectiveness of these programs in association meetings.

Media Packet

The more speaking engagements you have the better your media packet will be. Use the chapter on unabashed promotion to swell your file. Suffice it to say here that this packet should include a sample media release and recent media clippings. Don't use clippings more than a year old since they don't date well; the exception to this rule is where you have addressed a similar audience or organization where your prior experience is meaningful. Importantly, as you address associations, make sure their newsletters and publications cover you both in advance of your presentation and afterwards. These kinds of media are important for a packet, and you need to strive for this kind of related coverage.

Chapter 5

On photographs: unless a special brochure is being created for your program, a continuing education catalog almost never features the photographs of lecturers. An association, however, will probably need the standard mug shot, 5×7 inches or 8×10 black and white.

Audio Cassette(s)

An audio cassette is most important as you go into the association market. Association program planners want to know how you sound. There are several kinds of cassettes which you can have; an association will prefer you before a live audience for obvious reasons. You can also use an appearance on a radio show, particularly a call-in radio show where you had to relate to a live audience. In the case of the former, you'll have to arrange for your own taping; in the latter case, the radio station can make the tape of your show for you while you're on the air. Always ask them in advance because you occasionally have to bring your own cassette tape. Finally, some speakers create very elaborate tapes with a professional announcer and snippets of several programs. Whatever you do, never neglect the applause portions of your programs for this indicates a happy audience and that is something every program planner wants.

Video Cassette(s)

A video cassette is not absolutely necessary but it helps. You can, for instance, get one duplicated for about $25-50 when you are on a public affairs show on television. This is one good reason for going on such a program. As with radio stations, ask the producer in advance whether you can get a copy of the tape. Once you get it, always ask a reviewing association to return it to you. They are often careless about returning audio cassettes (and you should never send the original). A video cassette is larger and will probably be returned with less effort.

Testimonials

In the speaking business you need testimonials. Some people put them into a loose leaf three-ringed binder especially created for this purpose. The more audacious of my fellow speakers leave these on their office coffee tables so that people arriving early for appointments will lose no opportunity to discern how superlative are their virtues. Even I don't do this! Instead, I keep a simple manila folder filled with testimonials from both program planners and program participants. Again, in the beginning of your career you will have fewer of these testimonials and the ones you have will be disproportionately important. In your early years, there are fortunately several ways to beef up this testimonial file.

Get yourself invited to local organizations like Kiwanis, Rotary, Lions, &c. These organizations do not pay speakers but they can provide you with both experience and splendid letters of recommendation. Since you are not getting paid, you have every right to a letter of endorsement, but you're going to have to ask for it. The key constituents of such a letter are:

- number of people addressed
- audience response to you
- comments on how you handled questions and dealt with spontaneous audience reactions
- your handling of humor
- the relevance, timeliness and importance of your talk
- value of supplementary items like leave behinds, brochures, support materials
- ease to work with (most important for those who'll have to do so)
- promptness
- attention to the audience's needs
- your general impression on the audience
- the organization's readiness to invite you back.

This is a lot.

Chapter 5

Since you're going to have to ask for this letter in any event, don't hesitate to send along topics to the program planners which you'd like addressed in his letter of recommendation. Be frank about why you need these topics addressed. Say that you are developing your professional speaking practice and that you'll be including this letter in your portfolio.

One last point: always have the recommendor include his telephone number in the letter. I've always believed that written recommendations are not a very good judge of how a person feels. People these days hesitate to commit anything to paper that is not complimentary. Also, they don't really give the kind of information that applies to the individual situation in which you're interested. Thus, if you can and you are absolutely sure of the oral recommendation you're likely to get, include the telephone number in the original letter and in specific instances give out this person's telephone number personally to those who are seeking information about you. A positive oral recommendation carries a lot more impact.

Types Of Presentation

On the continuing education circuit, you can usually give only the following kinds of programs:

- one-day intensive workshops

- evening programs for 1-2 hours that extend over a series of weeks

- lecture series in which you give one of a series of presentations on a given topic.

There are exceptions to be sure. Some programs have overseas tours. Others are multi-day institutes taking place in exotic locales, but most of the programs given are along the lines of those above.

On the association circuit things are different. Here are some possibilities:

- one-day programs given regionally around the country to members

- one-day programs at conventions

- half-day convention programs

- keynote and other convention speeches.

One-Day Regional Programs

While colleges and universities are local, associations offer the speaker the tempting possibility of offering a single program around the nation. If you can develop such a program, you can enter into a relationship with a trade or professional association to carry it right to their members and so profit the association and yourself.

There are several benefits to this approach to speaking, and I'm amazed to discover that more organizations don't use it and that more speakers don't propose it. It offers the following benefits for the association:

- Good programs at affordable rates.

- It cuts the travel costs of members. It is, after all, a lot less expensive to send one speaker to 20 places than to send 20 organizations to one place.

- Programs can often be offered right on the premises of individual (usually institutional) members.

- Food costs are lower. Participants can brown bag it or an inexpensive catered lunch can be included in the price.

- Promotion is easier. A single brochure can be developed listing all the dates.

- Follow-up clinics can be held at the regional or national meetings to reinforce the problem solving information dispensed at the local sessions.

Chapter 5

- Such programs produce unrestricted operating revenues for an association at a time when this should be most attractive.

Such a relationship holds the following benefits for you. You should consider them, but of course there's no reason to expatiate upon them while speaking with the association. They can simply radiate a quiet glow within you.

- These programs produce a continuing source of speaking income.

- They are an ongoing source of promotion.

- You secure a good, strong track record which can be leveraged through Success Letters.

- You'll have access to audiences to which you can sell additional products and consulting services.

- Once booked in a given area, you can piggyback additional speaking engagements in that area since all your travel and accommodation costs will be covered.

Since there's so much to be gained from such a relationship for both you and the association, it behooves you to think through all the financial possibilities of the idea and its marketing and promotional aspects. Here's how.

Financial Possibilities

A typical package would look something like this:

You are retained by an association to provide 4 to 8 Problem Solving Process programs regionally. The association must tell you where the pockets of their members are so that the right places can be targeted. Usually they are in the big cities. A good package rate for those attending would be $250 for an organization sending 2 to 3 people. This would include materials fees and lunch and perhaps an after-program cocktail party.

You should get a straight $1000 per day plus materials fees costs (mine are the full prices of my books used by participants). You can provide the books without additional cost for the 2 to 3 people in the package rate. Others must pay for the books directly or the association can invoice them as you prefer.

Aim for 20 organizations (or single individuals) participating at this rate or a gross of $5000. The cost of organizing the program (promotional flyers, mailings, your transportation and materials fee) should be no more than $1500. Your speaker fee is $1000. The association keeps the remainder.

Is This A Good Deal For You, The Speaker?

You may argue: "Why can't I do all this myself and take all the money? Isn't the association profiting unduly?" Well, of course you can do everything. You can rent the mailing labels in some but not all cases. (Sometimes association lists cannot be rented.)

You can produce your own promotional materials and rent hotel space as discussed in Chapter 15. But you won't have the clout with the prospects that the association itself does. Doing your program with the association means that you "give away" a percentage of the gross proceeds to be sure but it has its advantages:

- You have to put up no advance money yourself.

- You have the endorsement of the association (good for future leveraging).

- You'll get promotion through the association which is also useful later.

- If the program is successful, they'll probably want to book you again for this or another program.

- You get a regular income plus profit from materials.

Chapter 5

- You can simply come in and deliver the program without much further ado and then go on to do more programs elsewhere leveraging the travel money you're being paid.

As a professional consultant to nonprofit organizations, I encourage all associations to get into this line of fund raising, that is, to consider fund raising in much broader terms than merely looking for standard individual, corporate and foundation donations. So should you. The numbers I've given above are real and would result in a nice profit at the end of the year for any association that enters into a serious Problem Solving Process talk program.

To be sure, your relationship with the association may not be quite so effortless as I've suggested. It's to your advantage to put in some time developing the program brochure, assisting with promotion and marketing and with media relations. You needn't worry about any of the other matters pertaining to a successful program.

Here's a good suggestion to give to any association where you have problem solving information that is useful to its members:

- Begin with a presentation on your topic at the annual meeting. Make it an overview.

- Follow this up with a series of programs at regular intervals with smaller groups of participants. All these programs will be arranged along the lines of the Problem Solving Process.

- Finish up with a review of the year at the annual meeting, problems encountered, and the successes and failures of those taking your programs.

If the association does decide to adopt this suggestion, don't forget to charge them for both the introductory and final programs which are essential parts of the package.

More Standard Fare

The model I've suggested above is one I am trying hard to popularize. If you really want people to master your Problem Solving Process information, giving it to them once and hoping for the best is not enough. Adult learners need both time to be exposed to new material and time to apply it on their own. Both are essential constituents of true technique mastery. Because all too many associations haven't yet figured this out, you have also to offer the standard convention programs. These include the one-day workshop, the half-day workshop, and the keynote or other convention speech. Since these have been discussed before, there's no need to reprise here. What is necessary is some discussion about where to find places where you can offer these programs.

Locating Association Clients

If you are going to find clients in the association market, you need to be aware of three key publications. I use them regularly:

- *Encyclopedia Of Associations,* 3 volumes
  Gale Research Company
  Book Tower
  Detroit, MI 48226

At about $220 this may seem too much for you to pay. It is a lot, but not if you plan to do much speaking for associations. Gale lists the associations, officers, publications and activities of over 20,000 organizations.

- *National Trade And Professional Associations Of The United States*
  Columbia Books, Inc.
  1350 New York Ave., N.W., Suite 207
  Washington, D.C. 20005
  (202) 737-3777

Chapter 5

The 1986 edition of this useful book is $75.00, plus $5.00 shipping & handling. One of its helpful features is that it is indexed by city so that when you are traveling, you'll be able to call ahead and visit the program planners while you're there. This book also lists the annual meetings and cities for many associations for several years to come.

- *Who's Who In Association Management: 1986-87 Membership Directory*
  American Society of Association Executives
  1575 Eye Street, N.W.
  Washington, D.C. 20005
  (202) 626-ASAE

$12 for members (membership is curently $140) and $75 for nonmembers. This lists the members of the professional organization for association executives.

It's important to put these volumes in perspective. No one who is seriously contemplating a career offering programs to associations can afford to be without them. By the same token, fully half the associations of the United States or more are not to be found in these books. Thus you must not assume that when you've got these you have access to all the places with which you'll want to do businesss. I have lucrative professional relationships with several associations not found in these books. Thus you must remain alert to the names of associations which may be of interst to you and continue to ask people what their professional associations are.

First Approach To Prospects

Just like in continuing education, you must review an association's programs to determine what kind of presentations they offer. As before, where a program is already being offered, you'll want to suggest yourself as a substitute. If your program seems appropriate and has not been offered, you'll want to suggest it. Start with the convention proceedings from the last meeting. Just call the association's main office or write and ask for it. An officious secretary will undoubtedly ask you why you are calling and will probably not send you the information if you say you're trying to become a convention speaker. Say instead that you are considering taking a booth at the next convention and that you wish to see the program for last year. Also ask for the name of the individual booking convention speakers. Get the individual's complete name, title, address and telephone number.

Once you've had the oppotunity to review the last program catalog, which is often a very extensive document, do the following:

- Write an introductory letter to the program planner. The larger the convention, the more these people work months and months in advance. Thus about 8 to 10 months prior to the next meeting is a good time to begin your selling process. Prior to that they are not ready for you; afterwards, too many decisions have already been made.

If in response you learn that the program is already fully booked let the planner know that you are available as a stand-in. Most convention planners are not able to assemble a program that undergoes no changes. Indicate your availability. You have a very good chance of being selected although if you are your name probably won't appear in the final program. Under such circumstances, if you are asked to make a last-minute appearance, request that your literature or at the very least a biographical write-up be put in the catalog as an insert. It's a reasonable request, although one the planner probably hasn't heard from anyone else unless he's read **MONEY TALKS**.

After having requested consideration as a substitute, ask from the planner the name of his successor. The larger associations appoint shadow convention planning teams which learn their tasks from watching the current team at work. If the association is already fully booked with speakers for the next convention approach the planners for the subsequent meeting. Also ask whether there are regional or other meetings between the larger annual conventions. There often are. While you should, of course, contact this individual as soon as possible to establish a connection, you need to understand that while the next convention is in the process of being assembled, no one is yet ready to do much about the subsequent meeting. So your initial connect is necessarily preliminary. When you do contact this meeting planner, get a date and time to call back when a more substantial contact can be made.

Chapter 5

Selling The Program Planner On You And Your Programs

Understand this: it's your responsibility to follow-up any letter you write to a program planner. Remember: they need you and they may even know they need you. But they don't always remember to pick up the telephone. So help them along.

Your Initial Telephone Contact

Of course you already know you are going to call in the morning and you know, too, what you're going to do if they don't return your call for you are now the master of the telephone. When you do connect, you need to ascertain the following:

- Which speaking slots are still available. A convention offers a good many opportunities for you, and you need to know what's available. As you move up the speaker totem pole, you'll want to target the keynote and other major addresses. Don't neglect the other possibilities.

- Find out which of your programs would be of most interest to the audience. Don't hesitate to make recommendations. You are, after all, the expert and you know what's timely. Be prepared to defend yourself!

- If there was a similar program to yours at last year's meeting, ask whether it will be repeated. If not, find out whether the speaker is unavailable, or the program did not work out well. The planner may have bad memories about this program; it's up to you to dispel them and demonstrate that your program will be decidedly different.

- Ask when the decisions are being made and what kinds of material the planner would find it helpful to review about you. Volunteer materials you have and which you'll be happy to send.

- Find out what speakers are being paid. Don't be shy about this. Usually what happens is that a program planner is given a totally inadequate amount of money with which to work. A disproportionate sum of this money is early allotted to the keynote speaker leaving smaller sums for all the other speakers. The planner you are speaking to, unless a meeting planner professional (a growing group), has no experience in knowing what you should be paid, but he does know what's left. You should find out and proceed accordingly. The advice which follows will help you fashion a constructive package deal.

The Deal

Is this convention worth doing if you're not being paid? The answer to this pivotal query is a resounding "Maybe!" It depends on these factors:

- Do you have a product or book available which you can sell on the spot? Is there any objection to selling it at the meeting?

- Can the association make booth space available to you at no cost or a reduced price?

- How will the organization be promoting speakers in its publications?

- Can you fashion a product distribution agreement with the organization which will result in money in your pocket?

- Will there be client prospects in the audience? Will you have sufficient information about them (names, addresses, telephone numbers) so that you can easily get in touch with them?

- Can you tape the program and sell that or will the organization demand taping rights?

- Would the organization consider the regional workshop arrangement discussed above?

Chapter 5

It should be clear to you by now that your opportunities are distinctly limited if you do not have a book or other product which you can factor into your reckoning. Without it, you are left to a straight fee arrangement with the possibility of follow-up for consulting or other service contracts. Unfortunately, however, most people offer services which are too high priced when the extra travel and other expenses are added to their cost so that getting clients from professional conventions is not a realistic alternative for many. Thus most speakers are left with the stark alternatives of cash or straight "professional development," which is another word for on the job training for the opportunities which really count.

At least see whether the organization can pay travel and other customary expenses, for then the meeting is surely worth doing since it is important to build up your credentials and your perceived standing as a speaker. Remember: once you are in the city where the meeting is being held:

- You can arrange some calls on other associations and organizations in the area for future speaking engagements, and

- You'll also be building up your frequent flyer bonus miles in the hope of getting to Rio without cost.

Finally, as soon as the convention date is booked, you can look into the prospect of piggybacking other assignments while you are there. A college which could not afford to bring you in because of your expenses may now be willing to make a date with you. Don't neglect these opportunities which should produce profit and new credibility to be leveraged for future assignments.

Follow-Up To First Program Planner Contact

Don't expect the program planner to sign you up right away unless you've been truly dazzling in this initial conversation, unless your information is hot and you have no competitors, or unless the meeting planner is desperate. Of course all these eventualities do occur, and you will occasionally benefit from them. Ordinarily, however, the planner has to go back and report to a committee whose members will be considering other speakers, too. Thus before you end this conversation, make sure you have a date at which you can call again and check on progress. Also make sure that you send all the materials that the planner wishes to review. Send these at once.

Other Ways To Get Access To Program Planners

Don't forget networking. Every person you know belongs to at least professional or trade association or union. Such organizations use speakers regularly. The trick is to figure out what you've got that would interest that audience.

Whenever you meet anyone complete an imaginary questionnaire. Find out the contacts that your friends and associates have. If something sounds promising, take the responsibility upon yourself to call and get the name of the meeting planner and the last program catalog as we've already discussed. Then get your friend to send an introductory letter on your behalf (See samples, page 274). This will be the hard part because very few people have ever recommended a convention speaker and have no idea that they could. Let's be very clear about this, however: as dues paying members of an association, your friends and their recommendations will be acknowledged by the responsible officers. After all, the members are paying their salaries! Members of organizations have influence they don't even know about! Use it on your behalf!

As I've said before, make it your responsibility to discover this kind of information about everyone you come in contact with. Use, too, the participants in your programs. Find out from them what associations and organizations they belong to and follow up appropriately. You'll soon find that you have more leads than you can conveniently handle.

As these leads come to fruition, don't forget to thank your original contact. You can do so in a way which is inexpensive for you and yet meaningful for the source. Invite them to attend one of your workshops as your guest, or give them an autographed copy of one of your books. These are gifts that will be talked about and which will redound to your advantage.

Then see whether they can give you some additional leads — to the corporate training sector.

Chapter 5

Selling Training Programs To Business: The Wide Variety Of Options

Don't make the mistake that so many trainers make, that is of conceiving of business solely in terms of the *Fortune* 500. Instead, remember that all sorts of corporations—from small businesses to nonprofit corporations to the country's titans — buy and use trainers. It's a multi-million dollar market. You can sell your training programs to:

- schools, colleges, universities and other educational institutions for their inhouse staffs and officers

- religious organizations

- all agencies of local, state and federal government

- hospitals and other health organizations

- training and personnel directors of companies

- executives in business and industry

- all other nonprofit organizations, &c.

Anyone who has a need can in fact become a client for you through a directed training program. The possibilities are staggering. Your task is to mold the information that you've got to see how you can make it appropriate for each of the continuing education, association and corporate markets. I'll use my fund raising program to give you an idea of how you can cluster programs and turn them into possibilities in each of these three areas:

- **In Continuing Education**

    I have one-day intensive workshop programs offered through continuing education centers, colleges and universities. These are marketed through catalogs and specific program brochures on the essentials of fund raising from individuals, corporations and foundations.

- **To Associations**

    Here I offer keynote speeches, lectures, convention programs and regional workshops on fund raising to specific target markets, e.g., "fund raising for the Congregational Church" or "fund raising for visiting nursing agencies."

- **Training Sessions**

    I offer programs to the boards of directors of individual nonprofit corporations on their role in fund raising. I train executive directors of a specific kind of agency, and I do training programs for businesses on how to make their philanthropy more effective.

As you can see, these programs are clustered; they are designed so that I'll have a significant presence in each of the three major talk areas. There are literally thousands of program clusters that can be created and as you develop your speaking practice and your expertise you'll be able to fashion several of them yourself. As a result you'll have maximum flexibility and the ability to take advantage of circumstances. This is important so that you'll become "recession proof"; you can promote those programs that seem most likely to be successful at any given time.

The problem with most speakers is that they haven't thought through all the programs they can offer in each of the three major fields. As a result they are attempting to sell too little and, of course, they meet with minimal success.

The Beginning

I know from experience that it takes time to fathom all the possibilities that you should be offering within each of the three major areas. Here, however, is the way to get started:

Chapter 5

Use brainstorming to help you maximize your options. Start with the general subject on which you intend to speak. ("Raising money from individuals, corporations and foundations.") Now list all those individuals who become involved in the process in some way: (executive directors, nonprofit trustees, directors of development, directors of public relations, corporate contribution officers, &c.) Now list all the ways you can get access to these individuals, all the relevant trade and professional associations, the publications they read, the meetings they attend, the direct mail lists on which they appear, &c. All this information is for ease of marketing and promotion. Once you have done this begin listing the wide range of training programs that you can create for each group. Here's a very partial list that would apply to those groups listed above:

- successfully raising money from corporations (directed to executive directors, trustees, and directors of development)

- successfully raising money from foundations (the same)

- successfully raising money from individuals (the same)

- successfully involving your Board of Directors in the fund raising process (perhaps simply targeted to executive directors)

- successful special events and how to create them (perhaps just for selected board members and directors of development or agency volunteers)

- successful fund raising documents and how to write them (for executive directors)

- masterminding the planning process (executive directors and selected trustees)

- creating an endowment fund (the same)

- successful community fund raising (executive directors, selected trustees, community volunteers)

- public relations and its relation to fund raising (directors of public relations, directors of development)

- "Becoming A Good Neighbor": Successfully Creating A Corporate Giving Program (corporate contribuition officers)

You get the idea. It remains to point out several things about this process:

- All utilize the Problem Solving Process methodology.

- All sell success. You are not in the business of disseminating information. You are in the business of producing a meaningful success. Stress the fact that you are the person who can do this and that your methods embody the means of achieving the success that the client wants.

- Don't hesitate to mix and match your programs depending on the time you have available, your audience, and its wishes.

Identifying Prospects

Once you have a preliminary list of your training subjects (for this is a list you will develop and elaborate the longer you are in the business and the more you know about your client prospects) and simultaneous to your marketing yourself to continuing education and association programs, begin to look for other training opportunities. In this section I am going to concentrate on the inhouse training possibilities, those programs you offer to an organization's personnel and leadership and that instruct them in your Problem Solving Process techniques.

Chapter 5

I must tell you something about this universe. There is no job bank with available openings. To be sure certain publications occasionally list an opportunity or two, but in most instances you create these training positions for yourself on an ad hoc basis: that is you respond to a perceived need of an organization and manage to make a convincing case that what you have to offer will solve a problem. Keep in mind that when you begin to do training programs, you necessarily must become a job creation expert: the individual who learns how to sense needs and create Problem Solving Process programs accordingly. On your ability to do so rests your success.

Networking Redux

It goes without saying that networking is where you begin. Listen to your friends as they talk about the problems in their offices. Listen to your clients as they complain about corporate conditions. Mull over how you can transform the information and training techniques you have at your disposal into a Problem Solving Process for these people and their organizations. Then use networking to get a hearing.

In case it is not by now obvious, let me explain why I place such great stock in networking. If you've ever tried to make cold calls to organizations, you don't need my explanation. You know that secretaries and other low level clerical types are paid to block you from getting through to decision makers. This is because people in organizations are in a state of stasis: comfortable stability and nonthreatening nonchange. When you come in to train people, you are necessarily functioning as a catalyst, a change agent. You can as a result expect resentment. It's not surprising, therefore, that no matter how needed your service there are those whose objective is to prevent you from offering it. This is where networking comes in.

With networking you gain Automatic Acceptance with decision makers. You will have what most sales people never get: a hearing. Make no mistake about it, this hearing is of the utmost importance for without it you cannot make your case.

To be a successful networker necessarily means, of course, asking people about themselves and keeping note of the connections they turn up. It also means using these connections on your behalf. Does this make you queasy? Alas! You'll have to get over the luxury of this squeamishness. Find out from the people with whom you deal the direct and indirect links they have with decision makers. Urge them to use these links on your behalf by following the stages of the Pyramid of Contacts. Write down this information for your permanent files and follow-up all the leads you are given.

Targeting Possibilities

The mistake most ingenue speakers make is that they spend money foolishly. They take out an ad in a professional publication announcing their availability. They do a great mailing to all likely prospects. Then they connive at other ways to waste money wantonly, usually to little avail. This is not the way to get clients. Instead target.

- Use networking to secure viable leads.

- Once you have given a successful program look for other organizations and individuals which are similarly situated and approach them with the idea of replicating your success for them.

- Deal with fewer organizations rather than more and follow through on them conscientiously.

Take as your objective the spending of as few dollars as you can and getting as many profitable speaking dates as conceivable. Then work hard to get that first speaking assignment. Regard it as the first link in the Great Chain of Possibilities. Leverage it to repeat the success and bring the Problem Solving Process information to others similarly situated. Promote the success to the relevant trade and professional associations. Identify individuals and organizations which have the problem you are addressing and create training sessions for their inhouse personnel and officers. In short, make a relatively limited body of information useful to its furthest extent. This is cost effective, inexpensive and productive.

Chapter 5

Differences Within The Corporate Training World

The leading difference in delivering training programs in the corporate world is that in many instances you will need to develop a survey questionnaire to ascertain what problems the client has, for it is the solution of these problems that will be the core of your session. Your training must be specifically directed to the needs of an individual organization. Making your program organizationally specific is usually not the prime consideration in the continuing education and association markets. Here it usually is. In short, you must be prepared to function as a consultant undertaking a needs assessment before recommending an exact form of training.

Note: you will occasionally be brought into a corporation where a needs assessment has been completed by another consultant before your arrival. In this case you'll need to review the following points:

- Who developed the questionnaire?

- Is this individual a recognized expert, someone who can be objective about the problem and its circumstances?

- Does the survey instrument measure objective or subjective data?

- Does it address a homogeneous audience?

- Was the questioner knowledgeable about the subculture of this audience?

- Are the responses a free expression from the personnel interviewed or did the presence of management skew the response?

If the answers to these questions do not meet with your approval, as the expert you'll need to recommend the formulation and dissemination of another survey document.

Note: it is beyond the scope of this book to advise on how to undertake a needs assessment. Here, however, is a handy reference guide which will be helpful when you have to provide this service.

Contracting With External Agencies by Richard A. Lombardo, Fawzi H. Hermes, and Vince L. Carney. Published by Learning Resources Network, 1983.

Thus, either you know what kind of training to produce because of an existing needs assessment which you can review, or you will have to develop your own ascertainment techniques and subsequent training program accordingly.

Selling A Package

If there is no existing needs assessment, try to sell the corporation/organization the following package of services:

- needs assessment

- actual training module

- evaluation of training

- subsequent check-up clinic.

Remember: each of these is in fact a separate service module and can be sold as such. There is, however, good pedagogical reason for attempting to sell all these modules as a complete package. You needn't point out the financial benefits for yourself!

Chapter 5

Needs Assessment

As a successful corporate trainer, you must come to work from what I call the Physician Mode. That is, you are the doctor who can help the indisposed patient solve a pressing and injurious problem. Under such circumstances, of course, you need to be absolutely sure that you are addressing the right problem and not rely upon your own hunches (informed though they may be) or those of the client. Thus a needs assessment of some sort is absolutely necessary. If the client doesn't have one that you regard as useful, propose doing your own.

Actual Training

Different trainers have different views on this subject: whether to hold your meeting(s) on site at the organization or at a separate place. Both can be successfully done so long as the program itself is properly arranged. Here are some advantages of an on-site program:

- People won't have trouble finding the location and can be expected to arrive promptly.

- They'll feel comfortable.

- Any supplementary materials you may need relating to the problem are probably readily available.

There are disadvantages, too:

- Participants already have their (usually bad) habits and may be less willing to alter them in their habitual surroundings. This may help defeat your necessary role as the catalyst.

- They may be interrupted during the course of the program to attend to their regular jobs thus interrupting the flow of your workshop and diminishing its importance.

Keeping these factors in mind and balancing them against the amount of money available and the willingness of management to assist you, you can probably minimize the negatives. If you do give an on-site program insist that there be no interruptions during the course of the day or allow for specified periods when participants can attend to other matters. Move the program to an area of the building that participants would not otherwise use, say the board room.

Evaluation

When you give a program for a continuing education facility or association, you can be certain you'll be evaluated. These evaluations are, after all, useful to you, too, and can be leveraged to get more work. You'll also be evaluated by participants after a corporate training session. What's different about this training session, however, is that you should also submit an evaluation of the participants upon completion of the program, something that will rarely if ever take place with your other programs. It's your responsibility as the designated expert to record your impressions and make suggestions about how receptive the participants were to the information and what should happen next to facilitate the important matter of bringing about success. What you write should be in the form of a "Success Report," a brief, pungent document putting forward all that was done right and that worked, that which was not so successful and why, and what needs to happen next to move towards the designated objective. This document should assist you in getting more work with this client and situations with others similarly situated.

Check-Up Clinic

We have already discussed the human limitations of adult learners and our collective inability to keep new information current for long, especially when we are being asked to change our habits. All trainers, therefore, need to insist upon a follow-up clinic at regular intervals, say three, six and twelve months after the original presentation. You need to know what is working and not working for the participants, refresh their memories and deal with the situations that have arisen as a result of implementing, perhaps incompletely or sloppily, your suggestions. These check-up clinics are in my view probably the most important part of the training, and, human short-sightedness being what it is, they are the most neglected.

Chapter 5

Payment Options

There are several different payment options you can use in the corporate training sector. They include:

- fixed flat fee
- fixed flat fee plus expenses
- per capita fee
- per capita fee with guarantee
- payment by results contract.

Fixed Flat Fee

As its name suggests, in this option you get a certain amount of money if the training program actually takes place. You supply the trainer or trainers, the materials, pay your own expenses and meet any other costs. You are paid a lump sum.

Fixed Flat Fee Plus Expenses

With this option, you break out all your expenses including transportation, accommodation, postage, copying, and materials but not the actual training fee. This is the arrangement I usually use.

Per Capita Fee

In this model you'll be paid a set fee for each participant. This is, of course, risky unless you have a guarantee of attendance.

Per Capita Fee With Guarantee

If you're inclined to do per capita fee arrangements, do ask for the guarantee.

Payment By Results Contract

This is not to be recommended because in most instances it will be difficult to determine the result level. If you adopt this as a method of payment, you must have control over how your suggestions are implemented so that there will be the necessary results.

Your Training Contract

The contract you establish with the organization you are working with should address the following matters:

- names of participating parties
- date agreement is signed
- term of agreement (when it will start, when it will conclude)
- when your training session/workshops will be given and where
- who will prepare the training materials
- who will own the rights to them

Chapter 5

- whether the client is getting one-time only use of materials (including evaluation forms, written documents, proposals, memoranda, booklets, video and audio cassettes, &c), whether they will retain all rights, or whether the rights will be shared and if so in what way

- who will conduct the program

- who is responsible for recruiting additional trainers if more than one is required

- how pre-workshop/training consultation is to be done and how paid for

- whether you will have ascertainment and testing materials

- whether there will be a follow up clinic, where, when, who will attend

- who will handle notification of this and all programs to participants

- who will be responsible for providing support staff, what kind it will be

- what the support staff will do, when

- who will the contact person be for the contracting organization

- how advertising and promotion will be handled if applicable

- how the facility will be set up and by whom

- whether attendance will be limited.

In addition to this break down of responsibilities between you and the contracting party, you need to specify:

- you are an independent contractor

- you handle your own workmen's compensation, insurance, &c., and that as a result of injury or suit you render the contracting party harmless from counter action

- which state laws are applicable

- the contract can be modified or amended only by the mutual written consent of both parties.

It is also a very good idea to include clauses specifying which expenses you will be compensated for and what will happen if the contracting party doesn't pay your invoice. You'll want wording saying that in such an eventuality you can take legal action and that the contracting party is responsible for legal costs, attorney and court fees, &c. It's a sad fact that some people won't pay their bills. You need to be prepared for action!

Note: For further information on contracts see my book **THE CONSULTANT'S KIT: ESTABLISHING AND OPERATING YOUR SUCCESSFUL CONSULTING BUSINESS.**

A Final Word On Training Programs

Once you have succeeded in offering a successful training program at one organization, don't rest on your laurels. Attempt to follow it up with other organizations. I begin each day writing five marketing letters to new organizations and media sources which ought to cover me. Follow this good advice! Develop your Success Letter, identify prospects, market and market some more! This is a slow moving universe; you have to spend the time not only perfecting your programs but identifying prospects and selling them on you and the disproportionate benefits you offer compared to your fee.

Chapter 5

A Few Key Resources

There are many, many books written about training but most of them won't be necessary for you. Here are a few resources which are:

- *Training: The Magazine Of Human Resources Development*
  50 S. Ninth St.
  Minneapolis, MN 55402
  (612) 333-0471

A significant resource that will address in detail many of the issues of this chapter. Subscribers receive once a year the *Training Marketplace Directory* which is packed with useful leads. *Training* also provides major conferences for people in the industry.

- *Training News*
  38 Chauncy St.
  Boston, MA 02111
  (617) 542-0146

A monthly newspaper for the training professional.

- American Society For Training And Development
  Box 1443, 1630 Duke St.
  Alexandria, VA 22313
  (202) 484-2390

An educational society for people engaged in training and development. Publishes the useful *Buyer's Guide and Consultant Directory* where your services can be listed.

Chapter 6

SELLING YOUR PARTICIPANT PROSPECTS: SECRETS OF CATALOG COPY, FLYERS, BROCHURES AND PAID ADVERTISING

If you schedule an inhouse workshop or training session at any organization you probably won't have to worry about assembling your audience. It'll be delivered to you. This is, of course, a superb way to do business and many lecturers and trainers live by seeking out captive audiences and catering to their needs. However, if you just do that it will limit your growth and the number of people you can reach. The truth is in this businesss you need to become an expert on the ways audiences can be produced. This chapter will help.

More On Catalog Copy

Most catalog copy as I hope I've already made clear is severely inadequate. It is written to impress other lecturers and not to sell the benefits to participants. Most academics, for instance, who write catalog copy feel it is *infra dig* to write clear, persuasive selling copy. Sales is something they wish to keep from the rarefied land of academe. This idea, of course, is nonsense. Don't succumb to it; do learn how to write the best, most sparkling copy you can. Here's what you need to include:

- title

- description of presenter

- main body of copy.

Title

As we've already discussed, it is your responsibility to conceive a title which is at once interesting and short. It should also promise a benefit to the participant or answer a question they have. As you know, I prefer titles that are in two parts: the grabber and the descriptor.

Description Of Presenter

People rightly want to know who's giving the workshop. They want to take courses given by people who can help them meet the objectives they have for the course. Thus stress the following points:

- credentials which relate directly to what you're offering

- prior employment experience which directly relates to course

- degrees which directly relate.

Credentials, you must know, are contextual, never absolute.

Main Body Of Copy

Your copy must be user centered and concentrate on user benefits. Whenever possible, use the words "you" and "your" in the copy. Directly address your buyer. Communicate a sense of connectedness and excitement about what's happening. Remember, too, that any sensible reader knows that if the course is successful it will be offered again by the institution (a very reasonable assumption). Therefore, there really isn't any pressure to take action now. After all, if it's not successful, it won't be offered again and your reader can reckon he hasn't lost much. If it is successful, it's sure to come back.

Chapter 6

You must keep in mind, however, that whether the prospect enrolls now is of very real importance to you. If you have an insufficient number enrolled, the program will be cancelled; at the very least your Success Letter will lose its impact if the course is only marginally successful. Thus, you must promote the feeling of urgency and the need to act now to an audience which instinctively knows better. How can you do this? Here are some ideas:

- Your words must be action words impelling the reader to do something — now!

- There must be a sense that a benefit will be lost if the reader fails to take action.

- You must play on the latent anxiety of the reader about what will happen — or not happen — because he fails to take immediate action.

Do any of the following circumstances apply in this case? If so, use them:

- Stress the infrequency with which this course is given.

- Emphasize the changing trends in the field and the need for immediate action.

- If start-up time is involved in realizing the objectives of your program, make sure the reader understands it's better to begin now.

In short, use those words and descriptors necessary to impart a need for decision, for movement, for action — now! I need hardly say this is hard to do even under the best of circumstances and most difficult when you are competing for the attention of individuals against all the courses in your catalog and all the other catalogs from this marketing area. Therefore consider using some or all of the following:

- Point out the usefulness of the material in helping the prospects secure their immediate objectives.

- Use participant evaluation comments from recent programs. One pungent comment is worth repeating in the copy.

- Cite the number of participants who have taken your programs.

- Give the number of years the program has been offered.

Remember: you always need to balance the need of the prospect for reassurance about quality and certain substance as against his need to act now. *N.B.* Don't forget on your participant evaluation forms to take advantage of the opportunity to ask your students to analyze your catalog copy. What did they like? What didn't they like? What other phrases, items would have been helpful to include?

Handling Publications

If you have a book, audio cassette, pamphlet, &c., which will be available to people as part of the program, always mention this in your catalog copy. It's a benefit to those attending and as such should boost sales. Always make sure that you provide the regular retail price of the material as part of the catalog copy, thus: "A copy of Dr. Jeffrey Lant's well-known book **THE CONSULTANT'S KIT: ESTABLISHING AND OPERATING YOUR SUCCESSFUL CONSULTING BUSINESS** is included in the program fee (regular $30 retail value)."

If the book is not being made generally available as part of the fee, add this kind of line: "Dr. Jeffrey Lant's well-known book **THE CONSULTANT'S KIT** is available for your purchase at the program." If you are planning to offer your product at a discount, make sure this fact is in the program copy. It's another inducement to attend.

Possible Objections Of Program Planners

Many program planners, come uncertainly from antediluvian times, do not like the notion that their brochures and catalogs are being used for the benefit of lecturers and program leaders. I remember in one instance at a college in South Carolina, the dean of continuing education deleted all mention of my books because he didn't want his brochure to be tainted with commercialism. This attitude is, of course, offensive; you need to mount a strong attack on it!

Chapter 6

The correct way of handling this situation is to write the copy yourself (this gives you the initial advantage). Mention your book or product as part of a sentence presenting your credentials: "Workshop leader Dr. Jeffrey Lant, author of the well-known book **THE CONSULTANT'S KIT**, graduate of Harvard..." In other words, properly sell your product as part of the credentials which make you the most credible person to offer your program. It's hard for a program planner to argue with this logic; some will, of course. Simply say, "The book is one of the strongest reasons why people will attend this course. From it they know that I am the expert!" From your standpoint, you want the product mentioned because you will get additional promotion and hence sales. It will make it easier to sell even if it's not included in the cost of your program.

Note: don't expect to have your way with catalog copy without a brisk discussion. Because the people you are dealing with are not marketing minded themselves, they often mistrust those of us who are. Use your selective hearing and do the best you can.

Associations, if possible, are worse. An association, for instance, will think nothing of asking a professional to come give a lecture for free to its members (this they deem acceptable behavior) but will take deep umbrage if this professional attempts to use the opportunity to bring something to the attention of his listeners if he is benefitting even though that very thing is of vital interest and significance to the members. I confess to you that I have never understood this twisted logic, but I can assure you it's prevalent and that you will face it. My advice to you is this: keep working against this arrogant stupidity. Marketing is in the best traditions of this country, and it's the very shortsighted who don't understand this and try to keep things "tainted with commercialism" at a safe distance. I believe this: so long as people feel comfortable saying "No!" and so long as the marketing is reasonable and not intrusive, I think any professional has not only the right but also the obligation to bring his products, services and messages to the attention of the broadest possible audience. Adopt this as your credo and work for it!

Self-Mailing Brochures

It is in the nature of catalogs for the copy to be severely limited, but if you remember at all times you are writing advertising copy, you won't fare too badly. Moreover, if you keep asking your participants for their opinion of the copy, you'll be able to refine it to the point of perfection.

Most brochures are boring. They have been written and assembled by people who have done too many and have lost all heart. They have been assembled too quickly and without understanding why people should or would pay over dozens or hundreds of dollars and what will motivate these important buyers to take action.

What I am about to tell you equally applies to any advertising form to be sure. But it is critical when writing brochures. Brochures and other mailing pieces are expensive, and there is no sense spending this money unless you are going to get a good response and whether you are going to present the best, most convincing information in the best, most convincing way. Otherwise don't bother.

Here are some things you should know before you begin writing brochure copy:

- Whether you are going to make a presentation through a continuing education program or an association, your host probably already has an outline in mind and may also have a standard format into which your copy is to be fit. There is little if anything you can do about this format. Do try, though: you don't want your program to look like the last 100 programs promoted by this organization.

- The people you deal with probably have lost all flair and zest and enthusiasm for their work. They therefore need your help. Be prepared to give it to them.

- Demand that you see the final brochure copy before it is printed. I have learned from hard experience that the brilliant, sparkling copy I write (and which has been approved by the sponsor) has a way of getting reduced to pabulum before publication. You be the last to review the copy. If you can't actually see it because of time constraints, you can request that it be read to you over the telephone. It's no bad thing in any event to have copy read to you since reading often exposes awkward and graceless prose.

Chapter 6

Preparing Scintillating Brochure Copy

I'm quite prepared to admit that writing scintillating brochure copy is a high art form. While you should aim to be the consummate artist, you need nonetheless to master the basics. Here are the leading points which should be addressed in your brochure copy:

- title program
- date
- time
- place
- sponsor of program
- goal of program
- want for program
- learning objectives of program
- learning methodology of program
- target population for program
- program presenter information
- program materials
- continuing education units and/or certificates of participation
- program schedule
- related programs
- deduction for educational expenses
- travel and accomodation particulars
- price
- credit card and other payment information
- advance registration discount information
- follow-up individuals
- telephone number
- address
- program sponsoring organization information.

Some of these points seem obvious and yet the absence of information or the difficulty in finding it on your brochures will cause people otherwise interested to pass your program by.

The Beginning

If the organization sponsoring you has a standard brochure format, ask for it. That will enable you to get a sense of how much space you have to provide the necessary information. Moreover, it will minimize the amount of time you need to spend preparing the brochure. Much of the information (contact person, telephone number, &c.) will probably remain consistent from program to program. Take advantage of this. This being the case you can spend the time you need to prepare the really important parts of the brochure, the parts selling benefits to prospects.

Hint: Before beginning to write, get a sense of how many words you need for each section. Writing good brochure and catalog copy is rather like writing a haiku.

Goal Of Program

Implicitly or explicitly each program has a goal. A goal is a statement of ultimate purpose of your program. You should be able to state it in a single crisp sentence. With my fund raising workshop, for instance, here's the goal: "To make disadvantaged nonprofit organizations more competitive in the race for scarce private sector funds."

Any uncertainty about your goal will be communicated to your prospects. If you feel such uncertainty, ask the prospects about helping you refine a concise goals statement. They'll tell you what goal you should have by telling you what objective they wish to reach.

Chapter 6

Want For Program

Note that I have used here the word "want" rather than need. People need many things and yet they are not always willing to spend their resources to have them. Thus you must persuade people that your program is not only something they need but also something they want. In this connection, your job is to persuade them that your program is the proper vehicle to take them where they want to go.

Sadly, I long ago came to the conclusion that no one really wants my programs. Let me explain this. They want the results which they can achieve because of my programs. They want wealth, financial security, professional recognition, fame, the satisfaction of doing good with and for others, &c. My program is just one of several ways to help them reach their objectives. The purpose of this section of your brochure is to convince people that in one place, in a well organized, well delivered way, and entertaining, too, they will get the information they need to help them reach their ultimate objectives.

Thus, people taking my consulting programs want financial independence, freedom from the traditional workplace and traditional employer-employee relationships. They want a detailed plan to which they can refer when they go out on their own that gives them a reasonable chance for success. They tell me this over and over again. These wants, then, must be spelled out in the brochure or in any of your advertising copy, or else your program and its enrollments will suffer.

The hard part comes, of course, when your prospects are vague about what they want. Here you must help them articulate their own wants and put them in a fashion they can earnestly and enthusiastically respond to. That's one service you often offer: articulating for those less articulate and thoughtful than yourself the goals and objectives they seek.

Instructional Methodologies Of Program

This section is where you say just how you will conduct the program. Remember: most people disliked their school days. They felt constrained, undervalued and as if they'd wasted their time. They came to associate the grotesqueries of the American educational system with knowledge itself, a distressing coincidence. Your job is to convince them that the instructional methods you'll be using will help them learn — and meet their objectives.

Here are some instructional possibilities:

- lecture

- simulations

- peer exercizes

- review of participant materials brought from outside or produced in workshop

- use of films, tapes, cassettes.

The key to selecting differing instructional possibilities, and there are many such, is this: will these methods help the participants reach their objectives for the program? If so, they need to be highlighted in the program's brochure.

Here's a popular selling point I often use and I commend to you: I ask participants to bring in their own brochures, marketing materials, letters, memoranda, contracts, business cards and other materials. If you have the kind of program where you can review the business, professional or personal life of the participants and give on the spot advice, then do so. Hint: this is an appealing selling point to be sure since people know very well they rarely get this form of interchange with an expert without paying a good deal for it. However, all will not take advantage of it through shyness. Thus you get the advantage of offering this benefit without needing to carry through with all prospects.

Chapter 6

If you, like me, intend primarily to use the lecture format, you will need an indication that your style is not dry-as-dust and hence repellent to your audience. In this connection you can insert a line like this into your brochure copy: "Dr. Jeffrey Lant is consistently rated by participants as one of the most lucid, enthusiastic, well informed and entertaining lecturers they have ever heard." Now let me say something else: don't wait and hope that someone will write this sentence about you for you. You have to do it yourself. You cannot expect that someone else will have the perceptiveness to write just what you need. This line is not, it should go without saying, mere hubris. It's designed to solve a problem that your prospects have: their distaste for the traditional classroom format. If you need a reason for writing such a line, there it is.

By the same token, if you are going to use films and other techniques which many people (including me) regard as diversionary at best, then you need to use a line like this: "You'll have the opportunity to learn from two special 20 minute films. Ann Smith, your instructor, was a technical advisor on these films and will supply background material about them which cannot be found elsewhere." Again, you must supply the relevant context to make the information meaningful.

In any event, you need a descriptive line or two detailing the kinds of instructional methodologies you'll be using and in upbeat language their benefit to your participants. This section becomes meaningful when you conceptualize their fears and anxieties and then make sure to polish them off!

Learning Objectives Of Program

What will participants leaving your program know and be able to do? In other words, what are they buying? To give you an indication of some of the characteristically inept brochure copy that is produced by even the most eminent workshop producers in this country, I'd like to cite some parts of a course description entitled "Designing and Planning Productive Meetings." I came across this description quite by accident in my study, but it seemed so typical I wanted to share it with you, not least because the company producing it is a household word in this industry. Here are the published outcomes they provided for this course:

"Participants will take away with them:

- a framework for designing meetings of any size or type;

- ideas for a variety of methods to begin and end meetings;

- ideas for creative start-up techniques;

- actual practice in designing a meeting of the participant's choice, at least in mini-form."

I hope by now I don't need to tell you that this is simply atrocious copy. Yet it's typical of the rubbish regularly published. Let me say as strongly as I can that all your program outcomes need to be as specific as possible. Use real numbers. Bring up common problems within your field and indicate that your Problem Solving Process program will solve them. Put these problems into priority order. Deal with the greatest fears and anxieties of participants. Here are just a few thoughts about how the mediocre copy above can be improved:

- Don't say "participants." Say "You!" You are talking to a real person. You must visualize this person and his problems, problems that you'll be solving. This is a critical error.

- Introduce key words into the copy, words like "profit," "achievement," "success." You are the magician who can produce these ultimate objectives. Capitalize on your strength. Write something like this: "Attending you will succeed in creating the kinds of meetings people look forward to ..."

Most people would agree that there are too many meetings and that these meetings accomplish too little, that attendance is often difficult to secure, and that attention is even more difficult to command. Yet, as a problem solver, you surely believe that there are ways of dealing with these common problems to make your meetings memorable and so help your own career. The hope that people have about meetings is that they can get their work shared, that they and their achievements will be noticed approvingly by their peers and superiors, and that they can therefore propel themselves ahead. *Pari passu*, their fear is that a badly organized meeting will cast doubt on their competence and at the very least cause them to be regarded as dull and not fit for advancement.

Chapter 6

All advertising copy, all brochure copy should therefore play on the aspirations and anxieties of the reader. It should also make the vague concrete so that people come away feeling they have bought something specific, not just general information. In this connection, here's how to rewrite some of the mediocre copy:

"At this workshop, you'll learn:

- four ways to arrange a meeting that will get the boss' attention and enhance the likelihood of a promotion

- how to set an agenda that commands attention

- fifteen meeting planning mistakes you've suffered from and how to avoid them

- those crucial fifteen minutes: techniques which will work for you and get your meeting off to a right start fast

- how to get the right people to your meetings time after time."

You get the idea.

The unsatisfactory brochure copy I cited above addresses itself to an impersonal audience ("participants"). Its outcomes are vague and unspecific. And worse, a benefit is suggested and then taken away: "Actual practice in designing a meeting of the participant's choice, *at least* (my emphasis) in mini-form." Instead, the copy writer should have said something like this: "Bring at least one example of a meeting you have to organize in the next month. Arrange it right in class and have the benefit of both instructor and peer suggestions." (Note: not criticism!)

Learning objectives need to be specific, measurable and packed with benefits to the participants. Build them around the anxieties of the participants, their own experiences and their aspirations not around abstract information you happen to have. Make the copy short, snappy and benefit-packed. Use action words and copy that lends itself to action task lists and ways that will help participants actually solve the stated problem in their real lives.

Target Population For Program

Be as specific as you can be about the kinds of people who'll benefit from your program. How's this? "Anyone interested in and responsible for planning meetings would find this seminar useful, different and productive." This is an excerpt from our now much flogged mediocre example.

It's too vague, of course, far too vague. Instead, visualize your audience and be precise about who you want to attend. Your Participant Profile should help you. Then write down their job titles. Specifically. Infuriatingly, people who give programs are often maddeningly unspecific about the exact job titles of the people they wish to be present. Perhaps they are just plain uninformed. But knowing this information is part of your job. Different kinds of people plan meetings, for instance. I can't believe that one program would suit them all or that even if it did the participants from wildly different backgrounds would feel comfortable with each other or regard the experience as satisfactory. Thus say instead, "This seminar is designed for Chairpersons of Boards of Trustees of nonprofit organizations, Executive Directors, &c".

Once you have a sense of what you want your audience to look like it will be easy for you to list their job titles or an appropriate description. Then you can always add a catch-all line at the end. That's basically what appears above. One further note: There is nothing in this brochure copy that indicates why the program is "different" or why being different is somehow meaningful. If you haven't proved the point in the copy, don't use the word.

The problem, of course, is that program planners, particularly uninformed ones, cast their nets as wide as possible in the search for participants. Don't you be one of them! You be as specific as possible. Aim for a particular prospect and do all you can to convince this person to attend.

Chapter 6

Program Presenter

In my example, this is what is said about the presenter, "She returned recently from a trip to China and Hong Kong where she studied management and training methodologies." What's relevant about this? I've said it before but I cannot resist saying it again: don't write the credential section for your benefit, to appear to be grand and important. Write it for the benefit of the prospect. In these circumstances your degree credentials are usually not meaningful. You're not applying for an academic job after all. You're letting people know what you've done that entitles you to be regarded as an expert in the area. As I reviewed our now beleaguered instructor's credentials from our example above, I found nothing that suggested she had any experience in planning meetings or that we should have any particular regard for her expertise. Thus, the credential section not only does not work towards her objectives, it actually works against them.

Ladies and gentlemen, I'll say it again and again! The credentials you present to your prospects must be relevant to the audience you expect to attract and to the program you expect to present. Each word, each "credential" must help to promote you as the expert on *that* topic, in that context. No one cares, frankly, whether you are a wonderful person or that you graduated *summa cum laude* twenty years ago. The myopia of many continuing education and association planners in disseminating this kind of information is predictable if disheartening. Now you know better.

Program Materials

The trick here is to ensure that people don't feel they could get the materials without taking the course. Or, if the materials are commercially available, that these materials encompass all the information that you the expert will impart. People often call and ask about a program they are considering attending, "Is your book **THE CONSULTANT'S KIT** available independently? What will I get out of the course that I won't get out of the book?" People quite rightly fear that the author of a book will simply repeat that material. They rightly find that offensive and wonder whether they wouldn't be better off getting that material even though they risk losing a bit from the day itself.

Do yourself a favor: make sure that you have additional material in the course that does not appear in your publications. Here's how the problem can be dealt with. "You'll receive Dr. Jeffrey Lant's well-known book **THE CONSULTANT'S KIT** ($30 retail value) simply by attending. Dr. Lant will also be providing his newest research findings on what makes consulting practices successful. Don't forget that you also have the opportunity to have this nationally-known consulting expert evaluate your own marketing and business development materials — a service that is well worth the cost of the course!" Make sure, in short, that participants understand they are getting something at the course they cannot get elsewhere.

Knowing this, you can see why the blurb on this point from our sample copy is so inept: "The basis of the seminar will be the book (title)... which has been co-authored by the seminar leader and published by..." Seeing this in print, why would any sensible person spend an additional $185 (the seminar's cost) when they could get most if not all the material by paying the much-lesser price for the book? I certainly wouldn't.

Continuing Education Units And/Or Certificates

Many associations as well as divisions of continuing education now offer continuing education units for noncredit courses. These can be applied towards relicensing in areas like real estate and nursing. Frankly, while it is no surprise to me that continuing educators are working like crazy to get more and more professionals mandated to take continuing education courses (and thus fill their classrooms), I've never found these CEUs a great lure. Unless people can get some direct job-related benefit from continuing education units, they don't seem to me to be very useful. Having thus pooh-poohed them, if you find they are available do use them. It can't hurt.

Try, however, for a certificate. Understand this: most continuing education divisions have certificates which are made up in advance for participants or sent afterwards by mail. From the institution's standpoint they are all very well and good since they promote the course and the program. Most, however, do not include the instructor's name. This has always been a sore point with me, and I hope you'll be equally aggravated. I realize the benefit of certificates, but I'd be more happy about them if they included my name as instructor (something they rarely do). Unfortunately it scarcely does to complain about this, since the universities usually have a good ten year supply on hand. Still, over time if enough of us do complain...

Chapter 6

The fact remains that if the participants are going to get a certificate of participation, it should be mentioned in the brochure. I like this to be boxed thereby calling attention to it and making it seem more important than it is. Personally, I now have a wall full of the things, and they don't do much for me. They rather remind me of the comment made by Lord Melbourne, Queen Victoria's first Prime Minister, about the Garter, England's premier heraldic order. He liked to give it, he said, because there was "no damned merit" about it. So do give certificates and do it with a flourish!

Program Schedule

Adult learners like to know exactly how their day is going to be arranged. Partly this is so they can make other arrangements for business and child care, &c. Partly it's because they don't like uncertainty. In either event it's often a good idea to publicize exactly how the day will be divided. Something like this will do:

"The workshop begins promptly at 9 a.m. (coffee from 8:30 a.m.) Lunch will be from 12 noon until 1 p.m. in the university's student cafeteria. Coffee will be available throughout the morning, and there will be a soft-drink break in mid-afternoon. The workshop will end at 4:30 sharp."

As you'll notice, food constitutes an important part of the program schedule. Sadly, many universities and associations, alarmed at the cost of such amenities, have abandoned them. This, I think, is a mistake. I'm not a coffee drinker myself, but it's a good way to have people get acquainted and break the ice. You should press for having it whenever possible.

These days you may also wish to include a line like this, "The seminar room will be divided into smoking and non-smoking sections." In time this line will be standard in all brochures.

Deduction For Educational Expenses

If people are using your course to improve their job-related skills, then they can probably legitimately claim the cost of the program as a deduction. Here's the exact language:

"An income tax deduction is allowed for expenses of education, including registration fees, travel, meals and lodging, undertaken to maintain and improve professional skills. (See Treas. Reg 1 162-5 Coughlin vs. Commissioner 203 F2d 307)."

I can't imagine any continuing education program that doesn't have this citation and exact wording on file, but you should have it, too. Besides, many associations don't have it, and that's a mistake.

Price Information

Notice that I have left the discussion of price to the conclusion, which is just where it should be. Naturally people immediately want to know what the program's price is. If they focus on price and not on the disproportionate benefit of attending, they may not come at all. Both of you would then be adversely affected. My preferred way of handling price is simply stating it and not discussing it. Don't attempt to explain your fee or provide a defense for it. Either the course is worth it — and you've proven it — or it's not in which case the price is too dear.

Whenever possible payment should be allowed by credit card. Fortunately most establishments are prepared for this, and there is little you can do if they're not.

Likewise, the organization will have its own way of handling follow-up information. Just make sure that it's included. It's absolutely necessary to have a specific individual responsible for handling your program and for fielding any questions that prospects may ask.

Chapter 6

Dennis Tarr, Dean of Continuing Education at Temple University in Philadelphia, once wrote an article in which he advised deans and directors of continuing education to try and register for one of their own courses. Try it yourself. You'll be amazed. I once called a major institution and asked for information about my program, a program which was then being advertised in the catalog. The woman at the other end of the telephone first told me there wasn't any program. Later she said it was cancelled. Finally she admitted (I will prod, you know) she didn't know what she was talking about. In real life, of course, your registrant has now quite properly concluded that you and your program are too much bother and probably not worth the money and has gone on to spend his discretionary income elsewhere. Thus: get a specific person and make sure that that individual's name and telephone number and address are on all outgoing brochures about your program.

I like to have my own telephone number included, too, for this reason: An individual calls the designated representative of the sponsor. That person tries to answer the question and cannot. If they're smart, they give out my telephone number and suggest that the prospect call me directly. But they are not, I confess, always smart. You should be, however. Say that you'll be happy to take direct calls about your program and get your telephone number enclosed. A subsidiary benefit of this arrangement, of course, is that if you are promoting products you can handle the sales directly, too.

One more thing about fee: most organizations are willing to give what is generally called an "early bird" discount, that is a discount if you enroll before a certain date. This date should be about 10 days or so before the program in question, in other words it should be a real date. Early bird discounts work. Insist on one. Make sure that if you get it, it's promoted right on the front cover of your brochure. Make it attractive and bold. If you are giving a $25 discount off a $150 program, as often happens, don't just say "Early Bird Discount," say something like, "Act Now. Save $25!"

Related Program Information

If you are offering another program through the sponsoring organization, this would be a good place to promote it. Or if the organization itself is offering something else in the same field, encourage the sponsor to promote it in your brochure. Remember: the sponsor does have other courses and you should be welcoming and receptive to their need to get maximum promotion. By the same token, don't hesitate to suggest that they do the same for your course on their other brochures. It helps, of course, to know their catalog and brochures so that you'll know where it would be beneficial to suggest this. Understand that this common sense notion may strike many continuing educators as novel, although it shouldn't. More and more of them should be catching on to the need to cluster their programs and promote them as a group.

Program Sponsoring Organization Information

Unless the organization sponsoring your program is very well known, include some validating comments about it in the brochure. Such boilerplate is generally available and simply added by the institution. Again, they need the chance for promotion and should be encouraged to take it!

Your Photograph

Many brochures feature instructor photographs. I myself have some mixed feelings about this. On the one hand, it is certainly gratifying to you to be identified as a celebrity, the cynosure of all eyes. On the other hand, I'm not sure it really adds much. I would, for instance, rather have a picture of the book that the participants will get by attending. That is a real benefit and will help induce people to come. Such promotion will also be more useful to you in the long run as it spurs outside sales. Whenever possible, then, attempt to persuade the sponsor to run a photograph of the materials people will get by attending. This is the line, "This copy of **THE UNABASHED SELF-PROMOTER'S GUIDE** is reserved for you...," or "You'll get this 366-page unparalleled public relations resource by attending ($30 retail value)."

Lay Outs

I am not, I hasten to add, an expert on lay outs. I'm always told that I err on the side of having too much copy on a page and that's probably true. However, I have personally never liked the contemporary trend to large white spaces and just a few words. Maybe it's just me, but I don't tend to respond to these kinds of ads. I want to know more, and

Chapter 6

I'm assuming that others want to know more, too. Still, now that you know this failing (if it is one!), I want to go on and introduce several different brochure possibilities to you. Before doing so, however, let me recommend two good resources on the subject from experts who will correct any idiosyncratic preferences on my part:

- *Designing Brochures For Results* by Linda G. Leffel
  Learning Resources Network
  P.O. Box 1448
  1554 Hayes Drive
  Manhattan, KS 66502

- *Better Brochures, Catalogs And Mailing Pieces* by Jane Maas
  St. Martin's Press
  175 Fifth Ave.
  New York, New York 10010

The Old Standard

We all get plenty of brochures. My best advice to you is to save them. I have a very scientific and orderly method of keeping these around; it's called a cardboard box and into this box go illustrations of brochure copy, arrangement and paper that works. And, I confess, illustrations of mediocre productions, too, to keep me on the alert and make me feel happy at my own good work. When you do this you'll notice that most of what you get is the familiar 4 x 9 inch self-mailing brochure. It has a cover, a mail panel and an inside made up of three mailing panels.

This format enables you to put all your basic "5 w" information (who, what, where, when and why) on the cover and the essential course and registration information on the inside. You can use the sixth remaining panel, depending on your lay out, as a teaser: "This copy of **THE UNABASHED SELF-PROMOTER'S GUIDE** has been reserved for you..."

There are several benefits to this brochure which is why it's used so regularly:

- It's a self-mailer, that is your mailing label can be affixed right to it.

- It's about as inexpensive as you can get.

- It can be used as a poster.

Chapter 6

Of course, the mere fact that it is so popular now almost works against it. It is not very original. So here are a few other alternatives:

SAMPLE BROCHURE FOLDS

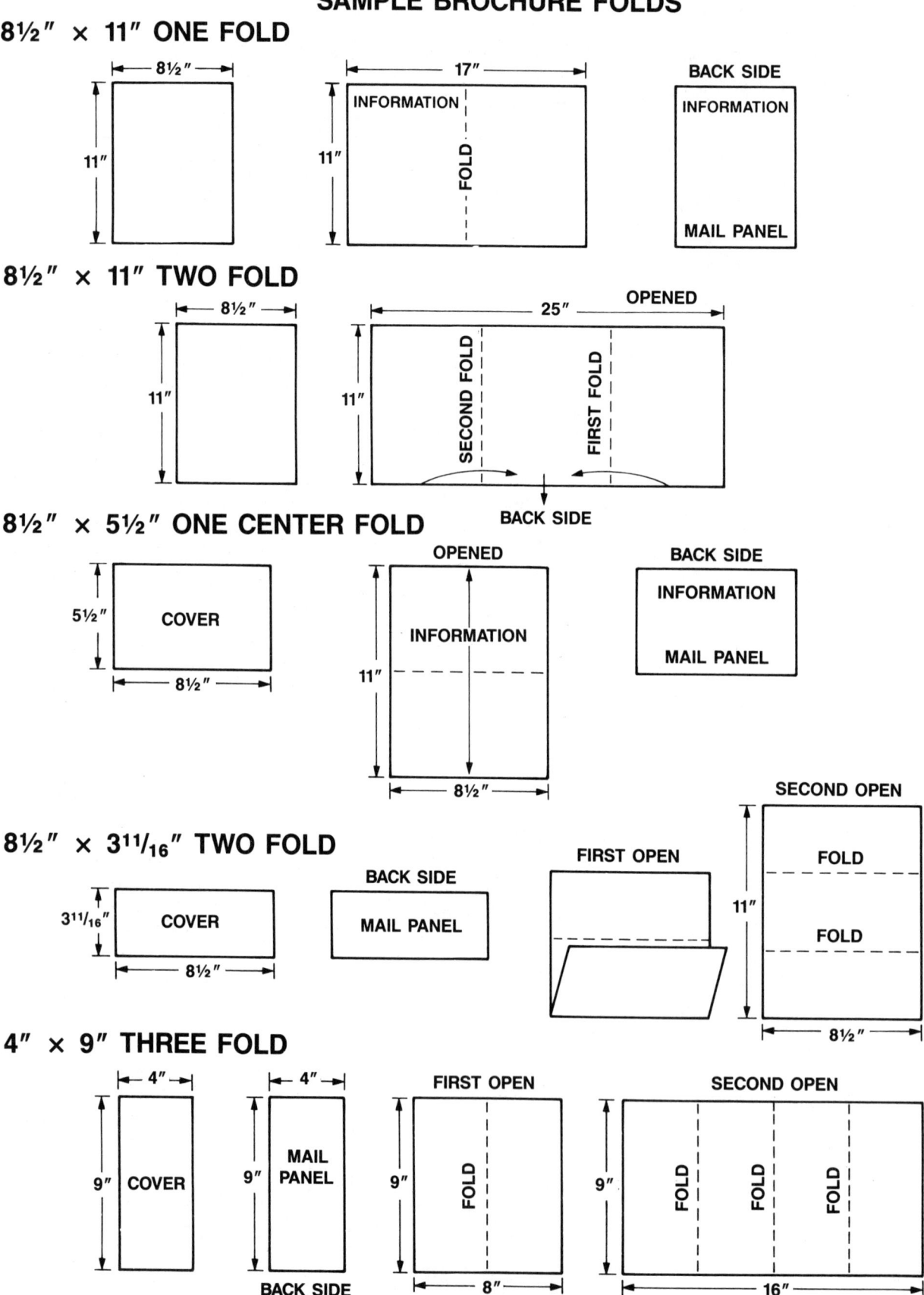

Chapter 6

I wouldn't get too creative if I were you though. If your sponsor can afford to go to extra expense on behalf of your program, what I would suggest is a special letter accompanying the brochure. In this case, in standard direct mail lingo, the brochure tells 'em and the letter sells 'em.

A letter accompanying a brochure is effective and should be used if resources permit. The letter needs:

- A good one or two sentence opening indicating to the reader that something exciting and important is about to happen.

- That the enclosed brochure lists the information that the reader needs but that the signer of the letter wishes to take this opportunity to point out several very special reasons why the letter recipient should attend.

Now stress:

- The timeliness of the material. Why this program, why now?

- The trends that have developed in the affected industry, its problems and developments which make this program important. Be specific! The more you can relate this seminar as a problem solving device to their problems — and hence opportunities — the better off you are.

- The fact that the instructor — you! — is superbly qualified to offer the information. My friend, now is the moment to toss your no doubt well merited modesty to the winds. You, of course, must draft this letter. But then you should have known that by now and at this point you should be adept at speaking about yourself in the Glowing Third Person, a new tense you've created. What you aim to impart in this section is this: you are the right person, you have the timely, valuable information; you will be offering not merely this information but outright solutions to problems and that participants will not get this opportunity again. Of course some of this material — perhaps all — is repeated in the brochure. Don't worry about that. Reinforcement is a key concept in direct mail promotion. This is a sales document in a more intense sense than the brochure is.

Indicate that registration is limited. Registration, of course, is always limited so this is scarcely a misrepresentation. If you know at what number you're going to cut off registrations, say so. *N.B.* As you get close to this number, you can send out a reminder post card or a short second letter indicating just how many spaces are left. At this point, you should also, if you're smart, schedule a second program within the very near future. Check with the sponsor. You've got a winner and you might as well press home your advantage while you've got it!

If possible, give a guarantee. The fact is too many people have been badly deceived and disappointed by workshops. They are rightly loath to turn over their money. The fact that you have a sponsor rightly reduces their doubts, which is, of course, one of the prime reasons for having a sponsor at all. The participant presumes, we hope correctly, that the program planner has ascertained the ability of the speaker to do what he says he can do. Nonetheless, there is still doubt. Therefore, I like an option which suggests that if after the first hour of the program the participant is not fully satisfied, a full refund will be made — on the spot, if possible! To be sure, most universities and associations are not geared up to provide this service. They'll make the registrant fill out a form and the check will be returned 6 weeks or more later. This is reprehensible and an outmoded way of doing business. The individual will be more likely to return to the sponsor for another course if this possibly difficult moment is handled with delicacy and dispatch. Of course, the participant will have lost some time, but he will not have lost his money, or what is more important, his dignity.

You should know that most sponsors are not prepared to give such a guarantee, and yet if it produces those two or three people sitting on the fence, it'll be worth it to you and to the sponsor, too. If you give such a guarantee, abide by it and repeat the guarantee at the beginning of the program. Not even one person in a hundred will take you up on this munificent offer unless, of course, you are ill-prepared and dull in which case they have a right to vote with their feet and not suffer with you.

Chapter 6

A Few Final Notes About This Sales Letter

- **Signature**

Many people could sign this letter effectively. But not you! The dean or director or program planner or head of the sponsoring organization should be considered. Also, it's perfectly acceptable to have a past participant do part or all of the letter (that is, review and validate a draft written by you). Of course the letter should be printed on the stationery of the sponsoring organization.

The tone of this letter should be upbeat and enthusiastic no matter how grave the problems being addressed in the program . In fact the more grave the situation the more necessity for enthusiasm and a sense that this workshop, this instructor can help salvage the situation and move things along again!

This letter along with the brochure needs to be sent about 6 to 8 weeks before your program and if possible a post card follow-up should be sent about 4 weeks before it takes place. (See samples, page 276 .)

- **Colors, Paper and Lay-Out**

These matters will generally be handled by the sponsoring institution. However, you'll want to have something to say about what they do. The fact is many continuing educators and association program planners have atrocious taste. Thus unending vigilance need be your motto.

Colors: Red, white and blue remain your best bets. They are patriotic, of course, but each of these hues has long, long histories. The colors you select need to match the kind of program you are presenting. Are you targeting mid-level executives or, perhaps, high school teachers? Colors may vary.

Paper: The best that can be afforded.

Layout: Let the sponsor lay out your copy but request that you see it before press date. Unfortunately this is often impossible, but I know from experience that you can spare the institution many mistakes if you do. I've actually had the unfortunate experience of having an organization print the wrong program description and announce a course I couldn't teach. It was clear to me they couldn't have read anything I mailed to them, and I wondered at the source of such breathtaking ignorance. You can bet your last dollar, it'll happen to you, too, unless you are unendingly chary.

Suggestions On Distribution

At long last the catalog or the brochure will be printed. This is a critical moment for you and one you need to be prepared to use to your advantage. There are several people to whom you should distribute either the one or the other. As soon as it's ready, ask for a number of copies, including at least 20 for your own purposes.

If others are considering booking you, under the guise of Assertive Courtesy send them the materials with a short "for your information" memorandum. There is something more interesting about a brochure when the event has not yet taken place.

Take this opportunity to send the brochure to program planners of continuing education and associations. Remember: you have now been validated by a program planner who has selected you and has thereby stamped you as an expert. You are now well situated to go forth and attract other assignments.

These brochures have a lifespan of about a year. After that people will begin to wonder what you've been doing with yourself lately. During their relatively short lifespan, use and reuse them.

Note: after the program takes place, particularly if it's been a success, ask the program planner to give you the extras. There are always extras. Take them out of the program racks. While they are of no use to the general public, they still are for you.

Chapter 6

Other Places To Distribute Catalogs/Brochures

Take it upon yourself to distribute catalogs and brochures to your friends and others who may be interested in taking your course. By the same token, you can also send a list of these people to the sponsor for mailing. The problem with doing this is that the sponsor probably won't even take the time to circle your program or otherwise mark it and that those receiving the material (unless it's an explicit brochure devoted to you) won't know why they've received it. A compromise is for you to go through a stack of catalogs with a "see page 7" and let the sponsor mail them for you. Unfortunately, each time you offer a program with the sponsor you'll have to remind them about this procedure. There seems to be no collective memory in this business. I wish I could get it across to each university and association with which I do business to send me a standing order of catalogs and brochures each time I offer a course, but this seems beyond their limited capabilities.

Finally, be willing to take bundles of catalogs and brochures to handy distribution points in your neighborhood. You cannot simply sit back and hope for the best as so many people on the speaking circuit. Why do they adopt such an unhelpful attitude? I find in my case that one of the most useful ways of helping is to stuff the appropriate brochure into book packages we are mailing with a special note inviting the person to attend. Yes, it takes time. It's also worth it! If your program is to be the success you want it to be, don't start prematurely thinking of yourself as a star — and hence above it all!

The Media

Because the next chapter goes into detail on the right and wrong ways of promotion, I shall not dwell on the subject here. Remember, however, that your workshop provides media with a convenient hook for a story, interview, or commentary. Use it!

A media release about your course is always a good idea and you are advised to create one. However, you can often get away with a letter and a copy of your catalog or brochure. Don't let the sponsoring organization alone send out such materials. Target selected media for your own attention. After all, you want to develop direct links with these sources. While a letter and brochure can be adequate, if you've got the time send a standard media release along, too: the story as you'd like it to appear.

Direct Mail

Even utilizing all these methods, you're still going to find yourself in the direct mail business. There is a lot written on direct mail, much of it suggesting that here is a business in which to get rich fast. The sad truth is that you can lose your stake in direct mail very, very quickly if you don't know what you're doing. Last year, for instance, a friend distributed 110,000 catalogs. They were very attractive and very expensive. But they returned only about 30 responses causing him to lose virtually all his investment.

Fortunately in the situation where you have a sponsor, you are not going to find yourself similarly afflicted, which is of course one of the benefits of not going on alone. However, if the sponsor doesn't make money the first time out, or close to it, there probably won't be a second time no matter how important your program. You, therefore, have a vested interest in insuring the success of the direct mail distribution. Moreover, if you proceed through all the steps of the speaker circuit and end up producing your own independent programs, you're going to have to become a direct mail expert to make money. And that's a fact.

There are really only three parts to direct mail:

- the offer
- the persuasion materials
- the list.

Chapter 6

We have already discussed the first two of these points. We have yet to discuss the third.

In selecting a list, your previous work to develop a Participant Profile becomes most important. You can provide this profile to your sponsor and have him contact a list broker (check in the Yellow Pages under "Letter" or "Mailing"). Most sponsors, however, and surely all those who do not have a regular catalog but who mail brochures, will have an ongoing relationship with a list broker. From the profile, which you will remember contains information on publications read by those you are seeking to attract, you can get the advice of the broker on which lists to purchase. List brokers either have their own in-house lists, which are usually less expensive, or they must buy lists elsewhere. You can also help them by reviewing Standard Rate & Data Service (3004 Glenview Rd., Womet, IL 60091. 312-256-6067). This company lists the availability of more than 25,000 lists.

In many instances it will behoove you to discuss your workshop and Participant Profile directly with the list broker. If possible, ask the broker to read you the first twenty or so names on the list. If the list is in your area, ask to be read the names from your own neighborhood. This year I was offering a special book offer to bookstores and had the opportunity to buy a list from a broker. Using this method on the stores in my own neighborhood I knew immediately that the list was all wrong for me; I ended up buying a more expensive but better list from a publication in the field.

Also find out from your sponsor what kinds of in-house lists he has available. More associations and divisions of continuing education ought to be in the list rental business. If they are not renting their names for income, suggest it. Such rental, by the way, can turn a marginally profitable program into a profitable one. Remember, however: a list ordinarily needs about 5000 names before it can be bought. Query lists, where an individual has simply asked for information, are not as valuable.

Some Suggestions

Here is a summary of ideas about how to get off on the right foot with direct mail:

- Develop your Participant Profile.

- Give this list to the program sponsor for transmittal to the list broker or go over it with a list broker yourself.

- Give the list broker as much information as you can about whom you are seeking to attract and what you know about these people.

- Have the list broker do some research and get back to you with a list of possibilities.

- Evaluate the possibilities yourself. Find out the minimum number of names in each case and determine whether it's worth it to pay that minimum.

- Ask to see a sample page from your neighborhood or area if possible. If you can't be given a page, then ask to have the first 20-40 names photocopied and sent you for review.

- Check with your program sponsor about in-house lists.

Knowing as much as you can about where the names came from and how much they've purchased lately is important.

More Tips

If you are buying the names of newspaper buyers from a certain area, direct some of your publicity efforts towards that publication and so reinforce the initial impression made by your direct mail piece.

Also, if you get most or all of your names from a single source, particularize the front page of your brochure thus: "You've enjoyed one of our programs before... and you'll profit from this one, too." That's a line directed at past buyers. Or try this one, "A program no intelligent reader of the *Wall Street Journal* can afford to miss!"

Chapter 6

Granted, there are some problems in using these methods. If you buy several lists, you'll have to change the code phrase during the printing process which means extra expense. However, the object is to touch the reader, to let him know that you've done your homework and are trying to reach out and make the connection. People do respond when special things are done for them. You task is not merely to do them, but to let prospects know you've done them.

"What Kind Of Return Will I Get?"

I consistently ask people in my consulting seminars what kind of return they might expect on cold direct mail, that is mail sent to an individual who didn't ask for it and doesn't necessarily know about you. The answers always surprise me by their optimistic, hopeful turn. They run as high as 10%.

On average, of course, on a piece of cold direct mail with the right offer and the right supporting materials sent to the right list, the response will be between 1-2%. This variable, needless to say, is tremendously important and spells the difference between just breaking even and making a profit.

It is perfectly obvious that when you put on your own programs you must be aware of this fact, but why bring it up here? Just for this reason: you want your sponsor's profit to be a good one so that they can afford to bring you back and book new programs, too. At some point, I assure you, one of these programs will fail and may have to be cancelled. If you have a good track record with an institution, they may not cancel the program but go ahead and lose money, partly to gratify the students, partly to gratify you. In my opinion it's always better to lose just half a loaf than all the income you expected from the program. This reckoning will happen less frequently, however, if you can help the program planners with direct mail consideration.

One good rule of thumb is this: a good conservative workshop planner will plan for a 1% return on direct mail advertising that will place the program within 1 or 2 registrations of breaking even. The difference, he reckons, will be made up from word of mouth, free publicity, friends of the speaker, &c.

Paid Advertising: Space And Classified Ads And How To Use Them To Promote Your Programs

Regrettably, I have long believed that many people simply throw away their advertising dollars. I have heard story after story of people who have paid good Yankee dollars for ad space that has not elicited a single call. This scarcely surprises me. Although the quotation is variously attributed, these words are true words, "50% of my advertising dollars work and 50% don't. Unfortunately I don't know which is which." Since P.T. Barnum is named among the fathers of this apt quotation, I'll send these words to you on his advice.

The great question is to know when to encourage your sponsors to advertise on your behalf, that is when they should invest money with the likelihood of a higher return. Remember this: if the advertising doesn't pay off, while you may not be immediately affected, they probably won't be able to take a chance on you again. Thus it is very much in your interest to make sure that whatever dollars are spent on advertising at least return and hopefully profit you and the sponsor.

The First Tip

Know this: advertising will never successfully sell an unpopular service or product. The word "unpopular," however, needs clarification. It could mean, depending on the circumstances, the right item at the wrong price; the right item to the wrong audience; the right item at the wrong time just as it could mean the wrong item, period. That's the trick of the advertising business. Why, then, should you consider buying paid advertising space?

Some Reasons

This is not a book on advertising and the question above has prompted entire volumes. Here, however, are a few guidelines:

- Consider advertising not to sell your program directly (particularly if it's a program selling for over $75 a day) but to elicit queries and expressions of interest from prospective participants.

Chapter 6

- Consider advertising when you have already sold a substantial fraction of the places in your program, and you want to alert the world of prospective participants that this is something very good they won't want to miss — but might.

- Consider advertising after your program, yourself, your book *or* the subject on which you are speaking has been the subject of local media coverage. This is called Piggybacking.

To Elicit Queries

It would be very nice if your targeted population simply bought your program directly from a newspaper space ad or after hearing a radio advertisement. But in most cases they won't. Thus the correct sales sequence should be this:

- Develop your brochure and supporting materials.

- Place your advertisement after you have evaluated the particular audience which will see it to ascertain that what you're paying to publish will in fact reach the right people.

- Ask interested readers to contact you.

- Suitably follow up such queries with a mailed brochure, cover letter and telephone call.

This kind of commitment and this procedure takes time. I am well aware of that. I know from experience, however, that too much is expected of a single paid ad even where the audience is enormous and you have reasonable expectations.

In this instance, how would such an advertisement be worded and where would it be run?

An ad properly defined is an appealing intrusion into someone's consciousness. In an instant, through a small space in print or an aural moment, you must establish that what you are offering fulfills a prospective buyer's need which, until that moment, he may have been unconscious of having. This is, I think you'll agree, a tremendous amount to ask of the medium.

An ad designed to elicit queries should include the following kinds of information:

- a good catchy headline

- a goals statement that appeals to the prospective audience

- specific learning outcomes

- highlights about the instructor

- past participant comments for validation

- the specifics of date, time, place

- complete follow-up information.

For example, here's what an ad intended to produce queries for my one-day consulting program might look like:

Chapter 6

ARE YOU SICK OF GIVING AWAY YOUR GOOD ADVICE?

"I was," says Joseph Smith of Point Summit, New York. "I knew people were benefitting from my knowledge — and I wanted to benefit, too. That's why I enrolled in The Lifelong Learning Center's workshop on 'Establishing And Operating A Successful Consulting Business'. Am I glad I did. It was terrific!"

Thanks, Joe. That's what nearly all the participants in this intensive one-day workshop have always said. And why not? Here's some of what they've learned:

- The 10 most common errors new consultants make in establishing a successful business — and what to do about them.

- Selecting a lucrative specialty: what's hot now, what's not.

- Getting retainer contracts: how to get your clients to pay you a monthly stipend.

- The three ways you'll get guaranteed free publicity from any media source to promote your practice.

- Building your business with independent contractors.

- Diversifying your practice: how to become recession proof as a consultant.

This program is designed for professionals in any field who want to earn full- or part-time income and take full advantage of what they know.

It's taught by Dr. Jeffrey Lant, nationally known expert on consulting and author of **THE CONSULTANT'S KIT**. Now in a 7th printing, you get the book (a $30 retail value) just by attending!

For further information and complete registration details, contact the Center at . . . . . . Ask for Gloria.

Call today! The last time this program was offered it was sold out. So, set Saturday, October 19th aside to attend this program.

Like Joe Smith, you'll be glad you did.

Admittedly, this is a lot of copy. If you don't have this much space, cut back in each category, but keep the flavor of this ad. You need to establish audience identification, prospective participant benefit, the value of the program, the knowledgeability of the instructor, and the need for immediate action. And you can't scare them off with the price, not yet anyway! They don't know enough to be quite snagged.

People will now call or write to follow-up. You are now assembling a prospect list. Use a variant of the brochure cover letter and get it out promptly, on the same day the query is made if possible. One benefit of using this approach is that you'll be able to get the telephone number of the prospect. Using the tenets of Assertive Courtesy, you can follow up the initial query and your letter with a telephone call: "I just wanted to see whether you received the information we sent."

At this point you'll discover whether the individual is serious about taking the workshop or whether it was just idle curiosity that prompted the initial call. Questions will emerge that the sponsor's program staff may not be able to answer. Thus, you as the leader must be intimately involved in the process of selling your program. Get the name of the person with the question from the program staffer and call up yourself. People will be impressed that you took the time to call (note: your call is a billable expense against gross proceeds); then you can effectively inform them why they should attend your program. In short, there is a substantial link between you and the prospect. This will also help on the day of the program because you won't feel you are confronting a room full of strangers.

Chapter 6

Selling A Success

Use paid advertising, too, to sell a success. People want to be part of a successful program, and it's both your job and that of the sponsor to give your program the aura of success that it needs to truly succeed.

There is, of course, something of this in the preceding advertisement. Push this factor farther:

- Produce background materials including your brochure.

- Mail the brochure.

- Once you've got half the number of participants you need to break even and you and the program sponsor feel reasonably comfortable that the program will succeed, *then* run your paid advertisement in the appropriate publication. It should frankly exude as much success as possible. Here are some possibilities:

"There are only 5 places remaining! Enroll today!"
"Last time this program sold out. Don't delay!"
"Dr. Lant's only New Jersey visit this year. Don't miss it!"

One way of being able to launch this program is to corral a captured audience. Try to get the program planner to offer a group discount and so attract a sizable number of participants. This takes marketing. As soon as your program has been accepted by the sponsor, suggest which organizations might themselves be interested in a group discount. Draft a marketing letter for the program planner (see samples, page 278). If you can get a large initial group, then you are well on the way to success and a Success Advertisement makes sense. One program planner I know even goes so far as to advertise programs which are "sold out" so that the next time they're offered people will hurry up and enroll for fear of being shut out. I myself haven't gone quite this far, but I understand the logic of the action.

As the responses come in, you'll still follow up just as before. More of any queries from a Success Advertisement will probably enroll right away, but you may still have to do some selling and wooing.

Any follow-up letter that was developed would have to stress the limited amount of space and the need for immediate action. In all situations, it is to the benefit of the program planner — and you! — to create an air of urgency and a need for prompt and decisive action. Stressing the limited number of places and the importance of the subject matter is a good start.

Piggybacking

I am a big advocate of piggybacking in all situations, both with advertising and with news and feature material. Piggybacking means taking advantage of an existing climate fostering interest in your subject as evidenced by news and feature stories in the media or by leveraging your paid advertising after having made an initial impression through free publicity. If you pursue this strategy, you must give adequate time and attention to getting the initial publicity you need. Here are a few possibilities to ponder:

- Write a Problem Solving Process Article (see Chapter 7). Follow this within a day or two with an ad promoting your workshop appearance.

- Is there a front page or significant news story on your topic? Piggyback on it with an advertisement about your program on the same topic.

- Get yourself interviewed or featured in a print media source. Follow up the story with an advertisement in the same section if possible.

Chapter 6

Notice that these examples concentrate on the print media. In theory this technique ought to work just as well with electronic media, but in fact paid advertising on radio and television for most programs is prohibitively expensive and is therefore rarely used.

In the eventual advertisement, link your program with the previous publicity:

- "As featured in Tuesday's *Boston Globe!*"

- Stress the timeliness of the program as evidenced by recent news articles.

- Stress the newsworthiness and importance of the speaker.

Advertising works, but it doesn't work all the time or consistently. Thus whenever possible, don't begin with an ad but use an ad to accentuate and develop your audience which you have begun to find in other ways.

Using Classified Advertising

It may not appear that the much maligned and lowly classified ad has much of a place in promoting workshop programs, but that depends on a few significant conditions. People read classified ads. I am myself an inveterate reader of them, and millions of other people are, too.

Clearly if you are promoting a local program, you'll want a classified in a local magazine or newspaper. If you are on the national circuit like I am, you can use the big magazines like *Popular Science, Popular Mechanics, Venture,* &c. The time to consider using classifieds, however, is when you also have a product to sell. I didn't begin to use them until I had a line of books available. Here's how it works:

I put the classifieds in in the usual way. One ad I've profited from reads simply, "Make money consulting. All fields. Free information. JLA Publications, 50 Follen, Cambridge, MA 02138." Depending on the publication and its circulation this ad costs between $15-$125 to run.

I have a packet of information which I send out promoting my books and consulting services. Also, if there is a program in the respondent's area coming up on this subject and if it's being promoted with a brochure (which is not always the case), I simply slip one inside.

More likely, I sent the names thus arriving to the continuing education offices of the various universities with which I do business. I let them send the catalogs, brochures, &c. The trick, of course, is that each outgoing catalog must be specially marked ("See page 7 for consulting program") or a letter must be prepared to accompany the mailing.

At best, I prefer the letter. However, the program planners, pressed for time, don't always take this suggestion. Many suggest that I contact these people myself. We proceed to dicker until we find common ground.

The point remains that you will be in a stronger position with potential sponsors if you say that you can present names from their marketing area who have already expressed an interest in the topic. This is particularly true if your course and subject area are relatively leanly supplied with mailing lists. That's something you'll find out from Standard Rate & Data or a list broker. In such a situation, your ability to supply the names of prospects may spell the difference between success and failure.

Chapter 6

A Word About 'Bingo Cards'

In the past I have worked with organizations which have supplied me with a quota of names each month (in return, of course, for a nice fee) of individuals who have indicated their interest in one or more of my subject areas. You've all seen what are called in the trade "bingo cards." They are run in *Parade Magazine* and come in the many card decks which are circulated today. Those with the card can check a number of items or subjects in which they are interested and the manufacturer will send information. Those using these cards are not, I think, good program prospects and you should avoid using this device. In fact, recently we experimented with a list of these names of individuals, all of whom had expressed interest in the subject of consulting. 500 letters were sent to invite them to a workshop and not one responded, a cautionary tale if there ever was one.

Classified advertising is cheaper and more lucrative, particularly when you figure in your prospective profits from book and product sales.

Remember: your goal is to turn a product buyer into a workshop buyer, too, and thus into an ongoing customer.

Being a media celebrity helps! In Chapter 7, you'll find out how to achieve this reachable eminence.

Chapter 7

UNABASHED PROMOTION

As a hereditary Scotsman in good standing, you should understand that I hate spending money, something my friends and associates will only too gladly attest! Perhaps this is one reason why I'm so enthralled with FREE publicity — that's to say promotion!

Let me tell you a little bit about my own romance with promotion and why I do it. I have been involved with the media for a long, long time, ever since grammar school in fact. More recently I have set as my personal objective being featured at least once each day in some media source — radio, television, newspapers, magazines and newsletters. For the last several years I have consistently met this objective and then some. Nonetheless, I don't regard this result as anything particularly praiseworthy since there are more than 100,000 media sources in this nation and an abundance of opportunities.

I have no doubt about the importance of free media as you enter the workshop business. The ability to work with the media to promote programs has constituted the essential difference between success and failure many times. Often this ability to generate free publicity has produced an extravagant success. On other less happy occasions, free publicity, though excellent, has not managed to save a program. And on still other occasions, a program which has received virtually no outside publicity — or even none! — has nonetheless been a profitable one.

It therefore seems to me that, as in other forms of advertising, pride of place must still go to producing the right offer at the right time for the right people. Which means that good publicity cannot necessarily save a bad program and by bad I mean one which is inappropriate, untimely or expensive.

Having said this, however, it is my firm belief that no workshop, lecture, speech or other program should even be considered unless you are prepared to promote it both before and after it takes place. Even if you have a captive, assured audience such promotion is still necessary because you must not see any speaking engagement as a single, isolated incident but rather another link in a great chain. This link, like all the links, can be leveraged so that you'll gain future clients. Free publicity, well considered and thoughtful, will help you achieve this object. Don't forget it!

Publicity And You: The Blocks You May Feel About It

Since my book **THE UNABASHED SELF-PROMOTER'S GUIDE** was published in 1983, I've had occasion to deal with many people through workshops, speeches and other contacts on the subject of the media. When I wrote my book I perhaps naively thought that every ambitious American, whether professional, small business person, nonprofit executive, politician, writer, &c — would immediately leap to purchase. In my moments of gilded reverie, when I considered that an article about me and the book was forthcoming in, say, a publication devoted to architects, interior designers, and planners, (all likely candidates for unabashed promotion and needing it desperately in a most competitive field), I idly conjectured that the entire readership would stuff my mail box with checks. Experience, dear readers, is not necessarily a bar to wishful thinking!

How wrong I was. The response to even the best articles or enthusiastic media praise (like that of Edward Schwartz on his "Mind Your Money" Show in KIEV Radio, Los Angeles who said, "This book is for everybody! I don't care what you're doing!") tended to be solid but not spectacular.

As this became an irritating pattern, I began to wonder what the problem was. It certainly wasn't the book itself since reviewer praise was unstinting, and I knew that people using the book were profiting from it (you readers tend to be a loyal bunch and quick to drop me a note or call).

Chapter 7

I remember, for instance, one evening in Boston at a cocktail party following a speech I had given a group of upscale professionals, each to me a customer candidate. One woman questioned me deeply about the book and its applicability to her field. She, a self-described matrimonial lawyer, then confessed that during the last year had spent $500 advertising her practice without so much as a single call. $500 wasted. Yet in the end she didn't buy **THE UNABASHED SELF-PROMOTER'S GUIDE** despite my best efforts and despite the knowledge that with her specialty there wasn't a mid-morning talk show in the land, radio or television, which wouldn't use her, thereby bringing her service and practice to the attention of tens of thousands of people.

As you may imagine this infuriating paradox intrigued me. Having seen it often and having considered it at length, I know that you need to consider the following points as you pursue the suggestions in this chapter and indeed the entire matter of promotion as it relates to your career and achievement:

"Promotion isn't for me. What I do isn't unique or special in any way."

I hear this a lot one way and another and it irks me. It's a sentiment that's so obviously beside the point, and it betrays a fundamental misunderstanding about the media and your relationship to it.

Media people tell me constantly they are tired of merely publicizing problems. They want to promote solutions, too.

You must look upon yourself, whatever you do, as an individual who has a solution to someone else's pressing problem. Your success in getting media attention is directly related to your ability to serve up what you know as a solution to a problem and to persuade the writer or talk show host that the problem is pressing and in need of a solution. That's it.

There is also something else going on here, a fundamental lack of belief in youself. I confess that this leaves me enraged. Most of the people I meet have such feelings of inadequacy that they are to a significant extent incapacitated. To succeed, you have to believe that what you are saying, that the programs you are offering, will solve people's problems. Your belief in yourself will grow naturally as you see that what you are doing works. If it works, then you are entitled to that belief and must call it up to work on your behalf.

Moreover, remember this: no one will dub you ready and worthy in this game. That belief must come from within you. The time you need it most, unfortunately, at the beginning when you are untried and relatively inexperienced, is just the moment when you've got it least. The solution? Self-belief, the sine qua non of personal and professional success.

"Other people do what I do."

For some incredible reason, many people I deal with seem to feel that before you approach the media, you've got to have a unique solution, a unique workshop, a unique service. How absurd! How many unique items are there in the world anyway?

The fact is it doesn't matter how many competitors you have, how many others are working in the field. You simply have to be the person who has thought through both the problem you are dealing with and your solution to it and made the approach to the media. This is probably not the first time that individual media source has dealt with either the problem or the solution, and it won't be the last. So don't worry about that. What you have to worry about is that at this particular moment, you are the one to get the coverage.

"Media people are piranhas. I don't want to be their next snack."

It's amazing to me how generally this opinion is believed and how erroneous it is. Most media, at least 95% in fact, are what I call Benevolent Media, meaning that their purpose is to put the subject (including the individual being featured) in the best possible light, not the worst. News media on the track of a sordid story are different, of course; they fall into the Woodward and Bernstein genre. What you want and are doing, however, has nothing to do with all this. You're offering a service, dispensing useful information and generally behaving like an admirable Crichton.

The kinds of media people you'll deal with most often, on-air talk show hosts, columnists, staff feature writers, newsletter editors and the like, want you to look your best and want the information you have available — your solution, remember — to get to the people who need it. In the process you'll get the promotion that is so much to your advantage.

Chapter 7

As you approach the business of promotion, always remember this: the media need you and what you know and your solutions to problems (in this case put forward through your talk programs) as much as you need them. Your credentials for approaching the media are not the degrees you have (although if you have them, they'll help) or the positions you've occupied (although being President of the United States is an advantage). What matters is your perceived ability to solve the problems of those reached by any given media source.

Thus as you approach this chapter, I want you to overcome your internal obstructions as soon as possible and get on with the job of getting yourself, your service, your product and all your talk programs known and promoted by as many media sources as you can and as are relevant to your prospects. Your success, after all, depends on it!

This chapter is designed to help you achieve this success by providing you with information about the documents the media need and their form, where to look for the right media sources for you, and how to convince them to feature you, and what to do as this featuring takes place.

Remember: the media attention you receive for any single program is useful far beyond that individual program. Media coverage establishes you as the recognized expert in your field. Not only does it discourage and infuriate your competitors (quite a nice subsidiary benefit of the exercise) but it lends credibility to your marketing efforts for future clients.

Note: In a single chapter I cannot cover all the ground on this subject that was so well covered in **THE UNABASHED SELF-PROMOTER'S GUIDE** nor do I intend to do so. If you're serious about promotion, serious about squeezing the utmost publicity advantage from your lectures, speeches and workshops, then read that book and follow its techniques.

The Documents You Need

Even though you may be making the bulk of your presentations through divisions of continuing education and trade and professional associations which themselves have publicity officials, you, too, must maintain a complete stock of background materials. One of the several keys to successfully getting publicity is this; you must have thought through:

- the problem you are attempting to solve

- the needs of the people with the problem

- how your methods solve their problems, and

- whether the individual media source you are approaching reaches the people with the problem you can solve.

This and all related material must be encapsulated into a series of well-written, fast-moving documents which can immediately be put to use by media sources. The critical conceptualizing about you, your problem, your audience and its problems must all be done before you approach a single media source. This is the strategic element. Thereafter all that you'll do is tactical: working with the media to insure that you and your problem solving process are featured in all those places where prospects might become aware of you. This is critical: if you have these materials ready and waiting, you'll be able to have the quickest turnaround time with media sources and will impress them with your grasp of their problems and your consummate professionalism. This in turn will make them more likely to want to help you.

Here are the necessary parts of your Basic Promotional Package:

- Problem Solving Process Article
- Standard Media Release
- Biographical Narrative
- Context Document
- Sample Question List
- Public Service/Calendar Announcement
- Photograph.

These are not, I want to say, all the documents the successful unabashed promoter will ever need. These constitute, however, the basic promotional package that will be helpful as you promote your workshop to radio, television, newspapers, magazines and newsletters.

Chapter 7

You Need to Master These Forms Yourself

Some people may ask why, if most sponsoring organizations maintain a publicity person, you need to learn how to do these things yourself. There are two good reasons:

1) the kind of publicity personnel you are likely to deal with

2) their investment in you.

Sadly, the kinds of publicity people you'll be dealing with are those virtually least suited to insuring that you'll get publicity. I have had to work with many such creatures and my experience has often been an unhappy one. That is because of the way they approach their jobs and their limited understanding of public relations and how to deal with the media.

Often these people are young, inexperienced, and unfortunately either lacking in creativity or hamstrung by rules which militate against it. Moreover, they all too often conceive of public relations as an effort defined by writing a lackluster media release and public service announcement and mailing these out without follow up.

It should be clear by now that I regard public relations and promotion entirely differently, as an action business in which you and public relations people working with you must be prepared to work aggressively to identify potential media sources and persuade them to carry the story you need. Merely mailing papers will not do the job, and you should never be content with public relations done on behalf a program which consists of this inadequate procedure.

The Problem Solving Process Article

You need to break into print because print will validate you as an expert. Sadly, most such articles take most people too long to write. This is unfortunate. Perhaps it takes them too long for any combination of the following reasons:

- They are seeking to impart information.

- They don't have a complete structure for doing so.

- They are afraid of others criticizing their style.

If this is what you're worried about, don't be.

The Problem Solving Process Article is primarily a publicity vehicle for you not a means of disseminating information. It gets printed because it seems to offer a solution to the reader's problem but in actual fact in generally offers too little information for the reader to base any constructive actions on it.

This article is important because it meets the needs of media sources (*i.e.*, seeming to provide solutions to problems) and it meets your needs, too: the necessity of promoting yourself.

Structure Of The Problem Solving Process Article

This article exactly follows the structure of the Problem Solving Workshop and answers the following questions for the targeted reader you are attempting to reach:

- Are you, the prospect, mentally prepared to do what needs to be done to achieve success?

- Are you technically prepared?

- Have you properly planned and done the necessary research to achieve success?

- Have you the right documents and do you know how to prepare them?

Chapter 7

- Have you got an Implementation Strategy? What is it? Logically, do you know what must come first, second, third, &c?

- Have you thought about how you will report success and to whom?

- How will you evaluate progress and at what intervals?

This is the skeleton of the Problem Solving Process Article. Make it part of your very fibre.

Under each point you, the writer, give 100-250 words of precise, specific information. The trick is: can the reader really hope to achieve success with even the best 250 words of advice? Hardly.

Understand this: media will never give you sufficient space so that you can actually solve problems. But you can indicate to the reader that you know how to solve the problem. If he is really interested in that solution he'll seek you out — at your workshop!

Length

Problem Solving Process articles can be quite short — 650 words. They are generally rarely longer than 1200 words. If there is a lot of material to cover, suggest a two-part series on your subject. This is advantageous because you'll be linked with your potential audience twice and reinforce both your standing as the expert in the field and their desire to connect with you.

Biographical Tag

From my standpoint perhaps the most important part of any article is the "biographical tag" at its conclusion, those few words that identify you and provide follow up information for your reader. When you are promoting your workshop or seminar program, a suitable tag might be: "Dr. Jeffrey Lant is author of **THE CONSULTANT'S KIT**. He'll be offering his next full-day workshop on "Establishing and Operating Your Successful Consulting Business" at Alma Mater on Saturday, October 21st. For further information call the Division of Continuing Education at 657-8930."

A Last Word About The Problem Solving Process Article

These articles should be written quickly. All the material that you have on your subject of expertise fits nicely into one part or another of our skeletal outline. This makes it easy to organize. Don't agonize over this article! Look upon it less as a means of imparting information and more as a sophisticated form of advertising which meets both the media's objectives and yours.

Standard Media Release

Most people misunderstand the Standard Media Release. True, it does often result in stories and if properly handled the story that's printed will follow identically from what you've written. But because it's standard there's nothing very novel about it; in fact, it often simply works more against you than for you if it's sloppy or disorganized. Nonetheless you have to master this form.

Note: the key to a good media release is that it should read *exactly* as you want the eventual story to read, word for word. Don't leave it to the imagination of reporters to rewrite. Do the story in a professional way yourself and you have a higher likelihood of getting the story you want. Remember, however, that in all circumstances dealing with the media you have no guarantee that events will work out as you wish. You can only do your best to insure that they do and mastering this form will help you considerably.

Chapter 7

Here's what you should include:

Contact: Name, title _____

Company/Organization: _____

Address: _____

Telephone number (business): _____

Telephone number (after business hours): _____

                                                  Release Date _____
                                                  (usually "For immediate release"
                                                  or for specific date)

SUMMARY HEADLINE _____
(typed in caps, gives
leading facts about story)

Date: City of origin _____

Body of Release

    Paragraph 1: Include complete name of featured individual or organization. Provide specific information on who they are, what the event is, where and when it will take place. This paragraph should include the 5 W information: who, want, where, when and why.

    Paragraph 2: If you are targeting this release to a specific media source (the most likely way to have it used), introduce the name of that publication into this paragraph. This indicates to the source that you are providing them with an exclusive.

    The name of your featured individual or organization must apear in this paragraph. Modify it with a significant fact which will underscore its importance. Next include a quotation from the chief individual associated with this project. This quotation should be directed to the most significant readers of the article. All articles have many types of readers. The unabashed promoter keeps in mind only those who can do him the most good: his immediate workshop prospects. The quotation in paragraph two should be directed to these prospects. It should hook their interest and compel them to pay further, closer attention.

    Paragraph 3: This paragraph gives additional significant information about the individual, organization or event being featured. It should add a further noteworthy fact about the featured item and another pithy quotation. If this release focuses on one individual, then this quotation should come from that individual; if an organization is being featured, it is perfectly acceptable, even desirable, to quote a second individual.

    Do not forget to add personal touches to this release. Remember: whenever possible, you are writing the exact article a reporter would write, not just including factual material. In the regard, it is desirable to add descriptive information about the featured individuals.

    Paragraph 4: Adds further, though less important, information of interest to the targeted population. Again, the name of any individual appearing in this paragraph should be modified with a significant fact that makes this individual more substantial to the reader or which adds to his credibility. Also, add another quotation.

Chapter 7

Further paragraphs: These indicate to the reader what you want him to do as a result of learning about your story. Include all necessary follow-up information: how much does your product, service, workshop, &c. cost? How can the reader get involved? Who does he call? When? Where? Look at this paragraph as a specific free ad and write it accordingly. Unlike advertising, however, leave out the hype; what media people want is just the facts.

The media release can be typewritten and offset print on your stationery. It can be sent out as part of a general mailing or targeted. It is my firm belief that a targeted release works best. Write your release with a particular media source in mind and follow-up accordingly. Keep in mind, however, that as your career as a promoter progresses, there will be times you'll simply want to send out an untargeted release. This is quite acceptable so long as you remember that the releases most likely to be used will be those followed up personally by you.

More Tips About The Standard Media Release

- Keep it short. 500 words, two typewritten pages, with 250 words per page double spaced, should be quite sufficient for any media release.

- Write it like a story. Don't just supply facts and expect the media source to edit and rewrite for you. Your copy should bear as near a resemblance to an actual printed story as possible, quotes and all. Don't forget this! Particularly weekly newspapers and other publications are understaffed and are most happy to use your material *exactly* as is so long as it conforms to their editorial requirements. It is your job to see to it that it does.

- Use only one side of the page for your release. If your release continues over two pages, at the bottom of the first page add the word "more" and continue at the top of the second page. Repeat your headline in caps and write "page 2 of 2". Once you have finished simply write the word "end" in the middle of the page under your last sentence.

- Double space your copy. If you are a particularly unsophisticated writer, triple space. This allows an indulgent editor to write a sentence the way it should have been written in the first place. Understand, however, that such editors are most rare.

- In spacing your copy on a page, always conclude with a complete paragraph. If this leaves an inch or two of white space at the bottom of the page, so be it.

Biographical Feature Story

A Biographical Feature Story is a profile of you written by you to influence what a media source might write or broadcast about you. It is you, the unabashed promoter, as you desire your media, your public to see you. This piece should be between 250-400 words in length. Any longer and you might as well begin your autobiography.

The Biographical Feature stands alone as a story. It must therefore be interesting, provide significant, appealing background information, quotations by you, a real feel for you who are. It goes far towards establishing you as a person who compels our interest and attention.

Paragraph 1: Just like a fishing hook, this paragraph must grab the reader. You need to stand forth from the first minute as refreshing, different, uncommon, interesting, significant, important, unique, likable. Nothing less will do. Answer the question, "Why would anyone want to spend time with me?" You're on your way.

Paragraph 2: Support data. Begin to develop yourself as a personality. The first paragraph includes many, perhaps most, of the 5 Ws. The remainder of the article continues to develop the last of these: why. While it is quite acceptable to include quotations in the first paragraph, it is mandatory that they be used in the second and subsequent paragraphs. These help establish a sense of conversing with the reader. Don't hesitate to give a sense of the utterly characteristic, engaging you. Bring in your working milieu, characteristic gestures, clothing, ways of acting. Again, the reader wants to see you as you "really are." What you produce, of course, is entirely controlled, but it must seem natural, uncontrived.

Chapter 7

Paragraph 3: Bring in facts of weight and substance which establish you as a figure of significance. While you want your readers, potential participants in your talk programs, to know that you are human, you also want them to be quite clear that you are a master of your trade, technically competent, a pace-setter, forerunner of the future we must all live with but that you truly understand.

Paragraph 4: Paragraphs hereafter should mix human detail with evidence of further technical competence and professional accomplishments. If you add just one fact demonstrating technical competence onto another demonstrating technical competence, you run the very real risk of losing your audience. Instead, bring forward some human facet with each one or two evidences of professional competence. Add a mildly self-deprecating quotation, a joke, perhaps, as yet more evidence of the "real" unaffected person beneath your staggering external bravura.

Subsequent paragraphs. You may want to include as many as 4 to 6 paragraphs in your biographical feature depending on the number of things you've accomplished which are worth having your workshop prospects know. These paragraphs should present a judicious mixture of hard fact, personal information and pithy quotations which give further evidence of the swell person you are.

Final paragraph. Inevitably the biographical feature concentrates on work, particularly problem solving activities. As an unabashed promoter and entrepreneur in good standing work may in fact be your chief hobby. Don't say so. Americans tend not to like workaholics. They make the common run of our countrymen feel inadequate and slothful. Which of course they are. They'll never forgive you, however, for pointing out the obvious; so don't do it.

Invent a hobby. Start working out. Cultivate esoteric flowers and carnivorous plants. Take up macramé. And don't forget dogs and children. They lend just the right note to a biographical sketch.

Like all other documents, this one should be typewritten and photocopied or offset printed on your stationery. You will want to make good use of it not only with print media sources but with those in broadcast media, too, who will probably just read chunks of it over the air. The closer it reads to an actual article, the more likely they are to do so. Toastmasters will also use it in introducing you before their organizations.

Context Document

Once you have suitably established who you are, you must clarify what your subject is and why it's important. Understand this: media people know surprisingly little about issues. That is why they have such short attention spans. They are experts in packaging and delivery, but most have ridiculously little background in program content. Even if they have good, well-rounded educations, however, (something we can only wish for), they would still not know about your subject as you do and would very likely have no idea of why it is important or worth dealing with. That's why you need a Context Document.

In about 250-500 words, provide information on:

- What your subject is.

- A definition of terms if your subject is likely to be unknown to the reader or listener.

- Compelling statistics about the dimensions of the subject. How many people are involved? How many of them are in the marketing area of the media source?

- How the subject relates to the listener population of the media target.

- Any other helpful information which clearly demonstrates to the reader the importance of the subject, the number of people affected by it, and why your program is of consequence right now.

Chapter 7

Here's what one of my own Context Documents might look like:

WHY TALK ABOUT NONPROFIT ORGANIZATIONS TODAY?

Everyone is affected by nonprofit organizations, everyone. They educate us from kindergarten through post-graduate school. They provide us with medical assistance. They enrich our lives culturally. They are our day care centers, churches, civic groups, professional and trade organizations. There are one million such organizations across the nation. Yet many of them are in trouble. They face:

- unprecedented federal government budget cuts
- state tax-cutting initiatives
- a lower return on their long-term investments
- higher personal costs
- fewer Americans giving to the charity of their choice.

24,000 of these organizations are in Massachusetts. What can be done to help?

Dr. Jeffrey Lant, president of a Cambridge management consulting firm for nonprofit organizations, knows the problems of the nonprofit world. He has also devised some timely solutions. The author of **DEVELOPMENT TODAY: A GUIDE FOR NONPROFIT ORGANIZATIONS**, Dr. Lant puts the problems in perspective and offers a series of constructive, efficient, economical solutions.

There's nothing new about nonprofit organizations. There is, however, something new — and dangerous — about their current plight.

This plight will be well known to members of your audience, for without exception the lives of every member of your audience are affected in one way or another by nonprofit organizations.

As a guest on your show, Dr. Jeffrey Lant will help them help themselves by offering not merely an overview of a troubled situation but also practical steps they can take to help their organizations raise money they need to provide the services that are so important to all of us.

Dr. Lant will be offering a one-day intensive workshop program on his fund raising methods at the University of Alma Mater on Thursday, September 18 sponsored by the Division of Continuing Education.

In connection with this appearance, you can bring this sought-after national expert on nonprofit America to your listeners and help solve their problems.

Note: You, the unabashed promoter, are clearly brought into the Context Document as someone who is an authority on the subject and can deal with it. Remember: media people are constantly publicizing problems. Through their public affairs programs, however, they like to suggest solutions, too. The Context Document allows the unabashed promoter both to suggest the importance and dimensions of the subject and how he as a problem solver fits into it. It gives media people the "hook" they are always seeking.

Sample Question List

The Sample Question List is particularly helpful at an interview itself, but it is also worth sending in advance of scheduling because it gives a producer or on-air host a fairly clear indication of how the interview will proceed and what material it will bring out.

Chapter 7

In preparing the question list, consider what a moderately intelligent, reasonably informed individual might know about your subject. Distressingly little, right? You cannot assume any prior knowledge about your subject. Thus the questions must begin at the beginning and carry through to unveil who is affected, how many are affected, what difference it makes whether the solutions of your Problem Solving Process are carried out or not, whether the current trend will continue or not, &c. Your interview must be an entirely self-contained package, even though it may only last 90 seconds. Clearly the shorter the interview, the more artful the process of producing this result.

Here's what a Question List might look like for me, if I were being interviewed in connection with a workshop on consulting:

- What is a consultant?

- Where did the word come from?

- How many consultants are there?

- What fields do they practice in?

- Can anyone be a consultant?

- What makes a successful consultant successful?

- Do you have any advice for beginning consultants? ("Yes, Tom, have them come right down to my seminar next Thursday at Alma Mater!")

- Can you run a successful consulting business from your home?

- Is consulting especially interesting to retirees and women who want to work part-time?

- How did you, Dr. Lant, get into consulting?

- What does your consulting firm do?

- You're the author of **THE CONSULTANT'S KIT**. What's that about?

- What special training do you need to become a successful consultant?

- I understand you're offering a program at Alma Mater. Tell us a little about it.

The questions you write are designed for several purposes.

- They give the broadcaster who might use them a framework and a sequence, thus making his job easier.

- The answers provide the listener with two kinds of information:

  - background material about the subject so that he has a listening context, and

  - follow-up information about you and your program.

The Sample Question List above is designed for an interview of about 30 minutes. 15-20 questions should be more than adequate for this amount of time given the fact that you must take into account commerical interruptions and the fact that the host will presumably have a couple of questions of his own.

Chapter 7

As you'll notice, the first several questions are designed to provide the reasonably intelligent but otherwise uninformed listener with a context so that he can understand and appreciate the information you're providing. The remaining questions, by and large, are intended to give you the chance to promote yourself and your program. The Question List is effectively divided between what the station sees as its first responsibility, namely providing listeners with valuable news and public affairs information, and your own needs and objectives as a promoter. The successful promoter early learns how to balance these potentially conflicting but actually quite symbiotic objectives.

Public Service/Calendar Announcement

Since you are participating in an event, don't forget to draw up a Public Service or Calendar Announcement. Ordinarily the media will not use such information if you are for-profit, but there are many exceptions to this rule.

Public service announcements are designed for broadcast media; calendar announcements are their print equivalents. In general these announcements should not exceed 50 words in length. The public service announcement when read should take exactly 30 seconds. A public service or calendar announcement should by typed and double spaced on your stationery and photocopied. It should include: the name of your sponsoring organization, the release date of the announcement, the address, telephone number, contact person and a headline suitable to be read on the air or printed in the calendar section. The text in 50 words should cover:

- who
- where
- why
- what
- when
- price of admission
- telephone number or other pertinent follow-up information.

Note: If this is a public service announcement, type the word "Announcer" in caps just before the text. If you have written this announcement properly, the announcer can read directly from your text.

Photographs

Calendar announcements should often be accompanied by a photograph, especially if the event you are promoting lends itself to pictures. (Workshops do!) Every unabashed promoter needs to make good use of photographs. Suffice it to say here that there are two good sizes for photographs: 5 by 7 inches and 8 by 10 inches. Your photographs should be black and white; horizontal shots are more popular than vertical ones. On the back of each photograph you send, place a sticker. This sticker should:

- identify the subject
- include the complete names of anyone pictured
- give complete details of the event in question
- give follow-up information including the name of a contact person and telephone number.

Do not write this information on the back of the photograph and do not type it. It will show. One final word on photographs: Do not expect them to be returned. They won't be. Keep your originals safely at home.

Note: you should maintain two kinds of pictures. One should be the standard head shot and the other should be an action shot. As a speaker in good standing your action shot will no doubt show you talking away. Eschew the microphone however. It looks microphoney.

Chapter 7

More About The Basic Promotional Package

The purpose of the Basic Promotional Package is to cause you to think through who you are, what you are doing, the problem you are addressing and the solutions to that problem that you have created. By themselves these are just pieces of paper, not very meaningful. The value of these documents comes from knowing when to use them, who to give them to, and how to follow them up.

To make public relations and promotion work for you, you need superb documents and an understanding of the action process of public relations. That is, mere paper alone will not be sufficient to insure the kind of promotion and publicity you want.

Getting Advance Publicity For Your Program

There are two kinds of publicity you want to get with every program you give: advance and after-event publicity. Never forget that! A single speaking engagement can result in dozens of articles and media interviews, enough in a single instance to establish you as an engaging, sought-after authority. Don't be one of those who feels comfortable because your program has generated a single story. The key is to have a single incident, a single program generate a niagara of media paragraphs and subsequent engagements.

Places You Should Be Covered

Here is a sequence of possibilities for you to work through beginning at the beginning and progressing to the truly meaningful:

Stage 1: Public Service/Calendar Announcements. All too many publicists think virtually exclusively in terms of these announcements. This is unfortunate for the programs they are working with. Each week hundreds of public service and calendar announcements are submitted to radio, television and newspapers. By far the greater part of these are never used. Thus, learn early not to rely upon a public service announcement and if you are working with an organizational publicist make sure he doesn't rely on them either. By the same token, don't neglect them altogether.

- Identify places where a public service/calendar announcement will reach your intended audience.

- Send all announcements in at least three weeks in advance so that they can be properly cycled.

Trick Of The Trade

If you are interviewed on a radio station primarily about one of your forthcoming programs, ask that your public service announcement be run too. You should phrase the point thus, "Have you received the public service announcement about my workshop?" You'll be told this, "I don't know. We get a lot of them!" Your rejoinder, "Well, I've brought you a duplicate and I'd be grateful if you'd use it."

The proper time to have this conversation is just before you leave a radio station having done a program. The host will be at his most grateful to you at that moment, particularly if the program was a good one; (it was, wasn't it?) Make sure you have that duplicate announcement with you to piggyback on your good performance. It will destroy the scenario, by the way, to have to write it out in long hand or mail it in.

Other Possibilities

Advance announcements of programs should be run by a university's newspaper and by the newsletter or publication of a sponsoring organization. Consider, too, what other kinds of publications might be interested in such announcements. The key to public service/calendar announcements as to all advertising is to select the proper publication for your information.

Chapter 7

More Advanced Advance Media

People consistently ask me how they can promote their programs on radio, television and in newspapers in advance knowing that every one of these media does not like covering a lecture or workshop program.

Well, it's easy!

To begin with, put aside the notion that you are ostensibly going to promote your program. That, of course, is the reason why you want to approach the media, but it is not the reason why the media wants you. Media promotes my programs in advance of their happening time after time. The key, however, is that the principal reason for my approaching them seems not to be this promotion but rather to impart problem-solving information. You must do the same!

The Key

The key is knowing whether the particular medium of communication you are approaching has a sufficient number of people in its audience with the problem you are solving. If so, you are a prime candidate for promotion; if not, don't waste your time.

The first mistake people make in this regard is that they don't consider all their available options. For example, I have often said that to a promoter the entity called by most a newspaper is an abstraction, quite meaningless, too. You cannot be interested in the *Boston Globe*. You have to be concerned about each of its separate components: news, features, sports, business, *etc.* More than that, you must review each of its writers, reporters, editors, columnists, *etc.*

The objective of the unabashed promoter is not just to be covered once by an appropriate newspaper or radio or television station, but rather to be covered by each appropriate individual connected with that media source.

If there is a trick to this business, it is this: that you must know all the different possibilities available to you and consider in advance of approaching them what your story is. Then spend your time selling this idea to a person you already know who can buy it.

Sources

This suggests the need to be familiar with a wide array of source materials. In assembling **THE UNABASHED SELF-PROMOTER'S GUIDE**, I discovered nearly 200 useful media reference guides, that is guides which list both general and very specific media contact information. I'm not going to list them all again, but here are just a few to be aware of:

- *Standard Periodical Directory*
  Oxbridge Communications, Inc.
  150 Fifth Ave.
  New York, NY 10011 (212) 741-0231

Includes information on over 70,000 magazines, journals, newsletters, *etc.*

- *Oxbridge Directory of Newsletters*
  Oxbridge Communications, above

Indexes over 8000 newsletters in the U.S. and Canada

- *Bacon's Publicity Checker*
  Bacon's Publishing Co.
  332 S. Michigan Ave.
  Chicago, IL 60604

Chapter 7

Covers trade and consumer magazines, daily newspapers and over 8000 weekly newspapers. Two volumes. A superb place for looking for places to promote products.

- *Gale Directory of Publications*
  Gale Research Co.
  Book Tower
  Detroit, MI 48226

Two Volumes. Covers over 23,000 newspapers and magazines. Inter-edition supplement and up-date service.

Once you have thought through what you are going to be presenting to media sources, you must take the time to understand what media sources you'll be approaching and why. In this regard, there is no substitute for knowing about them, and I suggest that you become like me an inveterate reader not merely of publications but of the people who produce those publications and a radio and television dial switcher par excellence until you know as much as there is to know about the places you want to be promoted.

Clearly this is not possible when you promote programs out of town. In those instances, you can ask people (I always ask taxi drivers, for instance) what programs are worth listening to and what subjects are discussed until you get a sense of other markets. It goes without saying that whenever possible you should peruse the media trade publications, too.

It is only once you have done this necessary homework that you are ready for the attack and for going after the utmost possible media exposure. Here is the order in which you will ordinarily get it:

- public service and calendar announcements (the lowest form of promotion).

- story in in-house publications of sponsoring organization. Look for an interview with you, publication of your Problem Solving Process article with side bar about your forthcoming program. Use a photograph.

- standard media release sent to targeted print media sources. If you have the time, particularize this release by inserting the name of the publication into the body of the text thereby indicating that this constitutes an exclusive to that source.

- approach to appropriate radio and television programs. If your program has wide popular appeal (health, finances, the family, career advancement) then there are definitely appropriate programs for you.

- approach to specific columnists and writers for print media sources, if your program has a sufficiently wide appeal.

Have A Target

When you launch a program you need to know several numbers:

- the break even number, the number that you or the sponsoring organization needs to break even and not sustain any loss.

- the "reasonable attendance" number. Remember: you are planning to offer your program again in the future, perhaps in the next 90 to 120 days. If you are being paid a fixed flat fee, it is not to your advantage to get as many individuals to turn out for this program as conceivable. Your sponsor will love you, but you will not unduly profit financially. Your objective in this case is to turn a profit for yourself and the sponsor but not to deplete the potential audience for your program. Remember: all programs, all programs!, have finite audiences. Your objective is to discern the extent of your audience and the rate at which it is replenished (both subjective judgments in most cases) and to create a situation where you can profit on a regular basis. In this instance it is better for you to get a reasonable amount of publicity than to use all your sources. Targeting becomes of the utmost importance.

- If, on the other hand, you are only going to be offering this program once then you go for as many attendees as possible.

Depending on your objective you will have a different approach with the media.

Chapter 7

As you might have gathered by now, I am in that middle group, in that I aim to produce my programs year in, year out, harvesting the return and making both the sponsor and myself a comfortable, regular profit. Therefore except for public service/calendar announcements, I do not suggest approaching every conceivable media source every time you present a program. This uses up too many possibilities and all too often a media source, particularly a *print* media source, will be reluctant to do a second story.

After you are in business for a time and have done some media, you'll have a sense of how many telephone calls you will get after you've done a program or had a media mention and how many of these will be translated into actual registrations. I wish I could tell you now how many that will be but unfortunately it varies widely. I can say this, however, your best possible position is where you are looking for about 1/3 of your eventual registrants from free publicity.

Selling Your Advance Media Sources

Once you have identified whom you want to be covered by, you need to convince them to put you on the air or in their print source.

Here then is the sequence of events:

- draft query/cover letter
- mail to media source
- indicate follow-up
- track down media source and sell.

Draft Query/Cover Letter

As before, the standard media release is the "tell 'em", your query/cover letter is the "sell 'em." Here's the kind of information a media person wants to know in this letter:

- why you have selected him as a target
- what you've got and how it fits in to his format
- the particular thing you want
- why you think it's appropriate
- how you will follow up this initial contact.

(See samples, page 266.)

Writing a letter like this is time consuming (not mentioning the amount of time it takes to know the things that must be put in it!) But the results are worth it! Remember: with a single interview or article you can reach literally millions of people, many of whom should be potential buyers of your workshop.

This letter need not be long, and it should not be dull. Remember: you are an interesting person. Moreover, it should suggest the timeliness of your material. Media people respond best to urgency, on the need to act — now! This must be communicated in your letter and short, crisp, lunging sentences are best for achieving this effect.

What Else To Include

With your initial letter include the standard media release. That's enough. You can indicate on a separate piece of paper, if you like, that you have other materials available, too. This shows that you are the complete professional. But

Chapter 7

don't send them. They are expensive, and you don't know whether they're necessary or not. The only exception is your photograph. Television people are concerned about the way people look. If you're decent looking, then you can certainly send that photograph along. I don't bother myself (not, I hasten to add, because I resemble a troll), because I regard it as a waste of money. Suit yourself.

Following Up Your Initial Letter

You can expect the media person to be difficult to reach. Most media people have appalling manners although in person they have excellent people skills. They know, even the most junior of them, that they are in demand and that you'll call back a dozen times if you have to (and you often will!) to get them. They can afford to indulge their taste for grand sloth. This is irritating and yet it cannot irritate you. You have to accept the universe you are trying to get access to for what it is and act accordingly.

Call and leave a complete message. Then call again. Then call again. Then write a note. Then call again. And so on until you reach the source.

If the individual you get access to hasn't read your materials, as is quite probable, don't attempt to explain them over the telephone. Arrange a convenient time to call back. Then make sure you do — at the specified time.

Remember this: the individual that you are contacting is an expert at words, images, communications, but not substance. Media people are sieves; you are the one with the substance.

Once you've got them on the line, explain why you've selected them as a possible interviewer or source and why the topic is timely now. Don't lead with your workshop program although it is certainly appropriate to let the individual know that that's the reason you've come to town especially if you don't get there often.

Three responses are possible from your contact:

- "I want to think it over."

- "Definitely not interested."

- "Yes, let's schedule."

"I want to think it over."

This, of course, is the most frustrating. I know it. As I wrote in **THE UNABASHED SELF-PROMOTER'S GUIDE**, media people like to keep many options for programming and articles available until their product is completed. This is because people cancel, events change, time moves ahead. They must be prepared. Thus it is in their interest to keep you in a holding pattern.

My experience is that about 1/3 of those who say they are interested will actually deliver what you want: the promotion. Nonetheless you must continue to act towards them as if you expect to get the interview, sending the necessary materials, telephoning back at regular intervals, jumping, in short, through all their hoops. This is the way this mirage-like business operates.

I have confessed that I am not a patient person and in such circumstances the full force of my full Type-A personality emerges. But just as I have learned to control myself so you will have to learn to control yourself, too. Never get angry; never let your irritation show. Never express the feelings you are quite right to have about this irritating muddle. Saying so will only damage your cause. I recall, for instance, a situation last year when I was summoned for an interview by a major national newspaper with an immense circulation. It was in Washington and the day was dark and very, very wet.

Chapter 7

I went at the scheduled interview time. No interviewer. No indication of where she was. I called later and she apologetically rescheduled for later that afternoon. I returned. No interviewer. I left through a downpour without an umbrella. I telephoned yet again (I kept imagining the very large audience and the thought went some distance towards pacifying me). I called from the antechamber of the Smithsonian. I was wet; a thousand screaming students surged around me. I could barely hear the interviewer who blandly informed me she had to leave for an "emergency" interview with Marie Osmond. This, of course, was intolerable on several levels. I said nothing.

Unfortunately, this story does not have a happy ending. The interview never appeared. Yet I realize that that is the way the business operates. Still, I trust there is a special place in the most severe regions of Hell for such creatures. In the meantime, however, I do what I can to keep these feelings to myself and so should you.

"Definitely not interested."

Don't be discouraged by this line. Remember this: people in the media change jobs with extreme rapidity. When they do opportunities open for you. When I was promoting **THE UNABASHED SELF-PROMOTER'S GUIDE** in Boston, for instance, I was told by a major television show that they were not interested in having me on. Not to worry. After a subsequent story about me in *The New York Times*, they were on the line to me with a pressing request for an appearance. I graciously acceded to their wish. What happened in the interim? Same host but a new set of producers and new slant to the show. And a new opening for me.

"No" to me with the media means "No, not now." So you must regard it. While the media seems substantial, nothing could be farther from the truth. Thus, when you are cast aside, don't argue. Don't plead. And don't, by any means, give in to despair. It is unfortunate for your immediate program, to be sure, but don't wory about it. Look for another source at the same station or publication — so long as it offers access to the right audience for your problem solving program — and wait, just wait, until the personnel changes, the program changes, the ownership changes or any one of a hundred other eventualities occur. Then stand forward again asking for the coverage.

"We'd love to do the story!"

This phrase entrances me and it will delight you, too. When you hear it you can, for an instant, give way to an irradiating sense of good cheer. After all, you've earned it.

Don't get carried away by the euphoria, however. Before this conversation ends you need to find out:

- whether the contact needs further information

- the date, time, and place of the interview/show and directions

- names and telephone numbers of anyone else who may be involved (*i.e.,* radio/television producer).

Also, don't be too profuse in your thanks. You're not sure yet whether you really have anything to be grateful for. That will depend on the program/interview itself.

The Program/Interview

You use five documents for the actual print interview or electronic media show:

- the Standard Media Release (which gets sent in advance, of course, to help sell you and what you're doing and taken in personally when you go)

- Biographical Narrative

- Context Document

Chapter 7

- Sample Question List

- Public Service/Calendar Announcement.

It is also a wise idea to take your photograph to any print interview and a copy of any recent Problem Solving Process article to an electronic interview.

Handling Your Interviews

Print and electronic interviews vary in their emphasis. Here are some tips you can use:

Print Interviews

Whatever you do or say or wear is considered fit material for use in a print interview. Remember that and act accordingly. Again, don't press the point home about your workshop. Instead follow the steps of the Problem Solving Process Article. Indicate that there is a problem. Tell what its dimensions are. Indicate how it affects local people. And indicate what can be done to solve the problem. Be specific, concrete, precise. It won't matter much. Very little of this resolute information will actually make its way into the article. The important point is to let the journalist know that you know what you're talking about. That sense will come out in the article and it will be to your benefit.

You will be asked by the journalist what brings you to town if you are not a local and what has caused you to step forward now if you are. Be frank. Say that you have a program forthcoming. The journalist already knows this, of course; after all it's plainly in your Standard Media Release. Make sure that the journalist gets the date, time, place and sponsoring organization and a follow-up telephone number. Most will print all this information or at least enough of it so that follow-up is possible for the reasonably intelligent individual.

Expect a print interview to take 30-45 minutes. Seldom do they last as long as an hour. Ask if the journalist wants your stock photo; at larger magazines and newspapers he may call in the house photographer. Leave your photograph just in case; there are people in this world (of whom, regrettably, I am one) who don't photograph well (too many curves, not enough angles). For us, it is important to hedge our bets: leave your own picture behind!

A Few Tips

If you can cite success stories with your problem solving process methods, do. Have them validated, however, by letters and other documents. Journalists know better than most that people on the lecture circuit specialize in glibness. You'll get a stronger more convincing article if you bring testimonials from satisfied users of your methods. However, remember this: if you provide this information (with telephone numbers, please), whatever the people say may fairly be used in any article. A sobering thought.

By the same token, if you have the names and telephone numbers (addresses are less important) of *local* people who have used your methods, bring these, too. Journalists like to add a local dimension whenever possible; you can make your story more believable and connective to prospective participants if it includes local success stories.

If the journalist doesn't ask you the questions you want to have answered, use the last five minutes to bring up critical information or to correct any misapprehensions that you feel may have taken place. Don't be defensive, however. Be upbeat at all times. All the information you present must indicate that you are an in-command expert, accessible, knowledgeable, experienced, that you have surveyed the local scene regarding your problem and that as the expert you have an understanding both of what works and what doesn't.

If you travel to this interview in the company of a publicist from the sponsoring organization (which will often happen), don't have that individual sit in on your interview. It makes you look as if you didn't know what you're doing and is a waste of time besides making a bad impression. Instead, that individual should be working the telephones. Position the publicist at a telephone and have her call radio and television stations with this lead, "Hello, I'm Jean Smith, public relations director at Alma Mater. I'm over at the *Hollywood Sun* right now with Dr. Jeffrey Lant who's being interviewed by the Financial Editor for tomorrow's edition. I wonder whether you received the information I sent you about Dr. Lant and whether you'd be interested in scheduling an interview." This technique works very, very well.

Chapter 7

Electronic Interviews

Electronic interviews are different and demand finesse as you handle them.

Here are some tips:

- As with print media sources, don't rely on the personnel you are dealing with to have any of the materials you have sent in advance. In all dealings with the media bring a complete duplicate set of materials. Always.

- Send all your documents in advance including:

  - Standard Media Release

  - Biographical Narrative

  - Context Document

  - Sample Question List

  - Public Service/Calendar Announcement.

Bring a complete set of these materials with you even though you have sent them in advance.

Before going on determine whether you will have the opportunity to spend 5 minutes with the host before air time. If not, spend them with the show's producer. Explain exactly what you've got and why you've brought it and what's in it. This may seem self-evident and oh-so-redundant at this point, but I assure you it isn't.

When you meet the host, ask whether he has these documents and go through the same routine. You have a mission with this program, and you need to insure that it's achieved. Remember this: the journalists and on-air hosts you deal with know that you've got a mission and they are generally willing to assist you so long as you help them achieve their objective, too: ostensibly solving the problem that you say (and they now concur) their audience has.

On the air, make sure that you answer all questions fully and as completely as time allows. Fortunately for you, time never does allow for a complete answer to a question, just the barest taste of an answer. That's to your advantage in several ways; you need to look upon your air time as a means of whetting the appetite of your prospective workshop participants. Don't be perceived as withholding information; that's detrimental to your perceived status as the confident expert. If you have callers, after you've had a go at their problem, don't hesitate to invite them to your program. By this time they really want to come and they want the information about how they can do so. This comes under the aegis of Assertive Courtesy, aggressively promoting your own objectives while seeming totally devoted to the interests of your questionners/prospects. This is just the way you want to be seen.

Don't use pronouns or other nouns that stand in place of the full proper name of your program. Never refer to your workshop as "it" for instance. Never say, "I'm giving this program next Saturday." Say instead, "My next program on 'Establishing and Operating Your Successful Consulting Business will be given'..." This is tricky and difficult, not regular speech. So what! Your aim is to give a complete mini-advertisement every time you open your mouth; the trick of the business is to make the advertisement seem like regular conversation and Assertive Courtesy. Oh, yes, there's definitely an art to this business!

If you have done the program before, talk about the success rate. Let people know that they have a problem, to be sure; also let them know that there are solutions and that yours work.

Always invite the on-air host to attend the program as your guest. There are several benefits to this. I guarantee you that this invitation is rarely extended and it will be appreciated. Remember: you want this person to become if not a friend then a good professional acquaintance. Second, if the person does come (and you're good, of course) you'll very

Chapter 7

likely get more coverage because he'll talk about the experience. Third, if he doesn't come, he will nonetheless probably be more alert to placing your public service announcements and generally being useful. Finally, you will be perceived as a gracious, considerate person. There's no harm in that either.

End by giving the telephone number again, twice. For those sluggards who write slowly and don't have a pencil, let them know that they can call the station for the details. This means that you should leave a complete information packet (at least the program brochure) with the secretary who takes calls for the station as well as with the program's producer. I guarantee you people who are interested in your program will follow up this invitation.

Further Notes About Advance Program Promotion

Get your print coverage first. Print coverage validates you as the expert and a source of significant information. Radio and television producers scan newspapers and magazines for stories so there is at least the possibility that your print coverage will produce electronic coverage without your having to ask for it. Electronic media people, often illiterate and closer to pure sloth than the run of mankind, are grateful for the work of print journalists; although they regard them as unfashionable and drab (a deadly state of affairs) they nonetheless rely on their work. Make good use of this reliance in pursuit of your own promotional objectives.

Thus, you are well advised to write your problem solving process article first and peddle it to the major daily and weekly newspapers. While the first is clearly a better place to be published, the latter will do nearly as well as a validating source. Once published you are ready to leverage your new standing and so get electronic media coverage.

Be persistent. Media people, the new, irresponsible aristocracy, expect to be courted. They know they have their highest value to you before they give you what you want and as they feel that courtship and veneration are their due they prolong your agony as long as possible. Remember: it's quite pleasant for them to have you hanging on their every word and generally indicating by every thing you do that they are people of consequence.

How long should you continue your promotion before the actual program takes place?

Continuing educators always allow for walk-ins to a program. Indeed, these walk-ins often constitute the program's profit and are most welcome. You should learn to welcome them, too.

This means that you should continue your promotion right up to the last moment. Personally, I am delighted to have the opportunity to promote a Saturday program on a Friday evening radio call in show, for instance, and you should be, too. My advice to you is that if you need the participants to make your program a success, then keep working at promotion right up to the end.

This includes trying to do radio programs from your own office to an out-of-town program location. These days more and more radio stations are equipped to do long distance interviews. Such interviews are ordinarily short (under 5 minutes) but not always. I have done them for as long as *four hours!*

No opportunity should be lost which will bring your topic of expertise and your program to the attention of prospective participants. Although once you have reached the enrollment objective you've set yourself, stop and hold further advance promotion until your next program.

Program Follow-Up Promotion

Some of the most useful promotion for you comes after a program has actually taken place. No wonder. Make no mistake about it. If you are on the speaker circuit, you cannot see any program you do as an isolated instance but rather must perceive its place linking you to programs in the future. Thus any publicity that takes place after the program is actually very useful for you even if you don't have a product to promote.

Use local coverage in future brochures and publicity pieces.

It's amazing to me how many continuing educators and program planners see programs as distinct and unconnected with what comes next. This is a great mistake. If a media source highlights you and your program, this is important.

Chapter 7

Say in an article in the local paper a writer said, "Jeffrey Lant's consulting program has helped people around the country launch successful practices." This line should become a headline in the next brochure. Media gives validation and lines like this can be used for years. Local media, however, are the best of all since people can identify with them more readily.

This includes radio and television. With radio, of course, you can get the tape (ask for it in advance and find out whether you need to bring your own cassette for duplication or whether the station will give you one). With television, you can simply write down a commentator's words from the program or else you can request a transcript. Video tapes, too, can be purchased but as you've already seen they are a bit expensive.

These electronic media folk cannot be neglected, not least because their comments tend to be the more effusive. Without fail, people in radio and television give me the biggest and best send-offs, perhaps because they are most closely related to show business. In any event, take down all the relevant comments and make sure the sponsor keeps them on file for the next program just as they should do with the evaluations from the participants.

Get reporters and other journalists to attend the class.

To be sure, unless you've got a special program, it will be difficult to get journalists to cover you in the classroom. Don't worry. Often it is possible to arrange for a free-lance writer to attend without cost in return for resolutely pursuing story opportunities. Also, if the college you are speaking at has a journalism or public communications school, urge that your program be made a class assignment and that the best efforts be submitted for publication. At the very least, you can get a review in the college's own paper.

More Tips

Get radio personalities to interview you while you are in town or to attend your course, even if their programs will air after your workshop. This will often be the case if you do Saturday programs, since many public affairs shows play on Sunday. Ask them to hold these programs (or re-air them since this is often done) in advance of your next workshop with a voice over or public service announcement giving the new program specifics.

Announce your successes in trade, alumni and civic publications. Give yourself an aura of success through after-program announcements.

Announce the success of your program by having the program planner send in information about it to "The Marketplace of the Platform." This is a special continuing feature of the International Platform Association (P.O. Box 250, Winnetka, IL 60093) which keeps meeting planners up to date on where you have spoken, to how many people, and how much you charged as well as your subjects.

Arrange for a Photographic Reception Line at your workshop. Have all the individuals from a particular town (or section, if from a large city) have their pictures taken with you. The caption should read, "Here is Bessie Smith of 4906 Woodward Avenue with Dr. Jeffrey Lant, nationally known author of **THE CONSULTANT'S KIT** at a recent all day seminar on 'Establishing And Operating Your Successful Consulting Business' at Alma Mater." For a Photographic Reception Line to be successful, all the photographs must be thematically unified (the same city), must have a standard caption which people fill out at the time the picture is taken, and the photographs must be developed and sent out promptly to the newspapers (which are usually weeklies).

Note: Don't expect to get these pictures in the biggest metropolitan dailies. Do expect to get them into the weekly and city sectional papers which habitually print them. You can be sure that Bessie Smith will be grateful for the publicity and will discuss your program. *N.B.* Since she's so grateful, ask her to send you a copy of the article and photo when it appears.

Do a Problem Solving Process Article that purports to be an extract from your workshop. "This article is based on remarks that Dr. Jeffrey Lant recently delivered in a workshop at Alma Mater on the subject of giving successful workshops and seminars. He will be offering this program again February 12th. If you're interested in participating, call the Division of Continuing Education."

Chapter 7

Final Notes On Successful Promotion

The key to successfully promoting your programs is to be creative and persistent. I find that most people are neither. Learn to think like the people you are dealing with. Do as much of the work for them as you possibly can. Act like the expert you are. And don't be discouraged when they decline to print or broadcast you. The nice thing about the media business is that the idiot who blocked you will probably be gone within 6 months. It's a thought I have learned to cherish.

Chapter 8

DELIVERING THE SUCCESSFUL PROGRAM

You have now succeeded in crafting a timely, desirable program, selling a sponsoring organization on the need for such a program and on yourself as the program's presenter. You have written deft brochure and ad copy, and you have succeeded through the equally creative use of the free media in attracting the right number of participants.

Now what?

It's time to turn your attention to the buyers of your workshop, the people who are rightly your most difficult critics or your most enthusiastic supporters. There are ways of insuring that that enthusiasm will be yours.

Advance Arrangements

It goes without saying that good planning helps insure a successful program. All workshop planners know that, and each in his way tries to insure this successful result. As much as possible should be done in advance, because you can be sure that the unexpected will continually occur on the workshop circuit.

Site Planning Particulars

When you work with a sponsor you ordinarily may have little to say about just where your workshop will take place. Most continuing education courses continue to be offered in regular college settings and when you speak at an association meeting you'll have to share the space which is allotted for that meeting. There's nothing necessarily bad about either alternative. The key to being a successful lecturer is to be flexible. If you can only function in a certain type of room with a microphone in your hand, you will be limiting the number and kind of programs you can put on. This would be a great mistake.

If you do have a choice, however, consider the following crucial points about room selection. Your room should be:

- In a quiet place. What does this mean? It means that it should not be in the university quadrant that gets the grass cut on a Saturday or that is next to a loud soft drink machine or a room full of high school superintendents singing over and over "To Dream the Impossible Dream." All these things have happened to me. (Fortunately in the last case, by the merest luck, the cacophonous choir changed to "We're Into Something Good" just as I stepped up to speak. Don't think I didn't make use of this felicity.)

- Near rest room facilities

- Closest to the entry/exit doors and parking lot

- Near a public telephone.

When you are planning the meeting yourself, you will have to insure these items, but when you are working with a sponsoring organization it is perfectly legitimate to ask them to see to it that the right choice is made. Most books will tell you to check out matters for yourself and in theory I concur. The problem in fact is that when you are working with faraway universities it is very time consuming to run down the right buildings and grounds keeper for an opinion. Get your program contact to do so.

Chapter 8

Room Arrangement And Amenities

Much has been written about the way room arrangement affects the success of a program. Here are the possibilities and their pros and cons:

- **Amphitheater**

    This is where you, the speaker, stand in front of a large room, usually in a theater or university lecture hall. The seats rise above you row upon row in a sort of fan arrangement. The benefit to this arrangement is that you know exactly how many people you can accommodate and these people will have a good view of you and the blackboard. Modern amphitheaters also have up-to-date equipment for audio visual purposes and comfortable chairs.

    The drawback is that there can be little or no interaction among people in the hall. You are the cynosure of all eyes. This may, of course, be exactly what you had in mind. That places a premium on your ability to be entertaining and even theatrical. Moreover, if you don't fill up a sizable percentage of seats it is difficult to engender the enthusiasm that will make your performance memorable.

Here are a couple of tricks to minimize the difficulties:

- Even if all the people in the room can't introduce themselves (a technique I like), then have them introduce themselves to the people on either side. This is an old technique from the more competitive law schools, you might remind your audiences. After the students have so introduced themselves the shark-like professor says nonchalantly, "Two of the three of you won't be here next semester." It's a sobering thought. You can then point out that that isn't the spirit in which you are approaching today's presentation. This comment has the additional benefit in these circumstances of dealing with the repressed fear which most people have in such circumstances. Remember: such rooms are often the university's chemistry hall, a place where there can be very few pleasant memories.

- If the audience is indeed small, exercise your prerogative as the leader and ask them to move to the front. It's a momentary inconvenience to the audience but will be forgiven by the collective enthusiasm engendered by you and your program.

    Remember: anything you write on the blackboard needs to be BIG. I have terrible handwriting, and I have learned to write as large as I can and pause so that people can write down the messages on the board. In such circumstances audio visual aids are most appropriate.

- **Classroom Style**

    We all remember this traditional form of seating which is often used for workshops, seminars and lecture programs. Tables and chairs are set in rows facing the front at which you'll be working. Often there are two or more aisles in the room. All eyes face forward and there are 3 to 5 people at an individual table.

The benefits of this arrangement are several:

- Almost all facilities can be arranged this way,

- It's quick and easy to do.

- Participants have a writing surface readily at hand and people nearby with whom they can get acquainted. (Note: this latter point is not of negligible importance. Two people sitting beside each other at one of my *Training Magazine* sessions have since been married!)

There are some drawbacks, too:

- People often remember their dismal classroom experiences. Many adults have unhappy memories of their schooldays and it doesn't do to rekindle them.

Chapter 8

- If you are expecting or desiring greater interaction from your group than the parties of two or three at each table, then this arrangement won't meet your needs.

- Classroom style is not really appropriate for a small group of 15 or less. In such circumstances you'd be better with a conference table arrangement which will permit interchange.

About half the programs I do are arranged in classroom style and I like it.

Tricks: Whenever possible and especially in a classroom situation with an audience of under 50 have each person stand (preferably) at the beginning of the program and introduce himself. Encourage people to get acquainted. This will mitigate the feeling of relative isolation that sometimes creeps into rooms arranged classroom style.

- **Banquet Style**

We have all been to banquets which feature small round tables of 6 to 10 guests. This is customary for association dinner meetings and can often be a difficult arrangement for speakers.

It also offers several benefits:

- People can talk to each other, get acquainted and communicate.
- It's convivial.
- It promotes team building exercises.

There are also drawbacks:

- This setup does not accommodate as many people as theater or classroom style.
- Round tables and linens are not always available.
- People at the front of the table have to crane their necks to get a view of the speaker.

There are some tricks of the trade for using this setup style:

- Since it's used usually when people are eating, make sure that the main course has been cleared before beginning to speak. It will reduce the amount of noise you have to contend with.
- Get people to introduce themselves at the tables. It always amazes me that introductions are not general at small tables but this often happens. Your job is to be the leader and a leader is gracious.
- If possible, circulate around the room as you speak. Don't stay in one place. Place the podium so that you can make eye contact with many people, if possible in the center of the room.

Introduce more humor than usual into presentations made in these circumstances. While humor is always necessary, people are more accustomed to having it when the tables are round.

- **Theater Style.**

This is another popular lecture/workshop model. This means chairs only placed in rows like a theater. Here are the benefits:

- You can accommodate many people.
- The focus is exclusively on you.

Chapter 8

Here are the drawbacks to this situation:

- The participants have no writing surface.

- There can be limited interchange and communication between participants.

- **Tables In A "U" Shape**

This arrangement is composed of rectangular tables with chairs set around them and one end empty. You as speaker can stand in front of the room or move about to the various tables. This is a good arrangement for a small group and one that allows for a good deal of participant-instructor contact.

A variant on this theme is a "U" made up of three long tables, two parallel to each other and the third at the farther end.

These settings are most appropriate for smaller groups in that they allow for maximum contact and warmth.

- **Chairs Only**

This setting allows for many participant exercises and for ease in shifting arrangements as your needs require. However, there is no writing surface in most cases and that means that a chairs only arrangement would not be appropriate for long programs.

- **Floor/Ground Seating**

I confess I don't like this arrangement although I can see its utility. It reminds me, I'm afraid, of too many touchy-feely exercises from the 'sixties. Nonetheless, if this casual effect is what you want to create then use this arrangement. Putting people on the floor or ground is a great equalizer.

Notes On Room Arrangement

As you are already well aware from programs you've attended, the arrangement of the room has much to do with the success of the program. Consider the following:

- Are you trying for a more formal or informal experience? Select your room arrangement accordingly.

- Do you want to be the focus of attention (is this necessary for the success of your program), or do you want interchange and communication among the participants? Select accordingly.

- Do you want participants to take notes or just remember what you and others say? Select your arrangement accordingly.

- Do you want to be able to move among the participants, to touch them? Motivate and persuade by the nearness of your physical presence? Select accordingly.

- Do you want participants to get to know each other? To become friends? Again, select the best arrangement.

I want to stress as strongly as I can that there is no "right", no "wrong" arrangement. Each of these can work for you. By the same token each arrangement can be wrong given the right circumstances. It is up to you to think through exactly what you are trying to achieve with your program, and what you want the participants to come away with and what effect you wish to create. Select the arrangement accordingly and advise your program planner.

Note: Each seminar leader becomes expert at moving furniture. You will have to be, too. To no one else (except the participants, remember, and they are voiceless at this point) is the arrangement of the room as important as it is to you. That's why you need to work with your program planner, sponsor or hotel staff to make sure you get what you want. Be prepared to roll up your sleeves. I've discovered that men who arrive early don't mind being asked to help move a bit of furniture. It make them feel useful (which they are!) and breaks the ice. By the time you've moved a few dozen chairs with a guy, you're friends!

Chapter 8

Room Amenities

Check to see whether:

- The room has air conditioning.

- If not, will the windows open?

- How long it takes a room to heat up if cold, cool down if hot.

The two greatest complaints which people rightly make are: the seats are uncomfortable and the air temperature is too hot or cold.

Other Room Amenities

Whenever possible arrange to have water available in your room. You're going to need it for yourself and it's a nice courtesy for those in the program. The water should be room temperature (which after a minute or two isn't a problem!) This is because room temperature water is best for your voice and produces the fewest side effects.

If the program is not taking place in a hotel or near a water fountain, bring your own plastic cups, at least so that you'll always have water available.

Remember: water itself can be used as a prop. When you are thinking through a question or want to pause a moment, you can pour yourself some water and drink it.

I gave a lecture at MIT a year ago or so on a day I was very ill. I'd been in bed all day sweating profusely; I knew there was no way I could get through the lecture without many liquids immediately available. The problem was exacerbated because the crowd of several hundred overflowed the available space and made the air fetid. There was no cup for water and the water fountain was not convenient. Solution? A bottle of Perrier water and a bottle opener. I used both as props and actually opened the bottle as the commencement of my talk. It was a superb thing to do. Several hundred people who will watch a speaker open a bottle of water will pay close attention to virtually anything he says, and I gave one of my best speeches that night — and then went home to bed to sweat some more!

Smoking

I am a nonsmoker myself, moderately militant too. Early in my speaking career a woman in a seminar drew attention to herself by demanding that the man next to her stop smoking. He did so but she said the remaining smoke was bothering her. With great disruptiveness she moved to a window in the Harvard Club where the seminar was taking place, thrust open a great window and for the remainder of the evening stood listening to the program taking audible drafts of air. It was the same evening a lady acupuncturist told me she'd exchange a copy of **THE CONSULTANT'S KIT** for the privilege of sticking several long cold needles into my succulent skin. I ignored the one, declined the other. However I learned my lesson.

Always ask what the policy of your sponsor is regarding smoking. If there is no policy, consider the following: at the very least divide your room into smoking and nonsmoking sections. Find out which way the wind will blow and station the nonsmokers upwind from it. Even if you yourself are a smoker, don't station the smokers near you. Smoking affects your ability to talk. And, of course, don't smoke yourself during your presentation unless you can do so as elegantly as FDR.

I make it a habit when arriving at any seminar site to inspect the room and remove all ashtrays. I inform the participants at the beginning of the day that smoking can take place (always put your prohibition in the most upbeat terms) but that your policy is to wait for the regular breaks and then in the corridor or outside the workshop space. Very, very rarely has anyone objected to this policy which, after all, is for the general good.

Note: make sure the ashtrays are out of sight of the workshop participants. Smokers are obsessive. If they see an ashtray they leap to the conclusion that it can be used.

Chapter 8

Instructional Aids

Research long ago concluded that if you want people to remember something just telling it to them has limited utility. Seeing is better. Best, of course, is showing them how to do it themselves, working with them to insure that they know what needs to be done and can do it independently. The latter is often a luxury on the talk circuit which is why I recommend follow-up "clinics."

Just what you'll use to show people will vary. Here are the possibilities:

- chalkboards
- flip charts
- overhead transparencies
- films
- slides
- various kinds of paper handouts ranging from single sheets to books.

Just when to use these materials is something of an art in itself. If you are trying to entertain your audience use:

- slides and flip charts with slides the better option.

If you are trying to impress your audience use:

- multi-image slide presentations.

If you are trying to persuade your audience use:

- slides
- overhead transparencies
- various paper pass outs.

If you are trying to inform your audience use:

- flip charts
- chalkboards
- overhead transparencies
- your own handouts.

Using, Finding And Producing The Instructional Aids You Need

My workshops, pure Problem Solving Process endeavors, are designed primarily to inform participants. This does not mean that I don't have to entertain, that I don't want to impress or that persuasion has no place, but it does mean that on the whole these are secondary to my main purpose of imparting useful information to participants. Thus it will be no surprise to you that I lean heavily on the use of flip charts, chalkboards and my own handouts, principally articles and books I've written. These, of course, I regard as critical for anyone who seriously intends to make money on the lecture circuit.

Chapter 8

This suggests that you must think through what you are trying to do at your programs (and this may vary from program to program) and plan accordingly. Once you have made your decision about your primary purpose then the following will be helpful to you.

- **Chalkboards**

These days the old standard blackboard has faded from the scene and even the phrase "chalkboard" is not quite as popular as it once was since many facilities are now equipped with special grease writing pens and facilities.

Here are some pros and cons about using this old art form:

- Boards are convenient because you can easily correct your mistakes, add or eliminate material at will or otherwise alter your message.

- If you are planning to use a board, make sure that there will be an adequate supply of chalk; (I've been in situations where the chalk ran out long before the day itself and we've been forced to launch raiding parties on adjoining rooms), or know where you can get some. Also, make sure the erasers work. Yes, it's still a problem just like in 5th grade!

- Chalk dust is annoying and interferes, in due course, with your ability to speak. Thus you will need to have water close at hand.

- Make sure that you write large enough. This is a problem I have. My handwriting is scarcely copper plate and I tend to write too quickly and too small. The best way of handling a chalkboard is to write your points out in large letters and move to the back of the room and see how they look. Put yourself in the place of people farthest away from the board. Even in the best of places, blackboards have not been designed for the convenience of the viewer.

- **Flip Charts**

Flip charts can be as simple as pads you scrawl on during the day or as complicated as mini works of art. It's up to you and your purpose. Pros and cons:

- If you write on your flip charts during your workshop as I do, it lends an air of spontaneity to the proceedings. The program does not look 'canned' (although in fact it almost certainly is). You should know your material so well that you are able to write it on your charts quickly, easily, thoroughly. This impresses an audience with your grasp of material.

- The benefit of a flip chart is that it can be moved around the room or more advantageously placed vis á vis your audience.

- Like a chalkboard, however, whether you prepare your charts in advance or write them up during the program, make sure the lettering is large enough. Generally you should have one idea to a page and no more than 20-25 words. Fewer in this case is better.

- If you are making up your own charts, carrying them will be a problem. You are best advised to buy a special carrying case for them. I have had some not terribly nice experiences with airlines when I carry my own charts and posters with me. Here's some advice. Remember: under ordinary circumstances your charts will be thrust among the rest of the baggage and being paper products they are at high risk. Even if you do have a special carrying case, check them specially at the flight deck so they will be hand carried on to the flight. Do this: at the check in deck in the airport lobby, ask for a special handling sticker. Get it from the lobby check in desk because the seat selection desk inside may not have it handy. Your piece will get special handling (that means, get carried on) if the flight is not terribly busy and if the piece can fit in to one of the plane's forward compartments. Note: it will be farthest inside the compartment. This means you'll have to wait until others are off the plane before you deboard. Even in these circumstances, put special corner protectors on your charts. These are the areas most likely to be affected, and there is nothing worse and more detrimental to your image than looking at charts which are unravelling before your eyes!

Chapter 8

How many charts do you need? That depends. I would say don't use more than 3 or 4 an hour and put only your most significant thoughts on them. If you are giving a 7 to 8 hour presentation that would mean you'd have a maximum of 32 charts, and I can tell you that's a lot to transport anywhere. Whenever possible, then, think up variations for yourself and other means of getting your point across including the other instructional aids in this section.

- **Overhead Transparencies**

There is an art to creating and using overhead transparencies. Fortunately there's a good little pamphlet on this art which you can get for free from the International Communications Industries Association (3150 Spring Street, Fairfax, VA 22031. 703-273-7200). This booklet is called "Basic Tips On Producing And Using Overhead Transparencies." I've selected below just a few of their leading tips.

Note: The ICIA also produces a number of other free materials which are most useful to those on the talk circuit. Here are those I think most valuable:

- "Basic Tips On Preparing For A Meeting That Uses Slides"

- "A-V Periodicals And Trade Journals"

- "Operation And Maintenance Of A-V Equipment, Materials, And Production Facilities: A Bibliography"

- "An Overview Of Audio-Visual Communications: A Bibliography"

- "Still Images For Projection: A Bibliography"

- "Basic Tips On Video"

You'll find these materials very helpful and the organization one you should know about. Again, here's what you need to know about overhead transparencies:

Preparation

- Keep your visuals as simple as possible.

- The type you use should be at least 18-point, that is 1/4" high.

- Use illustrations, cartoons, graphs, maps and charts whenever possible to supplement words and present numbers.

- Be aware of companies that have available ready-to-use motifs, designs and illustrations which you can incorporate into your overhead transparencies. One of the largest of these is Dover Publications (31 East Second St., Mineola, New York 11501, 516-294-7000) which sells over 300 books with over 100,000 such illustrations for which you do not need copyright permission.

- Use horizontal visuals for maximum visibility.

- Position your material in the upper portion of the transparency.

Preparing The Room And Equipment

- The screen, to be clearly visible to every viewer, should be at least 42 inches off the floor.

- If the projector beam doesn't meet the center of the screen at a 90 degree angle, "keystoning" (image distortion) will result. To prevent this, tilt the screen forward at the top or back at the bottom.

Chapter 8

- Use this simple 2×6 rule to select the appropriate screen size and seating arrangements: the distance from the screen to the first row of seats should equal twice the width of the screen; the distance from the screen to the last row of seats should equal six times the width of the screen.

- Tape the power cord to the floor to prevent someone tripping or knocking the equipment off the stand.

Slides

The key to using slides (like overhead transparencies) is to keep things simple. And practice! You don't want your slides coming out in the wrong order or upside down. You can prevent these and other debacles by getting the free ICIA pamphlet on slide use and abuse.

Pass Outs

I am a big believer in the value of pass outs of various kinds. These pass outs have great flexibility, are easy to transport, and can be used to punctuate your day and program. There are several things you should know about them, however:

- If you are speaking to a large group (250 or more), consider the advantages of a personalized memo to these people which can be passed out at your presentation. Such a memo simply expands upon and uses your usual information, but it gives the impression that you have customized your information, which perhaps you have! The cost of this is not great and can be charged back to the sponsoring organization in most cases as part of the materials fee.

- All materials you pass out should come on your stationery. Each piece of paper you distribute should have your mark on it. It consistently amazes me how even veteran speakers distribute their own materials without their complete name, address and telephone number. This is a mistake.

- These pass outs should generally not be distributed as a group but rather one at a time at the appropriate moment of your presentation. This is a nice way of giving you a breather and of impressing the audience with the importance of any individual document. "I am now passing out," you'll say, "a problem solving process article that I've written on this subject." Hold it up while the papers are passing. People always want to make sure they're getting the right thing.

The longer you are on the talk circuit, the more you will want to eliminate materials created by others (unless you are distributing them as per the next chapter) and the more you'll want to distribute your own articles and books. This will support and reinforce your status as the recognized expert and insure the attention of your audience.

How many of these pass outs should you bring? That depends, again, on your program. I think that one per hour is quite sufficient, which means 7 or 8 for a day's program.

What is the cost of producing these hand outs? Excluding your designer's layout fee (which you may be able to eliminate by doing it yourself), the cost of duplication is not excessive. Expect to pay $20-$25 per thousand sheets run one side 8 1/2 × 11" on a decent quality paper like that of this book. You can charge the sponsoring organization double this price as part of the materials fee. Don't feel squeamish about this. Your papers and materials have a value and if the participants will be profiting from them you ought to benefit!

It goes without saying that this is a way of continuing to benefit from articles you have written and even basic materials from your office; for instance, in my consulting workshop I use many of the regular forms, brochures, marketing materials, &c., which I regularly use in my business. This is a way of promoting myself, of course, but also introduces the participants to formats I've found helpful.

Note: many sponsors provide special workshop folders. If such is the case for your program, arrange to send your pass outs in advance so they can be collated in the folders.

Chapter 8

Instructional Aid Check List

For whatever instructional aid you use there will be problems. Each has benefits and drawbacks and the only way of insuring a successful result is to check and double check. This is easier to say than to do, as I am well aware. When you are doing programs regularly, it's easy to forget a point which in the result becomes crucial. So consult this list.

Chalkboards

- Is there one?

- Who has the chalk or grease pencils?

- Who's responsible for putting these into the room?

- Does this person have an emergency number where they can be reached during the program?

- Erasers, ditto

- Where's the drinking water?

Flip Charts

- Will an easel be provided or do you have to bring your own?

- Will a pad of paper be provided or do you have to bring your own?

- Are you sending your materials in advance? What is the complete shipping address? (Make sure the recipient calls you upon receipt so that you can make other plans if necessary. Don't wait until you arrive to find out that you don't have the materials you need!)

- Make sure the corners of your charts are protected.

- Ship them in special carrying cases with adequate packing.

- Use magic markers and other felt pens. Regular pens and, heaven forbid!, pencils are inadequate for this job.

Overhead Transparencies, Slides, Films

- Does the sponsoring institution have the right equipment? You will most likely not want to travel with your own.

- Ask if there is backup equipment available and who *at the time* of the program will be able to get access to it. Remember: many programs take place on week-ends when regular working hour telephone numbers and staff don't apply. You must be prepared for the off hours when you are working!

- Will someone be available to help you with the screen and otherwise provide technical assistance?

It goes without saying (does it?) that your greatest enemy in preparing a successful program is assuming. Don't. This chapter is lengthy; the reason is that so much can go wrong on the day of the program. Prepare for as much of it as you can.

Microphones

Your program will not be successful if people have trouble hearing you. The great days of the nineteenth century orators are gone. Even today's politicians have trouble projecting themselves a few rows without a microphone. I must say I despise them for their weak lungs; I myself try whenever possible to do without a microphone. There is something about a microphone which I find very irritating. It puts a barrier between you and the audience and so often makes a speaker look very, very affected. We are not, after all, crooners and most of us look decidedly silly with the microphone

Chapter 8

in hand. And please: stay away from those posed publicity shots with microphone in hand. It just looks ridiculous! Nonetheless, such diatribes aside, the microphone is a very useful piece of equipment and one that is a necessary evil on the speaking circuit.

Here are your five choices:

- Fixed lectern microphone. This is attached to a single spot like a podium. If you're dependent on this microphone, you're attached to this spot, too. These microphones are adequate if you are giving a presentation of about an hour's length, although even in these cases it is hardly ideal. A speaker succeeds by being able to reach out and touch the audience; if you are trapped behind a podium dependent upon a fixed point microphone, you will limit your ability to impress yourself upon the people in your audience. Avoid this if you can.

- Hand held microphone. You can move with such a microphone but you'll have problems with it notwithstanding. When you need to write (and you will if you're using a chalkboard or self-drawn flip charts), such a microphone causes problems. Such a microphone is awkward (and hence detracts from your status as the leader) and tiring, too. Avoid this one if you can.

- Lavaliere microphone. Although I detest the word (sounds pretentious to me), I prefer this device. This microphone has an attaching cord that goes around your neck and connects to the microphone. The mike hangs at your collar bone and moves with you — to chalkboard, easel and audience. I must say I am not one of those who feels comfortable in gold chains or anything else around my neck (too suggestive of the gallows), and while I understand the utility of this device I regard it as nothing more than a necessary evil.

- Clip on microphone. This is generally what's used on television programs. It's attached to your clothes at mid-chest with a tie-tack or clip. Since I like television shows, I prefer this kind of microphone. Unfortunately, many places just don't have it. Nonetheless, you still look a little silly moving about the room trailing a cord looking a bit like an electrified doll.

- Wireless microphones. Such microphones avoid the problem of the cord and of having them in hand, moving them about, wiring and attaching yourself, &c. Unfortunately, they are prone to picking up stray signals. In the middle of your splendid peroration, therefore, you are likely to be interrupted by a few squalid seconds of top forty tunes, by no means an uplifting conclusion!

As before, check with your sponsor to see which kind of microphone they have available. Try whenever possible to dispense with it altogether if you can. Start with a room of 25 people and see whether you can project your voice sufficiently throughout your program so that you don't need amplification assistance. Go as long as you can without it and only fall back on it when you need to. I can speak comfortably to 50 to 100 people without a microphone; (I also don't have the lungs of either Gladstone or Disraeli regrettably)!

Remember: you want nothing to stand between you and your audience. Your audience, your workshop participants want you to connect with them. They are willing to overlook poor grammar, a halting delivery, fractured diction so long as they feel your energy, your enthusiasm, your commitment to your topic touching them and your desire to help them realize the objectives of your program in their own lives. If the microphone helps you do this, then by all means use it. If it stands between you and your audience in any way, then work to eliminate it.

And don't begin your talk by touching the microphone, starting it on a screaming fit and saying "Can everybody hear me?" It's been done...

More Planning

Find out in advance who your program contact person will be. Get a day and evening number for this person. From this person find out:

- How far the speaking site is from the airport or from your hotel.

- Whether you'll be met at the airport (it's always better if you are).

Chapter 8

- If you're not being met, what's the best way of getting into town.

- Get confirmation information about overnight travel. Although I often try to arrive on the morning of a program, I don't recommend this activity. Try to take the second to the last flight so that there is a back-up if you need it.

If you cannot be met at the airport, try to arrange a brief get-together with your contact person before you speak. There are several reasons for this:

- You want to know as much as possible about the group you'll be speaking to.

- You are trying to make a friend who'll write you a good testimonial/endorsement letter.

- You want to network for future assignments and contacts.

- You'd like to come back and do this or another program again and you need to find out whether that's possible, deadline dates, &c.

Putting The Puzzle Together

Once you know when you'll be speaking, have your transportation and know how long it will take you to arrive in the center of the town *and* you have scheduled time with the program planner, round out your schedule with prospecting and promotional work.

Allow at least enough time for you to contact local media to make a final bid for coverage and to call associations. I like to leave a block of time, at least an hour, to call local associations and find out:

- the name of the program planner

- make initial contact if possible

- have the last meeting brochure sent me

- indicate that I'll be following up with my own materials

- connect with the newsletter editor.

You can easily call a half dozen associations and contacts in an hour and this at any one time is enough for me!

Remember: once a given speaking assignment is in place and the audience has been secured, it's your responsibility to look ahead to the next assignment. Always make the best use of your ground time.

Preparing To Leave: What To Take

Most often you'll ship your pass outs and books ahead. Don't ship all of them, however. Make sure to hand carry at least one complete set of your pass outs so that if your materials don't arrive or can't be found at the last minute (yes, even this happens!), you can get them duplicated on the spot. Of course, you'd better ask how this can be done if needed.

Also bring at least one copy of each of your books and other materials for sale and a quantity of order blanks. I'd like to say I never fail on this count, but I remember one day arriving at a New York City television station which had been sent, I think, 4 books and complete packets of material and not bringing any more only to discover that there was nothing on the set and they expected yet another book! I was the only one on the program without a dazzling literary bangle and I was angry!

Remember: in a worst case scenario you could probably work around the absence of books and written materials, but you don't want to lose all the sales and people won't buy unless they can see the product.

Chapter 8

Put together a kit to carry with you and consider adding some or all of the following items. Most are self-explanatory but perhaps a word or two is necessary for the rest.

- scissors
- pen knife (a key will also help to open boxes)
- cellophane and masking tape
- stapler (filled, please)
- hammer, screwdriver and nails if you have anything that needs to be hung
- measuring tape
- light bulbs, slide carousel tray, splicing tape and blank transparencies for your audiovisual needs
- white-out fluid
- needle and thread.

I shouldn't, but I will tell you this story: I was about to speak to the English Speaking Union in New York City one day and just as I got into the taxi I split my trousers right across the back. Of course I had no spare. Since I was late there was no chance even to put a safety pin to the problem in the men's room. Worse, there was no podium. I was supposed to speak standing up.

The solution? I grabbed an overstuffed, floral patterned chair, sat myself down and held a reading cum lecture from my book **INSUBSTANTIAL PAGEANT: CEREMONY AND CONFUSION AT QUEEN VICTORIA'S COURT**. Not a soul was the wiser. Lesson? Carry safety pins. If you don't, learn to improvise. Better yet, do both. Also bring:

- name tags
- change
- cash receipt journal (people like a receipt even after you've told them their cancelled check will do)
- pushpins and thumbtacks
- cassette tape and recorder (designate someone to handle this for you. You want a complete recording of the day for future use.)
- batteries
- small camera, film, flash cubes (you can run a modified Photographic Reception Line)
- lemon drops or other throat lozenges. Lemon works best.
- string or twine
- flashlight (yes, the lights will go out at some point. Count on it.)
- plain white 8 1/2 × 11 inch paper
- plastic water glass (real glass breaks)
- list of critical telephone numbers including your contact person, media and association numbers
- small travel clock with alarm.

Chapter 8

A Word, No More, On Clothes

When I travel I like to go light, very, very light. Whenever possible for an overnight I prefer to simply take carry on luggage, that's it. In either case, bring at least one complete change of clothes. Most times when I'm traveling on United Airlines one of the madcap flight attendants spills a drink on me. I've now come to expect it. And I plan accordingly. I still think it *infra dig* to go before an audience with deep discolorations on my clothes. Gentlemen can have gravy stains on their ties but there the obvious presence of food ends.

En Route

At the airport, buy a newspaper from the city you are visiting. Whenever possible sprinkle your talk with topical references. I look for information about fund raising drives, consulting and consultants, those who have obviously used promotional methods, &c. Whenever possible connect with your audience. They'll be grateful — and they'll understand more, too — if you make your examples topical. By the same token with a trade association, read the latest issue or two of their publication. Reading it on the plane will do if you haven't had time before, but do it.

Also, use the time on the plane for writing. This is the perfect opportunity to sketch out your next Problem Solving Process Article. I do it in a log that I carry which also contains the names and numbers of people I'm to contact. This log is valuable, too, because I have all people who want something from me write their request with complete follow-up information (name, address and telephone number) right in the log. I tick these items off as I finish them back at my office.

At the Program Site

Hotels and, worse, motels are nasty places no matter how grand. I believe that if I were to be blindfolded I could nonetheless tell you which chain I happened to be in by the smell. Each has a unique odor and a Holiday Inn does not smell like a Ramada does not smell like the Marriott but each is olfactorily reminiscent of its sister in whatever city it's located. Don't take my word for it. You'll find out for yourself.

Whenever possible, if you arrive the night before your program (as you ought) arrange to spend the evening with a friend or with someone you liked from your last program in the city. I can wholeheartedly attest that these people will be very glad to see you. You'll have a nice evening, get taken to a nice restaurant (yes, you are the guest, after all), perhaps see a bit of the city, meet some new people, and be made to feel like the visiting celebrity (which, after all, you are). In due course you'll be invited to stay in people's homes rather than in hotels. Frankly, I prefer this. This kind of evening puts you in the proper frame of mind for the day's work ahead. You'll be in high good humor, relaxed and eager to go.

The Day of the Program Arrives

- Have a good breakfast. As nutritional experts say, this really is the most important meal of the day and you mustn't skimp. You'll need it not least because you'll be having a light lunch if any lunch at all. Lunch to someone who is putting on a full day's program is an enemy. It makes your audience tired and it does you in, too.

- If you have nothing to pass out to early comers, buy several copies of the day's newspaper. If you are lecturing at a college campus, you'll have to get these at your hotel.

- If you are catching a plane immediately following your program, take everything with you from the hotel. You can in a worse case call a taxi to pick you up. Most likely, however, one of the participants will be only too happy to take you to the airport. It gives them extra time with their guru — you! In case you are the quivery type, like me, you can find out whether anyone is going to the airport by mid-day and then schedule a taxi if you don't get any nibbles.

- Arrange to arrive at your workshop site at least 45 minutes before the program, longer if you have to check audio visual equipment which can take a lot of time. Make sure that the room will be open, again a possible problem at a college site on a Saturday. Use this time to:

    - locate the rest rooms

    - remove the ashtrays

Chapter 8

- open the windows (if it's stuffy)
- find the soft drink machines
- find the chalk and erasers
- arrange the furniture like you want it.

Also, distribute your first pass out on the seats. Leave the seats in the back of the room without pass outs. People always want to sit in the back and near the door; (that's what they think of you!) Don't let them. Put your papers on the seats nearest the front. As you get busier and more people come in, whatever pass outs you are distributing first should be given to the person nearest the door who can become paper monitor for late comers. Don't let these inevitable johnny-come-latelies spoil your presentation!

Even if you are working with one or two people as support staff, it is very likely that you'll arrive first. When at last the support staff arrives, introduce yourself and find out the answers (if you don't know them already) to all the pertinent questions people will want to know during the day:

- validation for parking
- time of lunch, place, directions
- availability of morning coffee, afternoon soft drinks. Exact time expected, serving instructions.
- registration particulars for late comers if support staff leaves
- where evaluations can be returned. Mail address in case people want to send them in after the program (to be discouraged, of course, since they never do.)

Be nice to the support staff. If possible, introduce them during the day and publicly acknowledge their support. You may have to work with them again and even if you don't, it's still the right thing to do!

People will begin to arrive up to an hour before your program. If you turn into Michael Jackson, they'll come days before. Frankly, these early comers are a nuisance and yet you've got to be nice to them. This is what the newspapers are for and at least one pass out. Fortunately for me, when one of my books is included in the cost of the workshop, then this, too, is distributed at the beginning of the program, and I encourage people to look through it.

Introduce yourself to these people. This sounds obvious but isn't always done. Extend your hand, be cheerful, hearty and accessible. This is your job. If you need some help, you'd better be especially pleasant. You'll often have to pull tables and chairs into a better formation and this needs help. Ask them, too, about their own situations and jot down a note or two. Bring them into the presentation as you do look in their direction and speak to them. Again, connecting with your audience.

If you are bad with names like I am, ask them to repeat it and repeat it again. If there is a class list make a comment next to the name so that you can connect it to the face. If there is no list, circulate one. I generally use my log for a class list so that all the information I need is right there: name, address, telephone, business name, position, address and telephone. Ask participants whether they have any objection to this list being duplicated and find out whether you can get it to them that day.

Write an outline of the day on the chalk board or flip chart or distribute individual copies. Note each subject that is being covered hour by hour, the exact times of breaks and the end moment of the program. Adults crave this kind of structure. Begin any program longer than 45 minutes by going over this chart point by point so there can be no questions; (there still will be, of course, so you might as well expect them.)

If the registration team is leaving at some point and you will be left unattended (the common scenario at most colleges and many other functions), get an emergency number.

Chapter 8

Designate a spot in the room where people can put their own materials, business cards, brochures, flyers, &c. I believe in networking and I believe that the participants in programs should be encouraged to make contacts and profit from this experience in as many ways as they can. Help them!

Begin On Time

Many speakers make the mistake of waiting for latecomers. Even if your group is small and half the people have not yet arrived begin within 5 minutes of your starting time. If promptness is the courtesy of kings, it is also the courtesy of speakers. Moreover, don't make any special recognition of latecomers. If there are papers to be passed out, leave them with an individual in the back of the room; if there are registrations to be taken, leave them to the first break. In short, get on with the business at hand.

If you are being introduced, urge the person doing so to get going. The odium for starting late will not rest on this individual (who may wish to wait for the latecomers) but on you. If you are alone, stride up to the front of the room and begin. "Welcome. My name is Jeffrey Lant and I'll be your speaker for today..."

After you've had the opportunity to review the outline for the day, announce anything special that pertains to this program. With me that's the keeping of time. I don't own a watch myself and haven't for many years. In a college classroom, there's usually one of those great white faced instruments we watched through school. In a hotel, I have to appoint a time keeper. This person watches the clock for me.

Too many speakers are time conscious. This is a mistake. You need to be and remain audience conscious. It is nice, of course, if you can neatly divide your program into 55 minute packages as I try to do, but things don't always work out that precisely. You need to be alert to your audience and how it feels about the presentation. Perhaps you'll need a break at 40 minutes, for instance. But make sure that there is one after 55 minutes. It's the job of the time keeper to remind you and they are ordinarily punctilious about this job — after all they want the break themselves. When this person calls "Time!" you can conclude your thought and then break.

Have People Introduce Themselves

I have said in other places in this book that the most successful programs are those where people connect not only with you but with each other. If your group is under 50 and you have a day-long workshop, you should go around the room and have people introduce themselves to the group. Have them give their name, city, kind of business, reason for attending and any other information which will help them feel at home. Hardly surprising, there are those who will seize this opportunity to tell you and the rest of those present their life story. The best way of handling this situation is to cut in at an advantageous moment and say, "Wait a minute! Only I get to tell everybody that much this early in the day!"

There'll be a laugh, the point will be made and you can move on. Encourage people to stand up as they introduce themselves. If there is a participant list, encourage people to annotate it. The idea is to convey an atmosphere that it's encouraged to make friends, business contacts and to benefit from the day in all ways. People will take their cue from you, and this is the cue you ought to give them.

As people go around the room, interject your own comments. If there is something you'll be discussing during the day that seems particularly ápropos to that person, say so. Encourage them to pay particular attention to that section. Indicate that you are the people-centered leader and want to make sure they come away with the useful information they need.

If there are too many people to introduce the entire group in this fashion, have them introduce themselves to the people in their immediate area. Do what time and numbers allow to make them feel at home.

After the participants have finished introducing themselves, tell a little about yourself. Let them know why you are leading this program, your appropriate background and your expectations and objectives for the day.

Chapter 8

Also give your policy on questions. Questions properly handled are a great boon to you. They add an element of spontaneity to your program and allow you to be perceived as the people-centered leader you want to be. My own policy is this: I allow people to break in with a question at ANY time. If this question is premature, I urge them to hold it until a specific time. "Try the third hour when we will be dealing with just that point." Answer the question as fully and completely as you can. Don't hold back any information. Give the names and addresses of appropriate people, the complete names of books, &c. This is the moment to demonstrate your virtuoso knowledge of the subject and be truly helpful.

If you don't know the answer, of course don't babble on. Admit the gap in your knowledge. Everyone has them. However, let the individual know that the information he wants is available and that you'll get it to them. Pass the log book and have the question and questioner entered or have them do so at a break. By all means do what you say you're going to do. Nothing gives you more credibility than that.

Another way of handling the matter is to have the questioner annotate his business card and give it to you. The key is to get the question or matter that needs looking into and to give it your attention.

If at any time you make a factual mistake and catch it, admit the error! Do so with a little self-deprecating humor. Your audience won't mind and in fact will be grateful for the candor. Do not, however, go back and correct grammatical flaws, diction, mispronunciations (unless of names in the audience), &c. While devotees of Fowler's *King's English* will wince, unless you are teaching a program on the use of unblemished language, don't worry and don't try to correct yourself. It seems affected and what you are trying to do is get connected to your audience.

The First Hour

From experience I know that the first hour of any day-long program will be the worst. You should know this, too, and not be worried by it. One thing that might exacerbate a naturally rather difficult situation is that there might be someone present who feels the program isn't for him. As I've said before, as people go around the room you'll know immediately, if you have a clear sense of your Participant Profile, who these people are and you won't be surprised by what happens next.

Assuming that the program has a cost to it (and if not, why are you doing it?), this out-of-place individual will, if couth, seek you out at the first break and explain that the program isn't what he wants. That's fine. Don't fight it. Do try to find out what the individual's expectations were and see whether later in the day information that he wants will be forthcoming. If so, strive to keep the person present.

If you cannot keep the troubled soul, don't worry. After the first hour in my opinion the individual should be free to go and have his money entirely refunded. If you are working with a sponsoring organization, they'll undoubtedly have a policy on the matter which you need to know because it's not, in such cases, your decision. In this case, simply state the sponsor's policy and refer the individual to the appropriate person. Remember this: if the refund is not given promptly the individual will blame you and not the sponsoring institution. You are, after all, the leader. You can rest assured that this displeasure will be trumpeted about and may cost you future registrations. So do what you can to right matters immediately.

Ironically enough, even when people don't want to remain in the program they don't want to part with the pass outs. Be gracious about the loose papers but make sure you get paid for book, pamphlets, &c., just as you would with any customer.

Lunch

As I've said before, try to arrange matters so that you lunch with the director of program planning for the sponsoring institution. You need this time to impart a sense of yourself, your objectives for this program, and your suggestions both about how to improve attendance at this course and those new courses and programs you'd like to suggest. Have this individual if at all possible introduce you to the dean or director, the director of public relations and the support staff, too. These people can have a real influence on your success with any given program. (Remember my experience with that major southern university when callers asked about my consulting program. "Consulting program. Oh, that's been cancelled," which is of course your nightmare.)

Chapter 8

Program planners need a series of suggestions from you. If this program has been successful, they will want to reschedule. Don't assume this, but do bring it up for discussion. "I'd like to do this program again. When is your deadline for new courses?" Work on this short-term objective and get matters wrapped up while you are there. Take out your calendar and discuss dates and follow up this discussion with a letter.

There should be discussion, too, about a new program. Once you have proven yourself successful, push the discussion ahead. Transportation takes time. Whenever possible try to cluster your programs so that at a single stop you are offering at least two courses on related subjects. These can, after all, be marketed as a single package, perhaps with a special two-fer price.

Work on a long term program, too. In another chapter I'll be discussing the creation of annual institutes and conferences. Find out what the sponsor's capabilities are in this area, what comparable format programs they already have, and whether they would be interested in at least considering new programs. These annual programs take much longer to plan; conference planners, for instance, need as much as a year's lead time or even more. Plan accordingly.

Your discussion with program planners at whatever level, then, should be geared to:

- a repetition of your successful program

- testing a new program in the next available time slot (clustering your programs together and thus increasing your return on the time invested)

- probing for information about an annual institute or conference.

Although this seems like a lot of ground (especially if you expect a lightning introduction to the support staff), you will have no more than an hour to cover it and even less given that your partner at least will be eating. I suggest that you have a very light lunch, an apple and some dried fruit for instance and a multi-vitamin! Program planners err frequently by arranging for a heavy, hot mid-day lunch. This is bad since it makes your audience sluggish in the afternoon. Whenever possible, make sure that the food is kept light. A buffet is a very good idea. In winter in the snow belt, it can be supplemented with a hot soup. This is enough. The effect of a disastrous menu, however, is compounded if you partake. Don't! Keep it light. Frankly, you don't have the time to eat a lot and you don't need it, either. (Remember I told you to have a good breakfast!)

If the main program planner (dean, director, &c) is not available, at the very least meet with an assistant. In this case, leave a memorandum which discusses each of the catagories above. Sell the program assistant on the need for each of your suggestions; this person will now have to become your advocate and your lunch must be spent selling.

The Alternative

Unfortunately, your lunch period cannot always be used productively. Program planners may be unavailable or simply not working when you are on hand. This is a common problem for those of us who work Saturdays and evenings. There are people that I've worked with for years that I still haven't met. In such cases, you need to build a very good telephone relationship and keep in frequent contact.

If you cannot eat with the program planners, there are two alternatives: staying behind in the seminar room or lunching with the participants. It may seem obvious that you'd do the latter, but you can't always do so. If the room can be locked with all materials and personal possessions safely inside, then you will surely want to be with the participants. In a hotel, for instance, you'll surely be able to lock the room. But on a college campus, particularly on evenings and weekends, this desirable result is not always possible. Under such circumstances and given the number of light-fingered people in the world, I stay behind in the room so that people will not need to pack up. This isn't the best use of my time but it does have its advantages: there is nothing wrong with 45 minutes or so to yourself, to gather your thoughts, rest your voice and generally relax. Moreover, it does reduce the risk of problems. On one of the infrequent occasions when I did leave a room unguarded, a participant's briefcase was stolen. At a very prestigious university, too. What results when this happens is most distracting, not to mention the anger and pain of the sufferer. So it's better to play it safe.

If, on the other hand, you can take care of the security needs of the participants and lunch with them, do. There are real benefits to be derived by both the participants and yourself. Here's how to handle this situation.

Chapter 8

Expect to remain behind a few minutes after you have adjourned your presentation. People will have questions to ask you and there are always late housekeeping matters to attend to. You will therefore enter the eating area last. This allows you to pick the best spot to place yourself. My preferred strategy is to sit next to any people who I feel may not be entirely happy with the program, not sold on the value of the information, or otherwise in a state of embryo dissatisfaction. Remember: you want the best possible recommendations you can get and this may mean spending a little extra time with possible malcontents. Your lunch break is the time to do this.

In many cases, people may be simmering because they haven't had the opportunity to talk as much as they'd like. This is a very common problem. Allow them to use the lunch period to tell you how you should be presenting material, what personal experiences they have had that bear upon the subject at hand, and generally to act as sidewalk superintendents if they feel they must. Be gracious. Suggest to one or two of them with something of value to impart that they make a general announcement to the other participants at the beginning of the next part of the program. Coopt these people and make them part of your team. Be inclusive. Adult learners have varied experiences which they want to share. Where appropriate, encourage them to do so.

Spend roughly half your available time with the group you are lunching with. Make sure each member is heard; encourage the silent to open up. In such ways you are writing yourself good recommendations and, if you have products for sale, the prospect of future sales. Spend at least 15 minutes, one quarter of a one-hour lunch, circulating to the entire group. I table hop. I go from group to group making sure that people have enjoyed their lunch and answering any questions they may have. I encourage them to get acquainted and to network with each other for future assignments, jobs, &c. You are the master of ceremonies and it is your job to take care of these amenities. Enjoy yourself! I have found that I will probably never actually see 99% of the people again with whom I come in contact during the course of a workshop, lecture or presentation. My goal however, is not modest: I want to leave a lifetime's impression on them, make them feel that for however brief a moment, man or woman, I was there simply for them, that the full force of my being was directed to them and to them alone. Why? Not least because word of mouth advertising is still the most powerful promotional force and you can create it by making each person in the room feel special, wanted, desirable and of value. Whenever possible spend just a moment, you really don't have more, with each person and touch their lives.

A Note On Lunch

Often you will find yourself eating in college mess-halls. These are far nicer places than they were when I was an undergraduate although there has been no appreciable diminution of the grousing. Many colleges where programs are presented give people in their workshops tickets at the beginning of the day which allow them to go through the line. In such cases there should be no problems. However, others simply ask you to shepherd the group through and leave the number with the student monitor, who is, in my experience, inevitably dull and surly. Rest assured this individual knows nothing of your program and less about public relations. If you find yourself confronted by this recognizable type, ask for the manager. This person should expect you and will take care of matters. In a worst case situation (yes, even this happens!) keep the program director's telephone number with you so that a doubting official can call for confirmation.

Returning

Add the time it takes to return to the program facility plus about 7 minutes to the time at which you ask people to consider returning. The extra time, of course, is for a restroom break. Don't neglect this. For the participants or yourself! You need a moment, too, to renew your gloss. Take it. Unlike the lunch line, be first in this activity so that you can be back in the workshop area ready to take introductory questions and generally get the show moving again.

Afternoons in day-long programs are different from mornings. They are invariably less formal and stiff since people have now become accustomed to you, and they have begun to make friends with each other, too. Also, the food will make them sluggish. If possible, therefore, lower the temperature in the room, open the windows and otherwise get the air circulating.

Start the afternoon session with a reprise of the morning. Now begin to act the college instructor. Throw out a few questions to the group to see what they've learned. (You'll probably be appalled as I have been on a few occasions.) Encourage multi-part answers so that people can piggyback on what others are saying.

Chapter 8

Encourage those who asked you questions at lunch of general interest to ask them before the group. Ask your simmering malcontents to make their comments, too. In short, be the conductor of the orchestra letting each instrument have its say.

Begin the formal proceedings with a brief recap of what you have accomplished in the morning. It's a very good idea to let the participants know that they — and you! — have made progress and that they are getting their money's worth! This also provides you with a natural bridge which will get you into the material you are about to present.

The afternoon's program should be punctuated by a soft drink and juice break. This should be in mid-afternoon.

Winding Up

About 30 minutes from the completion of my program I begin winding down towards my conclusion. About this time pass out the evaluations which you want to have completed. Most evaluations are standard. Most, therefore, lack an important section which you'll need for the future. Ask people to add a comment about the day's program which you can use in promoting and publicizing the next program you give on this subject. As I've said before: program planners all too often see each program as distinct. As a professional lecturer, you cannot. The comments of satisfied users should appear in your next brochures and promotional pieces. Indeed, those who have satisfactory applied your methods are perfect to accompany you onto local television and radio shows. Remember the local angle. You are the facilititor, the midwife of people's success. This means that you have to be able to show evidence of success. Your program participants are that evidence.

There are a couple of reasons for passing out the evaluations at this point. Often people will have to catch planes themselves or otherwise leave early. You don't want to miss them! Also, if you wait to the last minute, you'll get many participants saying that they'll mail in the evaluation. They mean well, of course, but they won't do it. Just in case they insist, however, make sure that you have available the name and address of the program officer. Note: occasionally you'll have to insist that they mail them in. I remember one occasion at a university where program evaluations were done on a computerized form. Unfortunately the office had forgotten to provide me with the necessary pencils and, of course, no one in the workshop had any with them. I had an uneasy moment just then because it was part of the contract that there would be no payment without an evaluation! Fortunately, enough evaluations were returned so that I didn't become a test case!

Allot at least fifteen or twenty minutes for general, free-wheeling questions. I encourage people during the last quarter hour to ask questions on whatever subject they wish, something that pertains to the material in the workshop generally, or to their individual cases. If you have presented a lot of material during your program (as I do) there may be relatively few or even no questions during this period. Don't worry. All learners reach a point where they have learned enough for the moment and where they are suffering from 'circuit overload.' In such circumstances, be prepared to stimulate discussion by asking questions yourself. Or simply have some standby material.

The end of the day is an important part of the experience and must be planned. Don't just end. Conclude.

- Tell people you are grateful that they've attended and ask them to tell their friends.

- State your policy on follow-up telephone calls. If it is your intention to allow people to call you once or twice after the program to refine their understanding of certain information or ask a private query, then this really ought to be cited among the program's benefits in any promotional literature. "As a participant in this program, you'll have the opportunity to consult Dr. Lant afterwards by telephone to get follow-up information to this program."

People constantly ask me whether such a benefit might not become a leader nightmare with you being forced to take calls at any hour of the day or night for weeks afterward from exigent participants. This frankly doesn't happen. Most people don't make use of this privilege and when they do their questions are brief and specific.

Those having taken any program where mastery of the subject material is needed to insure success feel more comfortable and secure when this access is available to them even if they don't make use of it. Try this announcement, "Many of you will find that you have a question about how to make some aspect of this material work for you once you get home. My first suggestion to you is to study the pass outs and try again. Then if you're still having problems, feel free to call me at this number during business hours." The Accessible Expert at work.

Chapter 8

In the closing moments, also remind people that you are available on a professional basis to assist them with their problems. You don't need to overplay this, the more so since if you follow my suggestions you'll be contacting them again anyway. If you have an informational brochure on your business hold it up now and make sure that all the participants have it. Advise them to hold on to it for future reference. Business results from workshops months and even years after they take place. Don't oversell your services. It's not necessary. If you've handled the workshop effectively, you've already made the best sales pitch you can make and in any case a thank you letter will be sent afterwards.

Close with a good story, an amusing anecdote and an uplifting comment. I advise people in the last moments to begin to put into effect right away the precepts and techniques they have learned today. That the longer they wait the more difficult it will be, the more elusive their success. I encourage them to stay in touch with me, to let me know their successes and to advise me about their failures, too, in case I am able to be of assistance to them. I encourage them to become part of the extended network of individuals who have taken my programs and to use me as a resource. "If you succeed," I say, "I want to know because I'll hold you up as an example to those who follow you. If you fail tell me, too, since I'll use you as a parable." The line never fails to elicit a good hearty laugh.

After The Show Is Over

You now have several possibilities.

If you are catching a plane within the hour (a common scenario with me) then you'll have to leave promptly. Try to remain behind for at least 10-15 minutes to clean up the room (not necessary, gratefully, if it's a hotel but a good idea on a college campus), pick up your papers, the evaluations (which should be returned that day if possible) and anything else. Move the chairs back into place and erase the board and generally clean the place up.

If you have scheduled a consulting client (a good way to pick up some extra income and stay in touch with previous registrants), your picking up the room will help create a better atmosphere for the meeting that follows. Whenever possible, you should let previous participants in your program know that you will be available for a limited number of consulting sessions the day preceding your talk and immediately after. Aim for one or two of these meetings.

What I find often happens is that I schedule one of these meetings after the program for an hour and then arrange with the client to drop me at the airport. I don't charge them, of course, for car time but rather swap and save the taxi fare. It's a nice trade.

If you have neither a plane nor a consulting assignment, arrange to meet interested members of the workshop at a nearby watering hole for a drink or two. You'll find that you'll be joined by 6 to 8 people, usually among the nicest and most interested in you and what you're doing. This is a good time to do a little relaxing and cement your network, and I recommend it to you. Try to keep the place within walking distance so that people won't have to move their cars.

During this session as with other meetings throughout the course of the day, people will provide you with openings for future programs. You'll learn what college they attended, what associations they belong to, what friends they have in what places. This is critical networking information for you. Note it down. I find that at any given time I have such a wealth of networking information that it is literally impossible to follow up all the leads, yet I keep at it and do follow up many of them. These leads will assist in bringing you and your programs to the attention of individuals in a way that will help you get bought. Networking is an important sales aid. This is another good time to make use of it.

At Your Office: More Follow-up

Once you get back to your office there remains more to do to effectively make use of this program and conclude it gracefully.

- Make sure that you know how much the program grossed (easy enough to compute) and what the profit was for the sponsor (more difficult. You'll probably have to ask). This is the basis for your Success Letter and future leveraging.

Chapter 8

- Write the program planner a thank-you note. Even if they didn't do all you wanted, they probably did the best they could. In any case, make your letter warm. If this individual has done anything out of the way, anything particularly nice or has been peculiarly effective, then write a nice letter to the dean or director; if it has been way above and beyond the call of duty, write to the president of the university or the chairman of the board of the association. These kinds of thank you letters are rare and will be much appreciated. They may even become part of a personnel file and as such if you can possibly write one, do.

- Follow up the items the participants added to your log book. Send out all the materials and generally follow up. Particularly good leads should get a Monday morning telephone call. This impresses participants and it ought to. When a good lead surfaces I add the item to my Monday marketing list. Remember: we live in a slow and slothful universe. We all partake of these unhappy qualities but try to minimize your own. Get cracking as soon as you can!

- If media people have interviewed you, send them a thank you note, too. You'll need them again. Those of us on the national lecture circuit know that this vast country of ours is small. You'll be dealing with many of the same people for the duration of your professional life and these amenities will be most useful to you. Make use of them.

- Request extra copies of the program brochure or catalog for your files. You'll need them. Program planners always want to see what you've previously done. These copies will come in handy.

- Follow up your meeting with the program planner with a detailed letter or memorandum in which you discuss your next program, the new programs you've proposed and your long-term ideas.

- Take time to review your performance. I guarantee you this: Even if you delivered a Churchillian oration, there will be those to find fault and you had better accept it. There is a group of people in the world, unfortunately numerous, which regards a good comment as akin to noxious flattering and something therefore to avoid. Expect this kind. And ignore them. Ultimately, the evaluation that matters is the crisp, candid evaluation you give yourself. I'm not going to tell you that I don't read evaluations and that these evaluations don't influence me, don't occasionally offend and irritate me. They do. I'm only human. I take them, however, with a grain of salt, good and bad, because I know from experience what I did right and what I didn't. You'll learn this, too, and this feeling will be your inner compass, the necessary equipment of everyone who ventures out on the talk circuit.

A Few Concluding Remarks

Having delivered hundreds of programs now all around the nation, let me leave you with this thought and these stories. As you travel, expect the unexpected. You can be assured it will happen and you can rest assured that it will throw off your most careful calculations. The best thing to do is to keep a cool head and your sense of humor. As irritating items occur, the workshop participants will be evaluating you and as you handle this irritation so they will know how to evaluate all the glorious things that you say. Anyone can be turned out to look good á la Eliza Doolittle and to mouth the right kinds of words, but it is in moments of difficulty and distress that your real character show through. To wit:

- **The Case of the Exploding Commode**

One evening in Manhattan, half way through a consulting workshop, there was an explosion in the toilet attached to the hotel suite where the program was taking place. A quick look inside revealed the eastern equivalent of Old Faithful and a spreading gush of water. Repeated telephone calls to the maintenance staff of the hotel finally succeeded in bringing a squad of repairmen to the scene. All were Turks with only a smidgeon of English among them. The result, predictably, was chaos and confusion. But, folks, the show must go on even when a bevy of Musselmen decide to parlay at close quarters.

Solution: Ask the hotel for a refund. If that fails (as it did in this case), ask for a comparable credit on your next workshop (this worked). If that fails, write the national headquarters. Don't give way.

Chapter 8

- **Illness Is Your Friend**

I have written elsewhere that when you are ill is no time to cancel a program. Quite the reverse. Years ago I was invited to make a presentation at the Kennedy School of Government at Harvard on fund raising for alternative causes. The room was small and packed with fervent undergraduates who lent a fetid quality to the air which swam before my feverish eyes. I was that evening a member of a panel and spent the time before my remarks drinking large drafts of orange juice and praying for an early end to the proceedings. But I stayed. I can't remember a word of what I said. I do however know the result: another member of the panel was a woman who was shortly elevated to the presidency of her college. When she got her new job she promptly retained me as development counsel and workshop presenter, a job I hold to this day, years later. The reason, "Your grace under pressure," she said.

Solution: If you must be ill, be ill on stage. If you must die, do so from the podium. You'll be forever memorable and go on or out (as the case may be) with the envy and admiration of your audience.

- **Complacency**

I have written this book and I believe what I write and I try to live it, but I have my days, just like you will, when I give way to complacency. Inevitably this will be the worst day of your life.

I was giving a program recently on a Saturday at a large, prestigious eastern university. The program director assured me I would have no problem finding the lecture room and that all was being arranged to be not merely adequate but even munificent in honor of the kinds of people attending the program. I purred and lapsed into blissful stupor. When the director told me that she'd be out of town and that a friend would take over for her, even this did not phase me. Learn, reader, learn.

When I arrived on the Saturday, 45 minutes before the program, no signs were up. There was no indication ("you can't miss it!") where the workshop room would be. A campus policeman said I couldn't use his telephone because the line had to be kept open for emergencies (what was this?). At least I found the room and, lo and behold!, not only was it locked but it had been doubly sealed with a combination lock to which the hapless program assistant did not have the key. No signs, no room, no combination, no program director and, of course, a bevy of early participants judging me by what happened next.

Solution: get the program assistant to call the dean or even the president at home. (The person who knew the magic combination number was located on the operating table of her chiropracter!) Locate a new room. Get pieces of paper and tape to put up your own signs. Begin the program on time and let the assistant sort out the matter while you carry on. But by all means indicate that you are in control.

It is now, of course, a cliché that the Chinese ideograph for crisis is similarly the sign for opportunity. So it must be with you. Even though the information you'll be imparting throughout the day may be of impeccable worth, timeliness and value, your audience won't buy it if you have failed to sell yourself as the appropriate sales person.

Remember: a successful workshop or program represents the successful culmination to a series of successful sales contacts:

- a successful sales contact with the sponsor

- successful sales contacts with prospects

- successful sales contacts when the prospect is on hand and buys you.

These three prior sales are prerequisites before the necessary and important information you have will be communicated to the participant. Never forget this and act accordingly! Each time there is a question, an unexpected development or a crisis, anything that throws off your pre-established control, you will advance or fail by what you do. This is, of course, what makes each experience unique and challenging for you and why I find the talk circuit the greatest game in the world. Carry this book with you on your journey and you'll have the best chance of winning it.

REAL MONEY

Chapter 9

CASHING IN I: PROFITING ON THE SPOT FROM PRODUCTS YOU DON'T PRODUCE AND FROM THOSE YOU DO

Using the methods I have discussed this far, you should consistently make between $500-$1000 per day every time you work on the talk circuit. Even if you are committed to only doing a few programs a year, you can see what a nice difference even this level of commitment makes in your income.

But you can do much, much better. Sadly, however, many people on the talk circuit haven't learned how. There are many reasons for their relative lack of success. Some are selling the wrong program to the wrong people. Others stay too long with programs which may be successful but which appeal primarily to the lower price end of the market. Still others are not aggressive enough at marketing and thus fail to keep a steady stream of engagements. All these reasons can and do limit a speaker's success.

Worse, many people on the talk circuit just haven't learned how to profit from the sale of packages to their audiences. They rest on selling them a workshop participant ticket and nothing more. To succeed, however, means products: pamphlets, workbooks, books and audio cassettes being the leading items that should be included.

I hear all the time from the bright, talented, knowledgeable people who take my programs about why they are reluctant to take this move:

- "I don't have time."

- "I don't know how."

- "I don't have the money."

And a series of other excuses which inhibit an individual's success. Each of these excuses can be dealt with and must be dealt with if you are going to derive the full benefit from the talk circuit.

The Beginning: Profiting From Products You Don't Create Yourself

I don't think beginners should rush ahead and produce products which do indeed demand the investment of scarce resources. There are several reasons for such prudence:

- People in the early stages of a speaking career haven't entirely mastered their presentations. Thus elaborate materials based on this presentation (I exclude articles of course which are ephemeral) may become quickly outmoded.

- You may not have a clear sense of your market. The materials you develop may be overly theoretical, too general or, more rarely, too detailed for the audience you are addressing.

- You have only a limited sense of how many of these materials you can reasonably expect to sell in a year.

All of these are valid points which you need to consider. Don't let your enthusiasm carry you away into making investments of time and money which you may not, in the event, be able to recoup. Instead adopt the beginner's strongest suit: contract with those who have already produced materials until such time as these three points have been adequately dealt with and you are ready to proceed on your own.

Chapter 9

Contracting With Product Producers

It's curious to me how few speakers who have not yet produced materials of their own have still not contracted with others who have produced suitable materials for their audience. There are, I think, two reasons for this error:

- They aren't aware that such materials exist.

- They don't know what kinds of marketing and distribution arrangements are possible.

The first of these errors is unforgivable. All too many people on the talk circuit have ceased to do research and continuing education in their subject areas. After a time, it seems to me, speakers who may once have been fresh, vital and forward looking become complacent. "I know my material well enough to get by," they reckon, and along with this reckoning comes a creeping contempt for their audiences. These audiences, they think, are not bright enough to detect the speaker's sloth and out of date material. Such an attitude, very prevalent I'm afraid to say, will catch up with you. This is one reason why there is such a high turnover rate on the talk circuit.

Your job as an expert, for that is what you must continually remain as you put yourself forward, is to keep up-to-date on developments on your field. This includes knowing about new materials and products which will help solve the problems of your audience. How can you find these materials and products?

Finding Products

Materials and products are available everywhere. I am a voracious reader and I constantly put myself in touch with producers of materials, authors of new books, those people, in short who are or may be on the cutting edge in the fields in which I am interested and which my workshop participants should know about, too. Here are just a few of the available places to look for product suggestions:

Books

- *Books In Print.* Published by the R.R. Bowker Company, this volume and a series of others published by this well-known name in publishing will keep you up-to-date on available data. Also see *Publisher's Weekly* (published by R.R. Bowker, 245 West 17th St., New York, New York 10017). This, the so-called "bible of the book business", is where forthcoming titles are listed and often reviewed. If you want to distribute books, check out these resources.

- American Bookdealers Exchange (Box 2525, La Mesa, CA 92041). This aggressive organization headed by Al Galasso publishes both a magazine and a directory of publishers who are interested in drop shipping agreements. "Drop shipping" means that you promote and they'll ship for you. This, of course, is just what we're talking about!

- *Cosmep Newsletter* (P.O. Box 703, San Francisco, CA 94101). The publication of the professional organization representing small magazines and book publishers. Regular columns will inform you about what new books these often highly imaginative companies are publishing. All would, with enough prompting, welcome book marketing agreements. (A sample copy is free on request to publishers only.)

You've already been given the addresses of the *Oxbridge Directory Of Newsletters* and the Newsletter Clearinghouse. Don't forget to use them!

Audio Cassettes

Try Listen, USA! (60 Arch St., Greenwich, CT 06830; (203) 661-0101). They publish an extensive catalog which may have the kinds of tapes you'd like to sell. Tell Ellen Heffes I sent you!

Chapter 9

Products Of All Kinds

Try *Drop Shipping News* (Consolidated Marketing Services, Inc., P.O. Box 1361, New York, New York 10017). *Selling Direct Magazine* (Communication Channels, Inc., 6255 Barfield Road, Atlanta, GA 30328), and *American Drop-Shippers Directory* (World Wide Trade Service, Medina, WA 98039). These list thousands of product possibilities with addresses and follow-up information.

Catalogs

Catalogs are a good place to find products to distribute. At the very least the catalog publisher will forward a letter to the manufacturer who'll probably be very glad to hear from you. Here are some places to look for leads:

- *The $100 Billion Dollar Directories* (Publishers Services, 6318 Vesper Avenue, Van Nuys, CA 91411-2378). These books provide introductory information on 10,750 mail order companies. Write to Jack Erbe; tell him I told you to!

- *Mail Order Business Directory: A Complete Guide To The Mail Order Market* (B. Klein Publications, P.O. Box 8503, Coral Springs, FL 33065). Gives information on 10,000 mail order firms.

Using Your Resources

I want to stress that these are only some of the available resources, but these are some of the ones I regularly use and profit from. The way to approach these resources is intensely. While you are doing so, keep looking for new ones. Here's where I find my leads:

- newspaper business pages

- newsletters

- book pages and book publications

- at conferences in the exhibit areas

- through the package stuffers of other entrepreneurs

- from radio and television shows

- by reading my "junk" mail.

Keep a file of all the possibilities that exist in your field. And do, at the very least, write to the companies stocking this material and get complete information about books and other products that may be of interest. In this way you, like me, will come to have boxes and boxes of possibilities; there are always too many, never too few.

Now what?

Drop Shipping: When You Don't Want To Stock Materials And Products Yourself

I live and work in a condominium in the heart of a densely populated area. Space is at a premium. Many of you will be similarly situated. What then?

Easy. Try drop shipping. What this means is that you enter into marketing arrangements with manufacturers of products (books and other printed materials will be of especial interest) so that you can distribute information about the products but will not have to warehouse or actually ship them.

There are two ways of handling drop shipping:

1) distributing literature with the manufacturer's address

2) distributing literature with your address.

Chapter 9

In the past, I was keener on the first alternative than I am today. What this means is that the manufacturer (be he a publisher or whatever) will provide you with some quantity of flyers (250 is a good opening number) of the kind he customarily uses. You simply initial these flyers. Each month the manufacturer reports back to you how many items were sold and pays you your percentage.

Frankly this doesn't work as well as it might. Sadly, while many manufacturers are only too willing to have you distribute their materials in this way all too many are not as scrupulous about properly accounting for sales you have stimulated. Moreover there is no way to check. See for yourself. If you are offering a program and want to distribute information to participants, contact a manufacturer from one of the sources named and propose this relationship. If you don't get any response after 250 pieces are distributed, don't do it again.

How much should you be paid? Manufacturers have fairly well defined dealer payment schedules, but here are some guidelines. For books, don't accept less than 40% of the retail price and try to get 50%. This is fairly standard although major publishers may not want to grant so much. Similarly on newsletters, you should be able to get 50% of the sale price. Your product return will vary by category and will range between 20-50%.

Personally I am not undertaking any more of these arrangements, for the reasons stated above. I'm using the following one instead.

Distributing Literature With Your Address

If you want to be sure that you are properly credited for all orders, have them returned directly to you. The only variable in this case is who will bear the cost of printing the literature. I think my way of handling this problem is typical.

For each of the books I print, I develop a standard advertising form. (See samples, page 280.) I make this form available to vendors nationwide (including, don't forget, you!) who can insert their name and address and print from the copy. In these situations I give a 50% discount.

Keep in mind that the advantage of drop shipping is that there is a very limited expense on your part. Take my own case, for instance. For about $20 you can have 1000 flyers printed with your own name and address. Two sales of one of my $30 items and you've more than broken even and the rest that comes in is profit! Yes, drop shipping makes a lot of sense on the talk circuit and as you attend conferences, conventions, &c.

Note: it should go without saying that each book published in this country should have such an advertising form developed by its publisher. Most publishers however make no attempt to sign up vendors and get information about their products into the hands of prospective buyers through this very cost effective method. As you come to develop your own books and materials, don't make this mistake. As soon as you start writing your material, develop the advertising format to go with it so that even before your material is published you can begin to draw revenue from it.

Stocking Materials Yourself

Drop shipping works very well where you don't wish to carry any more than a product sample with you to a workshop. I use it with several items which help people establish a successful consulting business or any one of my other programs, but I never bring more than a single sample. There is, of course, sales information for everyone present. This is a fine way of earning extra money from those participating in your programs and assisting them with problems that are likely to arise in achieving success through your methods. Rest assured that only a fraction of those attending will follow up this material. Thus you will surely want to enter into relationships with producers so that their products will be written right into your program. This is particularly true with books and other written materials.

All publishers are equipped with a representative who handles what are called "special sales," that is sales outside the traditional bookstores. If you discover a book that you want to use as your text, the best way to proceed is to call the special sales representative and discuss your program. This person will want to know the following information:

- How many books will you need?

- How many are certain sales?

Chapter 9

- How often will you be doing this program and what kinds of sales can you project over, say, the next six months?

- What kind of credit have you got? (Expect to be asked for credit references and to be asked to fill out a credit application.)

The best way of approaching this situation is to identify the special sales representative and write a letter dealing with all these points. (See samples, page 282.) Most publishers in a situation where you are selling under 50 books (the numbers vary with each company) will want to give you only a 10-30% discount. Stand firm and ask for at least 40% (you want 50%, remember). 40% is the standard discount they give bookstores and you should at least insist on that. Moreover, if you are moving more than 50 books, you must remember that this is probably a sizable number for this title (unless it's a *New York Times* Bestseller). The only real question that needs answering is who pays the freight. Best answer: probably you! You will pay freight both to the seminar site and back to the publisher if you don't sell all the books. Fortunately with both UPS and special fourth class (book rate) U.S. post rate, this need not be excessive. Still, it reduces your profits.

One of the problems working with publishers is that they generally need to know 4 to 6 weeks in advance how many books you're going to need. I guarantee you that at that point you are almost never likely to know. In the continuing education world, you won't know until the program actually takes place just how many people you're going to need materials for. This makes dealing with the major publishers tricky and in the beginning you are certain to be over generous in the number of books you order.

Questions That May Arise

If you are dealing with a college, you can rest assured that they may be aggravated if they know that you are profiting from the sale of the text. This is because in ordinary cases text sales are handled through their regular bookstore which is probably getting a 40% discount (or less if it's a regular, high volume text book. Publishers give these what are called "short discounts.") The bookstore is losing profit because of you and you can expect the college's representatives to be irritated and to perhaps say so.

This is your case: Say that your availability is linked to receiving a certain amount of compensation. That this compensation can be outright (lecture honorarium) or a mixture of honorarium plus book sales. That you have selected the latter method because the book is necessary and the payment is direct from participants. If the sponsor remains adamant, you have two choices:

- Either you can delete the materials (thus depriving yourself of some of your profit), or

- You can ask for an increased honorarium to compensate for the loss.

It would be a mistake to delete the materials. If you have made the decision that they would be beneficial to participants, stand fast. You are the expert and the program planners in every case should defer to your professional standing and expertise. After all, that's why they've hired you.

Remember: most program planners have in their own mind a figure for speaker payment which they won't raise. They know that speakers, particularly on technical subjects, are very likely to need materials. Your point is this: as an expert in the field, you should be compensated for knowing which materials to use as well as for knowing how to present the overall program. Regrettably, though this is a perfectly reasonable position, you can expect many sponsors to cavil about it. Most are not earning princely wages and there is a built-in jealousy when they see you profiting as a double dipper.

Once you do get the book adopted, make sure that it's mentioned in the course description as a desirable extra and don't forget to give its retail value.

Something To Avoid

You will come up against program planners who will not budge on letting you sell materials as part of the course. Instead, they'll suggest that you sell them on the day of the program. Their ostensible reason will be keeping the cost of the program down to a reasonable level. Don't get caught in this snare.

Chapter 9

I know from experience that people would rather pay a higher fee on a one-time basis and be assured of getting the material they need (remember: you're the expert and you've said so) than to be harangued and harassed on the day of the program to buy. Besides, this kind of huckstering is detrimental to your image.

Now to be sure, I have to do this and you'll probably have to do it, too. The time to do it is with your own materials, those you've written, not with other people's. There is much less validity and more question when you are selling the materials of others than there is when you're selling your own.

Thus if you can't get the materials included as part of a program package, inform the program planner that you just won't be able to include them at all because the alternative is not consistent with the image you wish to present and that the participants will be missing important information. In such circumstances, make sure you impress upon the program planner just what effect their mindless ukase will have. I feel it my obligation to make them feel as guilty as I can.

Your Profit

How much will you make by following these various scenarios. Let me share my experience with you.

- Consider a drop ship agreement with a manufacturer who supplies you with literature which you initial. You'll get a 0.5-1% return if you have a sample present and clearly state why your audience needs this material.

- A drop ship agreement with a company in which you are given an advertising format into which you insert your name and address. You will do better with this arrangement. Expect anywhere from a 2-10% return depending on the clarity of your presentation and the product's ability to solve a perceived need of the audience. You will, of course, need a sample of the product on hand.

- Seller relationship with manufacturer where book or other product is available for all participants but not included in the price. If you can add key sections from this book to your presentation, charts, graphs, documents, forms, &c., and are willing to talk about these charts, &c., while a significant fraction of the participants doesn't have the book in front of them, you'll sell 50-75% of the participants.

Note: in the case where the book is not included in the course fee, to minimize your problems state in the catalog or brochure that that book is the course text and that it will be available for purchase on the day of the program. State the cost. Consider giving a 10% discount. Your sales will improve.

- Seller relationship with manufacturer where book or other product is available to all participants as part of the program price. 100% sales. In this case, make sure you actually use the book or other materials during the program. Otherwise, the participants will rightly feel that they have been pressured into buying something which is not after all very important.

Before we leave this section, I'd like to run some numbers by you.

Let's say that you have managed to persuade the program planner that a text not written by you is necessary in your program and that you have persuaded the publisher to give you a 40% discount. The book sells for $17.95 (a typical price). You are therefore buying them for $10.77 plus shipping. The program planner urges you to sell them at a 10% discount to increase the desirability of the program. You therefore sell them to participants for a profit of $5.39. In a program of 25 people you have thus grossed $134.75. Not bad, but not great either when you consider the:

- time you spent dealing with the special sales representative,

- dickering with the program planner,

- cost of returning unsold books.

Keep these numbers in mind as we move into the next section, and I think you'll end up at the same place as I am.

Chapter 9

Mainstream Publishing

This is not, fortunately, the time or place to tell you all that you need to know about how to publish your book with a mainstream publisher. For that there are two very good books already available from authors I know and can recommend to you:

- *How To Get Happily Published: A Complete And Candid Guide* by Judith Appelbaum and Nancy Evans. A New American Library paperback, this book is must reading for the aspiring writer or self-publisher.

- *A Writer's Guide To Book Publishing* by Rickard Balkin. A Hawthorn/Dutton paperback. If you want to publish a book with a mainstream house, I earnestly suggest you read this book.

Without question these are probably three of the most knowledgeable authorities on the matter of getting published. Another source is Leonard Shatzkin's book *In Cold Type: Overcoming The Book Crisis* (Houghton Mifflin). This book is a horrifying indictment of the way books are marketed and is enough to discourage even the most sanguine author. I must confess that I was depressed by it for days afterwards not least because I know the man is accurate and his unerring judgment about the publishing industry.

I do not intend to duplicate the books or arguments of these distinguished authorities. But let me say this: if you are going to profit on the talk circuit, you are going to need your own products, principally written ones. This leaves you with three options:

- Distributing other people's materials. This is a fine ancillary activity but is not recommended as your main related profit center for reasons which should by now be apparent.

- Publishing with a mainstream house.

- Creating your own publishing business.

Hints About Mainstream Publishing

I have published with mainstream publishers in both this country and the United Kingdom; my experiences were not entirely happy or in any way atypical. If you are going to publish with a mainstream house understand the following:

- Whatever the publisher says, you are going to have to become your book's principal marketing agent and make a substantial commitment in terms of time and resources to its success.

- If you leave your book to succeed or fail just in the bookstore market, the odds are that it will fail. As Leonard Shatzkin emphatically points out, only 2% of books remain in bookstores for more than 11 months. The rest are returned or remaindered or both. In either case, you, the author, lose. Thus you must be alert to the special sales situations, which, of course, gets us right back to the talk circuit.

If you intend to publish a book with a mainstream publishing house, you'll make your money in most cases on the talk circuit through the sale of books to workshop participants and the people attending the conferences and workshops at which you speak. Thus it's very important that you take a close look at the section of your publishing contract detailing the cost at which you can buy books from the publisher. You'll want to buy them for at least 40% off and over a certain minimum quantity, say 100, for a straight 50% discount.

Assuming you do this, let's go back to the example above where you were distributing someone else's book that retailed for $17.95. Let's now assume that this is your own title. In this case assuming a 40% discount (which is what you'll probably be forced to accept if you are a one or two book author), you'll be buying books for $10.77 as before. But in this case you'll also be getting a 10% royalty on the retail price (insist on this! not on the wholesale price) which amounts to an additional $1.80. Now you can feel better about offering that 10% discount which the program planner wants. Moreover the program planner is likely to put up less resistance against this title seeing that it's your book and you really are the expert you claim to be.

Chapter 9

On the sale of 25 copies (excluding freight costs which are an expense to you), you'll gross $134.75 plus your royalty of $45, a nicer return for you. One thing you should know about this royalty, however: in the ordinary publishing contract the publisher retains about 15% of gross sales against possible bookstore returns. Make sure in your contract that this 15% is not withheld on your special sales. These books are nonreturnable after all from buyers who have probably written in them. The full amount of special sales income should be paid to you each 6 months when the publisher pays your royalties.

Other Advantages To You With A Mainstream Publisher

Remember: most books will be remaindered at some point. When this happens, be sure to bid on your books. You will be able to buy your own books back from your publisher for between 10¢ and $1 apiece. Specify in your contract that if the books are remaindered, the publisher must give you the opportunity to make a bid on all remaining books, that you must be told the high bid (and that relevant papers concerning this bid must be shown you if you request) and that your bid of the same amount is to be preferred over a competitor's. The publisher loses nothing in this scenario and your ability to get these books is affirmed.

Just because a publisher is remaindering books doesn't for a moment mean that you have to lower the price of the book unless, of course, a significant number of copies has been sold to a remaindering house which will surely offer the books for a deep discount from their original price.

One mistake that authors make who buy their own remaindered books is to sell them at a deep discount. If the information has gone out of date, of course, perhaps it would be better not to buy them at all. But if the material is current, just give a courtesy discount of 10% or so, not more. If you give more you'll be lowering the value of the information in the eye of the buyer.

One More Benefit

At some point, most books go out of print altogether. This is a golden opportunity for you. Again, if your information remains current make sure that you have the opportunity to get the rights to your book back along with the publishing plates. Thus you can print from these yourself without incurring the high costs of typesetting. In this situation, you can change the frontispiece and launch your own publishing company. Make sure that this right is in your contract. Some unscrupulous publishers may claim that your book remains in print so long as there are just a handful of books available. To forestall this development, specify in the contract that the book shall be considered out of print as soon as on-hand stock drops below 100 copies and no further printing is scheduled or contemplated within 2-3 months. At that time, all rights revert to you, the author.

Note: try to persuade the publisher to draw up a standard 8½×11 inch advertising format sheet out of available advertising funds which you can print from and use on the lecture circuit. The cost of this is not high and the benefit to you can be great. When you are asked to give a lecture to a large audience, for instance, or when you are attending a trade or professional conference just as a participant, it won't be possible for you to carry sufficient numbers of your book for everyone much less to insure that they have to buy them. Thus you need just such a form for promotional purposes, to insure that all the people you come in contact with at least leave with basic information about your book.

Sadly, when you sign on with a regular publisher, you won't be able to sign up your own vendors; the profit margin just isn't there. Your vendors, remember, will need at least a 40% discount; individuals who are wholesalers buying from wholesalers will wish to buy books with a 75-80% discount. Only the original publisher can offer this kind of discount and expect to make even the slightest profit. This of course is just one of the several reasons why, ultimately, I advise you to become your own publisher.

Self-Publishing And The Talk Circuit

I am very much a believer in self-publishing and there are good sound economic reasons for my enthusiasm. I don't want to gild the lily, however; self-publishing is not for everyone. You can't make it work unless you are prepared entirely to take charge of your project and devote a significant amount of time to your marketing efforts. The bulk of these marketing efforts lie outside this book, but your talk circuit special sales do not. Such sales will help insure not only the profitability of your book but also the profitability of your talk appearances.

Chapter 9

In this section, as in other sections of **MONEY TALKS**, I am going to advocate a considered, conservative approach to the subject of publishing, one which will allow you to become familiar with the different aspects of publishing without plunging in with a major capital investment and the prospect of loss and confusion. Before you deviate from this plan, make sure you have very good reason for thinking a more aggressive course will pay off and not just cause problems.

In this regard, there are really three possible alternatives you can consider:

- booklets

- spiral bound workbooks

- perfect bound books.

Booklets

In the interest of fairness, I should say that I skipped this stage and that I have not myself produced any booklets. The reason is clear: while demanding limited capital and with a low per unit cost, the profit on these booklets is not substantial for most people. This is not to say that some people don't profit handsomely from the genre, they do. But for most people booklets are not a substantial profit center.

Still, there are other reasons for doing them:

- They are inexpensive. You cannot lose very much!

- You can learn the art and craft of publishing.

- You can begin with a booklet on your topic and develop it through the other stages until it becomes a perfect bound book. Thus you can raise some or all of the money you need for the next stage of your developing publishing empire through the sale of current product. This is an attractive advantage of starting small.

- You can use a booklet as a means of unabashed promotion with the media.

- Booklets can provide you with inexpensive inducements to attract workshop participants or can be included among course materials allowing you to be paid as part of gross revenues.

- Booklets can be marketed in other ways and provide you with ancillary income.

- Booklets do not usually present the storage problems that books do.

- Booklets are easier to update and revise than books thereby allowing you to keep your information current.

The negatives include the following:

- While booklets can sell for many times their actual cost, you have to sell thousands of them to make any substantial profit. In most cases this is unlikely to take place.

- Booklets do not provide you with the standing and status that a book does.

- Booklets cannot be marketed through bookstores and do not provide a sufficient margin of profit for other forms of cooperative marketing.

Still, if you understand that booklets and other simple information formats have their place in the publishing pyramid, that they may be the right place for you to begin when you're learning and that they can produce a financial profit, you may very well wish to produce one or two.

Chapter 9

Writing And Producing Your Booklet

By now it should be clear that the Problem Solving Process format enables you to organize all your booklet material and assist you in quickly writing your booklet. Booklets tend to take their authors too long to write and too often suffer from a lack of form.

Your reader should feel that you have an understanding of his problem and his objectives and that, under your guidance, he is progressing through a series of firm steps towards the solution he needs to achieve success. This is the benefit of the Problem Solving Process; it produces just this feeling of surety in the reader and allows you to get through the necessary material in an expeditious manner.

How much material is enough? Your booklet should be as long as necessary to impart the information the reader needs to achieve a solution to the problem at hand but still short enough to be comfortably read in a single sitting.

Working this out in pages is something of an art. Thus before writing your booklet, check with your printer to see how many pages constitute a signature, that is a division of the booklet. The answer is usually 4 in a booklet, although it may be 8. Thus booklets are ordinarily constructed in multiples of 4 or 8. You want to be sure that all the pages you are buying are in fact utilized and work for you. Make sure, then, that the following items are included along with your text:

- title page with your name, address and follow-up telephone number

- order page for additional copies

- page promoting your workshops and other talk programs. Ask people to write to you to get information on the nearest program in their area or to book you as a speaker.

- information about other booklets or books you have written or may be producing.

Ordinarily you'll still have extra space available. You may wish to use some clip on art to fill part of it. You know the kind: pictures of (usually Victorian) ladies and gentlemen, words, odd expressions, &c, that can be plugged into your text. I detest this clip art but many, many people like it. Moreover the Dover catalog I've already cited is free and if you're going to produce any kind of publication, it's a good idea to keep it on hand.

Cost, Profit

Just how much you'll have to pay will be determined by:

- the number of pages

- the weight of the paper

- the size of the booklet (5½" × 8½" or 8½" × 11" being common formats)

- the number of copies.

Personally, I prefer 8½ by 11 inch booklets because they are easier to annotate and a serious reader taking up a booklet wants to use it as a tool to achieve his objectives, which usually means using it for notes, &c.

More important is the number of copies to be printed. Don't print too many. The per item cost will drop, of course, the more you print and so your printer will try to beguile you into running a larger order. You may also be dazzled with the raw numbers of potential buyers in the universe who should have your booklet and probably can't live without it.

Just take a breath and pause awhile. Products are difficult to sell and need constant maintenance, marketing and attention. A good rule of thumb is this: don't print more booklets (or anything else for that matter!) than you can expect to sell in a year. Since you are probably not yet addressing large audiences regularly, I wouldn't advise you to print any more than 500 booklets to begin. This number costs more, to be sure, on a per unit basis but is easy to store, inexpensive to purchase and still allows you to make a profit.

Chapter 9

How Much Should You Sell Them For?

Booklets should be inexpensively priced. That's one of their attractions to the buyer.

Here is a suggested price range:

    8-16 pages $5-6
    17-48 pages $8-12
    49-65 pages $15-18

Those of you who are familiar with the booklet business may cavil a bit at these prices. I know that many booklets of the latter length are going for $20 nowadays or more, depending on the value of the information offered.

My rule of thumb for pricing all items goes like this: what is the disproportionate benefit compared to fee? If you have packed your booklet with immediately usable information including hard-to-get names, addresses, telephone numbers, follow-up information and material that the reader can use to profit from — now! — then you can afford to charge more if and only if you are aiming at an upscale audience. In this connection, I recently paid $25 for an 8 page type-written booklet that had 200 names and telephone numbers I could use in my business. In point of fact I had about 150 of them already but getting the remainder was worth it. Still, there's no way the publisher of this booklet is going to sell 500 copies a year, and I doubt whether he even keeps more than 100 is stock. Remember, however, that most booklets have low prices, under $5.

Note: for further information on producing booklets with information on writing, production and marketing contact J.E. Barnes, author of *How To Make Money Writing & Selling Simple Information*, RR #1-1434, Fort Ann, New York 12827. Tell Jay I sent you!

Spiral Bound Workbooks

I myself launched my own publishing arm with spiral bound (gbc binder) workbooks which were originally designed for clients and the talk circuit. I can recommend this form to you, although it, too, has some drawbacks.

- Such workbooks need not be typeset. They can, like booklets, be typewritten and offset print. This saves you money.

- The typewriting gives the information that "hot off the presses" look which can be a definite sales advantage.

- The workbook format allows you easily to update and rearrange your materials as the need arises.

- Your workbook will lie flat and thus be easy for readers and workshop participants to take notes in.

- Because the information suggests timeliness, it is easier to set the price according to my disproportionate benefit rule.

- Workbooks are relatively easy to store.

Here are the drawbacks:

- While workbooks are perfectly acceptable in talk program settings, you are probably cutting yourself out of other marketing situations particularly bookstores. The spiral spine does not allow for the title to be printed on the side and thus bookstores are forced to stock the book face forward. This is fine from your point of view, but from theirs it takes too much space. Also the spine does not allow for flat stacking.

- Outside reviewers and publications don't like this format. It doesn't look like a "real" book to them, damn their souls!

Still, given that your current purpose is to make more profit from the talk circuit, there are many advantages. Until such time as you wish to promote your book to other, outside sources this may be the way to take. I certainly found it so when I was starting out in self-publishing.

Chapter 9

Back in 1980 after publishing with both a major English publisher and an American mainstream house, I self-published my first book **DEVELOPMENT TODAY: A GUIDE FOR NONPROFIT OGRANIZATIONS**. It was designed as I've said for clients and workshops, and it worked very well. The book has since gone into the next stage of development (discussed below) but for someone who doesn't know the ropes this is a fine way of beginning and a relatively inexpensive one.

Writing And Producing Workbooks

I hope I don't need to say again that by following the Problem Solving Process format, you will be easily able to arrange your material and produce your book.

The key to writing anything, and particularly a more major project like this one, is to set yourself a quota each day and work hard to reach it. You will find that a good length for a workbook is from 100 to 200 pages typewritten, double spaced. This is between 35,000-70,000 words.

You should strive to produce between 500 and 1000 words each day using the Problem Solving Process format. If you do this you'll have a completed first draft in between 2 to 4 months.

Pack this workbook with exactly the kinds of information you find in my books, for they are models of their type:

- complete follow up information

- documents

- letters

- contracts

- memoranda

- marketing materials.

In short, include all the things that the person striving to solve the problem being addressed needs to do. The more "tricks of the trade" oriented your materials are, the better. As you succeed in reaching this objective, then you are entitled to use the Disproportionate Benefit Compared to Price standard and charge accordingly. I put a price tag of $24.95 on my typewritten offset print **DEVELOPMENT TODAY** (which then had 200 pages) because at the time it was first published the Reagan Administration (then in the process of formation) was announcing the first of its series of budget cuts, many of which were going to be adversely affecting nonprofit organizations. These organizations would pay what may seem a lot for a paperback book because it was just a drop in the bucket compared to their need for solving their funding problems. This book has contined to sell well each year since, and I anticipate that it will be doing so 50 years hence.

The availability of this kind of workbook will benefit you in several ways:

- If it's not available in bookstores, you can promote this fact and so attract individuals to your workshops. "You get a copy of **DEVELOPMENT TODAY: A GUIDE FOR NONPROFIT ORGANIZATIONS** when you attend this program. Not available in bookstores, this book by Dr. Lant contains all you need to know to raise funds now from individuals, corporations and foundations."

- It enhances your standing as the expert. The mere existence of this product helps in marketing you to program planners. Don't be shy about sending this workbook to those who are considering booking you as a speaker. It is proof that you are the expert you say you are, that you have considered the problem that your audience has, and that you know what to do about it.

- It creates a new profit center for you. You can now be paid as both lecturer and more significantly from the materials fee. While you make extra amounts of money, of course, from distributing other people's books and from those produced for you by mainline publishers and from your own booklets, a self-published workbook can significantly enhance your profit.

Chapter 9

Here are some numbers:

Let's go back to our previous example with a workshop of 25 people. Whereas the traditional commercial publisher was charging $17.95, you should consider charging more depending on the disproportionate value of the information compared to the price. I would raise the cost of the book in most cases to at least $24.95 as you see I did with **DEVELOPMENT TODAY.**

Using this illustration, here is the problem you face. Either the program planner can pay the full $24.95 as part of the materials fee, or he cannot. His thinking will involve his ability to add this cost to the overall price of the program and still remain competitive in his area. To this end, you have to convince the program planner that the book itself — demonstrating your standing as an expert and giving people access to material which will help them solve their problems — will in fact make the course that much more popular and so justify the higher price. If the program planner buys this argument, which is a valid and reasonable one, you have the extra benefit that now your products as well as the workshop are being marketed through the sponsor's promotional information and that you are likely to sell your material to those who cannot attend the program and so additionally profit. To handle this likely eventuality, make sure that all such calls are passed on to you. The best way to handle this is to have the program planning staff get the name, address and telephone number of this individual and pass them along to you. Your rationale can be that you'll attempt to sell the individual on attending the program. Unfortunately, most program planners will claim that they are too pressed to give the matter this kind of attention and that the best they can do is give out your telephone number and hope that the possible buyer does in fact call you. At least insist upon this.

Let's look at two possibilities:

- The program planner cannot pay you full price.

- He can.

He cannot...

Remember most program planners have a distinct nonprofit mentality: they are not entrepreneurs and they like getting things for free. This is insidious, of course, as you try to make money. You need to resist this curious thinking in as pleasant but forceful a way as possible. Even so, the program planners may insist for a variety of reasons on a discount ranging from 20 to 50%. Let's assume in this instance they get a 40% discount, the same as a publisher would give a bookstore.

You would be selling the books to the sponsor for $14.97 each for a gross of $374.25. Even this is a much healthier return than you get in the other situations.

He can...

Of course, if you get full price, $24.95, you'd gross $623.75, a very nice addition to your regular speaking fee. Keep these figures in mind!

Expenses

Of course, it costs money to make this money and the determining question is always: how much and is it worth it to expend this sum?

Even in a worst case scenario it shouldn't cost you more than $2-2.50 per unit to produce 500 copies of a 200 page typewritten offset printed book. This will also include your cover. This means that you'll get 500 books for a maximum cost of $1250 which in turn means that you'll need two workshops of 25 people each with the books included and fully paid for to pay this bill. This objective shouldn't be difficult to reach following the techniques of this book.

Chapter 9

The Ultimate: Perfect Bound Books

There is, I confess, something thrilling about writing and publishing your own perfect bound book that a mere spiral bound workbook can never equal. Most people have a very fixed idea in mind of what constitutes a "book." The spiral bound format doesn't quite qualify. But as with every other format there are pros and cons about this kind of book and before you decide to go ahead with this format you should have considered all of them very, very closely.

The Negatives

Perfect bound books are expensive. There's no way around that. These books need to be typeset which is in itself a major expenditure. Typesetting a book of this length, for example, can easily run $5000. Then, of course, there is the cost of the print run itself and the storage. You'll want to run at least 2000 books and you won't be able to fit this many books in your closets. Printing 2000 copies of a book this size will result in a per unit cost of between $3.50-4.50. Storage will run about $50 to $100 per month if you have to rent it commercially.

Given these costs you must set your pricetag realistically. Many books on the subject of self-publishing suggest that the retail cost of the book should run 4 to 5 times as much as its production price. Does this number make sense? Say that your typesetting cost is $4000 and you get a per unit cost of $4 (both reasonable figures) and that you print 2000 copies. This is an outright expenditure of $12,000 and this does not include the artist's fee for your cover. If you charge $16 per book, your may imagine that you could conceivably gross $32,000, but this is extremely unlikely. Remember: you will often have to give discounts yourself ranging up to 75-80% if you sell to vendors who sell to wholesalers and certainly involving 40% if you sell to bookstores. Even continuing educators, as we've seen, will often want a discount and if you sell direct at your programs, sales strategy often necessitates at least a 10% discount even there.

Most likely, therefore, you'll be grossing about $18,000 on this run. There'll be a profit, therefore, and a better one than if you left your money in a savings account, but you'll have to work for it!

These numbers suggest several things, then:

1) You need larger print runs and lower per unit costs, and

2) A higher retail price along the lines of my Disproportionate Benefit Compared to Fee Rule.

Unless you are prepared to consider both these aspects of the equation, you are probably better off remaining with a typewritten, offset print spiral bound book.

There is another negative in the perfect bound book situation which you ought to consider. When I originally published **THE CONSULTANT'S KIT**, it came out in a spiral bound workbook format and sold for $24.95. It sold very, very well, better in fact than I thought a book like that would. No fool I, I turned the book into a typeset perfect bound book and sold it for $30.

Several perceptive individuals urged me to be careful before I did this. The book originally had the look of *samisdat* literature, the kind of timely, informative material that looked like it was smuggled out of a gulag to an expectant world. People therefore didn't mind the mistakes in the typescript (and there were plenty!) because the material had the look and feel of authenticity, hence worth the price. It was big, thick, ungainly, and had the feel of real important stuff about it.

With the typeset version of any book, this feeling necessarily disappears. You are automatically competing against the high gloss books published by the major publishers and this is difficult to do. They have the human and financial resources that you don't have and a deep fund of expertise that as a beginner you just can't match. Fortunately, in the case of **THE CONSULTANT'S KIT** it hasn't seemed to matter; more than 18,000 copies have been sold.

Still, you need to consider whether by changing your format you will make up the increased expenditures with your book by opening up new markets either on the talk circuit or through bookstores and special sales. If you do not or cannot spend the time it takes to open these markets (and it is time consuming at first, not least because you have to learn the different aspects of the business that each entails), then stick with the typewritten offset print version. It can be much, much more profitable and much less aggravating for you.

Chapter 9

By the same token, be aware that perfect bound books do have advantages:

- They lie flat whereas spiral bound books are difficult to stack and store.

- They do open the possibility of many new markets including book store and catalog sales.

- If you are seeking outside press, reviewers and other writers will be more likely to regard this product as a "real book."

- They last longer.

- They look visually more interesting.

As you see, when you look carefully at the advantages of the perfect bound book, most pertain only to that moment when you want to move into new market situations that demand a certain kind of product. If you are concentrating on the advantages of the talk circuit, then you don't — at least for the moment — need to worry about these.

One final thought: putting your material into a perfect bound book probably won't greatly affect your sales at a workshop or other program. Your expenditure will be greater, to be sure, but your sales through workshops will be about the same as with spiral bound offset printed workbooks.

Book Publishing And Marketing Resources For You

There is a very healthy literature about producing and marketing books. While I still see some significant gaps in this literature, at least now, having advised you on what kind of book to publish if you are going to confine your sales to the talk circuit and mail order, I have plugged one of them. The following books and people will help you with matters of writing, producing and marketing your books:

- Ad-Lib Publications, P.O. Box 1102, Fairfield, IA 52556. The very knowledgeable John Kremer publishes many helpful directories and guides for self-publishers including a list of 68 key resources about publishing and self-publishing. Write for his complete list of publications including *The Directory Of Short-Run Book Printers* which provides a superb list of book manufacturers. (800) 624-5893.

- *Book Marketing Handbook* by Nat G. Bodian published by R.R. Bowker. Volume one deals with tips and techniques and volume two weighs in with over 1,000 more of the same. These books are expensive and are written in a low-key academic manner, but they are chock full of useful pieces of marketing information. Don't get them, however, unless you're serious.

- *The Encyclopedia Of Self-Publishing: How To Successfully Write, Publish, Promote And Sell Your Own Work* by Marilyn & Tom Ross. Published by Communication Creativity, 5644 La Jolla Blvd., La Jolla, CA 92037, this is one of the two best books on self-publishing. Tom and Marilyn Ross are an amazing storehouse of good ideas and energy. Be sure to write for their catalog.

- *The Independent Publishing Network Report.* Published bi-monthly by Russ Von Hoelscher at P.O. Box 546, El Cajon, CA 92022, this informative newsletter offers subscribing small publishers profitable marketing and production advice. Like the Rosses, Russ Von Hoelscher is a stemwinder with a thousand good ideas and many, many self-published books. Sample copy, $2.00 postpaid.

- *The Self-Publishing Manual* by Dan Poynter, P.O. Box 4232-37, Santa Barbara, CA 93140-4232. Dan Poynter is the guru of the self-publishing field. Like me, he runs a one-man operation and thrives while doing it. Dan's advice is top-notch; I use it myself. What I like about reading it is the sheer joy of sharing in his exhilaration. It's infectious!

N.B. It goes without saying (or does it?) that if you want your books to get the right kind of publicity, you'll need **THE UNABASHED SELF-PROMOTER'S GUIDE**, too. Surely you've already placed your order by now?

Chapter 9

Some Final Words About Books

Whatever you decide to do, realize that your first edition will be a learning experience. Realize that you'll make mistakes and that these will be more embarrassing to you than to others. If the information you are dispensing is valuable, people will overlook the errors. I know this, and coming to realize it was one of the most eye-opening experiences of my life. Many people have been more than generous in the development of my own publishing business and, for the sake of the material which I have insisted on keeping timely, have been willing to overlook technical production flaws.

You, therefore, must keep your customers focused at all times on the value of the information, on the difficulty or indeed impossibility of getting it anywhere else, and of the benefit it will bring to their lives. If this information is as useful as you say it is, don't give your books away except to those who can provide you with a disproportionate benefit compared to the value of the gift, i.e., to reviewers, catalog publishers, continuing educators, &c. Anyone else should pay the going price for which you need make no apology. Learn this lesson now and act accordingly; it will save you a lot of aggravation later.

One Last Word

It should be clear to you now, patently apparent in fact, that you need written materials of your own to truly succeed on the talk circuit. It should also be quite clear that if you don't have them you will be severely limiting your ability to succeed. This suggests that you should get started today outlining your book, gathering information, always concentrating on the insider's material which is difficult to get elsewhere, and on drafting your chapters.

Set yourself a date by which you want to have your first draft completed and work assiduously to meet this important objective. As soon as this book is well underway, you'll then want to begin on the audio cassettes, your next talk circuit profit center.

Chapter 10

CASHING IN II: PRODUCING AND SELLING AUDIO CASSETTES

Books, of course, are dandy, but you'll also want to consider producing your own audio tapes, tapes, that is, of your dulcet tones and hard driving technical information. There's a good reason for this. There are now, surveys show, as many audio cassette players as there are homes in this country and about half the cars in the nation have them, too. What staggering persuasion potential! The profit potential is there, too, as you'll shortly see. By following the steps in this chapter you can begin to tap it.

When To Begin

Let me say this: there's no earthly reason for producing audio cassettes until you have the means of selling them. While producing cassettes offers its own peculiar challenges, as you'll see, the matter of sales and marketing is yet more pressing. Thus until such time as you are doing speaking engagements on a regular basis, there is no need to produce audio cassettes.

Moreover, you shouldn't produce cassettes until you are confident that the material you are disseminating truly meets the perceived needs of your audience. I hasten to add this does not mean that you need to offer a "perfect" product. Or that you need to have mastered every detail of your field. These are objectives towards which you should never cease to strive, but it is, I think, fatuous to wait for that which is probably unlikely ever to be achieved, namely flawless perfection. Instead, use the following observations to create a production process for yourself that will allow you to profit even as you continue to learn your craft.

Step I: On-Site Tapings

If you have followed the steps of this book, you'll shortly be profiting from continuing education workshops just as I do. These programs will draw anywhere from 15 to 100 people. They constitute as good a place as any to begin mastering the tape process.

I recommend buying one of the good but inexpensive portable tape recorders currently available. I myself use the Panasonic model no. RQ-330 which retails for about $49. You should begin carrying this recorder to your programs and taping them right from the start. In the beginning, you'll use the tapes to perfect your presentation and delivery. Note the number of times you pause, hunt for a fact, catch yourself saying distracting little phrases like "um" or, worse, "right." In the beginning of your relationship with tape, the purpose is clear: to improve yourself and your programs. Until such time as you begin to be a polished platform speaker and to disseminate usable information to the audience without jarring interruptions or graceless delivery, that's the way it should remain. Fortunately, however, the more speaking you do, the sooner you'll be on your way to profiting from the tapes themselves.

When you're ready to do so, announce at the beginning of your presentation that there will be no audience taping allowed. Some people will object to this, but these are individuals who do not realize that the resultant tapes constitute a different form of property from the right of attending the program itself. Some speakers allow people to tape the programs in return for a fee which is about 25% less than the cost of their own tapes, the difference being to compensate the individual taping for the cost of materials. This, I think, gets cumbersome and can be distracting if the individual taping places his machine near you and gets up from time to time to change tapes. It's better simply to produce a master.

Producing this master need not be complicated. I find, for instance, that the quality of my little Panasonic is excellent and remains so as copies are made from it. Here's how to handle this situation:

- Produce your program on C-90 cassettes. I find Maxell tape quite suitable. Understand that if you are using this length, you'll have to break every 45 minutes and change the tape.

- You can handle the timing quite simply. Get a watch with an alarm and also appoint someone from the audience to monitor the time. After a while, you'll develop a feel for lapsed time. Always stop at about 44 minutes so that you can add a line at the end of the tape, "Please go on to the next cassette." Or "Please turn this cassette over to side B."

Chapter 10

- The cassette recorder should be placed at the top of the podium where you will do most of your speaking. You'll have to find out using your individual machine how great its reach is and choreograph yourself accordingly. It is important, however, that you repeat all questions from the audience as these will otherwise not be heard on the tape.

If you are taping, determine the length and format of your program according to the requirements of the tape. If you are doing a complete day's program, for instance, try to arrange matters so that you produce 3 complete tapes, 45 minutes per side.

Pricing And Selling

The cost of reproducing tapes in small numbers is great. This will, therefore, affect your pricing. Figure on spending about $5 to reproduce a single 90 minute cassette and about $15 to reproduce the three cassettes mentioned above. This is steep. Real economies in production will not take place until you produce at least 100 of a single tape. Yet until you are sure you can move that many there's no point in making this kind of investment. Here, then, are some suggestions:

- Sell the tapes to those who are present for 50% of the cost of the workshop itself. Collect payment for them on the spot or send an invoice. If you bill for the cassettes, you'll find yourself in the banking business as you extend credit. Better to collect in full before reproducing them. Also find out what the freight charges are (packaging and shipping) and add this to the cost of the tapes.

- During the course of the day and as soon as you are sure that your recorder is working properly, distribute to all in attendance a special order form for your tapes. Give them an inducement to buy today, a special workshop price. Since those attending your workshop will probably retain this flyer, consider increasing the price if the order is not placed at the class.

Benefits Of This Approach

Many speakers rush to produce audio cassettes too early. They are drawn by the smell of profit, impelled by the prospect of celebrity. And, of course, they end up losing their money as stacks of tapes are unsold. Don't do this. My scheme has the following benefits:

- It's inexpensive. Unlike creating a professionally designed, edited and produced tape (such as I shall discuss shortly), this method allows you to begin without significant investment and allows for the possibility of a quick return on what you do invest.

- You can probably handle the taping (as well as the sales and fulfillment) yourself.

- Even if no one buys the tape (always a possibility, of course), you can still use it as a learning device and keep it available to send to program planners who may wish to book you.

- You can use it not only to perfect future programs but also to help you craft the script you'll probably need when at last you do decide to opt for a professional product.

There are, to be sure, some drawbacks, too.

- The tape will expose you warts and all. This means that any false starts, graceless language, jumbled sentences and all the other inelegancies that occur on the podium will be enshrined for all time. This is, of course, unfortunate.

- Reproduction costs are higher than they would be if you were producing en masse.

These two problems will be rectified when you move towards producing an entirely professional product. Before you do so, however, you'll probably arrive at an intervening plateau which should for some time prove adequate for your objectives. As you produce more and more programs and tape them, you'll find your remarks and presentation becoming ever more polished. At some point, you will therefore tape a program that will suffice for a time even if it has some minor flaws.

Chapter 10

Sell this program to bring in the capital you need to produce your professional product. I am a great believer in developing one's own capital whenever possible, earning the money you need to make your products better and better yet. What I've just been presenting in terms of audio cassettes will allow you to move steadily ahead without investing large amounts of your own money into the enterprise, surely a laudable means of handling the situation.

Trading Up

At some point, however, your atavistic American desire to improve things, to strive for the ultimate, to seek the perfect will seize you and that which is good will be jettisoned in hot pursuit of that you now deem better. This is what our culture is all about and you are not immune to it. In this context, it means you'll want to move ahead to producing an entirely professional tape product.

This, I confess, I have not yet done. I have so far been content to use the methods discussed above, although I am by no means immune to my nation's insistent thrust for improvement. Since I have not myself produced a professional cassette package, rather than discourse idly upon the matter, I sought out Bill Guthy of Cassette Productions to assist me with this section. Bill is one of the nation's leading authorities in the matter of producing professional cassette packages, and I commend him and his services to you in several places following. What follows in this book, therefore, is the result of Bill's quite natural desire to produce the finest in professional cassette productions matched against the profoundly thriftist leanings of a skinflint Yankee. You are left to make the decision about which course of action to follow.

Helping Yourself

Having tapes professionally produced costs money. Bill Guthy is right, however. Once the decision has been made to do it, it should be done right. And right usually costs more. That's why I think there are two things you can do to help yourself as a first step to working with any professional cassette production and packing firm: scripting and taping.

Scripting

I have mixed feelings about using a script while taping your audio cassettes. On the one hand, it's safe. You know what you're going to say; it's right in front of you. You've thought through your program and you know what follows in sequence. On the other hand, unless you've practiced, your delivery can sound stilted and unnatural which means, of course, that you'll turn off your listener and diminish future sales. Let's see what we can do about this situation.

The first decision you've got to make is the format you want. Here are your options:

- straight lecture

- question and answer

- snippets of a live program with audience interaction

- some mixture of the above.

Straight Lecture

In this format you, the expert, present what you've got to say in a straight lecture format. Hopefully you'll use my Conversational Accessible mode of access to your audience rather than some martinet style reminiscent of a Junker academy. The problem with this format is usually that the speaker doesn't vary his delivery often enough and hence ends up boring the listener. This is where much platform and radio experience comes in helpful. If you decide on a straight lecture style (which is, after all, perfectly acceptable given the right delivery) make sure you modulate your voice, vary the delivery, use emphasis and tonal punctuation to aid in the listener's access to your material. This is where my Conversational Accessible style comes in. In this situation you are carrying on a conversation with the listener and as in any personal communication of this kind, you vary your delivery with the importance of the material and the degree of emphasis you wish to impart. Try this. It isn't easy and demands practice. If you have no experience reading from a script, it is easy to lapse into a dull, even monotonal delivery which is fatal to your listener's understanding and your future ability to sell more programs.

Chapter 10

Question And Answer

This format will help you and the listener. Some people find it easier to "talk to" their audience if they have a friend or even a small audience in the room when they're taping. You can also achieve this effect using the Question and Answer format. Recruit a friend with an engaging voice (use someone of the opposite sex if possible for broadest audience identification) and script all the questions for this person.

If this individual and you have any chemistry at all, a natural conversational dialog will result which gives the tape an immediacy which is beneficial even if there are some flaws in the product. It's important to engage your listener and sweep him into your world. The degree of connection between the questioner and you will help achieve this result.

Snippets Of Live Programs

Often you can realize the desired level of immediacy by using snippets of your previous programs. The more programs you've taped, the better off you are. These can be most useful for live applause and other audience responses and for a level of excitement and enthusiasm that usually only results when you are engaged with your auditors. Granted, the questions you are asked probably won't make it onto your tape, but you can always get a friend to reask them and use the answers you've already got.

My own preference is for either the first or second of these options. Customarily my workshop programs consist of 6 to 8 hours of straight lecture. I am therefore used to exciting an audience and engaging them. Until you are comfortable that you, too, can do the same, option 2, the Question and Answer format, probably makes the most sense.

Producing Your Script

Your script, need I say it?, should follow the several steps of the Problem Solving Process. This is yet another instance where this skeleton rightly informs your material. If you are using a C-90 cassette, your script should be about 42 to 43 minutes long. To get an idea of how many pages of script that entails, simply read from any book and count the words per minute. Always prepare a little more, since people have a natural tendency (which needs to be discouraged) to read a script more quickly than they would ordinarily talk it through. The extra two or three minutes should be divided for an introduction at the beginning and a short "go on to the next cassette" at the end. The final cassette should leave a longer pause for complete order information and any other particulars about you and your business that you want to include. (Don't forget your address and telephone number!)

If you are producing a cassette with a Question and Answer format, prepare three copies of the script, one each for you and your questioner and the third for the engineer who is taping you.

Generating The Master Tape

Up to now, there have been minimal costs to you. Now, however, the expenses begin to mount up. Because they do, you should have already given serious consideration to how you are going to sell the resulting product. Assuming you know how you're going to do that, how you're going to profit, then you can look at all the following expenses as a necessary and sensible investment. Otherwise, think again and wait until you're ready.

The first thing you're going to need to do is rent a studio for the taping. Check the Yellow Pages under "Recording Service, Sound and Video" or "taping." An in-studio session makes more sense than a live audience taping since under ordinary circumstances, you'll have more control in the studio and the resulting tape will need less editing. This, of course, saves you money.

In-studio time will cost you between $30 and $40 an hour. You should plan on being in the studio for two hours for every hour of finished program time. This will naturally vary with your preparation and polish. What you are paying for is the use of the studio and its engineer.

In working with the studio, plan to have your remarks recorded directly on to a ¼" open reel recording in one direction only. This provides better quality and allows you to go directly into the editing process without any additional transfers. Moreover, make sure that the engineer records your session with simultaneous cassettes. This will cost slightly more but you'll have cassette copies to listen to right away without the additional studio cost of reel-to-cassette transfer. Remember: when recording directly to cassette only, an additional "generation" or transfer is required to go to open-reel format for editing. You will need to use one 7" tape for each thirty minutes of recording at a cost of between $10 to $15 per tape.

Chapter 10

Editing The Master Tape

Once you've got the master tape, it's time to edit it. This is not a job you'll want to do yourself. This is the moment to find a company which can provide you with professional assistance. In this connection, I recommend Bill Guthy's Cassette Productions, 5796 Martin Rd., Irwindale, CA 91706-6299 (818) 969-6881. His is one of the few companies in the nation offering the complete services you need including taping, editing, and the production of professional cassette packages. Other suggestions are to be found in Dottie Walter's already-cited newsletter *Sharing Ideas*.

There are three kinds of editing: basic, perfect, and at the editor's discretion. Basic simply means removing the obvious imperfections from the tape, your stumblings, mistakes, and long pauses. Perfect means just that: editing for the flawless product. And, of course, editor's discretion suggests leaving the job to a pro after you've set certain guidelines. Of these, I suggest either the first or third. Leave perfection to one side, at least for now.

No doubt cost will influence your decision. You should know, then, that it takes between two and four hours of editing for each hour of finished material. Editing costs between $20 and $30 per hour, and you'll be liable to an extra charge if your original recording was done on a cassette. In this case, you should also expect to pay a transfer charge to a ¼" open reel of between $20 and $30 per hour.

You can make the editing job much easier (and hence less expensive) by working in the controlled environment of the studio. There you can without undue effort correct the mistakes that result even while reading from a script. If you notice the mistake, simply continue recording. Say "correction" before carrying on to repeat the same point. Moreover, make sure the engineer has been instructed to point out mistakes to you including any energy or voice level reduction. It is very difficult to sustain your voice over many hours unless you have considerable platform experience. But it's important for the listener to notice no dropping of your energy. Note: in correcting mistakes, do not back up the tape and record over previous remarks. You will induce extra noise and continuity problems by doing so. Just provide a signal to the editor and carry on.

Sweetening The Master

The editing process of the main program having been completed, you need to decide whether you want to add music and special effects, professional voice narrations and equalization to your program. These polish your product. Do you, however, really need to use them?

Music

Music, of course, can add a certain flair to your program. You may use it to introduce sections of your remarks or the tape as a whole or to provide what is called a "music bed" such as background sounds for relaxation and hypnosis programs.

Here are the considerations in using music:

- You may have to hire someone to make a music search for you to find out just the kind of thing to complement your program. Such searches cost between $20 and $30 per hour.

- You may very well have to license the rights to the music so as to be able to use it. This costs between $95 and $130 per master.

All these problems apply, too, to the use of special effects. One other problem is also applicable. Don't add canned laughter or applause to your program. It revolts people. An editor can use something from your own tapes and it'll sound more natural.

Chapter 10

Professional Voice Narration

From your script a professional voice talent generally on staff or on call at a recording studio can introduce you and your program at the beginning of tape one, side A. He can also provide "tape turnover" and "go to the next tape" statements plus what's called an "outro" at the conclusion of your program. This provides the listener with information about your other products and services and how to get in touch with you. A professional voice can also supply the necessary bridge between segments of your program or between studio and "live" material.

There are two charges to consider in connection with professional voice narration: the professional himself will cost between $40 and $60 per hour with a one hour minimum. You'll also have the usual charges for the recording engineer, equipment and materials as previously supplied.

Equalization

Equalization is a process of sound enhancement. It along with such signal processing devices as limiters, compressor-expanders and filters can remove excess bass and boominess and improve your signal-to-noise ratio thereby improving the quality of your recording. If you have recorded in a professional studio, you'll probably not need to worry about this; if your program has been done before a live audience, you probably will in which case you'll again be paying the usual studio charges.

Do you want these enhancement devices? Do you need them? That depends, I think, in large part on how you plan to market your tapes. If you, like me, will be selling largely to participants in your own programs or through mail order, you can probably dispense with them. Or you can compromise: ask a friend with a good voice to handle the narration for you. This should suffice.

Creating Dubbing Masters

Whether you use any sweetening devices or just an unadorned program, at some point a dubbing master must be created, that is the final tape from which actual cassettes will be produced. If you have not added sweetening effects, your one-track edited recordings are timed, split and transferred to two-track (that is, two sided) dubbing masters.

On the other hand, if you opt for adding music, sound effects or professional voice narrations, these recordings will need to be mixed with the edited source recordings to create a set of intermasters (also called safety masters). These mixed and edited safety masters are then timed, split and transferred to two-track dubbing masters. This way if the dubbing master is ever damaged, a new one can be made from your safety master without having to go through the time and expense of remixing the entire recording.

Whether these dubbing masters should be cassettes or ¼" open reel format depends on the system to be used for duplicating. If you plan to buy duplicating equipment, you'll probably need cassette masters. If you plan to have a professional duplicating facility handle your copies (but not the mastering), you'll need to find out what format they require. Indicate to them the quantity of tapes you are planning to produce as this may affect which duplicating system they use. In most cases a professional duplicating facility will want to produce the dubbing masters themselves from your edited, timed and split originals or mixed inter-masters.

Note: you should realize that most duplicating facilities can provide all the master recording services discussed in this section, but few recording studios provide duplicating services.

You should by now have a sense of how much this part of the process costs. Creating inter (or safety) masters and dubbing masters and transferral from one source to another costs about $20 to $30 per hour and takes between 1½ to 2 hours of mastering for one hour of finished material. As far as materials are concerned, you'll need one 7" reel for each thirty minutes in the inter-mastering process and one 7" reel for each sixty minutes (because recording is done on both sides) for dubbing masters. These cost between $8 and $12 per reel.

Chapter 10

Cassette Length Guidelines

Obviously before any final decision can be made about the dubbing masters, you have to consider just how many cassettes you want to produce. Equally obviously, this question involves pricing. There's a curious fact about the cassette business and its pricing. Buyers perceive value based on the number of cassettes rather than on the length of each cassette. Thus while three hours of finished program can be packaged as 2 C-90's, 3 C-60's or 6 C-30's, these formats are by no means equal. You may, for ease of packaging and shipping, tend to want to produce your program as the first of these possibilities. Think again! The rule of thumb is that each cassette whatever its length should be priced at at least $10. Given this fact, you want to arrange matters so that your masters should run between 30 minutes (15 minutes per side) and 45 minutes (22½ minutes per side) with more cassettes being the desired result rather than fewer. This is the first pivotal consideration in selling your cassette packages for the maximum profit. The second is the overall look of the package itself.

Producing Pertinent Packaging

As you can see, you are probably not going to want to handle the editing process yourself. Equally likely, you will probably wish to eschew the business of producing packaging as well in favor of selecting professional help. Yet in working with your professional consider just how much panache your packages really need. If you are selling tapes after a presentation, the presentation itself and the enthusiasm of your audience rather than the packaging will sell your product, and thus you may quite rightly feel that an understated effect is preferable. By the same token if you are selling by mail, it is your copy not the packaging which is most important. Only where the packaging stands alone, as it does in a retail establishment, must you aim for the most dazzling (also read expensive) varieties. In other circumstances, the effect should be solid but not spectacular. Keep this in mind as you work with professionals who may be tempted to sell you more than you need, in part because they are always aiming for the production of artistic packages, in part because they like the resultant remuneration. Having rendered this warning, here are several points I trust you'll find useful in addressing this issue of pertinent packaging.

Considering The Cassette Package

Most cassettes are packaged in a vinyl album. These albums, about which I shall have more to say in a moment, come in standard sizes designed to hold 2, 4, 6, or 8 cassettes. If you get terribly ambitious there is even a size for 16 cassettes. Cassette albums can also be produced with inside cavities, pockets and three-ring capacity to hold supplementary literature. It is generally advisable to include some type of bonus or even a simple personalized welcome letter with your package. Dottie Walters, for instance, recommends a technique she calls "The Grand Slam" wherein a book is offered as part of a cassette package and the only way to get it is by buying the entire offering. I must say you have to be pretty sure of your market to hazard a book's fate in this way! Needless to say, this quite inexpensive offering increases the perceived value of your product and the purchaser's ability to benefit from it. In general a supplementary booklet should increase your overall sale price by about $10. Thus a four-cassette album packaged with a printed booklet will sell for about $50.

The Vinyl Album Itself

A vinyl cassette album has a front, back and spine just like a book. You should plan on using at least two of these three panels to help persuade the buyer to act — now! Your objective is to convince the buyer that a disproportionate benefit awaits and to send a strong message of professional competence. Just how your album looks will be of the utmost assistance in sending this message. In this connection, there are two cover decoration techniques worth mentioning: silk screening and using a clear overlay with insertable graphics.

Silk Screening

Silk screening is the process of "printing" directly on vinyl. While you can use a wide range of colors, you are limited in that silk screening cannot be used to reproduce photographs. On the other hand, this is an economical process especially when you are producing 200 units or more. Also, because the vinyl is cut and screened as one piece, your three panels can be done in one pass at no extra charge. Thus if you use silk screening you should consider using all three panels and really getting your money's worth.

Chapter 10

Clear Overlay With Insertable Graphics

The second option makes use of a clear piece of vinyl sealed to the edges of the album to "trap" or "embed" printed cover sheets. Here you can use any graphics you fancy as you are printing on paper and can include photographs, four color printing and all the rest. Since 95% of the album vinyl itself is covered with printed paper that is itself covered by clear vinyl, the album color is not as critical. It should be neutral or chosen to complement the printed graphics.

You can have the printed graphics trapped or sealed under the clear vinyl on all four sides of each cover panel (front, back and spine) or purchase your albums with one side (either top or bottom) of the clear overlap open and so insert your own cover sheets. This gives you the flexibility of buying albums in quantity with the ability to change products by changing cover inserts. This works well if you are planning to create a library of products, and you are not sure they'll sell in equal numbers; (they never do by the way.) Make sure your cover inserts are printed on suitably weighted paper or you will not be able to insert them under the clear vinyl. Also, avoid inserts on the spine as they are harder to do.

Hint: Want a four color look but suffering from want of a four color budget? Try printing a one color front cover insert leaving room for a 3" x 5" or 4" x 4" full color photograph. Photographs can be produced rather inexpensively while the preparation charges for four color process printing are in the $500 range and printing minimums range from 1000 to 5000 pieces. Your less expensive photograph can be glued to the designated area on your front cover insert sheet. The insert can then be slipped under the clear vinyl on the album cover revealing no trace of the two pieces. You get a great full color look and the crackling smile on your face will be very real indeed. Simply leave the back cover insert in one or two colors.

Cover Messages

In all likelihood you will probably select the clear overlay option for your cassette packages. In either case, once you've decided what to do it's time to select the messages you wish to add. Here they are.

The Front Cover

The front cover should include:

- a large, well-done photograph of you. Use the hint above to achieve a four-color look. If you don't, don't forget that you can add variety through 20 to 40 percent screening of colors.

- main program title. This should be prominent. Use a grabber and a descriptor.

- your name and title

- one to three descriptive lines of copy that drive home to the prospect the importance of the program and the disproportionate benefit he'll derive from purchasing the product.

The Back Cover

The back cover should include:

- A small photograph of you in a different pose or setting.

- Your biography and credentials. This is the moment to establish yourself as an authority.

- Testimonials and referrals. Try to get someone meaningful in your field to offer a provocative endorsement.

- Program contents. Specifically list the key points covered in each tape and supplementary literature. As always stress the disproportionate benefits compared to the cost of the tapes.

- Provide your name, company name, logo, address and telephone number.

Chapter 10

- Add this line: © ℗ 1988 XYZ, Inc. © is the symbol for copyrighting printed literature and ℗ is the symbol for copyrighting a sound recording. (Note: To copyright your material file form SR with the United States Copyright Office, Register of Copyrights, Library of Congress, Washington, D.C. 20559. 202-287-8700. The fee is $10.

The Spine & Labels

The spine should include:

- main program title
- your name
- any possible catalog number.

Don't forget, too, to produce cassette labels for individual product identification. These should include:

- the main title of the overall program
- specific title of each particular side (if applicable)
- tape number and side number
- your name, address, telephone number and logo
- copyright symbol (for example, ℗ 1988 Jeffrey Lant Associates, Inc.)
- your photograph (if there's room).

Plan to print your labels in either one or two colors making use of screens and reverses to add visual appeal. Labels can either be printed on 12 or 15 up sheets for hand labeling or on rolls for automatic labeling equipment.

Working With A Graphic Designer

If you're like me, you'll need a graphic designer to help you plan all this and to put your message into the proper visual form. Provide your designer with a list of your objectives, guidelines, time schedules, copy and budget. Don't hesitate to give your suggestions about what you want, particularly the image you desire, but don't restrict your designer's creativity either.

Just how much will it cost to work with a graphic designer and achieve an original design? Here are some estimates.

For an original design, typesetting and paste up for up to three color printing here's what you can expect to pay.

Front, back and spine inserts with up to 4 cassette labels $285 to $350
　　　　　　　　　　　　　with up to 8 cassette labels $300 to $375
　　　　　　　　　　　　　with up to 16 cassette labels $325 to $425

Note: If you're planning four color printing your graphics will be about 30% more.

Production

Now you've done all the advance work. The next step is actually manufacturing your cassette packages. What follows is a chart of reasonable cost estimates for doing so. Remember, however, there are many variables to consider including the number of cassettes you want to have produced. Generally the lowest number would be 100; price breaks occur

Chapter 10

thereafter at 250, 500, 1000 and 2,500 units. Remember, too, you can save in subsequent production runs if you print more of your inserts and supplementary literature at the beginning. Here, then, are some estimates.

Quantity of 100 to 1000	Rough Costs	Recommended Sale Price
1 cassette package	$2.50 to $4	$10 to $15
2 cassette package	$4 to $5	$18 to $24
4 cassette package	$6.50 to $8	$35 to $50
6 cassette package	$8.50 to $10	$50 to $70
8 cassette package	$10 to $13	$70 to $80

These prices include the album (silk screeened or with clear vinyl overlay), duplicated cassettes (30 to 60 minutes each), one or two color labels for each side of the cassette, assembly and shrinkwrapping (a tight clear cover over the final product protecting it from dust and scratching in shipment). These prices do not include the printing for the album cover inserts or your supplementary literature.

A Reprise On Expenses

It would, perhaps, be beneficial to take just a moment and give a final look at the expenses you may have in producing your audio cassettes with a professional. The example below is based on producing 250 units.

Assume you produce three hours of finished material and plan to create a 4 cassette album with printed booklet. Let's say, too, you've used a professional recording service, professional voice narration, and albums with clear overlay requiring separate printed cover sheets.

Here's what your one time only charges would look like:

Record in studio (6 hours @ $35)	$210
Materials (12 7" master reels @ $10)	120
Editing (9 hours @ $30)	270
Professional voice narration (1 hour @ $60)	60
Materials (1 7" master reel @ $10)	10
Mastering (6 hours @ $25)	150
Materials (4 7" master reels @ $10)	40
Graphic design, typesetting, paste-up for front & back covers & labels	375
Supplementary booklet of 10 pages plus cover	275
Total:	$1,510

Chapter 10

Here are the product manufacturing and shipping charges:

	250 x $7.50 per unit	1,875
Printing costs for 500 sets of front & back two-color inserts		
	500 x .80	400
	supplementary booklet	
	500 x $1.50	750
Bulk freight charges $250 x .60		$150

(Note: these are the shipping charges the manufacturer bills to you. You, in turn, will bill individual customers for their orders.)

Total: $3,175

Total cost of project: $4,685

A Glimpse Of Profit

As you can see, breaking into the audio cassette business demands a significant investment. That's why I've urged you to be very, very conservative in your sales projections. However, once you are encountering significant groups of particularly upscale buyers, this move makes a lot of sense. In my illustration above, for instance, where you are selling units for $49, you need just 96 sales to break even. That would leave you with 154 units left to sell and a potential profit of $7,546.

Now take a look at your second order: your one-time only charges have been paid. Your printing is already in stock. Therefore it costs you just $2275 to produce 250 more units. You break even at 47 units and on your reorder you'll profit to the tune of $9,947.

Working With The Professional Production Company

Before leaving the subject of the professional cassette production company, I want to include just a few helpful hints about your work schedule and give you some information about a couple of their business practices.

It generally takes about two months once you've finished your script to produce cassette packages. Keeping this in mind, here's a schedule that my be of assistance when you finally do enter into a relationship with a company like Bill Guthy's.

Week one: Finish both the program script and the professional voice narration script. Record in studio. Select music or special effects. Provide editing guidelines. Establish the number of cassettes per package.

Week two: Do the master tape editing and approve the result. Write copy for the album covers, labels and literature. Brainstorm for graphic ideas and packaging options.

Weeks three and four: Do the mixing, mastering, and approve test copies. Approve the art boards. Make the final package selection. Order the vinyl albums and the printing for labels, inserts and supplementary literature.

Weeks five and six: Duplicate and label tapes. The printed cover inserts should be ready for album embedment during final heat-sealing phase.

Weeks seven and eight: The albums and supplementary literature are ready. Assemble the albums with cassettes and booklets. The product should be checked through quality control, shrinkwrapped, boxed and shipped to you.

Chapter 10

Helpful Information and Hints

- Make sure you review all the masters and any printing before these are finally produced. A wise production company will have you sign off on these in case there is a final error. Note: it's very easy to overlook an error at this point. Have a friend review materials for you, too.

- The company will probably want 50% of its money up front once the agreement is made to proceed and will probably want full payment before shipping the product. There's probably not much you can do about this on the first order, but try to establish credit terms.

- Product reorders take about 4 to 5 weeks.

- Unless you have specified otherwise, the production company will assume that all dubbing masters, original artwork and printing plates belong to them. While most companies should grant your request for a return of all materials assuming all outstanding debts are paid, you need to cover ownership and access in advance of production.

Doing Things Yourself

The thrust of this chapter has been largely towards working with a professional production firm. But I know that there are many who'll want to handle the taping and production of their audio cassettes themselves. This section is for you! Whenever possible we have added 1985 purchase prices for equipment, but it's obvious that much of this can be rented.

Recording And Editing

In order to record and edit your own high quality master tapes, here's what you'll need:

- an open-reel tape deck. Use this to record and edit your masters. Editing is not feasible in cassette format. Consumer models like those made by Teac, Akai and Pioneer are priced from between $400 to $1000. Semi-pro brands like Tascam (by Teac) and Revox can cost from $700 to $1800 or more. Your machine should accept 7" and 10½" reels of 1.0 mil tape such as Maxwell UD 35-180 for extended non-stop recording (about one and one half hours per 10½" reel at the recommended speed of 7½ inches per second). Be sure the mechanism has a cueing level for editing and that it lends itself to easy tape handling when making splices. The Revox B-77 (about $1800) is an excellent choice.

- a low-impedance condenser microphone. The Audio-Technica AT 805-S (about $65) can be used both at home and on location to record your presentation. This model has an on-off switch to conserve battery life.

- two 25-foot microphone extension cords. These allow you the flexibility of walking away from the podium and locating your recorder wherever you desire.

- an Editall aluminum splice block for ¼" tape ($18). This is a precision piece of equipment usually used with single-edge razor blades. (Avoid the quick-splice machine sold in stereo shops.)

- a cassette recorder. This is used to make original recordings on location and for recording dubbing masters for use on a high-speed duplicator. The Marantz PMD-221 is a versatile mono portable which can be used effectively. It retails for $275. If you would like the convenience of not having to flip your master cassettes, consider a quick-reverse stereo deck such as the Aiwa R550. This machine is not very portable, but at about $300 it's your best buy. Incidentally it takes the R550 just two-tenths of a second to switch from side A to side B resulting in almost no loss of content. If you want auto reverse capability and portability, Panasonic's model RQ 383 is quite good and available for about $90 to $100.

Chapter 10

- mastering tape. Use only good quality tape such as Maxell UD 35-90 (7" reels), UD 35-180 (10½" reels) or Ampex 407. For cassette mastering of spoken-word presentations, TDX ADK C-60 or ADX C-90 are excellent.

Recommendations for Your "Live" Recordings

Both for practice and ultimately for sale to your audiences, you need to record all your performances. In this connection, here's a kit you can put together for under $400 that will be helpful. For your tape deck consider the Marantz portable model PMD 220 or for auto-reverse convenience, the Aiwa R550 stereo deck or Panasonic RQ 383.

Use the Audio-Technical microphone AT-805S which comes with a number of handy accessories.

Include two 25-foot extension cables (such as are available at Radio Shack), one 15-foot electrical extension cord, and a small roll of duct tape to secure the extension connections against pulling apart and to tape down cables across walkways.

Finally, you'll need some TDX ADK C-60 or ADX C-90 cassettes. Try to avoid using the C-120 cassettes; their thin tape can cause problems.

Make sure your microphone battery is new and in place. Use the tie clasp and clip the microphone to your lapel close to your collar. Avoid touching it or letting other clothing brush against it during recording. Plug the other end of the microphone into the "mic input" on your recording deck. Set your recording levels to peak at 0db on the VU meter.

Now insert your cassette tape and play forward a few seconds past the leader tape. Press the record button or the record and play buttons together (depending on the deck used) and make a brief test recording to make sure you're recording. Rewind back and listen to what you've done to make sure your signal is loud, crisp and clear. Then go ahead and begin in earnest!

Duplicating Equipment

Duplicating equipment is available that will produce one or up to 32 cassettes simultaneously. Here are units to consider:

- Wollensak/Universal
  821 E. Artesia Blvd.
  Carson, CA 90746

  (213) 327-2303

This unit is very durable and reliable. It is expandable from 2 to 32 copies at a time and has built-in rewind.

- Telex
  Distributed by Long's Electronics
  2700 Crestwood Blvd.
  Birmingham, AL 35210

  (1-800-633-3410)

Model Copyette 1 & 3 weighs 15 pounds and is very portable. This system makes three copies at a time, has built in rewind but is not expandable to increase copies per master.

Note: Long's also has an extensive mail order catalog with recording equipment, duplicating equipment, blank cassettes, blank labels, &c.

Chapter 10

Blank Cassettes

You can purchase standard or custom length blank cassettes in either black, white, ivory or clear "reel" cartridges. Plan to record your masters and copies with the same brand cassettes in C-32, C-46 or C-92 lengths leaving about 10 seconds blank at the end of side one and beginning of side two. This will allow for slight speed variations in the duplicating equipment from slave to slave and insure that no program material gets cut off.

Pricing, of course, will vary with quantity, length and type of materials required. Try Cassette Productions for the best buy: 5796 Martin Rd., Irwindale, CA 91706-6299.

Vinyl Albums

Check the Yellow Pages under "looseleaf" or "book and catalog covers." Then check your local source against these suppliers:

- Blackbourn, Inc.
  10150 Crosstown Circle
  Eden Prairie, MN 55344

  (612) 944-7010

- International Binding Products, Inc.
  4600 Pacific Blvd
  Vernon, CA 90058

  (213) 588-6323

- Vinylweld
  2011 W. Hastings
  Chicago, IL 60608

  (312) 243-0606

- Sealtronics
  8633 Sorensen
  Santa Fe Springs, CA 90670-2680

  (213) 945-7655

Cassette Labels

Try the following:

- Audico, Inc.
  219 Crossen
  Elk Grove, Il 60007

  (312) 640-1030

Available in white and colored stock, 12 per sheet.

- Avery International
  150 N. Orange Grove Blvd
  Pasadena, CA 91103

  (818) 304-2000

Available in white labels only, 15 per sheet.

Chapter 10

Other Matters

As far as your graphic design, album cover inserts and supplementary literature are concerned, these you can handle with local assistance. You've already been warned, of course, that printers vary drastically in regard to capacity, price and service, so do shop around.

Once your tapes are mastered and duplicated, your graphics designed and printed, and your custom albums produced, it's time to label, collate and assemble each individual unit. Invite your friends round. It's time they helped you out.

A Few Words About Marketing

Whether you use a professional production company or do things yourself, you'll still find yourself facing a pile of cassette packages and the need to move them out to an awaiting world. As always, take a moment to congratulate yourself. You've reached yet another significant milestone in your talk career and you deserve to feel good about your achievement. Then get cracking. You have sales to make.

You should, of course, use all the suggestions in this book to sell tapes, but especially consider the following:

- Create a "Tape of the Month" Club where for an annual fee you'll send workshop participants and avid fans your latest thoughts. This is one of Bill Guthy's specialties, so ask him about it.

- Sell package offers of books and tapes. If you have a four cassette package with inserts selling for $49 and a $30 book on the same subject, create a special seminar price of, say, $60. I've found that offering this kind of discount prompts people to go the extra step and purchase more than they might otherwise have done.

- Make sure that each person in every audience is given an order blank for your tape packages. While many people are impulse buyers, may more need time to consider their purchases. I find that I'm one of a relatively few speakers to insist that my literature (a précis for instance) is given to everyone at any convention where I speak. Orders dribble in for months afterwards this way.

- Sponsor a prize drawing during the course of the day with a tape as your gift. This helps break the ice and draws attention to your product.

- Autograph your albums at the end of the program. Adults are shy about asking but once someone has done so, most people want their package autographed. After all, you are the celebrity, aren't you?

- For further information, we have, you guessed it!, a two cassette pack entitled "How To Sell Product From The Platform." This extensive guide to product sales by Mike Ferry is available for $20 from Cassette Productions Unlimited. It's just one more thing that very entrepreneurial, very intelligent fellow Bill Guthy offers.

I must say, in conclusion, I enjoyed working with Bill in compiling this chapter which owes so much to his keen grasp of the subject. I know you'll benefit from him, too, so why not contact him today in Irwindale? By the way, when you do, request a free copy of his very informative booklet *"How To Produce A Cassette Program And Never Leave Your Office."*

Chapter 11

CASHING IN III: SELLING AND SELLING SOME MORE

Part 1: Selling To Your Participants

You now have your Success Package. You've got what you need to succeed:

- You've got a designated audience. You know who your participants should be and you know as much if not more about them than they know about themselves.

- You've got the programs they need, that they crave. Not just one program either. Multiples. All designed to solve their perceived problems — now!

- You've had successful first assignments, and these you are continually leveraging for further successes. You have that most desirable of items: a track record.

- And you've perfected your sales materials and your sales pitch.

You're hot!

It should be very clear by now that the value and benefit to you of your program does not end after you take your triumphal bow to sustained applause. You have to see each program as part of a great chain of possibilities. Opportunities for you. Annuities for you. You must plan accordingly.

What's infuriating to me as I assess speakers is how little benefit they gain from a single performance. They act as if such a performance is entirely disconnected from anything that came before or will come afterwards. What a mistake!

Your first connection with an organization should not be your best. It is, after all, introductory. You need to nurture that connection and the people that that connection represents, nurture them so that they'll be receptive, welcoming to the other possibilities which you'll present. A successful presentation, therefore, is just the beginning of your harvest.

Consulting Opportunities

Many speakers enter into the talk circuit as a useful means of getting clients. There's nothing wrong with this; I advocate the procedure myself in **THE CONSULTANT'S KIT**. Here are some suggestions for succeeding with this objective.

No Hard Sell

I remember attending a workshop conducted by a consultant about a year ago. He was being paid pitiably little for giving this particular program and could recoup only if a sufficient number of participants enrolled in his individual counseling sessions. The program was to end at 9 p.m. and an hour later we were all still in the seminar room writhing, eager for what had now turned into an embarrassing travesty to end. The program was extended because the leader had not gotten his quota and kept giving more material to show people "how beneficial" the therapy sessions would be. "Here's just some of what you'll get."

The longer he talked, the more draining illustrations he gave of his good work, the less inclined anyone was to sign up. Finally he gave up in despair, looking (and no doubt feeling) pathetic. What went wrong?

There are ways to entice clients to want your service. There's a sequence you should follow to bring your services to their attention in ways which increase the likelihood they will buy your professional offerings:

- The course/program description should list you as a consultant or professional along with the name of the firm.

- At the beginning of the program or as part of the program pass outs make sure every participant gets a memorandum of your services and products. (See samples, page 284.) Start the program by going through this packet, holding up each piece of paper in it including this memorandum. This is Assertive Courtesy. "I just want to make sure that everyone starts with the right materials for the day."

Chapter 11

- If questions are asked of you that you deal with in your daily practice, say so. "I'm glad you asked that question, because that's a common problem that I deal with in my regular business. Here's how we deal with it." Don't attempt to evade the issue because it encroaches on your practice. People have paid to hear what you've got to say, and they want to hear it as specifically as possible. The way in which you answer this question will be of the utmost assistance to you in garnering clients. Withholding information at this point will damage your claim to be the in-command expert. Adult learners particularly like candor and they are usually smart enough to be able to discern when you are skirting a problem. Don't do it.

- Add a section to your remarks on how people should deal with a professional offering your service. Tell them how to find the right professional, the questions that they should ask, the services they should expect and both the pros and cons of working with a professional. For instance, I end every fund raising workshop that I give with this point: "The Use — And Misuse! — Of Consultants." This enables me, subtly, to market myself and my services while providing information of very real value to the audience. Invariably this information is appreciated, and it is not seen as a "hard sell." The audience appreciates that there are techniques to be used in finding a good consultant, and they want to know what they are. They also know that many consultants can be of very real value to their audiences, and they want to know how to make the best use of them and the possible pitfalls of the relationship.

- Do by all means indicate (as if the point hasn't already been made!) that you are available for private consultation. State your policy on short follow-up telephone calls. I am always willing to take short calls from people who have taken my workshops if a bit of information or a few minutes can help them solve a problem. This helps me build a relationship with the possible client. But if their problem needs some more detailed work on my part, I say so and suggest that that time is billable. There are no hard feelings here. Your job is to take the reasonable position and stick with it. Adults understand this and I have found will generally not abuse your reasonable approach. Under no circumstances however make a strong hard sell for your products or services. This is *infra dig*.

Develop A Thank-You Letter

After your program send a thank you letter to participants and ask them to stay in touch. All too many adults have had the unsatisfactory experience of participating in a program and never hearing from the presenter again — or only with another offer for purchase. Distinguish yourself from this bunch! Try to send a thank you letter. Tell participants you were grateful they attended. You should be: they provide you with your livelihood — or at least a slice of it.

In the letters I send (and I confess I am not always sufficiently organized or energetic to do so on all occasions), I try to include a piece of useful information for the participants. Usually this is a Problem Solving Process article I've written.

You can and should conclude this letter by saying that you hope that you'll have the chance to serve them in your practice and that you'll be in touch again about scheduling an intensive refresher "clinic." Advise your reader to keep this letter and the other materials you've passed out on file for future reference. Make them understand that what you hand out is not just an ephemeral flyer but something which can be of assistance to them when problems arise which are within your area of competence.

Should You Develop A Newsletter?

Many people ask me whether a newsletter wouldn't be a good idea for keeping in touch with people who attend one of your programs. My resolute answer is: that depends!

I myself don't have a newsletter, but I want you to know that they can be under the right circumstances a superb means not only of keeping in touch with your program participants but stimulating sales and more advantageous client relationships. Here are some of the reasons why you might want to consider producing one:

- You and your participants will remain in regular touch.

- You can offer your readers products (including your own) at special prices.

- You can notify them about your future programs.

Chapter 11

- Newsletters properly packaged can become the basis for books.

- They can themselves become an independent profit center, another revenue stream.

Ultimately, perhaps, this last point is the key one. As you might guess, I receive many, many newsletters; most are sent to me without charge by people who want me to peruse their work, perhaps contribute to their pages and otherwise be aware of their activities. I encourage this and when you produce such materials be sure to keep me in mind.

But remember this: I am not an idle recipient. Too many of the newsletters I see (both those without cost and, alarmingly, those with) are very thin on practical information and actually end up damaging their producers. Who would, I wonder, want to do business with such aerated vacuity?

Consider, therefore: is this endeavor actually in your interest? The only real reason for beginning a newsletter it seems to me is to turn it into a free standing profit center as soon as possible. Just merely keeping in touch with your mailing list, program participants, &c., is not sufficient reason for commencing what can too easily become a draining project. Rather, I think you're better off spending your time trying to sell your programs to colleges or trade associations.

Perhaps, though, some middle ground is possible. I think that your interests will be met, at least in the beginning, if you send out two or three times yearly a general mailing in newsletter format. Such a mailing, like the one I send to colleges, could perhaps have a special cover letter that would make it appropriate for trade associations and yet another cover letter suitable for those who have taken your programs.

If you decide to do even these mailings, however, aim for profit. At the very least do co-operative mailings with those who have products and services of interest to your mailing list. Identify publishers of books, for instance, of interest to your past participants. With 40,000+ titles published each year, this shouldn't be too difficult. Here's what to do:

- Get a publisher to supply you with a standard advertising format (or stat). You add your name and address to the form. If the publisher gives you 50% of the sale price, expect to pay for the cost of printing yourself. (This is the method I as a publisher use and I recommend it to you! Contact me for further details.) Make sure the publisher can mail books for you so you don't have to warehouse.

- If a publisher wants to retain all the revenues generated and will simply supply you with literature, he can be billed for being part of your stuffer program at about $30-50 per thousand pieces mailed. You must tell the publisher (or other product producer) exactly the size you'd like the literature to be and whether you need it folded and if so, how. The publisher in this circumstance pays you for stuffing and mailing on a per thousand fee and pays the other expenses himself (*i.e.*, production of inserts, shipping and folding.)

Here are a few further suggestions about this topic:

- Don't have too many inserts. It will reduce the response and hence make it less likely that your advertisers will participate again.

- Don't expect a miraculous response. A good one will run about 1%.

- Response will be better if you editorially endorse the product. It goes with saying that you should not do so unless you've used it yourself. In this connection, ask for a free product sample from the producer. Publishers will be the most likely to comply, especially if your mailing is likely to be productive for them. If you can't get the product free, ask for the dealer discount. You are, after all, thinking of becoming a dealer.

Remember: stuffer programs and cooperative mailings work, but an editorial tie-in makes them more productive.

Chapter 11

Selling Your Newsletter To Program Participants

Those of you who already have newletters should perceive the benefit of signing up your workshop participants as subscribers. In fact, it is very likely through this method that your long-term profit will emerge. Here are some hints:

- Give a free sample copy (or two, not more), preferably your most immediate past issue (not the current one) as part of the workshop. Make sure the fact that all participants will receive a copy of your newsletter is trumpeted as one of the reasons for attending. Hand them out first thing in the day so that during the breaks participants can peruse them.

- Make sure that each participant gets an order coupon among registration materials and other pass outs.

- Give some inducement for ordering today (the last two-three issues, for instance) or a special "workshop discount."

- This inducement might include a special discount on the book you've written or the ability to get a book on the subject produced by another publisher at cost. Make sure you tell the buyer what a good deal this is! It is!

- Give the prospective buyer a sense of urgency, a need to act — now! Say that the offer is good for today only.

- If you do intend to provide a rather longer time in which the prospective buyer can act, include another order coupon in your follow-up mailing. But be sure to include a time after which the special offer is no longer valid, say 30 days.

A Few Candid Comments About Newsletters

- Most contain too much fluff. The reason for newsletters in the first place is to provide useable information in a form that is easy to follow-up. Don't let down the side by providing anything less.

- Give disproportionate benefit information. Always indicate to the reader just what kind of benefit he can expect to gain by reading your newsletter and make sure you indicate the disproportionate benefits he can achieve by following your purchase recommendations, too.

- Always include complete follow-up information including name, address, telephone number and anything else that will be useful. I find it infuriating to get interested in a newsletter article and then not have this follow-up information immediately available.

- Give your readers deals they can't get elsewhere. This builds their loyalty. Make sure they can't get them elsewhere and make sure you tell them they can't!

- Make deals with product producers. A newsletter is your personal vehicle and you should profit from it!

Newsletter Resources

For information on producing a profitable newsletter, contact Howard Penn Hudson at The Newsletter Clearinghouse, P.O. Box 311, Rhinebeck, New York 12572. Ask for a complete list of his publications and programs. Tell him I sent you!

Developing Relationships With Your Participants

I have an amazing national network. At least once each day I hear from someone who has bought a book, taken a workshop, participated in a program. I learn from them — and they buy from me! It's a good relationship. I am not, I confess, nearly as well organized about keeping this network functioning as I ought to be. Nonetheless I am an enthusiastic advocate of remaining in touch with those who have profited from your programs, bought your products, or otherwise been changed and benefitted by you. Here are some ways to do just that:

- Let people know when you are returning to their area. Either send them a course brochure or arrange for a letter from you to be enclosed in a sponsor's catalog or brochure. People who know you and like you will act as your unofficial though potent advertising and sales force. Make sure they have the information they need to promote you. They will both recruit others to attend your programs and often come again themselves for a refresher.

Chapter 11

- Try to arrange to have past program participants get a special "refresher" rate, say 50% of the rate for first-time participants. This will encourage them to come back. The program they hear shouldn't be the same as they've heard before — aren't you adding new material and updating your information? — and therefore they are unlikely to be bored. Even if the bulk of the material is the same, however, they need to have it: all of us learn the best when consistently reexposed to material and given the chance to hear it again anew.

- Make consulting sessions available when you're in the area.

- Get the sponsoring organization to hold a follow-up wine and cheese party and invite not only those who have taken your current program but your "alumni," too. This is a very effective way of keeping in touch and very inexpensive. You can sell the sponsor on it be allowing them to have their literature on hand and by having one of their representatives give a 5 minute presentation about other programs which will interest your people. Even an ordinary lecture room can be used for this program, although you should try to have it in a nicer place if you can.

- Have a special limited access follow-up course. Sponsor this yourself (it's the easiest self-sponsored program to arrange). You can do this when you have a pool of about 50 or more people who are already familiar with you. (If you are selling books independently, of course, buyers can also be factored into your pool as workshop possibilities.) The way to handle this program is as a mixed lecture and consulting program using as case studies the actual situations of those who have attended your programs and are now out implementing your methods. I shall present more information on this alternative in Chapter 15, but suffice it to say that one very valuable follow-up program is what I call the "clinic," an opportunity for those who have heard you and learned your methods to be able to work with you in applying them. This kind of format necessitates an ability in you the presenter of quickly evaluating documents and situations and being able to render sage advice, options and solution techniques without the need for lengthy study and reflection. In other words, you have to know your field!

Other Means Of Staying In Touch

Within your home territory (or even on the road), sponsor your own cocktail parties. People's social lives have atrophied over the last several years but as far as I can tell they like parties as much as ever! Consider charging $10-15 per head for an open bar and limited attendance. You're the host and prime deal maker. Introduce people. Circulate! Move about and have a good time faciliting possibilities for your paying guests. Invite someone to speak on a topic of interest. There are a lot of people who'll come for free even if you're only having 25 guests, people like:

- your friends

- elected officials

- refugee diplomats

- authors promoting books

- university professors, &c.

Write them a slavishly flattering letter and don't let it bother you that you have no money for a fee. Flattery is often more useful than money in motivating people and you'd rather keep the cash anyway. The aim is to get a draw for your party and give it the right cachet. (Do give those promoting products the opportunity to do so and make sure every guest leaves with his promotional material.)

These kinds of parties cost about $200 to produce and that includes liquor (buy by the gallon), bartender (use students from a nearby college; mine, Harvard, has Harvard Student Agencies which dresses their help in dapper uniforms for the occasion), light nibbles, printing and postage.

Make sure your own products and services get promoted in your mailings and at the event, too.

Note: As you develop your own network, you'll be developing your own group of followers. Indulge yourself! Groupies are nice. Get some and enjoy them. Why let rock stars have all the fun?

Chapter 11

Last Words

Once you've connected with an individual through a program, don't lose touch. Look upon that initial contact as an investment that can pay off for you for the rest of your life. I do and this attitude works. Keep these points in mind:

- The people that you meet are links to new possibilities. Keep an open mind about these possibilities and encourage their development.

- Encourage these people to make deals with you. They have connections that you want to trade and professional organizations they belong to and that you want access to. They need your help in other ways. Swap.

- Stay in touch so that they'll buy your new books, services and programs.

- Keep your image as the skill model before them, the successful individual who can do things they want to do and who has solved problems they want solved. The more your participants believe this the more possibilities will develop.

Part II: Selling Your Programs To And Through Publications

It seems very curious to me that most specialized publications — and by these I mean newsletters and trade and professional publications — are reluctant to get into the workshop, lecture and convention business. Oh, don't misunderstand. Plenty are into it. I know; I'm associated with several of them. But it's really the old question of publications executives not knowing what business they're in. Personally, I think they are in the communications business, not merely the publications business, and this means they should also consider the wide range of talk programs and how they can bring useful information to their audiences. Sadly, this seems more obvious to me than to some publishers I've approached; some, but by no means all.

Much of what I say in this section will, I trust, be familiar to you already. I hope so. It'll mean that you are glimpsing the manifold possibilites of talk.

The Key

The key to selling programs to publications is being able to show them that your Participant Profile overlaps significantly with their reader demographics. Go back to Standard Rate & Data. Better yet actually review the publication with which you wish to be affiliated. The best way of doing so, of course, is to write to the advertising department or call. Say you're thinking of advertising; in a way you are. Don't forget to ask for the Rate Card. This contains critical information you need to know about the publication and its audience — your future talk participants. You can rest assured that this packet will arrive promptly, whereas if you tell the secretary what you are really doing, she'll be referring it around the office until next Thursday. Don't muddle her; just get the information you need!

A good way to begin a relationship with a publication is, of course, to get an article published in it. Use the Problem Solving Process format. Your review of the publication will assist you in determining what article they need and which you should offer. Make sure the initial article includes follow-up information so that the reader can get access to you. This is very important.

There will probably be a response to your article; usually a few people take the trouble to contact you. Offer them some follow-up information on the subject you've written about; this will induce them to write. However, even if there is no direct response, don't worry. It never ceases to amaze me how few people actually do what's good for them, which includes asking for information which will help solve their perceived problems.

Whatever happens — an avalanche of letters or a ringing silence — write a letter to the editor (intended for publication) complimenting the publication on its amazing drawing power. Publishers like laudatory fluff like this. Keep in mind that your first task is for the editor/publisher to like you. A letter like this helps move matters along.

Chapter 11

Always supposing that this publication is in touch with the right possible program participants who will benefit from the information you've got, follow up this introductory letter with a business letter to the editor on your talk programs. (Note: If the publication already has a talk program, convention, &c. address your letter to the program planner with a carbon copy to the publisher or corporate president and proceed according to the sales techniques you'd use with any other program planner. These people are, after all, already equipped to deal with future speakers and are probably actively seeking programs and those who can deliver useful and profitable information. It goes without saying that in this situation, you should first request a copy of the last program and review it before submitting any suggestions.)

Contacting The Publisher

If the publisher/publication is not now in the business of offering talk programs, your initial letter needs to accomplish several tasks:

- You must subtly move the publisher to an understanding of his real business (which in not just publishing items but solving a defined set of problems for his buyers.)

- You must indicate that you know what his audience is.

- You must show that this audience has a defined problem (and indicate how you know this).

- You must also demonstrate that there is an easy way of arranging your program and so solving this problem and one that involves limited expense and the possibility of profit.

This last point is, of course, critical. If you can persuade the publisher that you can in fact mount a profitable program with minimal effort, you should be able to sell the deal. (See samples, page 286.)

The Arrangements

As you know by now, there are certain tasks that need to be accomplished for a successful program to take place. Here they are:

- develop marketing copy

- design one or a series of ads to be run by the publication

- develop a registration form

- develop a registration confirmation form

- arrange for site, meals and other amenities

- designate contact person for oversight.

These points are the basics. Here are some more advanced problems needing solutions:

- arranging for materials

- if tapes are produced, determining who owns the rights (could be a problem with materials, too, in selected circumstances)

- determining your long term relationship with the publication.

Answers: What You Can Do, What The Publication Can Do

The biggest problem of working with a publication is that they will be worried about the amount of work that is entailed in producing a program. Of course, they don't want to work any harder, even for enhanced profits! They're only human, too! So you need to convince them that this is a project which can be undertaken with minimal disruption to the daily schedule and offers the possibility of a good return. If it isn't, don't say so and don't do it.

Chapter 11

What You Can Do

It really isn't that much extra work for you to help a publication put on a non-residential program. The bulk of problems in the talk world occur with things that have little if anything to do directly with the program itself: accommodation, travel, &c. This is where the problems lie.

Here, then, is what you can do to minimize the problems:

- You can help develop all marketing documents including space ads in the publication itself. Since you've already done your program previously, you have materials from which to draw. Besides, it's in your best interest to draft materials yourself; you'll get the copy you want. Be willing to pitch in on these tasks.

- Draft the brochure, if you're planning on having one.

- Draft the letter that will go to those requesting more information. Make sure that you are given as the resource to contact and that your telephone number is included. You know the program if you are giving it and you are, therefore, the best seller. Don't shirk!

- Help design the registration forms and registration confirmation documents.

What The Publication Can Do

Leave some of the low grade technical matters to the publication:

- booking the site

- handling on-site registration

- booking the amenities, including morning coffee, lunch, afternoon soft drinks, &c.

Is this all? Practically. What you want from the publication is constant promotion for your program. You are contracting with them because they have close continuing contact with an audience you want to reach and in fact it is this contact, this ongoing relationship that you are really buying into. And for this, you're thinking, I'm giving up a substantial fraction of the revenues? You bet your life! If a publication will make a real commitment to market your program(s), promote you and handle the mundane details (all of which they can do with minor disruption to their daily lives), you are getting a good deal and should appreciate it.

How Many To Give And Some Contractual Matters

My advice to you is to start small and work up. This is my consistent refrain, of course. You want a long term relationship with the publication to be sure. Plan for this. Work towards this. But start by delivering a success and, as usual, leveraging it to achieve your grander objectives. Thus here's an idea for your consideration: begin with a single one-day program in an area of high reader concentration, probably a large city. Try to have this city be one you are already visiting so that you can piggyback on an existing program and thus cut expenses. Or have it in your home town. Either way expenses will be low and this will help the program succeed.

The program should, of course, be on the topic of greatest current interest to your prospective participants and should offer the Disproportionate Benefit Compared To Price. A good price range for this initial program is about $100-$150 per day per person including lunch and materials. With, say, a program cost of $100 and just 25 people attending, you can walk away with $1000 for speaker fee and materials and so can the publication. The basic expenses, being fairly minimal, will be nicely covered.

If this program is successful you can begin to consider other ones. In fact, this consideration should begin the moment you know that this initial program is profitable which, of course, may be well before it actually takes place.

Chapter 11

To arrive at this result, however, you need to consider one pivotal point which will be of the utmost interest to the publication: how will its advertising/space costs be compensated? If the publication is paid full page cost rates for its advertising, you'll come up short. The publication will benefit but you probably won't. Thus the best arrangement is a package. Do something like this:

- You will undertake to deliver yourself, a minimum quantity of material packages (say 25) and have your expenses paid. You'll help with the design of materials as above and answer participant questions.

- The publication will undertake to promote the program energetically including space ads and editorial support, handle registrations, site selection and onsite registration, &c.

- Both of you will receive a fixed, flat flee equally 50% of the net after the deduction of outright expenses (hotel, meals, &c). This is equitable.

The Grasping Publisher

Sadly, all publishers are not fair and equitable or even sensible. Be prepared. Here are some suggestions:

The publisher may demand payment for advertising space. Fine. Figure this on the actual cost basis, not the retail price. In return, set your speaker fee so that with the cost basis price for materials you make at least $1000 for the day. Perhaps this will induce the publisher to be reasonable.

The publisher may not be willing to guarantee you any return for the day, in other words it will be mutual risk. If this is the basis on which you proceed, get the publisher to commit to a certain degree and frequency of advertising for the program. In other words, if you are going to risk your reputation get the publisher to guarantee a certain size and frequency of advertising to give the program a fighting chance. How many ads should there be? At least one in 4 issues. Also, get some editorial support, including an article by you. You might as well get something out of this.

If you do go into an arrangement with no guarantee of payment, consider this possibility: a fixed, flat fee up to a certain number of participants and then an escalating return depending on the additional number enrolling. If you must risk, then you should be compensated if the operation is successful and the publisher's own investment has been returned.

Tapes and Books

You must work out with the publisher who will benefit from tapes based on the program and to what extent. I suggest that the most equitable method is the simple 50-50% split after outright production expenses. You should retain the right to market tapes independently to others so long as this does not infringe the publisher's possible sales to publication readers. Also, you should both be able to market the tapes independently to other publications and associations. You cede 50% of revenues to the primary marketer and split the remaining 50% after costs with the publisher, thus leaving you 25% of the net. Remember: this can be a most valuable right, since those who don't attend will want the tapes, especially if the meeting is adequately promoted in the publication (nice pictures of smiling people, follow-up article, &c).

Of course, you'll also want to benefit from subsequent book and materials sales. You should get a guarantee from the publication that your book will be mentioned in a box or side-bar in the follow-up article and that sales will be directed to you so that you can derive the full benefit from the product.

Subsequent Programs

If the first program is profitable, it is worth repeating wherever there are significant numbers of publication readers. Never forget this!

Initial programs are always messy. People haven't yet learned how to work together. Mistakes are made. Advertising and brochure copy needs to be refined. The program itself may have bugs and irritating episodes. Such is the nature of the business.

But as soon as this program takes place, if the participants were basically happy and the program made money, you should review the matter and begin to identify new places in which it can be held.

Chapter 11

You now have a very significant advantage that you didn't have before: satisfied customers to leverage. You can now draw upon the comments and reactions of people who know they got their money's worth. What a blessing! To get this kind of reaction, ask for it. Make sure to make available a reaction form at the end of your program. Tell people that enthusiastic comments may be used as part of the promotional efforts for future programs in this series.

People love to see their names in print. Thus their comments will be more enthusiastic than they might otherwise have been. Tell them, too, to give their name and company affiliation exactly as they'd like it printed. Don't give way to the silly notion of printing this kind of review: " 'Wonderful program,' Mrs. S.D., Detroit." Fatuous, irksome and downright ludicrous this is and not at all worth printing. You'll get many good comments this way which are attributable to their authors, the program participants. You won't need an explicit release form from them either because you've already told them (right on the form!) that this comment may be used for publication.

How Many To Do

The question now becomes how many of these programs to produce. I'd suggest 5 or 6 in relatively quick succession, say every Friday for 6 weeks. This will get the information out to the participants at about the same time and means that all the programs can be promoted simultaneously. This will be beneficial to the publication. Also, this series in this way will not tire you unduly. If you are working the continuing education circuit on Saturdays, Friday — or Monday — is usually a good day on which to piggyback although, of course, midweek programs remain the most popular.

Of course once this sequence is successfully concluded, you should be considering what to do next. If the information you are offering needs updating, that won't be a problem. You'll be offering The Sequel. If it's evergreen material, you may have to think through a new offering. In this case, try passing around an ascertainment survey at the seminars to see which other problems are of interest to participants and what they might like to see you offer. It's their money after all!

One Last Point

As before, get an agreement from the publishing company on your continuing involvement in these programs. If your program is profitable, you'll want to insure the publication continues not only to hold the sessions but to use you, too. Don't have the dubious distinction of helping to launch a program in which you no longer are featured.

Part III: Annual Programs: Your Annuities

The problem with working with publications is that at some point they will want to bring in new blood, and you may be displaced in the process. This is a sad reality of the talk circuit and one none of us likes to contemplate. That's why we need annuity programs.

These are programs that are offered in conjunction with a sponsoring institution, year in, year out. The topic remains the same and the subject matter is updated with each passing year. Such programs are about as close as any speaker gets to an annuity and should be vigorously pursued.

The kinds of programs I have in mind I call institutes. They take place over several days, in a single place, on a single topic. They are sponsored year after year by the same organization and are marketed to the same target population. And, of course, they present you as their leading light and guru.

The key thing to keep in mind about this program is that there can be as many of them as there are marketing districts in the country or indeed the world. Thus the five day program that I co-sponsor with a local Cambridge college each year on fund raising from individuals, corporations and foundations can take place around the country, too, which is why I now make it available through my catalog of courses. The only real drawback is that there are only so many hours in the day...

This format needs to be differentiated from conferences and annual meetings. With those, people from around the country travel to a single place which alternates year to year. There are really quite significant costs involved in this kind of activity because it isn't cheap to pay for that much traveling and accommodation.

Chapter 11

Instead, my institute format involves you, the leader, travelling from place to place to offer the program and drawing your audience from nearby areas so that the amount of overnight accommodation and travel is really quite minimal if it exists at all. This is significantly different and makes the institute a format you should actively pursue.

Creating This Admirable Cash Cow

Surely by now it goes almost without saying that you will organize your institute along the Problem Solving Process lines. Beyond this, however, there are questions that need to be answered.

- How long should your program be? An institute is a more major time commitment for participants. I suggest 3-5 days as the appropriate length.

- Are there competitors to this program in the targeted marketing area? This is an important question but its answer is a little unusual. Take my fund raising program, for instance. There are any number of courses, programs and lectures on this subject taking place at any given time in the Boston area. There always will be so long as the need for funds remains acute in nonprofit America. There are, to be sure, competitors. But not competitors to the *format* I've developed. In considering the kind of institute to establish the question of format, especially where there are competitors, becomes of pivotal significance.

Again, consider the question of my own five day intensive nonprofit technical assistance institute. What makes it distinctive is the fact that each day 3 to 5 heads of foundations, foundation trustees, corporate presidents, corporate giving officers, philanthropists, &c., are brought in as panelists. No other program in this marketing area offers this kind of sustained acess to the kinds of people who are critical to the fund raising success of the audience and who are otherwise so difficult to reach. This significant point gives this program its niche and marketing edge. (In a moment, you'll see how to do the same for your institutes.)

In creating annual programs (and not only annual programs, either), it is important to keep in mind not only what you'll be offering but the distinctive way in which it will be offered. Thus a competitive topic per se is not necessarily a problem. A competitive format may very well be.

Developing Your Program

After you've decided what your program is to be about, *i.e.*, what problem it will solve for the participants, after you have developed and written down a clearly defined Participant Profile and know who else offers programs in the field in this marketing territory, you need to consider the format, just what will happen, in what way, by whom. When assembling an institute you have some flexibility that you usually don't have in shorter programs, and you'll want to take advantage of the possibilities to create something truly distinctive, different.

Here's a format to consider. It's one I use myself:

The institute begins each day with coffee at 9 a.m. I lecture from 9:30-10:00 on the topic of the day. From 10:00-noon there are two hours of expert panels, each panelist being primed to speak on the topic of the day from a "hands on" perspective, giving information that is not otherwise available and from their expert vantage point. From noon to 12:30 the institute participants have the opportunity to ask personal questions of the panelists who are warned that these questions will be incisive, that being one of the purposes of the program. Lunch is from 1 to 2. Participants lunch together. The panelists lunch with you, the leader. This is a good way to make new contacts and network for yourself.

In the afternoon you, the leader, conduct two hours of analysis of the panels and panelists and lecture with new information on the topic of the day. The day concludes with reading assignments for the evening in preparation for the next day's topic.

Variation: you can use the afternoon session to break down into work groups that will allow participants to confront problems pertaining to the day's theme and allowing for specific outcomes pertinent to their own situations. You act as facilitator and supervisor of activities.

Chapter 11

A Sponsor Or No?

Once you have done your homework, discovered who else may be offering a similar subject and in what way, have developed the program topic and content and drafted a program outline, your next decision is to decide whether you will seek a program sponsor or go it alone.

Pros and Cons

For Going It Alone

- All the receipts are yours. You need share no proceeds.

- You will probably find it more efficient not to have to work through a sponsor's support staff for whom your program will probably never be top priority.

- You have complete control over the production and marketing process.

- No questions will emerge as to ownership of tapes or other materials produced in connection with the program. They're yours!

Against Going It Alone

- Given your state you may have to register yourself and your programs (see Chapter 15) and pay a fee which can be several hundreds of dollars.

- All the expenses are yours, too, as well as the proceeds; you will have to have start-up money to cover them. These expenses may include:

  - the design and development of promotional brochures

  - purchase of mailing lists and labels

  - envelopes

  - higher postage costs (unless you are yourself a nonprofit organization)

  - cost of room, food, amenities, &c.

- You will have sponsor staff to assist you.

- You will be able to devote most (never all!) your time to creating and delivering a memorable program and not to the paraphernalia of production and marketing.

- With this extra time, you can find sponsors in other places for similar programs.

There is also another good reason for seeking affiliation with an institution, be it a trade or professional association or university. That reason is credibility. The talk circuit is rife with fast talkers, glib by nature, who often promise more than they can deliver, hence the rationale for entry by states into the business of regulating it. This phenomenon of course hurts us all.

Thus until you are a known quantity, I advise you to think most seriously about affiliating with an organization. It is generally worth "giving up" some portion of the gross proceeds in return for security of payment, staff assistance and an affiliation with a respected organization that will help secure your legitimacy and value in the eyes of other organizations in other places.

Chapter 11

Identifying Sponsors

Let me say this: any organization is a potential sponsor of an annual program and you'll use the same prospecting techniques to find the sponsor of an annual program that you do for shorter programs. The difference is that because these programs are more expensive, it takes the host organization longer to make up its mind and it needs even more of the usual information before doing so. Thus, consider starting at least 10 months before you want the program to take place and try whenever possible to make a personal presentation, at least the first time.

Getting Your Act Together: More Preparation Before This Important Meeting

It is already clear that there are many things to work out before you rashly approach any organization about sponsoring your program. Here are some more:

Fee

Figure out your daily rate. How much do you want to be paid for each day of the institute? Multiply this rate by the number of days of instruction. Add at least one day for preparation and technical assistance you will provide the sponsor on:

- materials development

- participant identification

- materials review

- creation of media packets and materials

- media promotion, &c.

You should also give consideration to having a subsequent event, a "clinic," four or five months after the annual event and you'll want to include your charge for this as well.

Note: As you can imagine, the first year of a program demands a significant time commitment from you and time and financial commitment from the sponsor. When the sponsor cavils about your charges, say that these upfront costs are higher in the first year than you expect them to be for later programs. Start right from the beginning by getting the sponsor to think about your program as an annual event in which certain expenses at the beginning can be amortized over the program's life. Don't allow your desire to launch this program overpower your common sense, however, in the sense of slicing your fees at the first sign of any resistance. If you really are the expert and really are bringing to the participants a Disproportionate Benefit Compared To Fee, you need to derive the full benefit from your status and information.

Hint: While you can and should break down these figures for yourself as above, it is advisable to present the sponsor with a single cost which represents everything.

Books & Materials

I generally make as much if not more at an institute from book sales as from my speaker fee. So will you. Take charge of the materials question from the beginning. An institute needs a variety of materials. Benefit from this. Try to have the full retail cost of your materials built in to expenses. Also try to control the question of producing and selling session tapes.

Publicity

The institute to be most useful for you (and to enhance your status as the perceived expert) needs publicity, needs particularly written press. Work out an arrangement with the sponsor about how the promotional objectives will be reached. It goes without saying that you should not frame these objectives in terms of your own status enhancement

Chapter 11

but rather suggest that reaching the proper audiences will work to the sponsor's advantage, as indeed it will. Your terms may include the need for a publicist or outright public relations assistance from the staff in terms of hours of work to be rendered and targets to be reached. As this is an important objective for you, don't neglect this point.

Rights To The Program And Your Future Relationship

Your objective is to secure an exclusive relationship with the sponsoring organization within a given marketing territory, say Boston. All other rights you need to retain.

You must also have a clear conception of your future relationship with the sponsor. You therefore need contract language that will give you first refusal on presenting this program again, that is that the sponsor must first give you the opportunity to lead the program again so long as the sponsoring organization is satisfied with your professional presentation and the profit margin. Thus you will not be dumped having launched the program for cheaper labor, a very real problem on the talk circuit. All too many of us (and I unhappily include myself) have successfully launched programs for institutions which, because they were unfettered, have seen nothing morally repugnant about jettisoning the creator because they could recruit cheaper labor. Yes, this practice takes place in the halls of hallowed academe which is not always a very nice or uplifting place to be.

All these points need to be clear in your mind before you approach any prospective sponsor. What must be equally clear in your mind is how the sponsor can profit financially from the program, how much he needs to invest in it and how many people at what cost need to participate to provide a good return on investment. In other words, you are in the strongest position as you understand your potential sponsor's business and means of achieving success.

Some Considerations

In regard to the question of profit, you should prepare a draft budget which, after all expenses have been taken into account, leaves the sponsor with a profit of at least $500 per day. Keeping this sponsor profit figure in mind will help you determine the possible participant cost and allow you to make a preliminary decision about whether this is a reasonable expense/investment for the participant especially given what you know about other, competing programs. If it is, well and good. The problem comes, of course, when the sponsor wants more profit and you determine that the target population cannot sustain a higher level of expense for the program. What then?

Some Options

- See whether your prospective sponsor is willing to market your program to interested trade and professional associations at a group rate. If you can increase gross revenues without increasing costs proportionately, you may be able to achieve your objectives and have the sponsor achieve his.

- Reduce the amenities. Have participants buy their own food. Tell them that you are keeping the costs down and that this is the way you've decided to do it. (Don't mention that this is also an expedient for keeping profits up, too!) Since the institutes I'm discussing are designed to draw people from nearby areas, they'll know where to go. For those who are interested in lunching together, you can make an arrangement with a local restaurant for table space.

- Have participants purchase books and materials directly. This is not an ideal situation, because you could end up selling them yourself, an undignified beginning. One possible solution? Add a separate materials fee to the cost of the program and have the institute sponsor collect it and pay it directly to you. Let them handle sales, too. They have the support staff after all that you lack. In any event, don't give up this important profit center. You need it and the participants will need materials.

Another Idea

If the sponsor won't build in materials fees and pay them direct to you, retain the taping rights. Tape the program sessions, including the panels, and sell them both to participants and others who may be interested. If the sponsor isn't helping you with materials, you may very well lose some revenue from participants who don't want to purchase the text. (Yes, it's amazing to me to see certain stoics sitting through a long course without purchasing the materials and then, at its conclusion, buying. It happens all the time.) You'll make up the difference, however, in tape sales.

Chapter 11

As you can see, when dealing with program planners expect to dicker. Lots of people actually like dickering. In any case, to make this process work for you keep in mind precisely what you have to have to make this program a success. Don't waver on this. And not just because you want to make as much money as you can, either; that, of course, is the American way. But also because if you leave the negotiations unhappy, your attitude will inform your approach to the program and get you started on the wrong foot. You and the program planner should both leave your negotiations satisfied. Be creative and be persistent until you both can.

Thoughts On Program Content: Securing People Participants Want To Meet

As you can see, one way of making your institute distinctive and thereby securing your niche in the market is to bring in experts and authorities who can be helpful to the participants but who are difficult to reach. I have already mentioned in this regard our annual fund raising institute in Boston. Each year on the 5 days of the program we invite 3 to 5 heads of corporations, corporate giving officers, foundation trustees, philanthropists, &c., to make candid presentations. These people are important and they are not easy to get access to. (Try it!) We secure their participation early in the year and add their names to our marketing materials as an inducement to attend.

And their cost?

Nothing! The best of all possible worlds; they help bring in paying clients and yet do not deplete our revenues. How can you achieve the same result?

- Draw up a list of those authorities who would add useful information to your program. You will need about twice as many names as you need authorities.

- These people should be from your area. Excessive traveling will discourage their participation.

- Snag one or two key people first. Then use them as the bait for the others. Significant people want to meet and hobnob with others they regard as important. Impress people with the credentials of your authorities.

- Make reasonable requests of them. Don't ask for an entire day. Ask for two hours and throw in a nice luncheon for them.

- Recognize their participation through the media. Professionals enjoy the gloss only media can provide.

- Write a warm and enthusiastic letter of invitation. It's hard to resist flattery.

- Once the program has taken place, ask your authorities to nominate or suggest others who could participate. Then network using the name of the nominator.

Aim high. The more successful people are, the less onerous their restrictions. They usually already have a measure of success, some financial security and acclaim, but this doesn't mean they have a captive audience on which to pour their good advice. The opportunity to do so is irresistible.

Final Notes On Institutes

I like institutes because I like knowing that each year at a given time I have a program in place that will produce real revenue, will be a promotion vehicle for me and my books, will have client prospects in the audience and which will enable me to meet people who will be useful in my various projects. Yes, I like institutes.

To make them work for you:

- Start with a single institute and leverage it into other markets.

- Always keep in mind your revenue objective for the program and factor in the various revenue streams (books, materials, tapes, clients) that will enable you to reach this objective.

Chapter 11

- Use the institute as the basis for unabashed promotion. No institute should take place unless you plan to generate publicity from it.

- Follow up the first institute with an evaluation process and work to produce a book of instructions for the next program. Begin planning for the next program about 6 months before it takes place.

Follow Up Clinic

About 6 months after the institute has successfully taken place, arrange a follow-up clinic. Invite to this clinic all those who have taken previous institutes and all the panel participants, too. Ask student participants to make presentations about how they have successfully implemented the techniques taught at the institute. This kind of showcasing is good public relations not least because you can invite some future participants to attend this clinic and discover how well their peers are doing. Envy breeds emulation.

Once you have begun to create successful institutes, institutes you produce over the course of the year in several cities, you can sit back and take a moment for a little blissful self-congratulation. You are on the way to making the talk circuit work, and work very successfully, for you. Now the trick is to figure out how you can achieve the same result, reaching hundreds if not thousands of possible registrants, without traveling yourself and without causing them to travel large distances, thereby raising their costs of attending your program.

That pleasant result, gentle reader, awaits you now.

Chapter 12

AUDIO CONFERENCING & VIDEO TELECONFERENCING: YOUR AUDIENCE OF THOUSANDS AWAITS YOU

Let's face it. There are some real advantages to being the star of an audio conference or video teleconference.

1) Your audience will be larger.

2) It will be national.

3) You can reach geographic places which are otherwise economically infeasible.

4) You'll make much more money through your fees and materials.

5) You should have a much greater return with tapes and other program spin-offs.

6) You will launch in a single stroke relationships with many universities, trade associations, &c., which can sponsor other programs.

7) You'll be promoted to much larger audiences.

In short, whatever benefits there are to doing a single program will be substantially magnified as you hit the national audio conference and video teleconference circuit.

A Few Words About The Teleconferencing Phenomenon

This really is something new. The technology which has made audio conferencing and video teleconferencing possible hasn't been around for very long and therefore there are relatively few 'experts' in the field.

- It's not yet dramatically profitable for the sponsors of programs. One reason for this unhappy result is that those who create programs don't allow sufficient time for those presenting the programs to promote them. Promotion is, of course, the essence of a successful program but the problems of promotion are exasperated when you deal with a national (perhaps even international) audience. Murphy's Law, always so applicable in human affairs, has a field day in such circumstances.

- There are relatively few programs existing. (This, of course, is good news for you!).

- The field is quickly changing.

Your Approach To The Market

There's no substitute for sleuthing. Before you decide to go ahead, you've got to know what else is being offered. This is not as easy as you might think. After seeking out a number of experts in the field, for instance, I still couldn't get a list of all the existing networks, that is to say the organizations that offer programming. This makes your job very tricky. However, you might look at the annual *Satellite Directory* published by *Satellite News* (Phillips Publishing, Inc., 7811 Montrose Rd., Potomac, MD 20854) to get a sense of what's going on.

Chapter 12

Just as you write to the program planners in continuing education to get hold of their catalogs for review, so now you need to do the same for the various networks. One of the largest networks, though still in its relative infancy, is the National University Teleconference Network, Oklahoma State University Campus, 332 Student Union, Stillwater, OK 74078-0653. NUTN, (pronounced "Newton"), is a network of over 200 colleges and universities nationwide which are equipped to receive audio and video programming. Currently, 35-40 institutions can produce and disseminate video teleconferences, while all can receive them. I myself have been a featured video teleconference speaker through Oklahoma State University.

In approaching NUTN or any other network for information, do the following:

- Write for information on current programming (within the last 6 months or so) to get an idea of what has recently gone out over the network.

- Find out what is being planned for the next six months. This information is generally available. You'll find out, for instance, the name of the program and the sponsoring university or organization.

- Either you can find out from the network directly who is sponsoring the program or who has created it, or they can give you a referral.

- In the case of NUTN, by writing to the national organization you can receive a list of both the advisory board members and a list of resource group members. Some 20 to 25 universities across the country are represented on these lists; one is likely to be within reasonable distance of you.

Once you've gotten this information, you'll discover a couple of things:

- Programming is currently sparse. This will not be the case for long. Right now because the medium is in its infancy, there is not a strong library of programs and therefore the chance of breaking in seems relatively greater. On the other hand, of course, there may also be a reluctance to move ahead on the part of a potential sponsor because profits have not been astoundingly high either.

After you've had the chance to review current programming, do the following:

- Get yourself on the mailing list of sponsors for future programs. You need to review as many brochures as possible to get a sense not only of programming but of brochure design and marketing.

- Attend an audio conference and a video teleconference in a field relatively close to yours. You want to review content, of course, but you should be more interested in how the day is arranged. Both these program formats lack the immediacy of the live instructor and like all media there are methods that need to be learned to overcome this drawback.

Begin To Conceptualize Your Program

Before you approach any program planners, you need to conceptualize your program. Not only what the content will be (that you should know already) but the format and delivery. Here are some possibilities:

- How long will it be? 6 hours is a good length.

- Who will deliver the program content? You will be the chief lecturer, of course. But you may wish to bring in experts on one or two subjects to vary the presentation mode.

- Will there be on site instructional personnel? Many programs use local experts and instructional personnel to lead exercises on site. Will you be the only person involved or do you want such instructional personnel to be involved? What will they do?

- Will the program be exclusively audio? Audio is cheaper. These costs will vary, of course, but an audio program will cost in the neighborhood of $5000 for 6 hours; the same video program may cost $35,000-$40,000. Given these numbers, unless you are a recognized expert on a sizzling topic, you may have to begin with audio.

Chapter 12

- The alternatives are: audio plus some video (pre-taped).

- Video teleconference.

A Few Things You Should Know About The Program Planners Before You Approach Them

These people are in the business of making a profit just like you are, and it's important for you to get a sense of how they do it. In the NUTN, for instance, the developer of the program puts up the venture capital and contracts with the instructor. He also hires the necessary staff (or uses existing staff), develops the marketing plan and sells the program to the second tier of sponsors, those who will actually sell the program to consumers.

The original planner makes his money by selling one-time only use rights to the program to the second tier sponsor. The cost of these rights varies, of course, but about $600 is a reasonable estimate (less per audio). Thus, if you are proposing an audio program that costs $5000 to develop (including your fees, development and marketing) this program would need about 13 sites paying $400 each to enable the program to break even. This may not seem an overwhelming number but remember this:

- Some sponsors, particularly in the university network, may already be running a comparable program with which they do not want to compete.

- Others have already committed their staffs to developing and promoting other programs.

- Still others just don't think your program will do well in their areas and decline to rent it.

In short, it's not surprising that the road to teleconferencing is not, so far, entirely paved with gold.

Knowing this, however, will enable you to frame your expectations more realistically and present a program proposal which does have a chance of succeeding.

The Three Tier Sales Process

In working within the teleconferencing industry three sales must be made or your program cannot succeed. Each is of pivotal importance.

1) You must sell your program to the first program sponsor, the sponsor, this is, who will bring it to the attention of the second program sponsors.

2) The first program sponsor must sell the program to the second program sponsor, the sponsor who will deal with the ultimate consumer.

3) The second program sponsor must sell the program to the ultimate consumer whose enthusiastic participation is necessary to ensure the success of the program.

Selling The Initial Program Sponsor

Anyone considering sponsoring your audio conference or video teleconference needs to know several definite things about you and what you've got in mind. These matters must be dealt with in an initial contact letter and in a subsequent meeting which should be face to face, if possible.

The initial approach letter to the sponsor should address the following points. Before sending it make sure that you are addressing it to the person who can give you the answers you need and who can move your project along.

- Indicate that you already have experience in presenting programs. Program planners, particularly at this level with the investment sums that are necessary for success, are very conservative people. They really don't want to take a chance on a neophyte and it's your responsibility to insure them that you're not one.

- Indicate that a problem exists to which you have the solution.

Chapter 12

- Indicate how many people/organizations have this program and how you have gathered these numbers. Developing a highly specific target market is essential to program success and it's important to let the program planner know that such a specific market exists.

- Indicate that you are the sought-after expert in the field.

- Indicate that you have done some preliminary planning for this program and that you would like a meeting at which to share your findings.

This letter need not be long but it should be crisp, knowledgeable and authoritative. (See samples, page 266 .)

Preparing For Your Meeting

Understand this, your initial meeting with the first program sponsor will not result in an immediate go ahead for a program. The best you can hope for is interest, even enthusiasm and a desire to proceed. You can help create this enthusiasm, however, by doing some constructive planning before the meeting takes place.

- It takes about 58 weeks for the NUTN network to work through all the stages of conceptualizing, marketing and producing a teleconference. Keep this figure in mind as you approach program planners. You need to be working more than a year in advance.

Prepare the following information:

- Précis of material on past programs you have given including program brochures, press materials, course outlines, &c.

- If you have testimonials and letters of support from past program sponsors, have them available.

- If you have the comments of satisfied students from evaluations, have them available.

- Bring your conception of what the day will look like and what kind of vehicle you wish the sponsors to consider.

- Provide the program sponsors with a "context document" which includes the following information:

  - The problem you'll be addressing.

  - How you know that it is in fact a problem. Use national magazine articles, newspaper features, books on the subject (including your own research findings, of course), legislative testimony, &c. In short, indicate that people of weight and merit are concerned about the issue you'll be addressing.

  - How many people have this problem?

  - Are these people readily identifiable (assists with list purchase and promotion if they are).

This "context document" is important. You have to assume that the program planners you are dealing with are intelligent, even sophisticated, but that they know nothing about the field of your specialization. Thus you need to provide them with the background information that will make it easy for them to understand that you are in fact addressing a significant national problem and that there is a readily identifiable audience who will wish to participate.

- **A Program Outline**

Conceptualize how you will arrange the day. What will you discuss in each hour and what specific program outcomes will there be for those attending? In other words, what will people learn and how will they get their money's worth?

Chapter 12

- **Provide Information About Yourself**

You need to present the prospect program planner with the right kind of material about yourself, material that is that indicates that you are:

- knowledgeable

- a known quantity

- a good speaker (indicate that a tape is available if needed and a video cassette if you are proposing a video presentation).

- **Information On How The Day Will Be Organized On-Site**

Think through what kind of on-site help you will need. Facilitators are those who register people and provide basic information about the location and its amenities and run interference for you on housekeeping details. Instructional personnel help deliver on-site exercizes that involve the participants after you have presented general information.

- **Information On Materials You Wish To Use, Why, And Their Availability And Price**

If you are the author of the materials yourself, you will surely want to include your own materials in your program. This makes good sense pedagogically and financially, too. You should be prepared to have a review copy of these materials; (they should be returned to you, of course, one way or the other). If the materials are available from a mainstream publisher, you need to confirm their availability and what kinds of arrangements can be made with the second tier sponsors. Will the publisher send books to each site? If so, who pays shipping? Can you buy books at 40% off and sell direct, &c.? These are questions you need to have resolved before you approach a program planner.

Looking over this list, you are perhaps groaning a bit. This is, you may well be thinking, quite a bit of work for what may be regarded as a gamble. I understand your sentiments. Understand, though, why I am advising you to do this work.

Program planners are continually having ideas tossed at them for consideration. Most are half baked but even the good ones are rarely supported by the kinds of material that the prospective sponsor needs to be able to make an informed decision. Be different! By doing this spade work, you increase the likelihood that your proposal will be seriously considered. Moreover, the mere job of sorting through your material and arranging it should point out flaws and shortcomings in your program and enable you to strengthen it before you've written anything. Thus you should be able to present a better case to the program planner.

Meeting With The Program Planner

As you know, I don't feel that it's always necessary to meet with program planners. As you become known on the continuing education and trade association circuit, you will often be hired over the telephone without undue effort. That's as it should be. In this case, however, try to see the sponsor. There are some good reasons for doing so:

- The amount of money involved here is greater than with your ordinary presentations. Thus sponsors need to be reassured not only about your formal credentials but about your powers of persuasion, showmanship and presentation. A meeting will enable you to turn a perhaps skeptical program planner into one of your strongest advocates.

- Arranging an audio conference or video teleconference takes time. Thus it is important, right from the start, to get a very clear sense of all that is involved in planning the teleconference and when things need to take place. During an initial meeting, which will probably take about an hour, you can get a clear picture of who does what, when.

- You need to know who you are dealing with and get a sense of the person's strengths and weaknesses. If, for instance, you are dealing with a continuing educator take notes. There is a lot of high flying talk in continuing education about teleconferencing and its benefits, a lot of entrepreneurial talk. In fact, however, many of those in this business remain stuck in pre-modern business attitudes: they have the rhetoric down pat, but you'll find that the slow, meandering pace of academe continues. If you have a sense that the person you are dealing with is not well organized and efficient, your working relationship might be a difficult one.

Chapter 12

- You can get a sense of the facilities that exist. Ask for a tour. Also, ask when the next program is being sent from this facility and, if things proceed well, ask to come in and observe. The more you know about the sponsor's operation, both managerial and technical, the better off you are. Fortunately, your anticipated remuneration, which can be hefty, allows for this investment and you should make it.

Handling The Meeting

During this important meeting be prepared to be brisk, businesslike, cool and, of course, exceedingly likeable. You are not, of course, the host and you should wait for the sponsor to take the conversational lead.

What is likely to take place is this: the sponsor will open with some general remarks and then proceed to tell you something about his operation. Because of your preparation you'll probably know most but probably not all that he tells you. Listen closely. This individual is the captain of his ship and is proud of his work. You can be sure of that. Listen for conversational clues about the programs he has produced about which he's proudest. That's probably his favorite subject area and if you can bridge from these programs to your own you're probably in a stronger position. Also, don't be afraid to congratulate this person on his success. The delivery of this compliment is a minor art form. You do not wish to come across as flattering and servile but rather as one professional offering a frank acknowledgement of a job well done to another. Look the person in the eyes and say, "I know how proud you must be of that job. I know how difficult it is to attract that kind of attendance and derive that level of profit. This is just the result I'm hoping for for our project." Show the prospective sponsor that your program can be another feather in his cap. Remember: sponsors probably have two reasons for taking on programs: 1) They feel they will be profitable, and 2) they feel that such a success will be useful to them professionally as evidence of their own creativity and intelligence. Appeal to both.

After this opening, the prospective sponsor will turn to you for an explanation of your objectives and program. Treat this moment as what it is: an audition. Pause if you must but fix your eyes on the sponsor's and make your presentation just as you would present your program material on the day of delivery. This is probably the first time the sponsor has seen you after all and first impressions are important. You need to come across as an individual who is at once knowledgeable about a subject which has a clearly defined audience, empathetic to the needs and objectives of the sponsor and of interest to a future audience. Also and significantly, worth the investment money.

You should have brought to this meeting two sets of all the documents you've prepared, one for the sponsor and one for yourself. Don't turn these over in advance of your remarks. Make your case first: why this is the time for your program. What the audience is and how you can get access to it. Your successful track record with the program elsewhere. The availability of promotional materials and all the other matters I've previously mentioned. At the conclusion of each point, *then* pass the sponsor the relevant document. The reason for this is that you do not want him to be flipping pages rather than listening to you. The documents are for later reference not for present study.

It is most important that you establish the fact that you have already had success with this program. Mention the institutions and places where you have presented it. Indicate that participant evaluations are available and that you've got a tape of a typical program. Stress the typical. You want to show that your average performance is superb.

Expect to be asked precisely how your program would be arranged and what kind of on-site assistance you'll need. Also review the materials situation.

By this point you'll have some preliminary expression of sponsor interest, if there's to be any at all. You'll know because the discussion will move towards the real issue: money.

There is no need for you to be uncertain or diffident about this subject. Both parties to this agreement (and the secondary sponsor who is implicitly present) enter into the agreement 1) because the program is a valuable one and 2) because it offers the possibility of profit. There is thus no reason to be squeamish about this subject.

Some Possibilities

1) If you have no book or other written materials which you can sell participants, you are at a relative disadvantage in this discussion. Remember that and plan accordingly! In this situation your fee range will be $1000 to $5000. You should hold out in these circumstances for the complete tape rights and you should also try to make an arrangement with a publisher so that you can recommend and benefit from a text.

Chapter 12

2) If you have written materials, it is entirely likely that far and away the bulk of your income from the teleconference will come from materials sales. For instance, while you might derive a $3000 to $4000 fee from a day's teleconference, if 1000 people participate (just 30 some odd at 30 locations after all) each of whom pays $20 for materials costs you'd derive $20,000 from materials, much more than your presentation fee. In this circumstance, you can expect the sponsor to attempt to scale down the materials cost. Either they will try to strike a deal with you and so benefit themselves or else they will say that the program cannot sustain this level of materials cost. As you enter into this question, you should have a figure in mind that is the lowest you can possibly accept from materials. Mine is 50% of the retail price of my books. You can look upon the matter like this: Since $15 per book is my irreducible minimum the real salesmanship in this case comes in persuading the sponsor to pay more than the minimum I need and more than he wishes to pay.

In such a situation, what you might suggest is a 50-50% split of net proceeds on tape revenue. This should sweeten the deal from the sponsor's vantage point and also give you more revenue. Plus, if you have additional products to sell at the program, you need to specify that revenues derived will be yours exclusively. The sponsor will argue that he has made the opportunity for sales available to you; you'll argue that the product was produced by you and that the right climate for sales was produced by you and that you should accordingly benefit. Your best tact: downplay the likely response from participants while expecting at least one third of them to respond favorably to additional offers.

Some Words Of Advice

Don't rush to resolve the financial questions at your first meeting unless your areas of agreement are firm and clear. What you can do, however, is this:

- Find out what kind of stipend the sponsor generally pays the lecturer. Remember this: unless you are a sizzling star (don't undervalue yourself, of course) you will probably get the sponsor's going rate. After all, the program has not yet proven itself and you are still, to the sponsor, an untested commodity.

- Find out what the sponsor's usual way of handling materials fees is. You are better off if your materials can be factored right into the course fee. What you do not want to happen is to have the local people try to sell your book and materials on the day of the program. You will suffer a clear loss in this circumstance and if you plan to use the materials you have the unfortunate situation of having some people with them and some without, the ingredients for disaster.

- Find out whether the sponsor makes tapes available to the participants and how this is usually done. This may be the most unusual point you advance since many programs are not put on tape and sold to the participants. This is unfortunate, of course, since adult learners need repetition of subject material and tape is an easy way of meeting this need as well as supplementing revenues.

- Find out whether you can provide general information on yourself, books and materials of yours, services, &c., to participants. Treat this as casually as possible although it is a nice revenue stream for you.

One other matter which will need eventual resolution but you can skip at your first meeting is this: if, say, 30 program centers do book your program and this program is adequately promoted and you have a book to offer, you can be sure that there will be calls from those who want the materials but cannot attend the course. You have three options. You can simply leave this matter out of the contract negotiations and later advise the sponsor that all calls of this nature should be directed to you. You can include a clause in your contract that all such calls be directed to you and that revenues are yours alone. Or you can split revenues according to some formula with the prime and secondary sponsors. Of these, particularly because the third option while seemingly fair is difficult to administer, I prefer, *faute de mieux*, the first.

What you need to take away from your initial meeting is this:

- How much will it cost for the sponsor to produce your program? While the sponsor may not be prepared to give you a final estimate at your first meeting, you can probably get a general one. Rest assured that the sponsor will not move ahead unless and until there is a clear indication of profitability and you must not only understand this but help the sponsor realize this reasonable objective. By the same token, you need to keep in mind that the sponsor would like to secure you, the expert, for the cheapest possible price. Various 'glamor variables' will be dangled before

Chapter 12

you as the quickwitted sponsor attempts to undermine your fee: a national audio conference or video teleconference will be good for your reputation. You'll get "lots of business" as a result. You will have been validated as a star. Lots of people will get important information from you and you'll be providing a public service. Don't let this aery hyperbole sway you in any way. It's just eyewash.

You want to derive the maximum possible benefit from the several revenue streams which make electronic conferencing worth doing:

- speaker honorarium

- materials fees

- tapes of the proceedings

- additional product sales

- future client relationships with participants.

The deal must be structured so that you meet your reasonable objectives in each category.

Another Possible Stumbling Block: Black Outs

If you go into your conversation with the prospective sponsor already having relationships with some of the target groups, how should you handle this matter? I have been informed by responsible authorities that there is nothing to be derived from embargoing or blacking out a program within a network, that those who would attend an audio conference or video teleconference are in fact a different market from those who need and want to see you in person. I treat this expert assertion with a grain of salt, however. Before you sign a final agreement with a general sponsor, contact your existing relationships and see how they feel about having a teleconference beemed in. You want to use this teleconferencing mechanism to open new markets for yourself not threaten existing markets and you must be clear that this is the result you get.

Another Financial Question

One other major financial question needs to be resolved and that is the problem of future broadcasts. The problem we humans have and have not yet satisfactorily resolved is the finite quality of time. The advent of audio conferencing and video teleconferencing takes those of us on the talk circuit at least some way to resolving this problem and you mustn't lose sight of the advantages of program replay.

In this connection, what you are selling to the prime sponsor and what in turn the prime sponsor is selling to the individual or secondary sponsors is one-time only use rights. That is the possibility of using and profiting from the program once and once only. In this matter of negotiation, your problem does not come with the second tier of sponsors but with the first. Make sure you sell him just one-time only rights, too.

Find out from the prime sponsor or network representative what their usual policy is on replays. How often are the popular programs reused and what financial arrangements are made with the experts delivering the program? I happen to feel that a program, while it will be taped and sold to participants, those who can't attend and others interested, should not be given again.

- The initial program is not the best program you're going to give. Moreover if you are in a subject field that changes rapidly the information will age.

- People may resent attending what amounts to an entirely canned program. They like interaction with the expert.

What you want, instead, is a "next teleconference" clause in your contract. Such a clause is designed to accomplish the following:

- If the prime sponsor decides to again market your program, you will be offered first refusal on presenting it and that the terms, subject to negotiation, will be comparable to the last occasion on which you offered the program.

Chapter 12

- If the program sponsor declines to offer the program again, you are free to offer the program elsewhere without penalty or repercussions. Oddly, it occasionally happens (to my utter consternation) that even though a program is profitable and of high interest to participants, a sponsor will decline to offer it again. While I cannot understand such myopic reasoning, you need to protect yourself against it. If a sponsor will not offer a program, you need to be free to take it elsewhere without penalty.

If, on the other hand, the prime sponsor wants a clause in the contract for reuse of the existing program (which will, of course, be on tape), here's how that clause should be structured for your benefit:

- **Fee.** If the program is sold for the same price to the second tier of sponsors, you should derive *at least* as much for your fee. There should be no question of reducing what you are paid. Moreover, given the fact that overhead and other fixed expenses will not pertain, you should request proportionately more. There is yet another reason for requesting more: you should have from the first presentation a group of enthusiastic reviews and participant evaluations. These can be used as part of your marketing and promotional efforts and will help spur the enrollment of new participants. Don't be shy about saying so. There are several ways of solving the fee question:

  - Find out how much money will be saved a second time given the reduction and elimination of fixed expenses. Request this much more money.

  - If the need for the material is still apparent, the participant reviews enthusiastic and the likelihood of selling the program enhanced, charge more for the program to the second tier of sponsors. Make a $400 program fee, $425 for instance. Let the prime sponsor benefit by keeping your contract as it stands and you keep the extra for yourself.

It goes without saying that all previous book arrangements, materials fees, tapes and other rights should remain constant unless you feel they can be improved in your favor without jeopardizing the contract.

Other Points Of Discussion

Without a doubt the financial and rights questions will be the most difficult to resolve and yet they will be resolved if you keep in mind both the interests of the prime sponsor and yourself and offer reasonable terms that will be mutually beneficial. I firmly believe this. The trick is to take the time you need, keep these mutual interests firmly in mind, and be creative in finding areas of agreement.

When at least these matters have been resolved there are still others which will need your attention. At this first meeting, and any subsequent meetings which may be necessary, you need to resolve these matters, too:

- Who will draft the marketing plan to the secondary sponsors?

- What kinds of on-site personnel are needed and what will they do?

- Who will draft the marketing plan that the secondary sponsors can use to sell the program to participants?

Here are some answers to these pivotal questions.

- **Prime Sponsor**

It is really the job of the prime sponsor to draft the marketing document that will convince the secondary sponsors to sign up for your program. But don't sit back and do nothing. I have advised you to prepare certain documents for your meeting with the prime sponsor. In these documents there is sufficient information for the prime sponsor which he can use in developing this marketing plan. I would suggest that you draft the initial marketing plan and let the prime sponsor edit it with you having the final approval. There are several reasons for doing this: you know your program best and you should be able best to articulate the reasons why people should attend and the benefits to the sponsors. Working together with the prime sponsor in this fashion, you'll be able to craft a persuasive marketing document.

Chapter 12

What's more important than the document, however, is what happens to it once it's written. Here you need the assurances of the prime sponsor that he will not simply rely upon your written marketing document to sell the program. It's insufficient. Telemarketing is necessary. These calls should be made by the prime sponsor and they should be accomplished expeditiously. The correct sequence then would be the following:

- You draft the initial marketing document (benefits to the sponsor, purpose of the program, audience, &c)

- This is edited by the prime sponsor and ultimately approved by you, then produced.

- This should be mailed along with a most persuasive marketing letter from the prime sponsor to the secondary sponsors.

- This letter and package should be followed up with a telephone call from the prime sponsor.

- As secondary sponsors sign up periodic follow up letters should go out with an intimation, more and more urgently stated, that time is running out for signing up. The prime sponsor should leverage the participation of the secondary sponsors to encourage still more secondary sponsors to sign up for the program. This method works although it is time consuming.

- **On-site Personnel**

If you are relying upon on-site personnel to assist in the delivery of program material, you need to draft the materials that they will need and any instructional sheets for them. This is clearly your responsibility. The need for such personnel should be a part of the initial marketing materials and as soon as a secondary sponsor has signed up, these personnel materials need to be dispatched. You should make yourself available to the secondary sponsors to answer their specific questions.

- **Secondary Sponsor Marketing Plan**

This again should be the joint responsibility of the prime sponsor and yourself. But you should try your hand at an initial draft. After all, by now this should be terra cognita to you. You've presented programs elsewhere. You've had an opportunity to evaluate which program brochures have been effective and which not. You know (or at least should know) which marketing efforts have paid off; these should all be part of the marketing materials. Moreover, since you have done the program before, don't hesitate to use past user comments to help spur attendance. People like to know that they are not guinea pigs for a new program.

Things You Want To Know About The Prime Sponsor

Typically the prime sponsor will, in one way or another, pepper you with questions making you feel by the meeting's conclusion that this has resembled the traditional job interview. Don't let this happen! While the prime sponsor has reasonable queries about you, you, too, need to know some things about the prime sponsor before any deal is finally consummated. Here's some of what you should find out:

- "How many programs have you produced?"

- "How many of the kind (audio, video, &c) that I'm here discussing?"

- "May I have the names of one or two of the presenters?"

- "May I have the names of one or two secondary sponsors that you've done business with?"

- "Would it be possible for me to review one or two of your past programs?"

- "May I see a sample marketing plan?"

Chapter 12

The way in which these perfectly reasonable questions are handled will give you a sense of the agency you are dealing with. You, too, have your reputation to protect and the more you become a fixture on the talk circuit the more zealously you will guard it. Most people have good intentions but all too many of them lack the knowledge and techniques of realizing them. Make sure you are not dealing with this kind of lamentable creature.

Another Matter For Your Consideration: Multiple Submission

At the conclusion of your meeting, you should have a sense of satisfaction and budding fulfillment. Before this meeting ends, find out what the next steps are:

- Who else needs to review these materials?

- How long will it take?

- When can you expect to hear?

Mutually agree that if you have not heard by that date, you'll call back. There is time pressure in this matter. Remember: it takes NUTN 58 weeks from start to actual production. Being human you have probably started this process on the 57th week and you're hoping to make up the time. But be realistic. A lot of people are going to be involved in the process of making you a star and all of them will have something to say, something to offer, some objection to make.

The question therefore arises: if this is the case, shouldn't I protect myself by multiply submitting my proposal and by carrying on on several fronts? The best answer is: that depends.

If you have not approached another prime sponsor, tell the person you have contacted that this is an exclusive contact. Give him a month in which to make up his mind. Factor this month into your calculations. Allow for the fact that as someone who has not been through this process before and who is not yet entirely accepted by the prime sponsor, there is always a high likelihood that your first proposal won't be accepted and that you will have to make another presentation elsewhere. So be it. But be prepared. At the end of 30 days, get the answer you need even if it's only "We can't make up our mind yet." In that case, submit elsewhere.

Before you submit elsewhere, however, try to get some evaluation of your initial proposal. If you sense a waning of enthusiasm or indeed that enthusiasm was never present, find out why. It makes no sense to go through the selection process again if, because of certain inherent flaws, the project will not succeed in being adopted. Find out what these flaws might be and adjust your proposal accordingly. *Then* write your introductory letters — to two or even three places. Time, after all, is of the essence unless you are extraordinarily well organized and working quite far ahead in which case you can proceed at a more leisurely pace.

The problem now, of course, is that these other sources are likely to be inconveniently situated for you. Should you spend the money to visit? I think not. Put together a convincing introductory letter. Follow with a telephone call and then send the packet of information you've assembled. Don't hesitate to try to network your way to an introduction if you can. In these circumstances that should be most influencial. You can then follow up by telephone.

Decline After Decline

If you get two or three declines on your proposal, something is wrong with what you are submitting. If you're like me, you'll probably be inclined to suspect the intelligence and even the paternity of those you're dealing with. Fair enough. I am firmly of the opinion that the entrepreneur has a spark of genius which is denied to others and which those others go to enormous lengths to snuff out. Part of what differentiates us from the run of common man is that we have a sense of possibilities and opportunities that others lack. Don't, by any means, lose this!

Do, however, allow for the possibility that, for now and under the current circumstances, your idea is not ready to be accepted. Go back and continue to offer the program through the trade, professional and continuing education markets and chalk up a new run of successes. As new program brochures come out, as new registration figures are run up, keep the prime sponsors apprised of developments. This is what I call Assertive Courtesy, and it's part of the business of changing minds.

Chapter 12

Also, don't hesitate, as you continue your spade work on the talk circuit, to open up new channels of communication with new prospective sponsors.

Find out, too, what kinds of development plans are of interest to prime sponsors and see whether you can dovetail your own programs and objectives into theirs. Program planners are no doubt myopic; see whether you can at least take advantage of it.

The stakes in audio conferencing and video teleconferencing are high and it behooves you to keep working to:

- Find out what individual program planners are interested in.

- Keep your lines of communication open to them.

- Continue to bring news of your successes to their attention understanding that persuasion and motivation are long term processes.

- Present other proposals which may stand a better chance of acceptance.

What continues to amaze me about the talk circuit and those who practice on it, is the short sightedness of many speakers. I know from experience that it can take a year or two or more to convince a program planner to do what I always knew was in his best interest. Don't lose heart and don't give up. Remain unflappable. Remain optimistic. Remain persistent. Also develop a good friend in the business with whom you can share excoriating remarks about the idiots you encounter.

"Yes! We Want You!"

I like success and I like moments when people say this to me, whatever the prize. I especially like it said when the returns are so high. But remember, there's many a slip.... and there remain many details to work out.

Here are some of the leading details which must be worked out. Find out when they need to be completed and who will do them. Allow plenty of time for both sloth and changing minds.

- Final development of complete program outline.

- Minute by minute break-down of presentation day.

- Packet to be sent to second tier sponsors to persuade them to come on board.

- Packet of marketing materials which these second tier sponsors can use in their own marketing efforts.

- On-site personnel training materials and study guides.

Inevitably, even though the actual broadcast date may be a year away, you will need regular, even frequent meetings with the program planner as matters commence. For one thing, you need to know how each of you works. Remember, too, that the more helpful you can be about developing the program and marketing materials, the more the final product will look like you want it to.

By the same token, don't do everything. There's no need to. Leave these kinds of decisions to the prime sponsor, always allowing, of course, for the option of speaking your mind when it's needed:

- What will the cost be for one-time only rental usage?

- What kinds of equipment will the secondary sponsors need for reception?

- How should the room be set up for best reception?

Chapter 12

- What kind of technical help needs to be available?

- What kind of audio voice modifiers and other technical equipment?

Learn, of course, as much as you can about these matters. You, too, have much to learn through this experience, and you should approach this event with the expectation that you'll be doing other audio and video conferences in the future and want to fashion yourself as the prevailing expert.

Tips On Marketing To The Secondary Tier of Sponsors

Let me say this as strongly as I can. Even if you draw up the most exquisite, telling and exemplary direct mail marketing materials clearly eduticating the need for your program, its audience and the profit protential for the secondary tier of sponsors, such direct mailing pieces will still not be enough to sell your program.

Face it. People are inundated with direct marketing proposals of all kinds and we have become numbed to them. What you've got to do instead is get the prime sponsor on the telephone and use telemarketing techniques to sell your program. This takes both the right mental attitude, time, and the correct approach. One of the things you're looking for in your initial meeting, and before you sign any contract, is a strong indication that the prime sponsor will enthusiastically adopt this kind of marketing approach.

Here's the way to make the system work for you:

Once you have entered into your agreement with the prime sponsor, he should approach a half dozen prime buyers of your program with a personal letter offering the program, perhaps even at a special rate (say 10% discount) for a quick decision. This letter needs to be a strong, incisive sales piece, and it should be followed up with a telephone call if need be.

The reason for this piece is this: if these organizations sign on early, you can cite this fact in the remainder of your marketing and sales letters. You can also breathe a little easier.

Most people don't want to be the first to do anything. That's a sad fact of life. So make it easy for them: urge them to a prompt decision by showing them that your program is trendy, popular, the thing to screen. As other sponsors sign up, use their names in the same way.

Also, use telemarketing. Have the prime sponsor call other possible sponsors to sign them up. If the prime sponsor won't do this for you, look elsewhere since they either don't understand or don't care how sales are made. You do.

Once you've signed up the quota of sponsors you need for the program, encourage the prime sponsor to send yet another letter to the remaining possible second tier sponsors and urge them to sign up — NOW! There are those sluggish individuals who habitually wait to the eleventh hour to do anything. But their money's as green as anyone else's, and you should do what it takes to get it!

You should not make these calls yourself, let's be clear about this. You're the expert, and it's just the slightest bit *infra dig* to go pandering for sales. Nonetheless you can be of enormous help during this period. You can supply the prime sponsor with ongoing information about why your topic is popular now and how your program will address the needs of the prospective audience. Moreover, the prime sponsor should make your name and telephone number available as part of his sales effort so that prospective sponsors can call to discuss content and approach with you.

A Few Format Suggestions

Whether you are doing an audio or video conference, don't do all the talking yourself. Unless you are a much practised speaker capable of wide modulations, inflections, changes of speed and color, it may become tiring for your audience to listen to you. If they once tune out, it's difficult to get them to tune back in again.

Thus: change your format in easy ways. Allow some time for straight lecture. Take advantage of interactive communication with the participants for questions. Bring in a friend and set up a portion of your program as question and answer so that another voice frequency is introduced and so your format doesn't end up boring the listeners. Adult learners are not used to sitting in one place for long periods listening to a single individual and unless you modify your format you risk losing their attention and thus some of the benefits that come from this kind of program.

Chapter 12

Last Advice

Enjoy yourself!

It is your responsibility to set the proper tone for your program. It should be infused with joy — the joy of learning and the joy of success. Too many program presenters are lethal, soporific and joy squeezed. Don't be one of them! You have much to be joyful about, much to be satisfied with as you approach this program or indeed any other program:

- You have an audience that has paid real Yankee dollars to listen to you.

- You have something important to tell them, something which will change their lives, lessen their anxieties and help them realize their proudest aspirations for themselves.

- You are deriving some substantial benefits yourself from the experience, both financial and psychic.

Now knock 'em dead. You're in the entertainment business. It's your responsibility to give your audience a good show and as you give them the information they want, in a form they can use, in a way they can appreciate, you will propel yourself ahead.

When you do, immediately sit down with the program planner and begin discussing your next idea. For now you've been vetted in a most demanding venue and as such deserve to be taken very seriously.

Chapter 13

STILL MORE POSSIBILITIES: THE LECTURE CIRCUIT AND THE TALK CONGLOMERATE

The Lecture Circuit

There is more than a little smug self-satisfaction to be derived from casually remarking to your seat companion on your seventh flight of the week, "What do I do? Oh, I'm on the lecture circuit." Even I am by no means immune to the joy of this disarming bit of oneupsmanship, for to be on The Lecture Circuit suggests, even to those with flatworm intelligence, that one is an individual of consequence whose well-chosen words are worth attending to. Now you and I know that that is the case, but the rewards begin to pile up when those less perceptive come to this necessary conclusion. The problem, however, is that it is not easy to attain this desirable eminence.

In part, this is at least partly because the lecture circuit itself is something of a mirage. Perhaps television is the culprit, but nowadays there are no sweeping national lecture tours comparable to those of Charles Dickens in the last century or even Dylan Thomas in the middle of our own. Yes, I think television is the culprit. Today the lecture circuit is infinitely less structured than it once was and infinitely more diverse. With all due respect to Gertrude Stein, there is a there out there, but it is harder to put your finger on.

That's largely because the number of possibilities has grown so dramatically. As Alexis de Tocqueville so sagely noted in the infancy of the republic, Americans love to create and join organizations. So much is this a national trait, that there are now more than 200,000 organizations across the country which need speakers and are happy to book them, speakers who speak on every conceivable topic. To be sure, most of these organizations don't pay their speakers and provide them with only the most trifling media coverage, if that. Yet even these organizations have their place in the lecture circuit for they are the seed beds for many who later triumph on the more lucrative end of the market. And because they have their place, I feel compelled to discuss them as soon as I've given you a few words of preparatory advice.

Preparing For The Lecture Circuit

Public opinion polls consistently rate public speaking as the top anxiety of most Americans. No wonder. With so many organizations seeking speakers and with so many Americans tragically inept on the platform, each day presents a breathtaking array of possibilities for my fellow citizens to embarrass themselves and undercut their professional standing simply by opening their mouths.

We have all been subjected to these public fiascos:

Mr. Monotonal whose every word is an unconsidered cliché and whose rigid body posture is reminiscent of a naughty eight year old before a deserved spanking. This frequent specimen hugs his much pondered and completely written remarks as if they were a life-raft in stormy seas; his limp attempts at humor come direct from a compendium of surefire funny stories, but with him they turn sour.

The Gladhander repulses us with frothy bonhomie and back slapping hail-fellow-well-met intrusiveness. Effusive and effervescent, with a cascade of jollities at the ready, in the presence of such a wonder, our hand stays stolidly on the wallet.

Ms. Meek tells us she is unworthy of the honor of addressing us and all too soon we are in complete agreement with this lady whose merits are obviously on sabbatical. Tentative, anxious to offend no one, cautious to a fault, if we are blessed by the gods she is also short but all too often her tormented meanderings take time and more time and still more until she finally comes to a tentative, sputtering conclusion.

You and I have both seen and been tortured by these and the other unfortunate types who proliferate at the lower end of the circuit. It is to differentiate you from these twisted specimens that I am advancing the following thoughts.

Chapter 13

Understanding The Lecture Mileau, Preparing Yourself Accordingly

Most lectures have a food component. Either they take place just after a luncheon or dinner. Or just before dessert. If it is the former, your audience is necessarily somewhat sluggish. If the meal has been good, they crave a stretch, a cigarette, a visit to the powder room. If the meal has been bad (which is all too frequently the case), they crave a scapegoat. On the other hand, if the food follows your presentation, a sizable percentage of their minds are focused on the sheer animal joy that awaits them and no matter how memorable your verbal pyrotechnics, no matter how utilitarian your remarks, the expected delight still stands to shadow your performance. All this must be kept in mind on the lecture circuit. Thus consider the following:

- You must be prepared to communicate your energy and enthusiasm to the audience, to awaken them from the counter pull of the sleepy digestive process and to attract them from the food which will shortly thrill them. If you are not prepared to engender excitement, enthusiasm, and energy, avoid the lecture circuit. You are doomed.

- You must understand that you are in the entertainment business. I have said this before, but this single fact is significant enough to be stressed. No matter how valuable the information you are imparting, how shattering the consequences of not paying attention, if you cannot deliver the facts entertainingly your audience will not attend to you and hence will fail to grasp your conclusions, too. As surely as Frank Sinatra or Johnny Carson, you, gentle reader, are in the entertainment business the minute you step foot on the lecture circuit.

- Don't attempt to communicate too much. In a single speech of forty minutes or so, there should only be one leading idea, an idea to which you return in many ways, which is supported by many examples and made enthralling by your ability to bring it directly in touch with the lives of your audience. One speech, one idea. Don't forget it.

- Get your audience to visualize your point. Speakers make the mistake of stuffing themselves and their presentations with statistics and cumbersome facts and yet these very facts and statistics all too often insure the failure of their speeches. You have only to look to the ghastly example provided by our last presidential debates in which both Messieurs Reagan and Mondale, although much practiced speakers, grossly mishandled their data to the detriment of their arguments and objectives.

  Your task is to get your audience to visualize the matter on which you are speaking and to make them understand what particular relevance it has for their lives. In fact, I go so far as to say that they must not only understand their importance, they must feel it. What I call Visualization enables you to bring about this result. Use one clearly considered example, perhaps in anecdotal form, that will for your audience become the prism through which all the facts and statistics you provide make crystal clear sense.

- Use the Problem Solving Process Format to structure your remarks. This, surely, deserves no further comment since you must be by now a convert to this method.

- Be brief and to the point. Start promptly and end on schedule. If you don't do this, expect trouble. After all, you are competing with a portion of the brain that is screaming, louder and louder still, "Feed me!" And in this battle, your luminiscent remarks don't stand a chance.

Mastery From The Platform

True mastery of the platform only comes from experience. The more speaking you do, the better you will be. Thus don't worry unduly about your early mistakes. Learn from them to be sure, but don't be depressed by them for as sure as I can be in this uncertain age, your early presentations will not be histrionically flawless. The trick is to keep what is good and get rid of the chaff. In this regard, here are some things to keep in mind:

- As you take your place at the podium, pause for a moment. Force the crowd to come to order, to silence itself to hear you. Use a glass of water if you need to and sip, slowly. Audiences are schooled in proper behavior, too, and will usually accord the speaker some courtesy in remaining quiet. But this doesn't last. If you get off to a bad start,this courtesy will evaporate like morning dew and you'll be faced with outbreaks of noise and perhaps worse interruptions. Learn to glare. If such outbreaks occur, stop and focus your attention on the culprits. So long as you haven't lost the entire audience, this tactic will swing the group sentiment over to you and you can continue. Remember: this only works once, or at the most twice. After that mere glares will not help you. Thus identify the exit before you go on.

Chapter 13

- Select two people in the audience as weathervanes, people whose faces you can review to see how long the listeners are responding to your talk. Select a happy face and a glum one, one that's easy and one that looks difficult. Appearances, however, are deceiving. Those who look most glum, even irritable, may simply have an unpleasant cast of face and may be the easiest to ignite with enthusiasm. However, you need these weathervanes to turn to at regular intervals to see how your talk is going over.

- Begin your talk by thanking the association by name for having you. Also thank the introducer, by name, for his remarks. Right from the start begin to introduce things into your talk with which the audience is familiar. It helps them accept what you've got to say and will act as a bridge into your materials. It goes without saying that you should check on the pronunciation of these names and if necessary write yourself a phonetic note.

- Practice leaning into your audience as you talk. People are more likely to do what you want them to do if you touch them. Since this is impossible when you're separated by the forbidding eminence of the podium, you must overcome this barrier by suggesting physical proximity. Particularly on important points, practice leaning right into your audience. This movement suggests intensity and importance.

- Set the structure of your speech from the first minute. Inform your audience why you have come and what you will accomplish in your speech. Listeners need structure. There are, of course, any number of speeches which you can give but arranging matters in this fashion will help you get started and keep you on track. In many of my speeches I begin with a global objective, a specific objective and a personal objective. This part of your speech conforms to the old triad, "Tell 'em what you're going to tell 'em." The other parts, of course, are "Tell 'em" and "Tell 'em what you've told 'em." This has never been bad advice.

- Write out your key phrases completely. I rarely if ever speak from a completely written text. Unless one has a vast amount of time for practice, one continually looks down at the text rather than keeping your eyes where they should be — on the audience. One also feels bound to the text rather than to exciting the enthusiasm of the audience. Thus, while you should certainly have an outline, perhaps three by five inch cards with your significant points, only your openings, your most stirring rhetorical points and your conclusion should actually be entirely written out. Since these may actually wind up in media stories, it is important that they be imparted exactly as you want them.

- Use self-deprecating humor. The audience knows that you are a (perhaps ephemeral) star and they are willing to recognize you. But they don't want you placed too far beyond them, and they'd like evidence that star though you may be you are also human and vulnerable — just like they are. Mildly self-deprecating humor is so important that before you use it, you should, if inexperienced, write it down. This is to insure that you achieve just the right balance: to indicate your essential humanity and connectedness with the audience but in no way to undercut your status as the expert and cynosure of all eyes. For, of course, that would never do.

- Practice using short sentences and action words. The Problem Solving Process format is ideal for giving the audience a feeling that you are the master of the subject, that a solution to the problem you are addressing is possible if your steps are followed. Don't detract from this result by using sentences which are other than crisp, active, thrusting. This kind of simple English is both graceful and effective. It also seems very difficult for most people to master. Perhaps they feel that their meandering circumlocutions are intelligent, sophisticated. In fact, the best English will always be the shortest sentences carried by the most active verbs to a conclusion which is readily at hand. Never forget this and whatever you do, practice fashioning such sentences until you are their master.

- Use visualization to bring home the forcefulness of your examples. Instead of saying something like "15% of children suffer from this disease" say instead, "How many of you have children?" Right off the bat this is a better technique, because you are engaging the audience. Given the right audience, a substantial number of hands will go up. Then say, "How would you feel knowing 5 of you have children with this affliction? Well, those are the numbers nationwide. One out of every 7 children." That's very dramatic. To be sure, this technique takes longer but remember: in a single speech you can make only a single point and you want this point to be remembered. Visualization intensifies understanding and increases the likelihood of retention.

- End by invoking the anxieties that your audience has about the topic you've discussed. End, too, by citing their aspirations — the objectives that they have for themselves. Let them know that by following your suggestions, their anxieties can be allayed and their aspirations realized. Let them know, too, that if they don't follow your suggestions that those anxieties will in fact become dread realities and that they will have only themselves to blame.

Chapter 13

I like this conclusion very much not least because it's a core element of my own philosophy that people working together can achieve the objectives they desire but that people refusing to take beneficial actions will themselves bring on the very anxieties that they most fear. Under the guiding principle of true social responsibility, I feel that the audience should be aware of both the possibilities, their role in realizing them and their responsibility for failing to act. This is an approach which we as Americans understand and are philosophically inclined to respect and it works very, very well from the lecture platform.

- Consider the matter of questions. Most books will advise you to take questions after your speech. I advise you to be selective about doing so. If you have just given a blazing oration and have left the crowd stunned, you don't want to take questions. An insipid, ill-considered question will destroy the mood which is an essential result of your speech. You can however, make yourself available afterwords — perhaps at a table where you're autographing books. This is my preferred alternative. On the other hand, questions may be advisable both to cement your bond with your audience and to respond to specific queries about your ideas. But as I've written elsewhere in this volume, effectively taking questions demands considerable skill. No wonder!

Some damned fool will try to get the better of you by tripping you up on a pointed question. These fools are most abundant and their reasoning goes something like this, "If I can trip up the speaker who's made such a good impression, I shall be generally recognized as being better than he is." If you sense that this individual is out to score off you, remember you have no responsibility to answer the question, merely to score first.

I have a technique for these situations. I allow my spectacles to slide half way down my nose so that I am peering over the top. I pause for a sip of water. I look the questioner closely in the face and then say a single word, "Sir!" (or of course, "Madam", for I can be flexible.) There are titters from the crowd which waits expectantly to see what happens next. Then I launch into my answer which may be less designed to impart information than to silence a pesky questioner with dubious motives.

My point is this: the question period is not designed solely to impart further information on your topic. That's only one objective. It should also be used to confirm your mastery over the topic at hand, further rouse the enthusiasm of your audience, and to keep the atmosphere intact which you have labored successfully to create. In short, even here you need mastery and control.

Now that you have prepared yourself insofar as you can for the lecture circuit, it is time to find the audiences on which to hone your actual skills.

Breaking In

Breaking in is not difficult. Most people make the mistake of thinking that they will need a great break to be launched on the nether reaches of the lecture circuit. Nothing could be further from the truth. With over 200,000 organizations existing across the country, there really is no absence of possibilities. The problem rather is how to move from the unpaid possibilities to the paid and how to derive the utmost benefit from those otherwise frustrating situations which involve no check. But let's get started before we tackle that problem.

Leads

There are two ways to get invitations to organizations and program planners: networking and direct approaches. My own approach is to use them both.

Networking

Networking, as you know, is a sophisticated game of leapfrogging that adults play to move themselves from where they are now to where they'd like to be via individuals they may or may not know. I use it continually and I suggest you do the same. In this case, begin soliciting information from your friends about the organizations that they belong to. I have never yet met an American who did not have at least one organizational connection, although I continue, like Diogenes, to search for this soul. More likely, the people you know will belong to many organizations. Your task is to find out what they are, how they operate and whether they are part of larger organizations, national or even international in scope.

Chapter 13

Here are the steps to take:

- Start getting your information. The best way to assemble information about the organizational connections of your friends, business colleagues, and relatives is to ask for it. Find out what organizations they belong to, how long they've belonged, how active they've been and whether they know the name of the program planner or will find out. Also, listen carefully as people talk. You'll find that people continually dispense useful information about their organizational connections; your task is to hear it.

- Once you've discovered that you've got a connection to an organization, press the point. If your connection fails to get the name of the program planner, you can call and ask for it yourself. Then draft an appropriate letter for your contact to send recommending you. (See samples, page 274). The letter is an Alternative Credential; it establishes you as an authority and it gives you Automatic Acceptance by the planner so long as the signer is held in at least moderate repute. Once this letter is sent along with appropriate reinforcing materials, you can follow it up directly.

No Contact: Making The Direct Approach

I like to use networking and prefer it whenever possible. But it always isn't possible to find a lead, try as one might. Thus, you've got to be prepared to master the techniques of the successful direct approach.

- Start with the Yellow Pages of your telephone directory under "association" and locate the groups in your community.

- Call to find out whether the organization books outside speakers. Find out the name of the program planner and write him suggesting that you appear.

- Follow up with a telephone call. Your reception may or may not be cordial (plan for the worst). Even if it's only lukewarm, don't worry. Many people have lamentable telephone manners. You have to expect that and use your selective hearing to move towards your objective — becoming the featured speaker with the minimum of difficulty.

Talking To The Program Planner

Whether you get networked in or make direct contact, at some point you will make contact with the program planner. This is an important conversation at any time in your career and a crucial one at the start. Your task is to find out the following:

- Is the organization interested in outside speakers? If not, don't hang up the telephone angrily. Say that you'd nonetheless like to send some material to keep on file. Say this, "People get sick and cancel occasionally, and you may like to know that there's someone local who's available to step in at the last minute." This is an Assertive Courtesy. It would be a real brute who'd dismiss this offer. Note: such brutes exist.

- How many people attend?

- Does the organization have a newsletter? Does it feature speakers?

- Is there a publicity committee to assist with advance publicity?

- Would there be any problem of your distributing information about your products, services or messages to the audience?

Use Assertive Courtesy to get this information. You don't need to be perceived as an unabashed promoter but rather as an individual in business to solve the problems of others. You're not interested in promotion for selfish reasons, oh no!; you want it because you wish to insure that all those who are interested in the topic, who need the information to solve their problems will in fact have it. You want to distribute your information not, of course, for self-interested reasons (heaven forbid!), but because, you'll say, the people in the audience always are interested in following up a presentation and like to have readily at hand the means of doing so.

Chapter 13

Always present yourself as the problem solver and all that you do as a means of bringing about an apt solution. There's absolutely no reason to appear self-absorbed.

In this connection, you need to keep in mind that you as a speaker will actually be solving the problems of two distinct audiences: those who are the program planners and responsible for organizing the event and those who will be attending the program as audience. Thus, never hesitate to offer your assistance in writing the media promotional materials. This, too, is an Assertive Courtesy and solves a problem of the sponsor, namely that he doesn't usually know how to contact the press expeditiously and effectively. To be sure, you have a smidgeon of self-interest in the progress, but why flaunt it?

Moving On — Moving Up

Most people stay in the larger, unremunerative sector of the speaking world too long. This part of the circuit has real value; that's undeniable. It offers you, the untrained speaker, lenient audiences on which to inflict yourself before you become suave, polished, and enchanting. You can take from it such critical materials as: media write-ups, tapes of your (we trust better) performances, testimonial letters of endorsement from program personnel whose meagre expectations were more than met and other evidence that you are in fact a comer. In this regard, professional speakers owe a debt of gratitude to the mashed potato circuit. But since this is not a tome for the sentimental, you don't need to pause too long in grateful recognition. It's time to move along.

Sadly, too many speakers, would be stars, remain too long on the unpaid circuit. Why is this? It's easier to get engagements, of course. Many are uncertain that what they are offering is in fact of value to the listeners, that there is a Disproportionate Benefit to the audience that they deliver. Or is it just that these poor souls have no vision of themselves as professionals on the lecture circuit? Whatever the reason, they dally too long in an area which has value to be sure but a highly focused value.

The time to move to paid engagements is when:

- You feel comfortable as a platform performer, when a hostile questioner can no longer throw you off the pace and render you abject with embarrassment.

- You have such supporting materials as tapes of presentations, letters of recommendation and publicity about your performance so as to substantiate the nagging question of program planners, "Assure me not only that you know what you're talking about but that you can deliver the material in a cogent, entertaining, thoroughly professional manner. Can you?"

- You will stake your life on the importance of your material and its inestimable value to your audience.

When this critical moment arrives, it's time to be the complete professional, which means getting paid for what you do. And for the sake of all of us in the profession, eschewing the coy or abashed in being straightforward and businesslike about the question of honorable remuneration.

Reaching This Result

This transformation will not occur overnight nor does it ideally take place on the telephone when someone says, "What's your fee?" Work it out deliberately in the quiet of your own study. Here are a few questions that will help?

- "What is the disproportionate value of the information I'm imparting? Can my audience go out and turn what I say into profit, success, health, an ultimate result of surpassing value? How do I know?"

- "Who else is offering information of this kind?"

- "What does that person charge?"

- "What is this individual's perceived status?"

- "What is mine?"

- "How much, then, should I charge?"

Chapter 13

Arriving at a fee is by its very nature a rather impressionistic, artful business. There is no scientific formula, but as you succeed in carefully answering these questions, you'll get close to a fair price.

In discussing an engagement with a program chairman, consider, too:

- Not just how long you'll be speaking but how long it will take you to prepare your speech. Can you remake a stock speech or must you fashion something new?

- Consider, too, the matter of travel. You should get compensated for expenses, of course, but what about for travel time?

- To expedite matters and introduce the necessary realism, I ask the program chairman, quite bluntly, what kind of budget he's working with. Inevitably, the answer is the same, "Too small!", "Very limited!" But you need to get beyond this to actual limits. Find out how much money was allotted for the time slot/format you are filling. Keynote speakers always are better paid than those who present workshops. You simply need to find out how much money was allotted for the slot you are filling and begin to construct a package. Here creative financing is usually essential. At all times you must keep in mind the amount of money that this single presentation must return and work to construct a productive package accordingly. Here are some possibilities:

Your fee for a presentation is $500. The organization offers $250. You say the fee is acceptable if:

- You are given ad space in the organization's publication to the value of $250.

- The organization takes a book distribution agreement and turns over the first $250 in receipts to you entirely and divides the remaining receipts by some pre-arranged formula.

- The organization guarantees the sale of $250 of your product. If this amount is not sold, then you will get the remainder from the organization.

- You are given booth space at which to sell your product.

- The organization will distribute in its newsletter or publication one of your flyers.

- You are paid in merchandise produced by the organization to the wholesale value of $250, note *not* retail. It should really cost the organization $250. Expect dickering here.

You get the picture. In this business, you have to learn to be creative. Fast! The important thing is that you as a professional disseminating information of value and significance deserve to be compensated for what you know, the way you provide it and how you perform.

Dealing With The Persistent Freebie Seekers And Those Who With The Highest Of Motives Would Starve You If They Could

Despite the fact that you have become a professional, individuals will regularly approach you who, with the best of reasons, will suggest that you speak to their group for free. With one kind of creature the reasoning is thus: "Everyone can talk. Even I can talk. Ergo, why should we pay a fee? Surely, one talking human is as good as another and will surely fill the bill. I just need a speaker." The proper response to this, were some of the best mores of the 18th century in effect, would be a good, sound thrashing. It's futile to try to educate this kind of idiot, and you shouldn't try. Be calm. Be cool. Be collected. If the organization is a good one. If the audience is to be a large one. If they have a publication of importance then see if you can construct a deal where waiving the fee will yet result in a good return for yourself. If so, despite the infuriating attitude, it may still be worth accepting the assignment. But be sure of the facts.

The second creature you will encounter is the friend who comes to you and attempts to persuade you that as a favor you should do the speech without charge. Such friends! Demur politely unless, again, there is something tangible, substantial and immediate that you can get. I'd rather have cash in hand than the prospect of a future favor, but you can make your own decision.

Chapter 13

Remember this: It's not always possible to work out a mutually beneficial arrangement. The creature who comes to you with the suggestion that you speak for free is offended (yes, this happens) when you suggest a package which will result in some benefit for you may not be possible to reason with. Being a reasonable man myself, it used to bother me that I couldn't make the other person see at least some fraction of my point of view. Now it doesn't. I have come to the firm conclusion that ignorance is not only rampant, in many it is irremediable and that it is only a question of time until one encounters such a specimen wearing the hat of the program planner. When you do, studied patience and resolute courtesy are your best defense.

Finally, remember this: If by some ill humor you do accept an assignment without remuneration, you will encounter the sad fact that those who pay nothing not only treat you with an infuriating casualness but make the biggest demands on your time and patience. Expect this. Learn from this. Avoid this.

Working Alone

Any speaker who is honest will tell you that booking dates on the lecture circuit demands commitment, resourcefulness, a vast reserve of good humor and the capacity to overlook faux pas, foolishness and fatuity. Some of these I have; others I have learned. All are necessary. Also, remember that it is more difficult to book dates on the lecture circuit than it is through continuing education programs nationally. That's why I concentrated my early efforts, and will always devote a substantial part of my attention, to this area. There's nothing very surprising about this.

In the continuing education market, you can come back several times in a single year with the same program. So long as the program is profitable, the prime sponsor will want you back and will work with you to continue your program. Thus, while it sometimes takes a while to sell yourself, once you are in and your program proves itself, you can expect a good long run with it, a nice return on your initial investment. This is by no means the case with single lectures. Many of them are just that: single. The organization having heard what you have to say, now wants to hear somebody else. Thus, the professional lecturer is constantly on the look out for new sources, new possibilities, empty platforms to fill. In this connection, the following resources are critical for success:

Association of College, University and Community Arts Administrators, Inc., 6225 University Ave, Madison, WI 53705-1099

If you're interested in doing programs in the arts and for arts administrators, here's the organization for you. Maintains an annual meeting with exhibit area, publishes a newsletter and other materials pertinent to the profession.

International Platform Association, P.O. Box 250, Winnetka, IL 60093

Gives perhaps the largest annual convention devoted to talk and speakers. Publishes regular newsletter.

Meetings & Conventions, One Park Avenue, New York, New York 10016

Designed for the professional meeting planner, this monthly glossy magazine publishes information of interest to the professional speaker.

Meeting News: Facts, News, Ideas For Convention and Meeting Planners Everywhere, 1515 Broadway, New York, New York 10010

Again, this publication is designed for professional meeting planners. It's free, however, by writing to the above address. Consider putting an article here if you can make the meeting planner's life a little easier.

Meeting Planners Guidebook: San Francisco, Bay Area & Northern California Directory, 180 Harbor Drive, Suite 112, Sausalito, CA 94965.

If you ever want to stage a program in Northern California, you'll need this book with its clear-cut and helpful information on meeting sites and a wide range of meeting services. If you're outside that area, you'll want it for its very complete bibliography of useful resources for speakers and meeting planners.

Chapter 13

National Association For Campus Activities, Box 11489, Columbia, SC 29211

If you're interested in speaking to college students (or playing music for them, juggling, &c), at some point you're going to have to be in contact with NACA. NACA holds both regional and national meetings where you can pay for the privilege of enticing the very spoiled student leaders who control big buck activity budgets. Sadly, NACA shows are often disorganized, which is something they need to deal with before some enterprising entrepreneur steals their business.

National Conference on Student Services, 6401 Odana Rd., Madison, WI 53719

Bill Haight, president of this for-profit organization, once told me he needed this book when starting out. Even without it, Bill, you've done all right! This organization is a good model of what you can do to establish an annuity program and create spin-offs from it. If you're interested in getting to the student market and can offer programs of interest to student services administrators, send your proposal in. 600+ student leaders from around the country attend this meeting. Also affiliated with the *National On Campus Report*.

National Speakers Association, 4747 North 7th St., Suite 310, Phoenix, AZ 85014

The leading national association solely devoted to the interests of the professional speaker. Gives regular conferences on topics of interest and maintains newsletter only open to members and their products.

Professional Speakers Showcase, Public Management Associates, 2014 Siegle Drive, Lemon Grove, CA 92045

Another for-profit venture that showcases speakers and helps bring them together with prospective booking agencies.

Sharing Ideas Among Professional Speakers, Dottie Walters Publisher, 18825 Hicrest Road, Glendora, CA 91740.

One of the best-know figures in the speaking world, Dottie Walters publishes this newsletter which you won't want to be without. In virtually every issue, I find a very good idea and so will you! Dottie also publishes many helpful books, tapes and other materials of interest to the aspiring and professional speaker. Ask for the complete list when you write her.

Successful Meetings, Bill Communications, Inc., 633 Third Avenue, New York, New York 10017

Another publication designed for the professional but where you can both find good ideas and leads and promote yourself to the right people.

Western Association News, Published by Marketing/Association Services, Inc. 1516 South Pontius Avenue, Los Angeles, CA 90025

Marketing/Associates Services publishes both this helpful tabloid and a special directory of speakers available to western associations. This publication could be improved by including all the addresses and telephone numbers of the associations and people they write about (hint!) but contains much good information notwithstanding.

Who's Who In Association Management, Membership Directory of the American Society of Association Executives, 1575 Eye St, N.W., Washington, D.C. 20005

You can get yourself listed here (for a reasonable fee) if you offer services that are of interest to the association market. I did and I actually got some business from the listing. This membership directory is useful to you for leads, of course. ASAE publishes many helpful books and booklets of interest to the professional speaker. Ask for the bibliography.

World Convention Dates, Convention World, Bayard Publications, 500 Summer St., Stamford, CT 06091

This book lists major conventions and the cities where they're taking place several years in advance. You can also get yourself listed in it (again, for a fee) and the specialties on which you can speak and your fees. I'm listed but I've never gotten a call. Still, I have found useful information in the book itself.

Chapter 13

Successful Auditioning

In many ways looking for a good booking on the lecture circuit is similar to looking for one in the continuing education market. But in one essential way it differs: the audition. You can get dates on the lecture circuit without auditioning; as you become more and more established that luxury will become your norm, but at the beginning expect to audition. As you can see from the above list, several organizations give you the opportunity to do so — for a fee!

Auditions are necessarily stressful. Those who can contain the stress and make it work on their behalf are better off than those who cannot. Before you even consider doing an audition take note of the following:

- An audition is just another link in the chain that a successful speaker must forge. If you think that you can give a dazzling audition then stand back and do nothing further for yourself, think again. Don't waste your time and energy performing the audition if that's your attitude! This is not a 1935 Busby Berklee film after all. To make an audition work, you have to use it. I start from the assumption that your audition will be good. What will distinguish you from the pack of auditioners will be your ability to leverage the audition into an assignment.

- Other people's auditions will be equally good. The more involved you become in the speaker circuit, the more you'll recognize that there is a considerable amount of talent about and that you are all in pursuit of scarce dollars. Thus you need to stand out from the rest not merely by the sheer brilliance of your performance but by the way in which you use this performance. You must make the decision not only to give a sparkling audition but also to work the conference at which you are presenting. How is this done?

- Develop a special conference flyer, a one-sided 8½" by 11" brochure which lists: the names of your presentations, lengths, information about the format, places where you have given presentations, the kinds of audience reactions you've had, &c. Make sure that your photograph is on the page along with a follow-up address and telephone. Just before you speak try to get this special information into the hands of your auditors. If you can't, then make sure it's available on literature tables and that you pass it out throughout the convention. Distinguish yourself from the other speakers. Be persistent. Be charming. Be different. Be persistent. While other speakers are at the nearest watering hole filling up, congratulating and commiserating with each other, keep on meeting prospects. I know what I'm talking about. When I'm at a convention, as I am regularly, my literature is everywhere as I am. I let people know I'm present and what benefits there are for them in becoming acquainted with me (read "booking me"). You do the same.

- Make sure in advance that the convention is attracting the kinds of people you want to meet. You have to know your audience profile backwards and forwards. If your buyers will be present, then you should consider going, too. If not, it's not worth going because even the most brilliant audition will be wasted.

A Word About The Audition Itself

The auditions are short. You may get 8 minutes, perhaps a quarter of an hour. Rarely will you have more time. That means that in a very short time you've got to leave a firm impression. Aim for this image: knowlegeable, engaging, enthusiastic, empathetic. Remember that you are really selling to two audiences simultaneously: the program planner who is present and the audience which he represents. You've got to convey the idea that you are a professional, easy to work with (not a headache like the last speaker he engaged) and packed with useful information, capable of being engagingly presented to the ultimate buyers.

If possible, go to a convention and listen to many auditions at least once before you do it yourself. Seek out the successful speakers and ask them what works. Don't befriend the losers; success is infectious but so is failure. Tape the good presentations. Get a sense of why they work by listening to the rhythm of the talk. Put your eagle eye on the clothes the successful speaker wears and the body movements he makes. See how the crowd responds. Find out, too, how the successful speakers work the convention, the kinds of materials they pass out and where they leave them, who they talk to and what they say.

Does this involve a certain amount of sleuthing? Absolutely! Does it come naturally? Perhaps not! But it is essential if you want to get your money's worth and get ahead.

Chapter 13

One final word: collect as many business cards and means of contact as you can from prospects. Expect to spend the Monday morning after the convention determinedly contacting them by telephone and letter to move matters along. If you really believe that you have something important to say; if you like the roar of applause and the green stuff that is your fiscal recompense for all this bother, you'll do all this and more to get bookings. You'll also account yourself lucky, since you might otherwise have to work for a living!

Making Speaker Deals

Speakers must become good business people. That means mastering the details of contracts and letters of intent which are just simpler contract forms although equally binding upon the signatories. Here are the matters which need to appear in the contract and which usually present the greatest problem or grounds for confusion:

- **Duties.** What exactly are you doing? Be very clear on the kind of presentation you are making, its length and format. This should be clearly spelled out in your contract. Oftentimes an organization would like its leading speakers to appear at special cocktail parties, dinners and other functions that take place the day or evening before their presentation. Don't let an organization simply drop this expectation on you. Be very clear about exactly when the organization wants you to appear, what functions they wish you to attend, and when and how they wish you to speak. All this should be specified in writing.

- **Fees.** If you are being paid a fixed, flat fee in return for your presentation, the wording of this section of a contract should present no problem. If, however, you are being paid through a mixture of outright cash and a variety of other arrangements (ad space, book distribution agreement, merchandise, &c.), make sure that all the neccessary information appears in the contract.

- **Expenses.** It's better if the organization buys your air tickets, books your accommodation, &c., but work out the details in advance.

- **Cancellation Of Event By Sponsor.** The sponsor should be allowed to cancel the event without any penalty up to thirty days before it takes place. Thereafter, however, there should be a penalty clause. On the rare occasions when I don't use this clause I'm always unhappy with myself. I booked a date with a major university last year and two weeks before, they cancelled because their *other* programs were not drawing well and they had no confidence that mine would be different. I had no penalty clause and thus the hapless program planner ended up wasting one of my prime fall dates. Don't let this happen to you.

- **Cancellation Of Event By You.** Use similar language as above. You should be allowed to cancel without penalty up to thirty days before the event and for a similar penalty afterwards. In the event of an Act of God, of course, the event being cancelled, there will be no penalties.

Other Matters

Be sure, too, that the contract specifies how your literature will be distributed, whether and where your books and others products will be sold and who will derive the benefit from sales, how tapes of your program will be sold and revenues divided, and how the matter of after event publicity in their publications is handled. All too many speakers think that an engagement is limited to booking and speaking. How wrong this is! The successful speaker sees the act of speaking itself as a critical part of the speaking process but as a part which loses a substantial fraction of its impact unless properly perceived as part of the great chain of possibilities.

In Hot Pursuit Of Lecture Representation

As you can imagine, doing all this yourself is exhausting. That's one very good reason why you should seek out at your earliest opportunity assistance with bookings. When is this "earliest opportunity?"

You'll probably consider yourself ready for representation before any representative does. A sad fact of this life. The fact is the earliest opportunity is when you can generate sufficient money on the lecture circuit to justify the time, involvement and commitment of a representative, an agent. Since most of these representatives are paid exclusively on commission which ranges between 10% to 15% of the value of the contract, you have to be doing quite a bit of speaking at a fairly substantial fee to justify anyone taking much interest in you. Which means, of course, that you'll already have had to hustle quite a bit by yourself before a lofty agent descends to grace your life.

Chapter 13

Identifying Prospects

Unfortunately there is no single resource you can use to find a lecture agent. The Yellow Pages (look under "Entertainment") provide one resource, but of course this is geographically limited. The best general list is provided by Dottie Walters; you'll get it when you subscribe to *Sharing Ideas* (still under $50 annually). (Note: Dottie Walters draws the distinction between a lecture bureau which works for organizations needing speakers and a lecture agency which works for the individual performer in an exclusive or nonexclusive relationship.) Richard Weiner also provides a partial listing in his very helpful *Professional's Guide To Public Relations Services* (Public Relations Publishing Co., 888 Seventh Avenue, New York, New York 10019). There is no list, however, which tells you generally what the agencies are looking for now and so helps you focus. In **THE UNABASHED SELF-PROMOTER'S GUIDE** I include some information of this kind based on a questionnaire I sent to many lecture agents, but, frankly, the return was not great. Thus, you're in for quite a lot of effort in finding an agent.

Once you've perused these resources, it's time to make an initial contact with the agency for like anything else, you can't make your most effective presentation until you know their interests and operating arrangements. Thus your first letter should include the following (see samples, page 288):

- Indication that you are already a professional speaker

- How many speaking engagements you do yearly

- Names of some of the larger organizations booking you

- Fee range

- Topics on which you speak

- Indication that you are now looking for representation for further bookings

- Request for further information about this particular agency so that if there is a match you could be back in touch. The information you need includes: current areas of interest, whether the agency wishes exclusive or nonexclusive representation, what kinds of materials agency would be interested in reviewing about you, possibility of entering into a relationship if materials submitted are of interest.

Now because an agency wishes to be absolutely sure that you are in fact an expert in your field and a certified platform performer, you should add a page indicating that certain materials are available upon request. These materials should include:

- photograph

- tapes of programs (be specific about programs, dates, organizations. These tapes should not be more than a year old.)

- context document which puts your leading program(s) into perspective. Why is this program important now?

- media materials including standard media release, biographical narrative, sample articles (list publication and date). Again, keep these up to date.

- samples of articles by you on your subject or your books.

There is no need to send these materials in your first letter. After all, you have no information indicating that the agency really is interested in your subject or would even consider adding another client.

A Candid Look At Agents

As you begin to deal with agents, you must know something of their world, make up and ecology in order to deal with them effectively.

Chapter 13

- They are ordinarily consultants who are paid by commission. Thus they must be careful about whom they take on as clients and on whom they expend their limited time, consideration and energy.

- Agents receive requests daily from people who are shamelessly ill-prepared for the paid lecture circuit but who preen themselves on their indispensability. The sheer bulk of these letters has made agents very cautious about taking on anyone as a client until they are fully satisfied about the individual.

- In this regard, every agent, however grand, has in a weak moment perhaps to please a friend or client, taken on a new client who has proved to be disastrous and a waste of time. Thus, agents have learned to move slowly in a world that is at its best extraordinarily slow moving. An agent will move at a snail's pace until certain about both your credentials and your ability to provide a scintillating platform performance.

Thus, as I have discovered, it takes a long, long time to perfect a relationship with a lecture agent since they must first review your credentials, then establish the need for your information and expertise, come and listen to you and insure themselves that your are indeed good and marketable, and then must do all the necessary marketing to the appropriate markets. Yes, this is a very time consuming, drawn out process.

You must understand this as you begin your relationship with an agent which is why I'm including the following candid advice:

- Unless you become the darling of America with a horde of devoted followers, you should not and cannot leave the sole marketing of yourself to an agent. I have never discovered an agent, and never expect to, who will hold your interests as dear as he holds his own or who understands your market as well as you do yourself. That is why you should seek multiple nonexclusive relationships with agents rather than one exclusive connection. And why, equally importantly, you cannot afford to stop handling your own bookings (at least to some extent).

- Understand, too, that you have to remain in constant touch with your agent, making suggestions, offering possibilities, keeping your credentails up to date, handing over new and more exciting press materials and tapes and so keep the fire burning under him. There is almost always an educational element involved in an agent-lecturer relationship. The agent will educate you to the harsh realities of a very competitive business, and you must continually instruct the agent about the importance of your information and the possibilities that exist for disseminating it. Both are neccessary constitutents of a strong relationship.

Initial Letter Follow Up

Because there are so many well qualified speakers battering down their doors, even the least reputable, least well organized, least useful lecture agents are besieged with letters and pleas for assistance. This condition of events has inevitably made them more slothful, more arrogant and less businesslike than they ought to be. Thus consider yourself most fortunate if your initial letter is answered in the proper spirit and with the information you have a right to expect. If it is, consider yourself blessed and understand that you probably do have a very saleable program. Congratulations!

For the rest of you, however, don't feel unduly neglected if you must follow up this initial letter with a telephone call. Expect it in fact. To make the best use of this call, which is, after all, costing you money, make it with the questions of your letter written out and before you. Write down the answers. What you are looking for is an indication that your subject is of initial interest and that the firm is looking for new clients. This may not be much, but it is enough to start.

I must remind you now that you are in for the long haul with this or any other booking organization. You need them more than they need you initially. In infuriating ways the agencies will let you know this. So much for collegiality!

If you are given an opening, it is your responsibility to follow it up, quickly, efficiently, thoroughly with all the information that the agency requires. For ease of follow up make sure that you don't end this initial telephone conversation until you are clear about how long it takes the agency to review materials and whether they are good about getting back to you with a preliminary evaluation.

I suspect that the agency doesn't exist that won't tell you, with the best will in the world, how efficient it is and how certain you can be of a return response. It goes without saying that the minute you hang up the telephone, most of these promises are as easily forgotten as they were made. Thus, again, it's your responsibility to wait the required amount of time and get back to the agency to see how things are coming along.

Chapter 13

In the interim there are things you can do to help your case. Using Assertive Courtesy, make sure to send along program announcements of your latest speeches, a tape of a particularly good performance, media materials, new stories by and about you, &c. Indicate in short that you are a person of consequence and, importantly, determination. It's especially important to keep in touch if you are giving a performance near them. Make sure an invitation is sent and if they can't come, you try to stop by, get acquainted, and support yourself.

Breaking Through

Using these grinding methods, you will finally get through. At last an agent will wake up to the fact that you are knowledgeable about your subject, a polished and entertaining platform speaker, that your subject is in demand and that you are not going to give up. All of these are equally important in achieving success. As soon as this initial breakthrough occurs, the discussion gets serious for both you and the agent. You particularly need to focus on precisely what the agent can and will do on your behalf and on the essentials of your business relationship.

Analyzing The Agent

Since there is no degree, no credential, no licensing procedures, anyone may call himself a lecture agent. Thus you can and must expect those in the business to run from the sublime to the ridiculous. If you have a clear vision of yourself as someone who is to be on the national scene for a sustained period, you must be assured that the company with which you do business is in fact reputable. Thus do the following:

- Have the agent walk you through the entire process of your relationship step by step. Don't be hurried through. You need to know exactly who does what, when including:

  - responsibility for photographs

  - write ups for brochures and marketing pieces

  - selecting booking targets

  - booking transportation and accommodation and reimbursement of expenses

  - how payment is handled and how long it takes

  - who handles publicity relations with the sponsoring organization.

These are matters which are essential to your success as a lecturer.

Look at an actual campaign on behalf of another speaker. See what is put out and inquire who is responsible for each phase. Understand this, however: at no point can you divorce yourself from the process. You are and always will be a crucial part, and it is in your interest to be actively involved in all phases of the campaign.

Finish your talk by getting the names of at least three speakers the agency represents. Call them and discuss their situations. See if they're really happy, really getting bookings, and ask what kinds of problems are typical with the agency.

The Bottom Line

Many of you may be thinking about going on the speaker circuit because you feel it's glamorous, because you like the sustained applause of enraptured strangers, because you have something to say and you want people to master the world according to your particular point of view. Fair enough. These things never entirely wear off and for many speakers remain perhaps the most important ingredients in their decision to lead the crazy quilt existence of the professional lecturer. But let's not be coy about it: the money is a consideration, isn't it? I know it is for me. Thus, this is an area in which you need to be very, very clear.

Chapter 13

- **Agency Fees.** Perhaps because there are so many more speakers than speaking opportunities and perhaps because so many agents are not very successful, a reprehensible practice has sprung up in recent years: registration fees. Beware of them. I am not saying that every fee in every situation is necessarily bad, but that you had better be sure that your fee and that of other ingenue speakers are not keeping a sleepy enterprise in business. Be sure that you're getting your money's worth.

- **Commission.** Lecture agents, like their book counterparts, are bit by bit raising the fees to 15%. 10% is still standard but it won't be for long. Again, this is partly a function of lack of business and the need to take their profit out the hides of the speakers. Another regrettable trend.

- **Percentage Of Product Sales.** There are some agents who demand a percentage of product sales produced by a speaking engagement. These fees range from 5% to 10%. I oppose them and so should you. True, you may not have been responsible for getting the assignment but you are the author of the book and you should derive all the revenues. Resist this importunity strenuously. Do the same with tape revenue. It belongs to you.

- **Expenses.** Don't advance the expense money yourself. When you are working with either a bureau or an agency, it's their responsibility to cover the expenses. Stick to your guns.

- **How You'll Be Paid.** The commissioning organization will pay the lecture agency directly and the agency will pay you after deducting their fee. You should be paid promptly. Insist upon it and have a penalty clause in your contract for late payment.

- **Self-Made Bookings.** You should not have to turn over to your agent a percentage of any contract that you book yourself. Why should you be penalized for working for yourself, expecially when at the beginning of your relationship you can't be sure your agent will really produce for you?

A Few Other Points

In determining the bounds of your relationship with your agent, make sure you have an agreement on the following points:

- Nothing should be sent out about you until you've had the opportunity to review it. Remember: you know whom you're trying to teach and what they're interested in better than the agent. If you don't, you shouldn't be on the lecture circuit in the first place.

- Get your agent to tell you why you're not booked as well as why you are. Perhaps there is some problem that you can straighten out. Knowing why you fail to get bookings is equally important as knowing why you do, but you can bet that an agent will not without prompting provide this critical information.

- Have a periodic review of the agent's activities and your overall relationship. You need to know what an agent is doing on your behalf and what marketing plans he has for you.

Relationships between agents and lecturers can and do go on for years. But like any other relationship they take work. An agent is a marketing expert — or should be. You however must work with the agent to insure that the right product is being marketed and in the right way.

Establishing Your Own Speaker Conglomerate

By the time you've mastered the preceding sections of the book and put them to good use, you're going to know a thing or two about the various aspects of the talk circuit. You should profit accordingly, in all ways.

Moreover, if you're using direct mail to promote yourself to continuing education departments or trade and professional associations, you could probably use some additional programs to offset your costs and bring in additional profits. And frankly, you deserve a day off now and then and the only way you're going to get it — and keep the profits rolling in — is to have somebody else earning for you. Creating your own speaker conglomerate might be the answer.

Chapter 13

By this I mean establishing a stable of other speakers with a defined audience, a Problem Solving Process presentation, the expertise to render such a presentation meaningful, and a refined platform manner. A person like me, for instance! (Yes, I can be one of the people you add to your conglomerate. Let's talk about it.)

Identifying Speakers: The Ones You Want, The Ones You Don't

It should by now be perfectly clear that there are far more speakers competing for the paid speaking assignments than there are assignments. This situation won't change in the future except to get worse. (After all, this book alone will launch thousands of well qualified professionals on the circuit without a commensurate rise in the number of possible assignments!) Thus if you have an entrepreneurial streak, it won't be hard to find speakers to peddle. Here are some places to look:

- trade and professional meetings

- programs in which you've participated and where a speaker or two has impressed you

- authors whose books you've enjoyed but who don't make much of a splash on the talk circuit.

No, identifying speakers won't be difficult. They abound. Identifying speakers you want, however, is another matter. For one thing, they ought to have a saleable product to offer their audiences, a book, for instance, or a tape. The reason for this is clear: those who are themselves the recognized authority as proven by a book are easier to market than those without this badge of authenticity. As such, you will derive a higher price for their services and, importantly, you'll be able to put in the subsidiary revenue stream of the product itself. This is a critical variable.

Already you can see that I'm going to be shifting my advice to you as you become, in this instance, the agent of the lecturer-agent duo. Whereas I said before that when you do business with a lecture agent you should under no circumstances consider giving up a percentage of book and product revenues, here I'm suggesting the exact reverse. Take advantage of the plethora of good speakers and their need for assignments. Take a percentage of product sales.

Auditioning Speakers

Whoever the speaker, unless a recognized star on the talk circuit, you need to proceed in a businesslike way. Request and review tapes, letters of recommendation, press materials, books and articles. Even if you've already heard a speaker, it's not a bad practice to take a look at these materials which ought to confirm your initial impression. It's just common sense.

Once you've decided that the person is someone you think you can sell consider the business relationship. Note, I said "sell." There is much important information that ought to be communicated and there are many people who are good speakers who can't be sold because the market isn't interested. You need to keep this sad fact in mind and act accordingly.

Business Matters

- **Fees.** Don't charge a speaker an upfront fee for becoming associated with you. This is not, after all, your primary business. If you are particularly hard up for cash, charge the lecturer a typesetting fee for including his write-up in your regular mailings. This should be minimal, about $100 per page. This situation works well when you find that you're going to have a mailing going out with the final page blank. Rather that waste the space, add the description of another lecturer's program and charge for typesetting. After all, you've already bought the paper and the postage won't change.

- **Payment To You.** If you're working in the continuing education market, you can make quite a deal for yourself as the agent. Many speakers are quite happy to work for between $400 to $500 a day plus expenses. But you can sell them to continuing educators, depending on their credentials and the cost of the program, for at least twice this amount plus a materials fee, from which you should also benefit. This is considerably better than the 10% to 15% which is standard for a lecture agent. Keep in mind, however, that in standard lecture settings, your fee will be closer to the usual, although you can still profit from a percentage of product sales. Note: this percentage should be at least 10% and may be as high as 40%.

Chapter 13

- **Lecturer's Responsibilities.** The first responsibility of the lecturer, of course, is to show up prepared. Don't deal with the proliferating numbers of the infuriatingly casual who have no sense of the importance of time, dates, contracts and responsibility. They can cost you a substantial sum in direct and indirect loss. Bind the lecturer to you. If the lecturer cancels, however, there should be no penalty if the cancellation is up to thirty days before the date. On the other hand, make sure to include a clause that the lecturer has no claim against you if he is not used because the program is cancelled at the last moment. Particularly in the continuing education market, decisions about whether programs will be run or not are often made on the day before. Continuing educators live with this uncertainty and so must you and the speaker.

- **Noncompetitive Agreement.** It's important that the lecturer not be allowed to have independent business access to the sponsor. I have strong feelings about this. If I've made the contract for the speaker, I want to benefit from the relationship now and for the foreseeable future. Just how long should this be? Consider: a continuing education relationship can go on for years. The hard part is breaking in. Once you do and the program is successful, you can expect to be the leader until registrations dip. You should benefit throughout this period and at the very least for three years. At least insist that for the next three years all programs for this individual with any given sponsor be booked through you or that the agreement has been breached.

- **Expenses.** If you are dealing in the noncredit continuing education market, these sponsors are not prepared to pay in advance for transportation and accommodations. Thus you must either pay for or charge these expenses yourself or have the speaker do so. Be clear about this policy. Speakers will want you to assume the expenses; you should try to get the speaker to put them on a major credit card for repayment. If these items are charged, however, either by the speaker or by you insist upon prompt payment by the sponsor. And good luck to you! Universities are infuriatingly slow about payment. They make a habit out of a payment system which if they themselves had to suffer from it would produce an immediate strike. So much for the humanity of the academy.

More On Marketing

The best way to market any speakers with whom you are associated is to sell them on you own lecture tour. Do so immediately after you've spoken. As I've already said, be sure to schedule a meeting with program planners following your own presentation. That's when they are most under your influence, most excited, most enthusiastic, most receptive about what you've said and about you. Discuss future presentations of every kind, including those by your associates. Handle your own needs first. They are preeminent. But when you've finished with your own agenda, make some more deals for your associates. You'll be listened to because of what I call the Principle of Automatic Acceptance: the planners already know that you can do the job and they presume that you would only suggest those who are likewise up to the mark. Don't disappoint them! In the long run, if you suggest people who are not up to your level, you'll only be hurting yourself and damaging your credibility. Don't forget this!

One Final Word

Make sure all payments go directly through you. You pay the speaker both honorarium and expenses and the sponsor pays you. There is no need, none at all, for you to discuss with the speaker just what benefits you are deriving from his engagement and you need to make it clear to the sponsor that you're handling all business matters for the lecturer. You may have a moment's pause if you're profiting more than 10%. Don't. Remember, it isn't the amount of time it took to make the deal that you're being paid for, it's the amount of time, commitment, preparation and intelligence that you've spent over the years to know how to structure the right deal in the least amount of time. This is what makes you a professional, and you have a right to be compensated for it.

Chapter 14

TAKING CARE OF BUSINESS

To succeed as a speaker you need a systematic plan and a clearly stated dollar objective for yourself as well as technical proficiency on the platform. Make no mistake about it: the speakers who succeed in this rigorous business are those who not only perfect their trade but perfect their business practices, too. That's why a book like this one would be incomplete unless there was some discussion about how to make yours a successful business operation. Sadly, I continually meet speakers who, while concentrating on their technical proficiency, have little or no sense that they are actually running a business, too, and a demanding business at that. Don't let this happen to you. It won't if you have clear objectives that you work at meeting.

Setting Your Objectives

All speakers, ingenues or grizzled veterans, need specific objectives and periodic reviews to insure that these carefully considered objectives are in fact being met.

Here's an action plan to follow:

- Begin by reviewing your last year's effort on the talk circuit. How many engagements did you have? How many were you paid for both by direct payment and through such revenue streams as books and tapes? With what frequency did you speak? To what kinds of organizations?

The goal of these questions is to give you a composite picture of the current state of your speaking practice. This should provide you with benchmarks from which to improve. Don't worry if the answers show a fairly meager rate of employment and a trickle of revenue. Everyone starts somewhere and so long as this is just a start and not the result after a strenuous year of activity, so be it. The point is to have a clear understanding of where you are now and where you've just been.

- Once having completed this review, and you should do so at least once a year, set down your objectives for the next year. Here the utmost specificity is recommended. Don't just set a goal of one presentation per month; you need to be more specific that that. Write down:

  - the number of presentations you'll give

  - at what frequency

  - to what kinds of organizations

  - what kinds of programs you want to deliver

  - with what level of remuneration

  - from what revenue sources (speaker honorarium, book deals, subsequent book sales from organizational publicity, &c.)

  - overall dollar return from speaking for the year.

You cannot arrive if you don't know where you're going. This cliché is true. It's your responsibility to set your agenda clearly and concisely. One thing that never ceases to amaze and frankly appall me as I lecture about the country is this. People often say to me, "Oh, it's easy for you now to get engagements. After all you're established!" This comment is infuriating.

I wasn't born established. I don't find speaking engagements taped to my bed when I get up. I work at getting them, day in, day out. I have a vision of myself on the lecture circuit, a vision which includes precise numbers about how many engagements I need to give and with what kind of return to meet my overall goal. This vision existed before I had a single engagement, or at least some part of it did. So it must be for you. You've got to believe in yourself and this belief will precede by a considerable period the first indications that success is indeed possible.

Chapter 14

By the same token the objectives you set must be realistic. If you have only so far made unpaid presentations before groups on the mashed potato circuit it's unrealistic to assume that your income from speaking will be $25,000 the next year. $5000 is probably a more realistic objective given all the specific information that you have to follow in this book. Moreover, don't forget that it takes time, a lot of time, to do the necessary marketing, networking, and promoting of programs and this time must be figured into your planning process.

Having set out a precise plan for yourself with precise dollar objectives, now draft a preliminary marketing plan. In due course creating this plan will become second nature to you, but at the beginning it will seem a unique, unprecedented form of drudgery. It is, however, absolutely necessary.

Say that you have set as your goal making the following presentations with the following returns:

i) 1 workshop at a professional association in your field, dollar objective (honorarium alone) $750

ii) 3 noncredit continuing education seminars. Two colleges. One course to be repeated twice. One new course. Objective $750 each, total $2250

iii) 6 unpaid speaking engagements on the mashed potato circuit. No direct revenue. $2000 in subsequent product and service sales to those in audience.

Total objective for year $5000.

This, I feel constrained to say, is a very modest plan and one that you really ought to realize even if your experience is very limited.

Now the question becomes setting your marketing plan to realize these objectives.

To realize objective (i), here are some of the steps you should consider taking:

- Write an article for the organization's newsletter and follow up to program chairperson.

- Network through a member of the association or contact with program planner.

- Write a direct sales letter from you to program planner with telephone or appropriate in person follow up.

Just how much of this do you have to do? In the beginning you probably don't know and neither do I. It depends on a number of factors including the kind of presentation you are proposing, whether this presentation deals with the felt anxieties and real aspirations of your proposed audience, whether you are perceived by the program planner as a professional, whether you have competitors and what they may be doing. These are all factors in your success. After a time you'll come to have a keen understanding of how they advance or inhibit your success. That's one reason why you need to keep at it.

To realize objective (ii), here are some steps you should consider taking:

- Review university noncredit continuing education catalogs in your area. If there is a hole, write a strong sales letter to the dean or director and request a meeting. Before you do so, however, make sure you've thought through your presentation and developed the necessary marketing documents previously discussed. Program planners in this arena work about 6 months in advance. You could have one program in about 6 months and another at the end of your twelve month cycle, always assuming that the first program went over well. (You need contingency plans in case it doesn't). Once you've been hired at one university, you can approach another in a noncompeting marketing area and proceed with dispatch. The fact that one place has hired you makes you more attractive to others so long as you've done your homework and are not asking for something that you can't have.

- Network. Get alumni from the college to write to the dean of continuing education on your behalf. Use your own college as a starting place. Get participants in the continuing education program to write on your behalf, too. These letters will provide a sufficient entry point.

Chapter 14

To realize objective (iii), here are some steps you should take:

- Write cold direct sales letters to the program planners of local organizations in which you feel that you can sell products and services to the audience. Arrange for an appropriate experience; this includes publicity and getting a list of participants. See if you can sell products right on the spot. If not, make sure you get participant addresses to follow up.

Ultimately as your speaker business grows, you have to factor in other matters, too:

- How many mailings will you have each year?

- When do they have to be sent?

- To whom will they be sent?

- What return will you need to make them profitable?

- What kind of follow up must you do with these mailings?

- How much telemarketing do you have to do? How many calls to schedule an engagement?

- How many articles in professional publications does it take to stimulate a single engagement?

Again, at the beginning of your career you don't know the answers to these questions. By being in business and working your business, however, you will get the answers you need and be able to plan accordingly. Thus it's crucial to work your business.

Arranging Your Perfect Day

In your mind's eye, I know you have a vision of yourself before a teeming crowd strewing rose petals in your path after having been captivated by an unparalleled speech. A big fat check awaits you at the end of a day which has been a swirl of gratifying activity and the tumultuous approval of thousands. You are a romantic, aren't you!

The fact is, the professional speaker's ideal day is actually a wee bit different. As often as humanly possible it should be divided into the following three critical activities:

- marketing for new speaking opportunities

- doing product and program research and development for the future

- delivering a program on the talk circuit.

This is truly ideal.

Marketing

To make your speaker business a success, you must always be marketing and promoting it. This must become second nature to you or else you will not become the success you want to be. Here is a task action list that will help you reach your objective:

- Start each day with marketing.

- Send out your query letters to future speaking prospects.

- Follow-up such letters with telephone calls and personal visits where necessary.

Chapter 14

- Make your telephone calls between 9:30 a.m. and 11 a.m. so that your prospects have an entire day in which to return your call.

- Identify and contact in the same way media sources which you feel should cover you.

- Network among your friends and colleagues for leads and follow them up.

I begin each day at my typewriter warming up with a series of marketing letters. Most of all I want to make sure that I am continually keeping my name alive before the individuals who can invite me to speak or who, in the case of media, are responsible for enhancing my reputation as someone worth inviting.

These query letters are photocopied and filed accordingly to an elaborate ritual: they are tossed into a cardboard box marked "prospects" which gets fairly loving attention and is constantly thumbed through and updated. Telephone numbers where available are written right on the copy so that all the information I need is at hand. The key is to assume that none of your letters will ever be answered. This infuriates me, but it's a reality. If you want to make contact, take responsibility for making contact.

As you devote more and still more of your time to the talk circuit, your marketing activities will grow. Twice each year an entire day or even more is taken up handling the mailings that I send to trade and professional associations and colleges. Other times, I have to continue my marketing at trade and professional associations and through colleague meetings. The important thing is to work at it and to have a system.

In this regard, I advise you, too, to maintain a log of telephone calls made and where actual matters stand. I maintain my log in three monthly editions and go back from time to time to recheck entries and contact yet again individuals who have not been able to give me a positive response — yet.

This work is laborious, and it is often irritating. You can expect contacts to take a long time to mature and thus as part of your marketing effort you have to master the intricacies of Assertive Courtesy. You must continually be in touch with those who can sponsor you with billet doux containing evidence of successful presentations, articles by and about you and other indications of your galloping success. Many people are squeamish and fainthearted about keeping in touch this way with people they don't know and they may feel they're bothering. Not me. I have long ago recognized that most people are well meaning but slothful, most need frequent kicks to spur them to action, most, in short, are disorganized, inefficient, uncertain, and undistinguished. All the things, come to think of it, that you don't want to be. So you must contain your rage and press on until such time as you get the result that you had every reason to regard as reasonable from the first minute.

Product And Program Research And Development

It is often said by some leading speakers that they have a hundred names for a single speech. If this is so, it's reprehensible and evidence of a certain foul slackness. Don't be this way. Today people want more than this; they want and need hard, specific, immediately usable information. And you need to be the master of providing it.

This information ages, however. If we live in an age of extraordinary informational richness, so, too, we live in a period of extraordinarily prompt information obsolescence. You must be prepared for this, which means spending the time you need to keep your information current in whatever form you offer it.

Here is your task action list:

- Develop new and related programs of interest to your primary audience.

- Develop suitable written materials and tapes for this audience.

- Keep them all up-to-date.

I can speak feelingly about how demanding and time consuming all this is. But this is the price we pay for remaining on the cutting edge. Moreover it is where a substantial amount of your profit comes from. Thus you must regularly set aside time for product and Problem Solving Process development. You must learn to see yourself as a conglomerate, a Mobile Mini Conglomerate, and fashion products and program processes accordingly.

Chapter 14

How much time should this take? Unfortunately, there is no good answer for that. But you'll find that the talk circuit has a certain rhythm which should assist you. The period between September and June is the truly active part of the year with breaks for Christmas, early January, Easter and the other major holidays when the business slows to a trickle. This is the period to set aside for research and development as is the summer when I find myself doing the bulk of my editorial work. In fact, I make it a point to spend the lion's share of the summer months actively pursuing material and writing for my next book. So should you.

You will find that when you are beginning, trying to hold down a full time job or raise a family or both, your free time is precious and very, very limited. You have to make the commitment to use the time you have available and make the best of it. This is easier to write than to do, but I know what I'm taking about.

Delivering A Program

At last we come to the place where you thought you might start, actually delivering your program. In some senses this is a culmination and in every sense it ought to be a moment of triumph and satisfaction for you. Whatever you are being paid, be proud. You've earned it. But don't let this stipend become a satisfier; let it be a lever and a spur to further achievement.

It would, I think, be quite mistaken to see any speaking engagement as the culmination of your work. It's better to see it as part of a circuit of continuing possibilities, part of a success sequence. What I mean is this: any given speaking engagement should also open substantial marketing possibilities as well as new avenues for research and development based on conversations with program planners and prospects from your audience.

After you've spoken, you'll be meeting with program planners and during this meeting, a critical one, you should be networking for new assignments, solidifying the details of publicity and promotion emanating from this engagement, and discussing what other programs you can offer to this and related audiences. Marketing, research and development, and program delivery are intricately intertwined and a single speaking engagement can and should result in advances in all three areas.

Sadly, you can succeed in all these areas and yet have your overall business fail through poor management and oversight. That's why you need to master the essentials of running a demanding small business so that you can continue to shine on the talk circuit, not once but regularly.

Business Nitty Gritty

Many things effectively destroy small businesses. I know. I spend a considerable portion of my waking hours helping to launch businesses and helping to sustain them. Previous chapters have dealt with selecting a specialty, marketing it, promoting it and diversifying from it. This is not enough to ensure success. You've got to organize your speaking business and tend to it just as you would in any other field. This is true whether you intend to operate a part-time home-based business or take on your new career as a full-time assignment.

As you know, I operate my business from my condominium in Cambridge's busy Harvard Square area. There are many advantages to doing so: I save days during the course of the year from not having to commute. This gives me a real jump on competitors. Further, I work at my business daily. I'm at my work during regular business hours — and beyond — and have the discipline not to slip away during the day to watch a soap opera or two (fortunately, in any event, I detest the genre). To make any business work, you need determination, commitment, enthusiasm, and good operating practices. To make a home-based business work, you need a carefully calculated myopia so that tasks which would otherwise unnerve you (dust on the dining room table? heaven forbid!) you learn to comfortably ignore and carry on with the more pressing matters of the day. You also need to master the points on this list:

- **Name.** In the speaking business you are and probably always will be the chief product. Thus, name the business after yourself. I did and there are good reasons beside outright hubris for doing so. You'll be spending a lot of time and energy promoting yourself, and you want people to find you quickly, easily. Selecting another name than your own will interpose a barrier between you and the buyer which you don't need. The only good reason for not naming the company after yourself is your fear of failure and later public ridicule. Burn your boats behind you and face the future confidently. Use your own name.

Chapter 14

- **Banking.** Once you've settled the name, establish your banking account. In this country there is fortunately precious little to do about setting up a business. One of the things you do need is a separate bank account. I'm still amazed at my colleagues who run their financial activities out of their personal checking account. This is, I suppose, satisfactory if you only plan on giving a speech or two a year but not if you intend to begin deriving regular revenue. Before opening your account, shop around. Banking services are proliferating these days and you might as well get the best possible deal.

- **Check Book.** I use what's called a One-Write System and the one I use is put out by McBee Systems. Checks cost about 8¢ each. The benefit of this system, which you can also find in most stationer's shops, is that while you are writing your check a thin carbon strip on the reverse is recording the information on a monthly cash disbursements ledger. Also the system has columns where you can keep running totals of both deposits and expenditures by category: rent, electricity, postage, &c. This is a very handy, not very expensive system which should save your bookkeeper time when it's time to do quarterly reports.

- **Bookkeeper.** You don't need to begin with a bookkeeper if you plan to do only a few speaking engagements a year. I'd like to suggest, however, that you divest yourself of life's nagging inessentials as soon as possible and concentrate on what you do best: conceiving programs, marketing programs and delivering programs. The other things are not as important and surely not as glamorous. You ought to recruit people for your Mandarian Network so that you don't have to do them. A bookkeeper, who will charge you between $8-$15 per hour depending on your area of the country and work load, is in my eyes a necessary expense.

- **Accountant.** You may or may not need an accountant. I use an accountant to do both my corporate and personal taxes, but he's not cheap. Make the decision about whether you yourself know enough about business planning and the available deductions, depreciations and detail of tax law or whether it would be cost effective for you to hire an accountant. Accountants cost at least $50 per hour and you'll probably need one for between 5 to 10 hours yearly. If you know where you're going an accountant can be of the utmost value in helping you get there, but I have to confess that they are not very good at initiating ideas themselves.

- **Expense Records.** Every small business book has the same good advice and I have to repeat it, too: keep good records of your expenses. These should include (but not be limited to):

- accounting and bookkeeping expenses
- advertising
- briefcase
- business books and publications
- business related entertainment
- Christmas cards for business associates
- computer
- consulting fees
- conventions and trade show expenses
- corporate fees
- delivery charges
- donations
- dues to professional organizations
- educational expenses including seminars, workshops, materials
- electricity
- equipment leasing
- freight and shipping
- gas
- insurance premiums (including disability, special rider on homeowners policy, health insurance)
- interest on business loans, late tax payments and business charge card payments
- IRA or Keogh account deposits
- independent contractors
- legal and other professional fees
- licenses and permits

Chapter 14

- mail list development, rental and maintenance
- maintenance contracts on office equipment
- membership fees in business-related organizations
- office furniture (to be depreciated)
- office maintenance help
- office supplies
- postage
- product displays
- professional services of artists, designers, copywriters, free lance writers, &c.
- rent
- research and development expenses
- stationery and printing
- taxes including sales, state income, corporate, &c.
- tax preparer's fee
- telephone including long distance services
- travel expenses connected with business

Some of these items are self evident. Some, however, need a few words of explanation.

Licenses and Permits

Many speakers work from premises which are not zoned for what they do. Most small business books will advise you to check with your local town hall to see what licenses and permits pertain to your work. This is, of course, good solid advice. See whether you can afford to ignore it! Fortunately speakers and writers won't under ordinary circumstances have a lot of traffic through their offices and thus you can take a calculated risk and go ahead without filing the necessary paperwork.

If this course of action makes you nervous, then have your lawyer call up and see whether your town has a "special exemption" process that enables you to carry on with your work without fear. It will involve, however, the possibility of a hearing at which your neighbors get the chance to air their feelings, if they have any. Again: don't make the call yourself. Your lawyer can do so without using your name.

Business Form

Since 1982 the advantages of incorporation for small businesses have been minimized. There were, it seems to me, only two leading reasons for incorporating: protection from suit and certain financial planning advantages. Given the litigious nature of our society and the vulnerability of those who hold what I call "very closely held corporations" where they hold all the stock, this first "advantage" is nugatory. If someone wishes to sue you, they're going to sue you whether you have a corporation or not. Moreover, given the nature of our work speakers are as unlikely to be sued as anyone. Remember however: if you provide your audience with specific advice which they utilize with disastrous results, you have theoretically given them grounds for an action against you. The correct way to handle this aspect of incorporation is to lay out for your attorney all that you plan on saying and doing and get an opinion of whether establishing a corporation would be valuable for you.

On the subject of financial planning, you should consider either running an unincorporated company or what is called a "Subchapter S" corporation. In either case the income the business makes is subject to the same rate of taxation as you are personally. Again, your accountant is the right person with whom to discuss incorporation since this may be a valuable way to save money, reduce the burden of taxation and plan for the future. A corporation is not, repeat *not*, of value to everyone and you shouldn't automatically assume that it's going to be useful for you.

Chapter 14

Pension And Deferred Compensation Plans

One of the advantages that corporations used to have over unincorporated businesses was their usefulness in enabling entrepreneurs to create better pension plans for themselves. This is no longer the case. The Tax Equity and Fiscal Responsibility Act of 1982 (TEFRA) was passed to bring about a parity between the Keogh plans of unincorporated business and existing corporate plans. Thus the maximum contribution for a defined contribution Keogh plan was increased for plan years beginning on or after January 1, 1984. The contribution can now be the lesser of $30,000 or 20% of net compensation.

There are other possibilities for you to consider, too. The Simplified Employee Pension (SEP) is a device that you can use with a corporation and that permits you to put aside up to 13.0435% of your net compensation up to $200,000 of salary yearly. 401(k) pension plans can be run separately or in tandem with an SEP account. This is yet another pension option.

My intention here is not to advise you on which of these several options you should adopt. You and your accountant need to discuss your long range objectives and how the various options will help you realize them. Rather, the point is to get you thinking about how your speaking business and its lucrative sidelines can be used for securing your long term objectives and how you should take advantage of these vehicles to reduce present taxation of either an incorporated or unincorporated business.

One final word: Don't forget to open an Individual Retirement Account (IRA), too. The last statistics I saw show that only about 15% of taxpayers use an IRA. What's the rest of the population doing? Using an IRA along with the vehicles discussed above will enable you to shield a truly substantial amount of capital — even if you can't deduct your contributions from your taxable income — and to develop a very comfortable old age, indeed. Look into it!

Taxes

This is an unpleasant subject to be sure, but one you must become knowledgeable about. After all, the implications of ill-preparedness are even worse than the disease itself.

Here are the taxes you need to know about and some places to get assistance and information:

Federal Taxes

These include:

- Owner income tax (or if incorporated Corporate Income Tax)

- Social Security tax (FICA)

- Federal income tax withholding (if you have employees)

- Unemployment tax (if you have employees).

If you're incorporated...

Think carefully about whether incorporation makes sense for your long term objectives. Discuss your situation with your accountant and weigh the pros and cons. A corporation is a legal entity and it needs perpetual tending. If you decide to go ahead and establish a corporation, here are the taxes you'll pay and how often you have to do so:

- File for a Federal Identification number. This is the equivalent for a corporation of your personal Social Security number. To get one, file form SS with the Internal Revenue Service. Once you've filed for this number, you'll begin to receive regular forms from the federal government concerning your business.

Chapter 14

- Each month in which you've paid yourself a salary, you'll be responsible for paying the Social Security tax and the federal income tax withholding for yourself and any other employees. As of January 1, 1988, the maximum Social Security tax has again gone up, this time to a base of $45,000. Although there is some talk about moderating the Social Security payments for the self-employed, those of us with small corporations continue to be double taxed, to owe, that is, the amount we would pay as employees and that of the corporation, too. This is an intolerable situation and we should be hotly indignant about it. Keep pressing your federal representatives to do something to mitigate this injustice!

These payments, by the way, must be made on the 15th of each month unless the tax you owe is under $500. In this case you pay as soon as the tax exceeds $500. On the other hand, if you have a particularly lucrative month and find yourself owing more than $3000 in tax, you must pay what you owe within 3 days.

- Federal income tax withholding. Your accountant or bookkeeper will advise you how much income tax must be withheld each month based on your salary. These payments are made directly to your local bank which acts as the depository and which gives you receipt of payment. The due date is the 15th of each month for the month preceding.

- Federal unemployment tax. The IRS has instituted a new coupon book for ease of paying Social Security, federal income tax withholding and your federal unemployment tax. This latter tax is paid during the first quarter of your corporate year during which time you'll be paying .008% of the first $7000 of your salary to the federal government.

- Corporate income tax. If you are incorporated and have had a good year (and you should have, you know, following my advice), the feds will want their share of your prosperity. The corporate income tax is based on your profits. Don't worry about getting the necessary forms. The government will be sure to send them to you towards the end of your corporate year.

If you are not incorporated...

- Owner income tax. All the income you make from your business during the calendar year must be added to other sources of your personal income and, after deductions, you must pay taxes accordingly based on the IRS schedule for the year.

- Social Security taxes. As an unincorporated sole proprietor, you'll probably be filing what's called Schedule C along with your 1040 tax form. This is the "Profit (Or Loss) From Business Or Profession" form. As soon as your profit on Schedule C is at least $400, it's time to file a Self-Employment Form along with your regular income tax form and pay into your personal Social Security account. As a self-employed individual, you'll be paying roughly twice as much as your colleagues who are employed by standard corporations. Again, this is discriminatory and unjust!

Your payments will be made quarterly as part of what is called Estimated Tax Payments. These payments from self-employed people are due quarterly on the 15th of April, June, September and January. There's a penalty for not paying taxes when due as well as for underestimating them by more than 20%.

Use your accountant to help you figure out how much to pay each quarter and also review the IRS publication #505, "Tax Withholding and Declaration of Estimated Tax." (See below for ordering.)

On The State Level

The situation functions much the same at the state level as on the federal. Here the following taxes may be due:

- income tax

- sales tax

- unemployment tax (if you have employees).

Chapter 14

If you are incorporated. . .

You'll need to apply for a state identification number which you can do through your department of revenue. You will then receive the necessary forms usually annually or quarterly from your state so that you can pay your state income tax withholding.

- Sales tax. Of the 50 states, only Alaska, Delaware, Montana, New Hampshire and Oregon do not have a sales tax. This is a tax levied against the ultimate purchaser of products such as books. As you go into the materials business with tapes, books, manuals, &c., you need to be aware of the sales tax requirements of your state and, perhaps, locality. Apply to the department of revenue of your state for what is called a Resale Tax Number. This number "permits" you to act as one of your state's tax collectors and gives you the inestimable privilege of remitting payment to them quarterly through special payment forms that will be regularly sent you.

- Unemployment taxes. You need to apply to the Division of Employment Security or like titled office and inform the registrar that you are newly incorporated and would like to begin to make payments into the state unemployment fund on a regular basis. Again, the state will supply you with the necessary forms on a regular basis. Thus you can begin to make unemployment payments. This will prove most beneficial if you as a corporate officer decide to lay off you the corporate employee and reduce yourself to unemployment. Given this Alice in Wonderland situation, it's quite proper to regard this little item as a burdensome tax and not as a benefit.

If you are not incorporated. . .

As an unincorporated individual, your state income tax will be paid annually and you will have no unemployment taxes to pay. Your sales tax situation will, however, remain the same.

Local Taxes

It may be that your state or locality requires payment of an annual inventory tax on property. This would, of course, include books! Check with your accountant to see if this kind of inventory tax applies in your area. And if it does, have a thorough end of the year sale. Do, please, let me know. I love bargains!

Further Information

For further information on the deeply arousing and unpleasant subject of taxes, you can get information from both the Small Business Administration and the IRS. The SBA publishes "Steps In Meeting Your Tax Obligations" along with other business management aids many of which are free. Call 800-368-5855 and ask for their complete title listing. Two IRS guides list their assistance titles: #910 "Taxpayers Guide To IRS" and #552 "Record Keeping And A List Of Publications." #334 "Tax Guide For Small Business" will also be helpful. You can obtain these and other free publications by calling your local IRS office and asking for the "Forms Area" number.

More Mundane Matters

- Postage.

Don't forget to apply to the Post Office for a bulk rate mailing permit. The fee is currently $40 annually and is good only from January 1 to December 31st. There is also a one-time only registration fee of $40. Remember: your permit automatically expires December 31st even if you've bought it the day before. In the speaker business you'll be doing, one way and another, a lot of mailing and a bulk rate indicia is an absolute necessity. For information about mailing, you may subscribe without cost to the "Memo To Mailers", U.S. Postal Service, P.O. Box 999, Springfield, VA 22150-0999.

- Educational Training

Any courses, workshops, seminars or lectures you attend and any materials you buy for upgrading your professional skills are tax deductible. Those that you use for entering the profession are not.

Chapter 14

- **Insurance**

If you are working full time and arranging your speaking activities on the side, you'll probably be adequately covered by health and disability insurance. However, if you are doing business in your home, you'll still probably want to get a special rider on your homeowner's policy to cover accidental injury. If you are planning on a speaking career full time, then you really should check with your insurance agent about available health and disability options. Do, please, shop around. Prices and coverages vary considerably.

Last Words

As should be clear by now, even a part-time speaking business demands your full attention and commitment. This is not something to be undertaken lightly, and the government, if no one else, fully expects those who enter into business do so understanding they have myriad responsibilities which must be met punctiliously. Remember this, however: the country was built by business people and they have not, as existing laws and regulations make plain, been entirely unmindful of their interests. There are real advantages, many financial, the government allows us. Don't be one of the sluggards who refuses to see the advantages that exist within the system and fail to profit from them.

Some Helpful Resources

There is, to be sure, an avalanche of material on business development nowadays. Much of it is hardly worth the notice. Here, however, are four sources of useful information which I can heartily recommend to you:

- *Home Made Money: The Definitive Guide To Success In A Home Business* by Barbara Brabec, Betterway Publications, Inc., White Hall, VA 22987. Barbara knows what she's talking about, and she does so in a direct, no nonsense manner. I can't conceive of anyone with a home-based business who wouldn't profit from this book. The resources section is quite simply superb.

- *In Business Magazine,* Box 323, Emmaus, PA 18049. This and its sister publication *Sideline Business* were made for you. Jerry Goldstein, the publisher, is a bright fellow, and I recommend you keep in touch with him and his fine publications.

- The National Association For the Self-Employed, P.O. Box 612067, D-F-W, TX 75261 (800-433-8004). This is perhaps the nation's largest organization for the self-employed. If offers health insurance benefits and conventions and a fine newsletter called *Small Business America.*

- *Small-Time Operator: How To Start Your Own Small Business, Keep Your Books, Pay Your Taxes & Stay Out Of Trouble* by Bernard Kamaroff, Bell Springs Publishing, P.O. Box 640, Laytonville, CA 95454. Perhaps the most successful small business publication of all time, this volume by Bernard Kamaroff is absolutely necessary. Tell him I said so!

None of these resources is expensive. All are designed for people like us — the go-getters who built this country and who set out to succeed knowing that we can do so if we get just a little help from our friends.

Chapter 15

ON YOUR OWN: SUCCEEDING IN SELF-SPONSORED PROGRAMS

I've left this chapter for last for a good reason. Sponsoring your own programs is the last thing you should think of, not the first. Other books on the subject of workshops and seminars make it seem that this is where you begin, break in. This is decidedly wrongheaded.

Self-sponsored programs have made a very select group of people very wealthy, but there are usually special reasons for their success:

- The programs follow a national best seller written by the program's inventor.

- There is intense popular interest on a given subject that cannot be satisfied through regular talk channels.

- There is limited competition in the field.

These conditions obviously do not pertain for very long and very few people are in a position to benefit from them.

Sadly, though, the optimists in this business predominate over the hard-headed realists. During the writing of this book alone, I have been approached by several would-be seminar entrepreneurs who without adequate forethought launched self-sponsored enterprises — and came to grief.

- An exercise expert from Southern California was impatient to begin a fitness program she thought was "hot." She did not want to wait the 6 months or so it would take a local college which had expressed interest to arrange and promote her program. She called me 3 days before her program when there were just 6 people and sought my urgent advice. Now, really, I am not a miracle worker!

- The college professor and psychologist from New Hampshire who with a group of colleagues launched a program on sexual fulfillment inviting the media to a special pre-session conference on the subject. No one came. What had he done wrong?

- The midwestern entrepreneurs who approached me: one is a physician, the other a fitness consultant. They had taken ads in a series of local newspapers for an important new program only to play to consistent audiences of under 10 and some evenings as few as 2 people. Where had they failed?

Let me say this. Not one of these people is stupid. All came to me financially poorer and wondering. Since they remained convinced about the worth of their ideas, what had gone wrong? What should they do?

Multiply the experiences of these people by thousands during the course of a single year and you not only have an avalanche of waste and distress but one of the principal reasons I have written this book!

Proceed With Caution

Before you decide to operate a free standing program, reread the preceding chapters and consider the following:

- Self-sponsored programs have a very high risk of failure.

- You are probably unknown to the audience you want to attract. The indifference of this audience to you and to the benefit you are offering is staggering and beyond your immediate comprehension.

- You not only have to master the arts of attracting audiences, you need also become adept at the matters of successful program arrangement, both of which demand considerable skill.

Chapter 15

- You must succeed in mastering these skills in a very short time under increasingly intense pressure perhaps aggravated by frustration, irritation and outright anger.

Consider whether you have the time, mental resources, commitment and financial backing to deal with these problems or whether you are not better off systematically mining the nation's continuing education facilities, trade and professional associations, publications, &c. All the already existing vehicles which would in return for a percentage of the revenues, do your prospecting for you or give you access to existing audiences.

So that you know and fully understand my bias on this matter, understand that of the many programs I do during the year — 100 and more — I personally present only one or 2 and in such relatively favorable circumstances as I'll explain to you shortly.

This is not only because I like being the performer rather than the organizer (although I confess there is something very nice about arriving on the scene in a strange city to discover a freshly scrubbed audience expectantly waiting for — me!) I need organizational skills to succeed, too, but they are the skills of identifying and persuading program sponsors in a very competitive market to hire me. Let these organizers then collar the audience and (working with me, of course) prepare participants for the program they want, need and expect.

This method, which I earnestly recommend to you, demands limited upfront money and should, if properly handled, produce regular revenue for you. It leads to a remunerative and personally fulfilling full or part-time job. For 99+ out of 100 readers, this should be sufficient and, at least for the moment, you'll leave this potentially dangerous chapter alone.

Since You Cannot Resist Reading On

Wasn't it Oscar Wilde who said he could resist anything but temptation? Since you, like me, march to the beat of a different drummer, I know that at the very least you'd like to learn how to make self-sponsored programs a success. I have at least offered the necessary caveat about your considering them.

Beginning

Whatever you do on the speaking circuit, don't commence with self-sponsored programs, I implore you! This is truly a suicidal impulse. Begin by launching your program through a sponsoring organization and getting an idea of how successful it is. By this I mean not only how people like it and respond to your material, but also whether the sponsor made money, how much, and for what level of effort.

You must be strict with yourself on these points. I like entrepreneurs and I deal with thousands during any given year. But as a genre we suffer from galloping optimism, the deep and abiding belief that people not only need but actually crave what we have to offer. This optimism is, of course, essential to our success, but it often leads us to make errors that the more cautious avoid. So be cautious, until you are sure.

Find out the following information about presenting your programs:

- space rental costs

- per participant food and beverage costs

- number of catalogs and brochures mailed? Number of participants responding per hundred (or per thousand) mailed?

- cost of mailing list rental

- cost of newspaper or other paid advertisements

- interest of media in promotional information sent.

Chapter 15

As you put your program and subject under the microscope, consider the following: Are there competitive programs? Is your market already saturated? Consider, too, who actually comes to your programs. Are there clear demographic trends in terms of age, sex, education, financial status, occupation, residence? If so, such information will give you an idea of how to promote a free-standing program.

As I wrote earlier in the book, get this information from your program participants. Pass out ascertainment surveys and keep doing so until you have a clear idea of who your participants are, where they come from and why they come. This is essential.

Dipping Your Toe In The Water

The easiest and least expensive way to test the water and see whether a free-standing, self-sponsored program will be successful is to organize a "clinic," an intensive follow up program for people who have already attended one of your programs. These clinics have real pedagogical and psychological value. All learners and particularly adult learners need periodic refresher courses. To improve their skills, they need the opportunity to return to their daily lives and begin implementing your problem solving processes, and then they need to return to the source not simply for information refinement but also for psychological renewal and rededication to success. You, your clinics, provide both.

Organizing Your Clinic

You should consider organizing a clinic after you have made constructive contact with at least 100 people who have enrolled in your programs (or, indeed, who have read your books) and who have had at least 6 months, but not more than one year, in which to master your techniques. These are people who now know they need you.

Contact these people with a letter about 8 weeks before your program is to occur. (See samples, page 290.) Here's what the letter should contain:

- Indicate that those attending your program have suggested the follow-up.

- You want to provide it.

- Suggest that a one day follow-up will be held at time, place, date.

- Give an indication of the program content. This content is important. It should at once promise refresher information about what you have previously imparted as well as your own newest material and the opportunity to engage in constructive case study work on their own situations and circumstances. Tell your prospects you want them to bring in specific materials and details from their own lives to be reviewed and to provide some of the basis for general discussion.

- Indicate that space is limited. Say exactly how many people you will enroll. Make your limits clear and stick to them.

- Ask for an early response to this letter. Indicate urgency and the need for a decision. The benefit of the clinic is that at an often ludicrously low cost, it provides an opportunity not simply for instruction but for consultation and the benefits that accrue through group learning situations. These are powerful inducements for attending, and they should be clearly stated in your initial letter of invitation.

Chapter 15

Note: You can also use, as I often do, a date selection process offering prospects two dates from which to select. I ask them to send a check and indicate a date from among two possibilities and a third category ("either date is fine with me"). I promise not to cash the check until at least 10 people have indicated they will come. This is the number I think is necessary for satisfactory group dynamics.

The Second Letter

I try to organize these clinics so that I'll make $1000 for the day, my usual target. If my initial letter to at least 100 prospects gets at least 5 responses, I know the program will succeed. Then it's necessary to send a follow up to the remaining 95 urging them to attend and reminding them that registration is strictly limited and that the benefits are astoundingly disproportionate to the fee. Also, if you have given prospects two dates from which to select in the initial letter, you must now announce the firm specifics of time, location and date.

How Much To Charge

I prefer charging between $75-$100 for a day, a price which means that for an audience of 15 or so, I should be able comfortably to net $1000. This would not ordinarily include book and other subsidiary revenue income generated on site either. I need hardly say that while the profit is comfortable the value is superb given the range of seminar offerings on the market nowadays.

The only variable is how much your original program cost. If it cost participants between $50-$75 (or, heaven forbid, even less!), you'll need to set your price lower and either be satisfied with grossing less or knowing that you must promote the program more. (Telemarketing? A final post card reminder?) I don't know about you, but I haven't a lot of time to do this, and so I prefer a marginally higher cost for participants.

More About Clinics

Knowing how much to charge is not the only decision you have to make about your clinic. You need to make a decision about the style of your clinic, the amenities you will offer and the location.

I prefer the "no frills" variety of program. People know that they themselves are paying for the three course luncheons, the three-ring binders and the three martinis following the program. They, or their bosses. This, of course, makes a substantial difference to them. If people are paying for themselves, as they often are with my programs, I aim for a "no frills" variety. The theme is this: you are paying for hard, useable information. If you want anything extra, you have to pay for it yourself. It's the same kind of theme that PeoplExpress or similar air carriers use in their advertising, and it works.

This kind of program can be held in your own offices (or home) or in a low cost hotel facility. Just what facility you rent should depend on where your participants are coming from. Don't make the mistake of so many seminar entrepreneurs and rent the most expensive facility in the center of the largest neighboring town. This isn't necessary and is often most inappropriate for the kind of clientele you seek to attract and the purpose of the meeting.

One more thing: offer no apologies for the site, the lack of amenities, the rather stark nature of the program. It's not necessary and is actually demeaning to you. Your objective should always be to impart the best information at the lowest cost and at a reasonable profit for yourself. Let this be your perpetual objective.

Free Standing, Self-Sponsored Programs For Those Who Don't Know You

Now, truly, this is where the game gets risky. The stakes, to be sure, can be significant, but so is the risk. What you're trying to do is among the most difficult of tasks: get people who may be interested in the topic to part with a significant amount of money in the hopes that you are the right person with the right material to satisfy their needs and meet their aspirations. You must do this in the face of many competing programs (not just in the same field either), with people who must be convinced by a very few words to take the action you suggest. Yes, this is difficult and very risky.

Homework, lots of homework, must precede this decision as well as the entrepreneur's gut instinct that the need exists. You need to have offered your program previously through a sponsoring organization, need to have ascertained critical information about how profitable it was and how it became profitable, and need to have a clear understanding

Chapter 15

of who came and why and what they liked and didn't like. If you have gathered all this information and the prospects still look favorable, then it is time to test the waters for a completely self-sponsored program appealing to new people who have had no previous contact with you.

As you begin this process, understand that your research has not ended and that your initial programs, however successful, must be analyzed and refined to perfect the process. Arranging successful self-sponsored talk programs is a tinkering business and one that is seldom, if ever, entirely refined and cemented.

The Pilot

You can tell me now and in detail just who should attend your program and why. The more specific you can be about your program participants the better. Now you must seek to get access to them. There are two main ways of doing so:

- brochures and other direct mail pieces

- newspaper and other paid advertising space ads.

Direct Mail Pieces

Direct mail can work for seminars and workshops despite all the competition if you have considered the following points:

- The list. Are you certain that the profile of the list to which you are mailing is the profile of the people you wish to attend your program? Make sure it is because if you are wrong, your program has a very limited likelihood of success. I have found that list brokers on the whole are apathetic and listless about providing the kind of exact information I need. Perhaps they don't have it; perhaps they are merely slothful. For whatever the reason, I am myself all too often left with an incomplete sense of what the broker has available. In this situation, pull back. At the very least have the broker get the first page, 44 labels, of the list so that you can review it. This should help give you an indication that you're on the right track.

- The price. From talking to my colleagues in the seminar business and reviewing an abundance of brochures, it is clear to me that the programs worth promoting are the programs worth putting a substantial price tag on and by this I mean a price tag in excess of $150 per day. If you don't, you will find it difficult to make a profit for your time and expenses. Lower fee programs work relatively well when an organization is prospecting to tens of thousands through a catalog for a noncredit continuing education program. In such circumstances proven "cash cows" support the marketing and prospecting for new programs. This is as it should be.

Where you are promoting a single workshop, you don't have that certain "cash cow" working for you offsetting your other expenses. Thus the likelihood of failure is substantial.

In such circumstances, set your fee as high as you can. You should have an idea of how high that would be. You ascertained for that didn't you at your previous programs? So you should know at what level you begin to encounter serious customer resistance.

Remember, too: you can conceive of means to lower the resistance by adding premiums and other registration inducements. If, for instance, you could show that adding $15 to your expenses to take advantage of our dealer discount for **THE UNABASHED SELF-PROMOTER'S GUIDE** would enable you to charge an additional $30-50, it would be worth it, wouldn't it? Well, think about it!

The point is this: many entrepreneurs who present self-sponsored workshops, have a curious idea about price. They set their prices low in a misguided attempt to attract business. This low fee, unless in a special circumstance like a "clinic" where participants should know you, usually doesn't work. People suspect the value of your information; ("If it's so good, why doesn't he make us pay for it?") You leave yourself a paper thin margin of error.

What is happening nationally these days in marketing should interest you, too. More and more marketing efforts are being directed at the most affluent, those with the most discretionary income. You, too, must turn your attention to the most affluent part of your market, understand what they want and need, and the disproportionate benefit they

Chapter 15

will get from attending your program. Then write scintillating marketing copy to communicate all this in a few diamond bright paragraphs.

The Brochure Itself

I have discussed brochures previously and you already know about Jane Maas' book on the subject. This section, then, is by way of being a refresher. Here are some suggestions:

- Collect all the seminar and workshop brochures you can. Keep them in a special place. Read them and mark the sections that most appeal to you. Writing convincing brochure copy is an art with scientific aspects. It's an art that you must master.

- Make sure that both the aspirations and the anxieties of your client population are addressed. People will attend your program to deal with both.

- Quantify the results. Instead of saying, "You'll learn how to write articles the media will accept," say "You'll learn how to master the only three media formats you'll ever need."

- Use action verbs to indicate participant outcomes.

- Demonstrate that these participants will not be the first to take your program and benefit from your methods. Your audience will not appreciate being guinea pigs. You have to show them they won't be.

- Indicate what they'll get from attending that they can't get anywhere else. Emphasize the unique aspects of your program.

- Consider the tone. I like using this one: "If you're not serious, stay home. This program is for those who seriously want to get ahead, who want success — now! — and who know that it takes hard work and mastery of the critical subject areas to be found in this intensive program."

- Give people a reason for responding now, either a special registration price before a certain date, a free gift or other inducement.

After your prospects have read your brochure, they should see in you not merely the repository of useful information but the critical vehicle and means of helping them achieve whatever success, whatever tangible success your program offers. This is critical: you must be the dreamspinner for your audiences, the individual who helps them see more clearly their own vision and who is the midwife for their dream, the person who helps bring it into being. If you can help them visualize their dreams and offer them a reasonable chance of bringing this dream into existence, then and only then will you succeed in getting them to part with a sum of money which otherwise will be too significant to part with.

One of the masters of this genre is Anver Suleiman (The Marketing Federation, 7141 Gulf Blvd., St. Petersburg Beach, FL 33706). Suleiman produces a useful newsletter for those interested in producing seminars and workshops and annual programs on how to make your programs more successful. He brings his high ticket program to your attention not once but time after time, perhaps as many as four mailings within an 8 week period. Each of these mailings communicates a sense of excitement and enthusiasm. They cite previous satisfied customers and critical objectives which will be realized through your attendance. This is the kind of material you need to review and learn from.

Note: I am not saying slavishly to copy it. Your task is to develop a style with which you feel comfortable, which is attractive to your customers, and which intensely communicates that you have the right program at the right price at the right time for your audience. This brings success.

I know this. During the course of the year I review hundreds of program brochures and advise many who are seeking to create and market programs. I'm convinced of this: most seminar entrepreneurs wound themselves. They have an inadequate perception of their audiences and no good reason why these hapless folk should plunk down perfectly good Yankee dollars for the program in question. These entrepreneurs write copy that would be useful only to those who have trouble sleeping at night. They expect that far more people will respond to their whimsies than is ever reasonable. Beware! My experience shows that you, too, could let this happen. Don't!

Chapter 15

A Few Words About Lists And Returns

This is not a book about mastering direct mail marketing. Yet if you expect to make a success of any self-sponsored programs promoted by direct mail, you must learn the ins and outs of this costly promotional genre.

Your expertise must deal with the following topics:

- How to find a reliable list broker.

- How much to pay for lists.

- How to evaluate the success of your mailings.

Here are some thoughts on each of these critical topics.

Finding a reliable list broker

Almost daily now I am inundated with direct mail circulars that promise "newer, fresher, proven" lists. Most end up in the circular file. I honestly believe that most list brokers want to help you. After all it's in their interest to do so; a happy, prospering customer will secure my business. But I've been disappointed in the quality of the advice I've received from such brokers. All too often they seem not to understand what kind of lists are available and the profile of the individuals and organizations who will receive your mailings. Under the circumstances, I advise you to do the following:

- Tell the broker precisely whom you are aiming to reach. The more specific you can be the better.

- Then ask him to search his files to determine probable lists that meet your expectations.

- Ask whether you can have a single page (44 labels) run off from the list(s) in question so that you can get a sense of whom/what you are mailing to.

This last point I have come to regard as crucial. Now having done quite a number of mailings, I can tell from a single perusal of a page of labels whether this is the right list for me or not and get a clearer sense of what the broker is selling. If this list cannot be run off for you, at the very least have it be xeroxed or read to you over the telephone. Yes, it's an inconvenience for the broker; no, they probably won't want to do it. But press your point. I shall never forget my discomfiture, irritation and annoyance when after having ordered a set of labels of nonprofit organizations to find interspersed more than 100 chapters of the Empire Loyalists organization. Not at all what I had in mind!

Cost

List costs vary. They vary depending on whether the broker you are using has to buy from outside his own organization or whether he has what are called house lists. Most lists rent (not sell, please note) for one time usage from about $50-$75 per thousand names. Geographical selection and format (pressure sensitive/peel off and cheshire labels) cost extra as does a "slug line" wherein you indicate the exact individual or office that you wish to receive the mailing. You will probably be asked to pay up front on your first order; thereafter you can establish suitable credit terms. I have discovered that list brokers are fairly lenient about collection terms and have learned to give you the time to mail and await returns before themselves demanding payment. The problem, of course, comes when the mailing doesn't draw.

Success

As you already know I'm generally optimistic, feeling Micawberlike that "something will turn up." That's true in almost all areas except direct mail where I've learned from experience to be cautious and very, very conservative. If you are succeeding in drawing a regular 1 to 1.5% response from a list, congratulate yourself. If you are drawing this response and still not making money, don't assume that mailing more pieces will improve matters; think, instead, about raising the price of your offering.

Chapter 15

What I've discovered about mail order is that people are scandalously addicted to tall tales. The truth is that mail order is a quick way for you to lose your money and that most people do. I often suspect that there is more money to be made from telling people how to make mail order work than there is from working in mail order. A cynical observation, perhaps, but nonetheless true and why there is so much literature about on the topic.

A Few Typically Candid Words From The Author

Given the treacherous undercurrents of the mail order business, I would be very, very careful about how I used it to promote a seminar or program. I myself now use mail order promotion regularly, but I do so with substantial high ticket items. My most successful direct mail pieces are where I offer myself, specifically my lecture and workshop programs as the offer. In this case I mail out roughly 2000 pieces to the nation's colleges and know that I'll break even if a single college books me and their program actually takes place. That's not only because the cost of the program is high but because, all things being equal, the buyer will not only buy once but for a span of years. To give you some idea of the return here, on my last college mailing, mailing to a market where I am at least relatively well known and have a very solid track record, I pulled 10 responses. That result warmed the cockles of my heart although it was only ½ of one percent of those I mailed to. I hope you get my point.

- Market by direct mail only high ticket programs.

- Market only to those who you are sure are interested in the program (perceived anxiety/aspirations) and who can pay the cost.

- Expect no more than a .5% return. Calculate your break even point on this basis.

- Add low cost premiums (like this book!) to beef up the perceived value and bump up the cost.

- Don't hire the most expensive facilities but project an image of lean and hungry intensity and information richness and density.

- Don't make this the only program you put on. If you put all your eggs in one basket, you could end up having to make omelettes sooner than you wanted.

- Do evaluate your findings and reevaluate them. Direct mail is necessarily an action business and demands continuing scrutiny and consideration.

Direct Mail Resources

Many, many books and articles have been written about this enticing subject. Here are two places, however, to look for solid information at reasonable cost:

Premier Publishers, P.O. Box 330309, Fort Worth, TX 76163. Ask for information on their five handy books entitled *How To Write And Design Money-Making Response Advertisements; 59 Response/Profit Tips, Tricks, & Techniques To Help You Achieve Major Mail Order Success; How To Make The Successful Transition From Small-Time To Big-Time Mail Order; The Success How-To's Of Money Making Direct Mail*, and *How You Can Write Winning Sales Letters*.

TOWERS Club Newsletter. This is published by Jerry Buchanan, a spry old salt if there ever was one, who offers mail order information in this and other publications including a helpful booklet on the mistakes you're likely to make and how to avoid them. Write him at P.O. Box 2038, Vancouver, WA 98668 and get the complete list of his publications. Tell him I sent you!

A Different Wrinkle

One way of getting program prospects is through running classified ads in such major magazines as *Popular Science, Popular Mechanics*, &c. Here's how to make this work: Once you have a product, produce a classified ad which will cause people to write you for information. While you will have to develop a response packet, these names are also prospects for your talk programs.

Chapter 15

- You can and should pass them along to the program planners at universities and other talk facilities with which you are dealing so that a special letter can be sent to them along with your program brochure or catalog.

- You yourself can mail directly to them with or without a letter when you're holding your own program.

Don't make the mistake of the aspiring ingenue (including me!) that all those responding are in fact real prospects. There are people, numbered perhaps in the millions, who simply enjoy getting mail and who therefore go to great lengths to write to entrepreneurs like us to get their jollities. Your return rate from this group, therefore, will probably be about the same, say 1 to 2%, as it would be from any other group. The difference is that a single workshop enrollment from this bunch should pay for at least a couple of month's worth of your ad. Thus it's probably worth pursuing them.

The Newspaper Gamble

You've probably seen the seminar entrepreneurs who promote their programs through the daily press. This may be the image and objective you want for yourself. Fair enough. Only remember that my special preconditions for success (best selling books, &c) are very relevant in these circumstances. I have myself run programs around the nation from large space ads in daily newspapers, and I have a clear sense of the risk, the need for capital, and the likelihood of success. It goes without saying that you substantially increase the former and threaten the latter if you proceed in this area without a great amount of experience.

Starting Off Small

Newspaper space ads cost a considerable amount of money. If you are holding a program in your home city, you will get the local advertiser's rate; if you move to another state, you'll have to pay the national rate. To give you some idea of what you can expect to pay for a major metropolitan area, consider that a 4" x 6" ad (about half the size of this page) in the *Boston Globe* in the Financial Section costs about $1800 for a week-day and nearly $2100 for Sunday.

This is money that must be paid in advance before your ad is run. Now within the profession it is well known how certain dubious seminar promoters finagle this matter. They kite checks by writing a check from a New England bank account for a California newspaper and the reverse. In this way, too, they seek to present themselves as local businesses. This doesn't work very well. I have watched two national seminar promoters collapse in disgrace and go into bankruptcy using such methods. Yes, the serious consequences of a misstep here are considerable. I therefore suggest that you begin by using either a weekly newspaper or else a suburban daily read by the kinds of people you are trying to attract.

Selecting The Newspaper

Don't begin your seminar program out of state. You simply don't know enough about the areas, the newspapers, and the places of residence of the people you want to attract. Success, like charity, begins at home. In case you don't know all the local newspapers hie thee to your local library for the most up-to-date edition of Standard Rate & Data. This will include a complete listing of possibilities and advertising rates. But do more than this: call the local newspaper you are thinking of using and talk to their advertising department. Unlike the editorial branches of newspapers which I have discussed in **THE UNABASHED SELF-PROMOTER'S GUIDE**, you will find the advertising people responsive and easy to work with. They suffer from no inflated notions about themselves and their importance. Which is a distinct and refreshing change.

Particularly if you are new on the job, don't hesitate to make an appointment to discuss your situation. Remember you are not merely buying one ad, you are trying to launch a program with potential national significance and you want to get off on the right foot. Here are the matters you should discuss:

- size

- location

- set up

- combination rates.

Chapter 15

Size

Your ad needs to be big enough to have an impact on the prospective participant. How big should this be? Your ad should be at least 3″ x 5″. This is big enough to enable you to pack in sufficient convincing information and make an impact with the reader.

Location

This is an important point. A weekly newspaper or a small suburban daily will have limited sections but you need to approximate the ultimate location that you'd like to run your ad in: living, financial, or sports (if you are keen in reaching a mainly male audience).

Set up

People who do national seminars have gone to the cost of having a professional designer lay out and design their ads for multiple use. If money is not an object (!), you can do the same thing. But since it is, what I advise you do to is work through the copy yourself (to be discussed momentarily) and ask the advertising department of the newspaper for lay out assistance. Occasionally they will charge you an additional typesetting fee but this is usually in the price. They'll be happy to follow your directions about set up. After all, they really do want you to be happy — and to bring your business back.

Ultimately, however, if you are going to be running your program on a regular basis, you should probably bring in a professional designer who can help you set up the ad for maximum impact and utmost creativity within the limited confines of the space available.

Combination Rates

Be aware of this: a single insertion of an ad in a newspaper will not ordinarily be sufficient to bring about the desired response. That's why you should inquire about a newspaper's combination rate, the rate that is for running the same advertisement twice. This rate is always better than the actual cost of running the same ad twice since the paper gives you an inducement for spending those extra dollars. For most seminar entrepreneurs, double exposure is of the utmost necessity. Moreover, this exposure should be in two distinct parts of the paper, a result the combination rate usually allows.

The Copy

Begin clipping all newspaper program space ads. When you're working on your copy, lay them out on the kitchen table and review them carefully. What makes one stand out from another? It'll be, I'll bet, the apt use of the following:

- Anxiety/aspiration axis. What are your prospects anxious about? What is their aspiration? Both must be addressed, boldly, straightforwardly and subtly in your text.

- Your credentials. People want to know who you are. Most of them will never have heard of you before. They want to know enough about you (25 words worth) to convince them that you are a respected individual, knowledgeable in the field and not a glib fly-by-night.

- Comments of participants. Prospects want to know that others have profited from what you've got to say. If you can insert the names of people from this marketing area, do so.

- Tangible benefits prospects will leave with. Tell people exactly what you're going to give them, why they need it and how they can profit from these benefits. Let them know that the program is a beginning, not an end, a lever from which they can profit. Let them know that others are already doing so, thus increasing the pressure on them to get along, too.

- Reason for attending now. If you are traipsing around the country, people may reason that if they don't get you now they can come back later. No! Your prospects need a reason for enrolling today. This reason can be a special gift that they'll get now, a likely change in the situation you are addressing that will affect them, a real reason that compels them to act today.

Chapter 15

- A premium. People like freebies, always have, always will. Give them a special gift for attending. What kind of gift? A pamphlet with hard-to-find names and addresses pertinent to the topic; a calorie counter; a bibliographic resource. Something that's inexpensive for you and yet useful for the participant. Don't forget to have your name and address and telephone number emblazoned on this premium. It's a good source of advertising for you.

- Deferred payment. We are a credit hungry nation. You can benefit from this fact. Give people the opportunity to attend and pay much, much later — the wildly alluring inducement of credit.

- A money back guarantee. Because people don't know you and because seminars cost a lot of money, you need a method of soothing the doubtful and dubious. A money back guarantee will help do this. "If for any reason you are unhappy with this program after the first hour, tell me and I'll refund your money. No questions asked." That's pretty direct.

Some Variables

The items above don't change. They are the heart of your program. Other items do change, however, including:

- Multiple programs. If you are holding the same program in the same area on different nights, you'll need to list the places and times. This step comes later, however, once you are sure that the program will in fact prosper.

- On-site versus advance registration. You'll feel better if you handle registrations in advance. Give people a reason to register early (a $10 reduction in the cost will do it, or the free gift I previously discussed). You'll get a sense about whether your program will go or not. I know the tension of having on-site registration only because I did a series of programs this way and it's very nerve wracking. Don't forget that even if you have advance registrations, you'll have to be prepared for walk ins, too, since in this business people often make up their minds to attend at the last minute and you have to be prepared for them. This means, of course, that you'll need to include a telephone number. A good way of answering your home phone (assuming you haven't installed a business number), is simply your name, "Jeffrey Lant speaking." Since your name appears in the ad copy this will do. If you are working from home, keep those adorable toddlers away from the telephone; their endearing chatter shatters a professional image. In due course, you'll want an 800 number when registering people from out of state. You can get a service which will handle your calls for under $1 each.

Another Costly Variable: The Law

The minute you begin to put on self-sponsored programs you are potentially subject to your state's licensing procedures. Not all states have them, but those that do (most of the bigger ones) have guidelines for the licensing of speakers. The state's argument goes something like this: "We have the right to regulate all speakers and insure that participants get the information they're paying for and that the people delivering the program are responsible, honorable and knowledgeable. Where a speaker works for a college, university or other education facility, we delegate our right to this facility in the hopes that it will put on only useful programs that satisfy the just needs of the public for information. Where, however, a self-sponsoring entrepreneur is involved, we insist upon doing the licensing and regulating ourselves."

Ladies and gentlemen, this is a growing movement across the country and on the surface of it these rational arguments are most appealing. Like many rational movements, however, in fact the introduction of regulating bodies has confused the issue and created as many problems as may have been solved.

A Typical SNAFU Snaring The Law Abiding

The Commonwealth of Massachusetts, a state which prides itself on its progressive tradition, has such regulating rules. One thing that it requires is that the facility which you rent for your program have proper fire protection equipment and be recently inspected. A colleague swears that having booked a program at a prestigious local hotel, the state licensing authority asked for the hotel's latest fire inspection report as part of his application to present a program there. The report was posted in the lobby in a glass case. The hotel's management was incredulous that the state wanted it and was not as cooperative as it might have been. In the end, the fire report was photocopied and sent on to the state which was satisfied, but much general inconvenience had taken place.

Chapter 15

Requirements

The kinds of programs which are most often regulated are business, professional and financial programs. If you are planning on offering this kind of feature, then check with the Attorney General of the state in which you want to offer the program. If you are offering a motivational program, there seems less need to register. For instance, the State of Minnesota exempts motivational programs from their licensing procedures but does have statutes dealing with other kinds of programs.

The Massachusetts statute seems typical. Even if you are only offering a single business-related topic, you must seek registration as a business school and pay all the fees that such full-time enterprises pay. This is, of course, absurd and an indication that the law was written by people who had no understanding of this business. It makes no sense to lump an independent speaker who gives two or three lectures a year in a given state into the same group as business schools and other continuing enterprises. If there must be regulating procedures, then they should make sense for the circumstances and have fees and requirements that are sensible for those being regulated. Since they don't, regulation introduces a whole new element of expenditure and risk into this business.

The Risk Of Not Registering

Seminar entrepreneurs are understandably reluctant to talk about the times they've been busted for failing to register and complete licensing procedures. However among speaking professionals (usually over cocktails late at night) stories do circulate about our peers and the occasions when their programs were shut down by the local police or sheriff because they failed to have the necessary permit or that they were forced to pay the fees before they could continue their programs. To put it mildly, this would be an embarrassing situation. I have solved the problem by working through organizations that are themselves licensed and where I function as an independent contractor. This is the easiest way out of the difficulty. Another means is to note the affiliations of independent seminar providers, many of whom have set up nonprofit organizations to market their programs, and see whether you can make an agreement with one of them and take advantage of their licensure.

For most of us, however, paying each state several hundred dollars yearly for the privilege of making our presentation really doesn't make sense. Most speakers don't have that kind of money multiplied by the number of states in which they want to do business. As a direct result an absurd law, originally designed for good, forces well-meaning people into the position of scofflaws and the possibility of embarrassment, fine and, perhaps, worse. Are you sure that an affiliation with a local college wouldn't be more sensible for you?

Arranging The Facility

Assuming that you are determined to proceed having considered all the risks as well as the possible rewards, you now have the inestimable delight of arranging a facility and all that goes with it.

The Place

One critical mistake seminar entrepreneurs make is to begin by renting the most impressive and expensive space they can. Usually this is in a central city location hotel. This is right, of course, for some programs but not all programs. I co-sponsored a very successful one-day intensive program for executive directors of visiting nurses agencies a year ago. There is one visiting nursing association in Boston; there are dozens in the metro Boston area. We selected Braintree, a suburb of Boston, as the right place for two reasons: 1) it was more accessible for those we were targeting as prospects; and 2) we received an infinitely better deal on the hotel, food, beverages and other amenities. It may fulfill your self image to lecture in the grand ball room draped in cloth of gold, but it's probably not a necessary expense.

A Check List For Facilities Arrangement

Here are the things you need to arrange with the hotel or other facility when you book it. You should consider confirming these items on your own form so that you can place it on file with the facility and thus have a reasonable expectation that matters will be arranged the way you want them:

Chapter 15

- name of person who'll be handling your program
- his telephone number
- date of function
- date function confirmed
- name of your program as you want it posted in the lobby (keep to about 6 to 7 words with your name)
- number of people for whom the room should be set up
- way in which you want room set up (theatre, classroom, &c)
- number of additional chairs you want present in back of room for use if need be
- name of room to which you have been assigned
- tables (specify length needed) at back of room (for sales) and at front (for pass outs)
- name of person who handles acceptance for deliveries (your books and pass outs)
- table top lectern
- microphone (kind)
- overhead projector for transparencies
- blackboard and chalk
- projection screen
- flip chart
- room should be set up so that latecomers enter from the back not the front
- registration table: length, number of chairs needed, waste basket
- where this table should be put (inside or outside room)
- time room is to be ready
- where telephone is located. Make sure that the hotel places no calls to you during meetings but does deliver written messages.
- ash trays. Where do you want them? (One side of the room only, please, to pacify nonsmokers, or, like me, no ashtrays at all.)
- where water will be placed
- if you are doing two programs on a single day, hours when room will be vacant for cleaning.
- the kind of beverage service you'll need. Note: order half as much coffee as you think you'll need and the smallest cups you can get. Keep your morning coffee on hand all day and supplement with afternoon juice and soft drinks.
- the kind of guest room you want. Indicate that you want the corporate rate and that if there is a form to fill out you want it sent. Guarantee this room for late arrival.

Chapter 15

Finally, ask for a précis of the charges for facilities rental, beverage service, guest room and anything else you may want including equipment rental.

Finding The Right Facility

There are two ways you can use to help find the right facility for your program:

- Take a look at the annual facilities guide published by *Successful Meetings* (Bill Communications, 633 Third Avenue, New York, New York 10017). This will give you a good list of possible meeting places and information about them.

- Call the city's convention bureau and ask where these hotels are located with reference to the kinds of people you're trying to attract. The convention bureau will usually not give you a recommendation about the kind of place to rent, but their information along with what you find in *Successful Meetings* will probably be sufficient to enable you to make a choice.

Other Matters

Here are a few other things you should consider providing to make your meeting a success:

- Directions to the facility. Can the facility provide you with a directional map? If so, this can be mailed to participants with their program confirmation notice.

- Registration helpers. If you anticipate a crowd of over 20 people, you're going to find it difficult to register them, answer questions, and generally handle the arrangements yourself. Get a temporary employee to help you. You'll need about two hours of time.

- Credit card payment. Those who accept credit cards for payment at their seminars report that this service has helped their sales. You can apply at your bank to offer Visa and MasterCard. Of course, you do pay a fee for this service, and as the fee varies with the bank, it pays to shop around.

A Word About Shady Characters And Their Machinations

Sad to tell, there are people who will write a check knowing they don't have the funds to cover it. My advice to you is to expect some of this. How much? That depends on your audience. One of the skills entrepreneurs have to develop — and do — is their ability to learn who is likely to bounce a check. You develop a feeling that's seldom wrong. In my experience, men are far more likely to write a false check than women, although others may dispute this.

The correct way to handle checks is this: ask the writer to endorse the check with his driver's license and another form of personal identification and a telephone number. Even so, some slippery characters will elude you. Accept it as the fact of doing business these days. I'd say that one in 200 people will do this and while you can try to get back the money, it's very difficult. After a couple of letters, and a nice nasty one to get the matter off your chest, write it off to experience — and vow to get even in another life.

The Two-Step

The program above involves payment either in advance or on the spot for one or a series of lectures. There is another possibility, one practiced by a few of the best known names in the talk business: the Two-Step. It would be wrong to conclude this chapter without a few words about how it works.

You are no doubt at least familiar with the genre wherein an engaging entrepreneur invites you, usually via your daily newspaper, to a program ordinarily held in the evening at a plush nearby hotel. This program is free and it promises the delights of the Mahometan afterlife. It's also a come-on designed to entice you with the prospect of obscene and immediate benefit if you'll only sign up, at a hefty price, for the next program which will truly reveal the necessary secrets which insure success.

Chapter 15

Perhaps you detect in my language a flicker of disdain about this genre, but in fact I have nothing fundamentally against it. It's used by many entrepreneurs but particularly those with real estate interests (the ubiquitous "no money down" crew) and others with financial schemes. You should use it only when you are a mature and experienced seminar promoter.

The success of the Two-Step usually depends on the following factors:

1) A name presenter you've heard or read about. Ultimately, of course, this well-known personality may cease to provide actual programming and delegate the actual talk to "clones" who make the pitch. Even so, it is the originator who is featured in the ads, rarely the clones.

2) A system which has been publicized through the mass media, perhaps through a book, on a topic of wide public interest.

3) A very engaging, compelling, charismatic lecturer whose game as the consummate salesperson is to tease and excite you with the benefits to come — tomorrow, of course — when the real action takes place.

4) The availability of high priced materials on the subject which can be sold to participants as a package. The price of these materials is stiff, of course, because it's set according to the benefits you've now been taught to believe in, if only you follow the method.

Very few people can convincingly carry off the Two-Step, at least in part because the sales aspect must be unrelenting, otherwise the entrepreneur has lost his money. After all it's the prospects who are paying for the ad campaigns which are always substantial and expensive, and if they don't pay there will be a terrific loss.

If you are even considering this, I advise you to move slowly and carefully. Go to not one but several different Two-Step programs. Don't just go to the free night, either. Enroll in the entire program and go wearing two hats: as a doubting prospect and as a potential duplicator of the seminar method. Take extensive notes. Meet the leaders. Buy them a drink and get them to open up about their work. Talk to the participants about why they attended. Be thorough. After all, you're not just out for an evening's amusement. Be hard headed. You must have good, solid answers to the following questions:

- Do I have a program, a benefit if you will, that will draw large numbers of people?

- Can I develop a product, usually a book, that will launch me by bringing my system to the attention of the public in a sustained way?

- Do I have the financial reserves it will take to launch expensive advertising campaigns in cities nationwide?

- Do I have it in me to be not merely upbeat but a charming, insistent salesperson and to tickle, entice and persuade people to spend their money on me and my program? Or would I find such a role demeaning and embarrassing?

When you've taken a long hard look at your prospects, your message, your financial resources and your personal ones, and you've become a polished platform performer then and only then will the Two-Step even begin to make sense.

CONCLUSION.....

A Moment For Exaltation — And Gratitude

There comes a moment when you can do no more. You've planned. You've promoted. You've taken the last look at the facility, moved chairs into place and adjusted the flip chart. Perhaps the situation is not perfect, not just what you envisioned in a palmier moment. Every lecturer has horror stories about the talk circuit: about rooms that smelled like mediaeval Parisian sewers, that were as dark as fish tanks, of staff who were torpid and abrupt, and of participants you sensed would be difficult — but were worse. Yes, we all have tales like this.

Nonetheless, you've come a long way to arrive at this point and now is the time to spend just a moment being glad and grateful, for a moment is all you have before you begin to speak, before you arrest every eye and become the ardent dreamspinner of every person present who has chosen you, you!, from among a throng of competing possibilities and whose life you may, you will!, alter in perhaps subtle, perhaps momentous ways.

You owe these people, your present audience, your future followers, a disproportionate benefit for investing in you, even if you are suffering from frustration about conditions, irritation from mistakes, disappointment because there are fewer expectant faces in the crowd than you'd have liked. Like the trooper you are, or the trooper you are becoming, you'll give them what they've come for. Because that's what being a professional is all about. And you are the speaking professional par excellence.

Perhaps this book, a very opinionated work to be sure, has helped and will continue to help you achieve your laudable objective. If so, let me know. For like your most devoted friends, I'm waiting to see just how well you do. Indeed, as someone who may have helped propel you on your way, I look forward to the pleasing interlude when I, too, may sport in the afterglow of your brilliant aureole.

SAMPLE SECTION TABLE OF CONTENTS

Essentials Of A Letter To A Program Planner Asking To Be Kept In Mind If A Vacancy Develops 264

Sample Letter To A Program Planner Asking To Be Kept In Mind If A Vacancy Develops 265

Essentials Of A Proposal Letter To A Program Planner 266

Sample Proposal Letter To A Program Planner 267

Essentials Of A Success Letter 268

Sample Success Letter 269

Sample Program Catalog For Your Lectures, Courses and Workshops 270

Essentials Of An Introduction Letter On Your Behalf 274

Sample Introductory Letter On Your Behalf 275

Essentials Of A Sales Cover Letter Being Sent From A Program Planner To Prospects Along With Descriptive Information On Your Program 276

Sample Sales Cover Letter Being Sent From A Program Planner To Prospects Along With Descriptive Information On Your Program 277

Essentials Of A Group Discount Sales Letter 278

Sample Group Discount Sales Letter 279

Sample Advertising Format For Your Books And Products 280

Essentials Of A Letter To Publisher Special Sales Representative 282

Sample Letter To Publisher Special Sales Representative 283

Sample Précis Of Products And Services 284

Essentials Of A Letter To A Newsletter Publisher Suggesting Talk Possibilities 286

Sample Letter To A Newsletter Publisher Suggesting Talk Possibilities 287

Essentials Of An Introductory Letter To A Lecture Agent 288

Sample Introductory Letter To A Lecture Agent 289

Essentials Of An Invitation Letter To Clinic Prospects 290

Sample Invitation Letter To Clinic Prospects 291

Essentials Of A Letter To A Program Planner Asking To Be Kept In Mind If A Vacancy Develops

- Letter should be typed on your official stationery (as all the letters in this section should be.)

- Tone should be brisk, upbeat. Remember you are not simply applying for a position. You are indicating that you can be helpful to the program planner in the future. Expect to be warmly received.

- Begin by showing you are aware that someone else is offering the program but that you'd like to offer it when the suitable moment arrives.

- Give an indication of your credentials and experience.

- If you have other courses you'd like to offer, say so.

- Indicate how you'll follow-up this letter. A telephone call is usually sufficient. Unless you are offering several programs, there is probably no need for an immediate interview.

SAMPLE LETTER TO A PROGRAM PLANNER ASKING TO BE KEPT IN MIND IF A VACANCY DEVELOPS

Dear Program Director:

I read with interest in your recent catalog of your program on "Establishing And Operating Your Successful Consulting Business" taught by Dr. Jeffrey Lant.

I wanted to write and let you know that I, too, have a special knowledge of the field of consulting. I have written two articles on the subject (one of which is enclosed) and have been a management consultant for the past 7 years.

It occurs to me that you might be willing to keep my name on file to offer this consulting workshop in the future in case Dr. Lant is unavailable.

Moreover, I should welcome the opportunity of discussing with you two related ideas which would be of interest to those enrolled in the consulting program: "The Golden Oldies: Developing Long Term Resources Through Financial Planning" and "Small Business and Professional Marketing and Promotion." I notice neither of these programs is currently offered.

I'll telephone next week to discuss these matters.

Sincerely,

Instructor Prospect

Essentials Of A Proposal Letter To A Program Planner

- Your tone should be forthright and authoritative. You are the expert after all.

- Begin with an indication that you have perused the institution's existing materials and that what you are about to propose does not now exist. If it *does* exist, make sure you immediately let the reader know that it does and why you are yet writing.

- Suggest why now is the appropriate time for this program.

- Tell what you've got in mind.

- Provide information on who you are and provide contextual credentials which plainly indicate why you're the right person to offer this program.

- Include sample catalog copy as supplementary material.

- Indicate how you'll be following up your letter. A personal meeting is advisable. To this meeting bring information about target groups (including any special connections you have to them), promotional ideas and anything else which you think will help get people to attend. These need not be sent in your initial letter.

N.B. With little alteration this format is suitable for query letter to a media source you want to cover your program.

SAMPLE PROPOSAL LETTER TO A PROGRAM PLANNER

Dear Program Planner:

I have reviewed with considerable interest your current catalog of noncredit offerings. Having done so, I find you are not now offering a course on "Financial Planning For Working Mothers." May I propose one?

As you are probably aware, women now constitute a majority of the workforce. Moreover of these fully 60% are working mothers, often heads of households. This phenomenon is a growing one as the enclosed story from this month's *Working Woman* magazine indicates.

Sadly many of these woman have inadequate financial planning devices. This lack of forethought and planning leaves them and their children very vulnerable to any change in the nation's economic condition.

I think I can help rectify this problem.

I would like to present a one-day noncredit workshop targeted to working mothers of any age. As you can see from the enclosed course description, I shall impart an explicit life's plan that is adapted to a working mother of any means and income level. Given the needs and circumstances of the targeted group, I feel a Saturday program would be best.

I have myself been a financial planner consultant for 3 years now; previously I was working for my M.B.A. degree at Alma Mater which I received in 1979 with a special emphasis in estate planning. I have seen the need for this course so often in my practice that at last I've decided to step forward to offer it.

I would like very much to meet with you and discuss the particulars. I'll call you in two weeks to see about scheduling a meeting.

Sincerely,

Instructor Prospect

Essentials Of A Success Letter

- This letter should breath confidence and enthusiasm. After all, you are now a tried and true veteran of the talk circuit and as such deserve to be treated as a colleague.

- If you know that the program planner for whom you have worked is known to the person you are contacting, say so. Ideally your employer will be willing to call ahead on your behalf or at the very least write a glowing testimonial letter. Even if the individuals are not personally acquainted, try to discover whether they belong to the same professional association. This kind of collegial connection suggests familiarity.

- Indicate that you've just completed a successful program at Alma Mater. Provide the number of participants and the revenue gross.

- Suggest that as this program is not being offered by this institution (you have checked, haven't you?), you'd like to present it. Give your reasons why you feel the program will succeed in the new place.

- Include copies of the catalog or marketing materials used to sell your course. These will have the complete course descriptions.

Note: It is not necessary to include any press or media promotional materials. You should, however, indicate they are available. Furthermore, you need say nothing about your credentials. Given your demonstrated success, you have now automatic acceptance.

SAMPLE SUCCESS LETTER

Dear Program Planner:

I am writing to you at the suggestion of Dean Cathy Smith whom I understand you know through LERN, the Learning Resources Network.

I have just finished a successful program for Cathy entitled "The Book Biz: Essentials Of Producing And Profiting From Self-Published Books." Last Saturday 26 people participated at a cost of $125 and the gross was $3250. Cathy was quite pleased with this program which I shall again be offering with her and which I am very anxious to take to new publics.

Having reviewed your catalog, I find you have nothing similar now offered. Given the relative similarity in your marketing area to Cathy's, I feel sure such a workshop would do equally well for you in the next term.

To begin with, I am enclosing a copy of the course catalog and an outline of the day which was given participants. I would like to retain both. There are, of course, other promotional and marketing materials available and a complete tape of the day should you care to see them.

I'd very much like to discuss this course with you and shall telephone you in a week to ascertain your interest.

Sincerely,

Instructor Prospect

SAMPLE PROGRAM CATALOG FOR YOUR LECTURES, COURSES AND WORKSHOPS

Jeffrey Lant Associates, Inc.

NEW COURSES AND OLD FAVORITES FROM JEFFREY LANT ASSOCIATES — THE SEMINAR PEOPLE!

To: Continuing Educators and Trade and Professional Association Program Planners
From: Dr. Jeffrey Lant
Re: Programs Now Available From Jeffrey Lant Associates, Inc.

A few general words about who we are and what we do.

Like you, we're in the talk business. For about a decade we've been offering programs in a variety of formats across the nation. We have experience creating popular lectures, short courses, workshops, teleconferences, and institutes. We know what you need from us. And we provide it.

Dr. Jeffrey Lant, President of JLA, is well known in the continuing education community. He began creating programs while a graduate student at Harvard; following graduation he became program coordinator in Boston College's Evening College, where he really learned the business.

Since then he has worked with individual program promoters, colleges and universities and trade and professional associations nationwide. His programs all have these objectives:

- to create an enjoyable learning experience. Jeffrey knows that people come to programs to learn and also to have a good time.
- to meet the financial objectives of each program's sponsoring organization. Programs cost money and need to earn money. Jeffrey knows this and wants to help you meet your financial goals for the program.
- to organize the program with the least possible extra work for you. Jeffrey knows you have a lot of other things to do, too little time to do them in and too few staff. That's okay, because, as a continuing education professional himself, he can help. And does.

PROGRAMS WE NOW HAVE AVAILABLE

"Succeeding In Your Own Part-Time/Full-Time Consulting Business."

Presented by Dr. Jeffrey Lant

This is Jeffrey's perennially popular program. This program was developed over 10 years ago for one simple reason: professional people wanted to know how to get more benefit from their problem-solving expertise. This one-day intensive program gives them exactly what they need to know. In it, they find out:

- what it takes to succeed as a consultant in their field
- how to position themselves in their market place
- how much to charge
- how to develop a Mobile Mini-Conglomerate, and make money from a variety of problem-solving formats, including tapes, workshops, booklets and books and products their clients need;
- how to work with clients to get results
- how to get repeat business
- how to establish the right form for their business and run it for the least expense.

And, of course, much more.

Course Text: This workshop uses Jeffrey's popular book **THE CONSULTANT'S KIT: ESTABLISHING AND OPERATING YOUR SUCCESSFUL CONSULTING BUSINESS.** Over 25,000 people are currently using this book to make their consulting practices — whatever their field! — more profitable. It's the *only* book on the subject recommended to new and aspiring consultants by the U.S. Small Business Administration and is also recommended by *What Color Is Your Parachute?*

(617) 547-6372
50 FOLLEN STREET, SUITE 507 • CAMBRIDGE, MASSACHUSETTS 02138

Jeffrey Lant Associates, Inc.

"Cash Copy: How To Write Every Marketing Document You'll Ever Need So Your Prospects Buy NOW!"

Presented by Dr. Jeffrey Lant

Every business in America — profit or nonprofit — pours often staggering amounts of money into marketing communications, including brochures, cover letters, annual reports, response cards, fund raising proposals, advertisements, *etc.* Most business people find out by costly experience that what they're producing doesn't work, doesn't help them sell their products.

That's why Jeffrey developed this intensive one-day program. In it, you'll learn the secrets of writing marketing copy that sells and creating marketing documents that will get people to buy your offer. You'll:

- find out the problems of your current marketing documents;
- discover what can be salvaged, and what needs to be redone;
- learn what it really takes to get your prospects to buy;
- realize the difference between a product or service feature and a benefit — and learn how to create benefits that will get your prospects to buy!

Additional subjects include:

- mastering the essentials of writing headlines and testimonials; creating offers; putting pep into everything you ever write; making people want to take action NOW to get what you're selling, and creating a marketing plan that reinforces your message.

Special Feature: Participants are encouraged to bring samples of their current or draft marketing materials for Jeffrey's critique. Tape recorders are encouraged!

Course Text: Jeffrey's new book **CASH COPY** is a permanent guidebook for participants on how to create marketing materials that sell their product or service. This is Jeffrey's ninth book, and it deals with one simple, but profoundly important, business problem: how to get your prospects to buy what you're selling NOW.

Note: A special section of this workshop can be arranged exclusively for nonprofit organizations.

"Money Making Marketing: How To Find The People Who Need What You're Selling And Make Sure They Buy It"

Presented by Dr. Jeffrey Lant

As a result of the entrepreneurial upsurge of the last decade, literally millions of Americans have gone into some kind of business for themselves. Most have no formal marketing training and little understanding of what they need to do to promote a business and get a continuing stream of prospects and buyers.

That's why Jeffrey developed this course.

This one-day intensive workshop provides business people (whether profit or non-profit) with the essential tools they need to:

- turn a one-time buyer into a repeat customer;
- get prospects to become buyers, and
- get people who have the need for your product or service to identify themselves so you can launch the sales process.

Unless you can solve these three problems, your business will fail. Just as upwards of 80% of new small businesses do, within the first two to three years of operation!

In this workshop, you learn how to:

- determine which markets there are for what you're selling;
- find out what they want — or what's bothering them now — that could be the basis for their buying;
- develop a marketing plan based on the Rule of Seven, so that you connect with your prospects the right number of times;

(617) 547-6372
50 FOLLEN STREET, SUITE 507 • CAMBRIDGE, MASSACHUSETTS 02138

Jeffrey Lant Associates, Inc.

- master the essentials of developing marketing copy and creating marketing documents;
- get free publicity for what you're selling;
- write classified and small space ads that get results;
- upgrade a one-time buyer into a continuing customer;
- get prospects to buy NOW.

And, as usual, much more.

Note: A special section of this workshop is available exclusively for nonprofit organizations. It's entitled "Successfully Marketing Your Nonprofit Organization."

Course Text: Jeffrey's book **MONEY MAKING MARKETING: FINDING THE PEOPLE WHO NEED WHAT YOU'RE SELLING AND MAKING SURE THEY BUY IT**. 285 pages devoted to exactly what you need to do to sell more of your product or service for the least possible cost.

"Succeeding In Your Own Mail Order Business".

Presented by Dr. Jeffrey Lant

Despite recent postal rate increases, mail order is a growing business with well over $100 billion in annual sales. Moreover, it's a business that you can run from your home on a part-time basis without employees. In other words, it's ideal for the small-time entrepreneur — if he/she knows the secrets of what it takes to make money in mail order, and how to avoid its expensive pitfalls. In this intensive one-day workshop you'll learn what you have to do to make money in mail order. Find out how to:

- select profitable products and make deals with distributors;
- develop a line of products;
- write mail order copy that gets people to respond *now;*
- turn a one-time buyer into a repeat customer;
- get free publicity for what you're selling;
- rent the right mailing lists — and avoid the wrong ones;
- make extra money by renting out your own house list.

And much, much more.

Course Text: Jeffrey is at work on his own mail-order book. Until it's published, he selects the best of what's currently available as the course text. This selection varies depending on the state of the market.

"How To Raise Money For Your Nonprofit Organization From Corporations, Foundations, And Individuals"

Presented by Dr. Jeffrey Lant

Most of America's nearly 1,000,000 voluntary organizations rely — either wholly or in part — on funds raised from corporations, foundations and individuals. Raising this money is a difficult and demanding task, which is one of the reasons why there is such a heavy turn-over rate among development personnel and so much burn-out among executive directors and board members. They need to know how to get the money they need with the least possible exertion and expense.

That's why Jeffrey developed this intensive one-day workshop for board members, executive directors and development personnel of nonprofit organizations. In it you'll learn how to:

- determine what you should be raising money for — capital, project and operating objectives;
- write the winning fund raising proposal;
- select the right corporations and foundations to approach for funding;
- turn a no into a yes, if you get turned down;
- build a relationship with a funding source so you get continuing funding;
- select names and build a mailing list of potential donors;
- write copy that gets people to give;
- get your board of directors involved - and what to do if they're passive.

And much, much more.

(617) 547-6372
50 FOLLEN STREET, SUITE 507 • CAMBRIDGE, MASSACHUSETTS 02138

Jeffrey Lant Associates, Inc.

Course Text: Jeffrey's book **DEVELOPMENT TODAY: A FUND RAISING GUIDE FOR NONPROFIT ORGANIZATIONS** (now in a Revised Third Edition) is the nationally-recognized source of information for raising money from corporations, foundations, and individuals. 278 pages long, it's packed — just like all Jeffrey's books — with samples of proposals, cover letters, and other necessary fund raising documents.

OTHER PROGRAMS

We have other programs available, too, including:

- **"How To Write A Book That Makes You Money."** This one-day program is designed for authors and publishers who don't just want to do a book, but want to make money from their creation.
- **"How To Keep The Members You've Got And Recruit More."** This program is designed for association executives who are interested in member retention and recruitment.
- **"How To Sell Your Product Or Service Using Free Media."** Based on Jeffrey Lant's book **THE UNABASHED SELF-PROMOTER'S GUIDE**, participants learn how to connect with their prospects, buyers, donors, and clients through every kind of free media, instead of spending their own money on paid advertising.
- **"How To Advertise And Promote Your Small Business."** Tells participants what they have to do — using both paid ads and free publicity — to connect with their buyers and get them to buy what they're selling.

Special Features Of These Workshops

We understand what you need from us and have created a number of special features not available to you anywhere else. They include:

- access to our mailing list. We have a list of buyers of Jeffrey Lant's books and people who have responded to our various promotions. We will happily supply you with the names and addresses — on pressure sensitive or cheshire labels — of the people in your marketing area. There is a running charge of $15 for this service.
- publicity articles. We have a list of business articles available that you can use to promote these programs. Jeffrey's Sure-Fire Business Success Column currently runs in about 100 publications and electronic databases nationwide and reaches more than 1,500,000 people monthly. We are happy to make these articles available to you for publication in local papers, particularly business papers. We will inform you how to swap these articles for ads that promote the programs.
- shipping books in advance. We are happy to ship books in advance to all participants if you send us their names and addresses.
- premium for early sign-up. We have Special Reports available on a wide range of business subjects which you can use as a premium to induce early sign-up.

Some Specifics

We understand different institutions have different ways of handling payment. We are happy to accommodate you. We need to be paid a minimum of $1250 daily (plus customary expenses), but have several ways of reaching this objective:

- Fixed flat fee
- Fixed flat fee plus book revenue
- 50-50% split of all revenues (workshop and book) with your guarantee that we will be reimbursed at least $1250 for a day's program should revenues not reach this level.

Now What?

Please call Dr. Jeffrey Lant at (617) 547-6372 so we can discuss which programs you'd like to present and when you'd like to do so. Audiences around America consistently give top marks to these programs. And we can prove it!

Find out for yourself; call now and bring these programs to people in your community!

(617) 547-6372
50 FOLLEN STREET, SUITE 507 • CAMBRIDGE, MASSACHUSETTS 02138

Essentials Of An Introduction Letter On Your Behalf

- This letter is properly understood as an exercise in Assertive Courtesy. That is, the writer must act as if this letter was invited by a program planner who should be grateful to have it. Why? Because using this suggestion minimizes his own effort. Thus there is no need for an apologetic meekness in this letter. The writer is doing the reader a favor. About the favor simultaneously being done you, the less said the better.

- The writer should present your name forthrightly and in such a way that there can be no question but that you'll be invited.

- Follow with an indication of what you'll discuss and why it's of immediate interest to the audience if this is not self evident.

- Indicate who will follow up and how.

Note: People asked to write this kind of letter tend to procrastinate, not least because they don't know what to say. Not to worry! Write it yourself or photocopy these pages as apt models

SAMPLE INTRODUCTORY LETTER ON YOUR BEHALF

Dear Program Planner:

You are always asking members of our organization to bring good speakers to your attention. Now I'd like to do so. I'd very much like to have my colleague and friend Jim Peters asked to come.

While Jim can speak knowledgeably and engagingly on several subjects, I think our members would be most interested in his work in assisting independent crafts people make more and more lucrative catalog sales.

I know that our budget for speakers is limited, but Jim is well worth our investment. I've given him your name and telephone number and asked him to be in touch. He can provide you with further information including a tape of a recent program he did at Alma Mater.

Sincerely,

Your Friend, Organization Member

Essentials Of A Sales Cover Letter Being Sent From A Program Planner To Prospects Along With Descriptive Information On Your Program

- This letter should be at once enthusiastic and indicate that the problem faced by the target population will be dealt with through this program.

- It should provide convincing facts about your background demonstrating that you are both an expert and personally compelling.

- Indicate why this program is particularly timely just now.

- Point out a few special features of the program that make it an especially good idea to attend. Include instructional formats, materials and, of course, actual learning objectives to be achieved.

Remember: This is the "sell'em" part of the package. Leave all the details to your brochure or supplementary information. In this letter aim for excitement and action.

SAMPLE SALES COVER LETTER BEING SENT FROM A PROGRAM PLANNER TO PROSPECTS ALONG WITH DESCRIPTIVE INFORMATION ON YOUR PROGRAM

Dear Prospect:

It is with great pleasure that I invite you to attend a forthcoming workshop on "Fund Raising For Visiting Nursing Agencies" being given by Professor Don James here at Alma Mater.

You may already be familiar with Dr. James and his work with visiting nursing agencies. Last year he was keynote speaker at the annual meeting of the Visiting Nursing Association. Moreover, this is the second year he has presented this program for us. We invited him back because of the excellent reviews of your colleagues in the field.

With increasing federal government cut backs and with the reduction of medicare reimbursement, we know this threatens to be a difficult year for you. That's why we were especially anxious to have Dr. James return.

As you will see in the enclosed program brochure, we have thought long and hard so that you'll profit from the day's program. We have made a special point of including not just workshop but also consultation sessions. Here are some of the topics that will be addressed:

- a four-part planning process to insure you are seeking the right amount of capital, project and operating money;

- a tested method for Board selection, involvement, and training;

- an inexpensive screening process to target the right corporations and foundations for your approach.

Dr. James is a scintillating speaker who is both professionally knowledgeable and personally engaging. If you have not yet had the opportunity of listening to or working with him, please accept our invitation to do both now.

Sincerely,

Program Planner

Essentials Of A Group Discount Sales Letter

- Like all sales letters, this one must communicate excitement and benefits. That shouldn't be too difficult to stimulate. After all the prospect is not only getting a shot at attending something in his direct interest but at a very special rate.

- The first paragraph should present not only the basic facts but present the added reason for this group's particular interest, that is the discount.

- Subsequent paragraphs should give an indication of the course content. If a program brochure or more detailed outline is available that, too, should be included.

- Make sure the discount is real and attractive. If it is, stress that it is.

- Indicate how and when you'll be following up.

Note: Often associations may not avail themselves of this special offer preferring instead to create programs especially for their own members. That's fine so long as your sponsor is prepared to market you to them and take a lecture agent commission. If all else fails, see if your program can be promoted in the organization's publication.

SAMPLE GROUP DISCOUNT SALES LETTER

Dear Association Executive:

In May we are having a special one-day workshop entitled "Money Talks: How To Create A Profitable Workshop Or Seminar In Any Field." For this exciting program we have invited author and lecturer Dr. Jeffrey Lant to be with us as workshop presenter. We'd like you and your members to be with us on that day at a special group rate.

We feel sure your members would profit from hearing Dr. Lant, whose definitive book on talk you probably already know, give practical, detailed information on:

- creating programs that sell

- mastering the Problem Solving Process workshop, the key to talk circuit success

- training yourself to give effective presentations

- identifying and selling sponsors for your programs.

And, as always, much, much more. This is information that will enable your members to profit now and for years to come.

We shall be advertising this program to the general public for $150 including a copy of MONEY TALKS and all amenities. But if at least 10 members of your association sign up, they may do so for the special group rate of $100 each.

I shall be calling you shortly to ascertain your interest. If for some reason you cannot take advantage of this offer, I'd like you to know that we can work with you to create a special program for your members with this well-known speaker.

I look forward to speaking with you.

Sincerely,

Program Planner

SAMPLE STANDARD ADVERTISING FORMAT
(Note the space available for your name and address. If you'd like to distribute this or other of our forms at your programs, let me know. JL)

"**MONEY MAKING MARKETING** is the most practical, information-packed guide to business success I have ever read."
Best-selling business writer Robert Bly.

The **one book you must have** if you want to increase the effectiveness and cut the cost of identifying your buyers, selling to them once, and selling to them again!

MONEY MAKING MARKETING
Finding The People Who Need What You're Selling And Making Sure They Buy It

By **the author you've learned to trust** for delivering the most solid, practical, thorough, and imaginative business how-to information: Dr. Jeffrey Lant.

Over the past 8 years, Jeffrey has become known as one of America's most unrelenting and creative marketers. Now, in one thick, information-rich book — the kind of book he's become known for — Jeffrey lays out the marketing secrets you *must* know to make your business a success!

MONEY MAKING MARKETING is made up of 11 info-packed, profit-making chapters.

- Discover step-by-step guidelines on handling your **marketing research for the least time and financial commitment** — even when you hate market research;
- Learn precisely what you need to know about **connecting with your buyers the right number of times** so they'll buy what you're selling;
- Get what you need to know about **creating inexpensive and persuasive marketing documents**, documents you can use again and again;
- Understand exactly **what you need to know about copywriting and headline writing**, and how to focus on the buyer (and not yourself) to convince him what you're selling solves his problem;
- Master guidelines for **getting free publicity** on radio and television and in newspapers, magazines, and newsletters for whatever you're selling;
- Find out what it really takes to **make classified and small space ads profitable** for you;
- Acquire the information you need to **use the telephone profitably**: to sell to existing buyers, get back buyers who have drifted away, and prospect for new customers;
- Know the **profit-making ins and outs** of co-op advertising, direct response card decks, premium advertising, and trade shows and exhibiting;
- Realize what you need to know to **make money with mail**: how to write effective direct mail copy and to whom and how often to send it;
- Learn how to **create a profit-making catalog**;
- Understand what you need to know about **making money from talk programs** of every kind;

And **much, much more** — including sample forms, letters and documents you can use right now to get your marketing effort off to a fast, profitable start.

MONEY MAKING MARKETING is a unique book. It's written in Jeffrey Lant's typically *information-rich, high-energy prose.* Like all Jeffrey's books, this one doesn't just tell you want to do, it gives you the *precise step-by-step information* you need so that you can do it — now!

Each copy of **MONEY MAKING MARKETING** comes with two guarantees. One is Jeffrey's Pledge: "**This book, like all my books, does what I say it can do. If you don't think so — for any reason — return it within thirty days for your money back.**" Moreover, if you have a question about any technique in the book, **Jeffrey invites you to call him and pick his brain.** How many other authors offer you this service? You already know. Precious few!

So, act now. The ability to identify your buyers and sell to them once and then sell to them again is what distinguishes those who are successful in business from those who aren't. Now, using **MONEY MAKING MARKETING**, you'll be one of those who knows precisely what to do and precisely how to do it profitably.

"**MONEY MAKING MARKETING** is spectacular! Lant has really 'laid it on the line' for anyone wishing to make a living from his-her own business today. Lant's book is the best I've seen on marketing — and I've seen them all!"
Tyler Hicks, publisher of *International Wealth Success Newsletter*

Order Coupon

❑ Yes, Jeffrey, send me right away a copy of **MONEY MAKING MARKETING: FINDING THE PEOPLE WHO NEED WHAT YOU'RE SELLING AND MAKING SURE THEY BUY IT.** I understand that if I'm unhappy with this book for any reason, I may return it for a full refund within 30 days. $32.50 postpaid.

Name _____ Company _____
Street _____ City/Town _____ State _____ Zip _____
Telephone ( ) _____

Make check payable and return to authorized representative:

I prefer to use my ❑ Visa ❑ MasterCard Card# _____ Expiration Date _____
Signature _____

If You're Really Serious About Business Success, Connect With One Of America's Most Thorough, Useful, And Profit-Making Authorities: Dr. Jeffrey Lant.

You probably already know about Jeffrey Lant. His Sure-Fire Business Success Column runs in over 90 publications nationwide. *Over a million people each month get their business get-ahead information from him.* If you've read his stuff, you know it's *packed with solid step-by-step techniques* to help you build the most profitable business, in the shortest possible time, with the fewest mistakes.

If this is what you want to do, then you should be profiting from the five volumes in his nationally-recognized "Get Ahead" Series.

❑ **THE CONSULTANT'S KIT: ESTABLISHING AND OPERATING YOUR SUCCESSFUL CONSULTING BUSINESS.** Now in an 8th printing, this is the *only* book specifically recommended by the U.S. Small Business Administration for new and aspiring consultants in any field. **Thousands and thousands of people nationwide are now profiting from the precise steps in this book.** 203 pages. $32.50 postpaid.

❑ **THE UNABASHED SELF-PROMOTER'S GUIDE: WHAT EVERY MAN, WOMAN, CHILD, AND ORGANIZATION IN AMERICA NEEDS TO KNOW ABOUT GETTING AHEAD BY EXPLOITING THE MEDIA.** If you want to reach every person whose problem your product or service can solve and want to keep the cost low, get free publicity for what you're selling. This book — **the most complete and innovative ever written** on this important subject — shows you exactly how to do it. 366 pages. $32.50 postpaid.

❑ **MONEY TALKS: THE COMPLETE GUIDE TO CREATING A PROFITABLE WORKSHOP OR SEMINAR IN ANY FIELD.** Talking is now a multi-billion dollar industry. *Changing Times Magazine* says this is the most complete book ever written on how to get into it part- or full-time. We agree! It's **astonishingly complete.** 303 pages. $32.50 postpaid.

❑ **TRICKS OF THE TRADE: THE COMPLETE GUIDE TO SUCCEEDING IN THE ADVICE BUSINESS.** Takes up where **THE CONSULTANT'S KIT** leaves off. If you have problem-solving information at your disposal and want to profit from it, use the book expert after expert agrees is **breathtakingly complete.** Never *give* anyone a piece of your mind again. Now sell it to them for what your information is really worth. 315 pages. $32.50 postpaid.

❑ **MONEY MAKING MARKETING: FINDING THE PEOPLE WHO NEED WHAT YOU'RE SELLING AND MAKING SURE THEY BUY IT.** Jeffrey's newest book is just like the rest: **packed with information.** Use it to target the people who need what you're selling, make sure they buy it, and transform them into a steady buyer. Gives you inexpensive, effective techniques for every kind of marketing. Exhaustive. 285 pages. $32.50 postpaid.

❑ **SPECIAL FIVE BOOK OFFER.** Now get all five volumes of Dr. Jeffrey Lant's Get Ahead Series for just $145 postpaid. Just like getting half of one of these over-sized books free! Information you'll profit from for a lifetime for pennies a page.

All books come with Jeffrey's Unconditional 30-Day Money-Back Guarantee. "These books do what I say they can do. If you don't agree, return them for a complete refund."

Order Coupon

❑ Yes, I want to profit from Jeffrey Lant's Get Ahead Books. I have checked the one(s) I want.

Name _____ Company _____

Street _____ City/Town _____ State _____ Zip _____

Telephone (   ) _____

Make check payable and return to authorized representative:

I prefer to use my ❑ Visa ❑ MasterCard Card#_____ Expiration Date _____

Signature _____

Essentials Of A Letter To Publisher Special Sales Representative

- This letter, like all the letters in this section, must be sent to a specific person. Get this individual's name and title before writing.

- Keep the letter brief and direct. You're making a business deal and needn't supply your life story.

- Include the name of your program, the places it has or will be offered, and the number of copies you'll be needing.

- Get the company's policy on freight, returns and credit.

- Always ask about related titles.

Note: If you are not including the text in your course, see about getting a review copy and order blanks.

SAMPLE LETTER TO PUBLISHER SPECIAL SALES REPRESENTATIVE

Dear Special Sales Representative:

This letter follows our telephone conversation today. You will remember that I am interesting in using your book *Midwives: The Definitive Guide* for my training program.

Currently I teach three all-day workshops on this subject at universities. I enclose the marketing materials for the latest of these. Average attendance is 25. I should like to include your book in the course. I would like to secure them at a 50% discount and have you ship direct to the universities. Please advise me on how freight charges and returns can be handled. Further, I would like to file a credit application with you if this is possible. Kindly send me one.

If you have other titles on this subject which might interest my audience, please let me know.

I look forward to doing business with you.

Sincerely,

Workshop Instructor

SAMPLE PRECIS OF PRODUCTS AND SERVICES

Jeffrey Lant Associates, Inc.

This is the kind of simple two-sided 8½" × 11" flyer you can create for all your programs before developing the kind of full-fledged catalog of products and services that appears on page 293.

A SPECIAL MEMO FROM DR. JEFFREY LANT

This is a précis of the books and services provided by Jeffrey Lant Associates, Inc. Produced in response to many queries, it contains information about the various ways we can profit together.

Books: JLA Publications, a division of the firm, produces the following titles. All costs are postpaid!

- **MONEY MAKING MARKETING: FINDING THE PEOPLE WHO NEED WHAT YOU'RE SELLING AND MAKING SURE THEY BUY IT.** 285 pages tell you exactly what you need to know to sell your product or service for the least possible cost. $34.

- **TRICKS OF THE TRADE: THE COMPLETE GUIDE TO SUCCEEDING IN THE ADVICE BUSINESS.** Use this giant 315-page guide when you really want to know how to profit from your problem-solving information. $34.

- **MONEY TALKS: THE COMPLETE GUIDE TO CREATING A PROFITABLE WORKSHOP OR SEMINAR IN ANY FIELD.** Make money with lectures, workshops and seminars. Everything you need to know! 292 pages. $34.

- **THE UNABASHED SELF-PROMOTER'S GUIDE: WHAT EVERY MAN, WOMAN, CHILD AND ORGANIZATION IN AMERICA NEEDS TO KNOW ABOUT GETTING AHEAD BY EXPLOITING THE MEDIA.** Stop buying paid ads. Promote your product or service with free publicity using this definitive 366-page guide. $34.

- **THE CONSULTANT'S KIT: ESTABLISHING AND OPERATING YOUR SUCCESSFUL CONSULTING BUSINESS.** The one book recommended by the U.S. Small Business Administration to new and aspiring consultants in *any* field. $34.

- **DEVELOPMENT TODAY: A FUND RAISING GUIDE FOR NONPROFIT ORGANIZATIONS.** Tells you what you need to know to raise money from corporations, foundations and individuals. 267 pages. $28.45.

- **THE COMPLETE GUIDE TO PLANNED GIVING: EVERYTHING YOU NEED TO KNOW TO COMPETE SUCCESSFULLY FOR MAJOR GIFTS.** Debra Ashton's mammoth 407-page resource tells you precisely how to raise major gifts for your nonprofit organization. $38.50.

Book Distribution Agreements: You can make money selling our books. We give you a minimum discount of 50% and will ship for you. Contact us for complete details!

Consulting Services

We can help you reach your objectives through a variety of consulting services. Ask for complete details.

- Want more people to buy what you're selling? Let us help you create all your marketing materials, including cover letters, brochures, flyers, advertisements, annual reports, media kits, and response coupons.

- Need money for your nonprofit organization? We can help you raise the money you need from corporations, foundations, and individuals.

(617) 547-6372
50 FOLLEN STREET, SUITE 507 • CAMBRIDGE, MASSACHUSETTS 02138

Jeffrey Lant Associates, Inc.

Services To Periodical And Electronic Database Publishers.

We know you're always looking for top-quality material for your publication. We can help.

We'll happily provide you with *free* articles on a wide variety of business get-ahead subjects. Written by Dr. Jeffrey Lant, these articles are currently carried by about 100 publications under the title "Sure-Fire Business Success" and feature information provided by recognized experts in many areas. Contact us for details.

Workshops And Seminars

Dr. Jeffrey Lant is one of America's top-rated platform speakers, presenting up to 100 presentations annually at trade and professional associations and through colleges and universities nationwide. A recognized expert in continuing education, honored by the Learning Resources Network for his contributions to the field, Jeffrey works with you to present programs whose participants always rate them highly. Complete details available upon request.

Stay In Touch

We do regular mailings to our clients and friends. Please make sure we have your current address.

If you want more information about any of the subjects covered in this precis, please contact Dr. Jeffrey Lant at (617) 547-6372. We are always happy to hear from you!

(617) 547-6372
50 FOLLEN STREET, SUITE 507 • CAMBRIDGE, MASSACHUSETTS 02138

Essentials Of A Letter To A Newsletter Publisher Suggesting Talk Possibilities

- The tone should be upbeat and positive. You're offering, after all, a new source of revenue and profit with minimal risk.

- Begin by getting an article in the publication, a Problem Solving Process article on the theme of your program or related to it. Without this article, you'll have to spend additional time establishing your credentials and the thrust of your program. In this case, try sending the catalog from one of your programs. With the article, you're one of the family and can move right along into the business and marketing details.

- Tell what you've got in mind.

- If necessary, suggest why such a program is timely now.

- Provide a glimpse both of future prospects and the limited risk involved in this one. Both aspects of the matter are significant.

- Give every indication that you know how to arrange matters with the least disruption and expense. Having mastered this book, that should be easy to do.

- Indicate how you'll follow up.

Note: A variety of this letter is perfectly suitable when proposing an audio conference or video teleconference to a sponsor. The difference is that you'll have to demonstrate that prior programs in traditional format have been successful.

SAMPLE LETTER TO A NEWSLETTER PUBLISHER SUGGESTING TALK POSSIBILITIES

Dear Publisher:

Recently *Innkeeping America* was good enough to run one of my articles about "Off Season Marketing For Inns." Evidently this article hit a real chord with your readers since several have written asking whether I had further information on this important subject. In fact I do. I have a one-day workshop on the topic.

I would very much like to discuss with you the possibility of entering into a relationship with you and *Innkeeping America* to bring this information to your readers. I have offered my course on small business marketing and promotion through two universities, and there is no reason why it can't be effectively done through your newsletter.

What I have in mind is this: I shall give the workshop and will assist in writing necessary ad and promotional copy. You can promote it through the newsletter with both ads and editorial support. To test the waters, we can run a single program. If this succeeds, I'd like to offer several across the country. I believe that the program should be taped and that that tape can be sold to those who are not attending.

This program can be arranged without overtaxing you or your staff. Having read Jeffrey Lant's book **MONEY TALKS**, I feel confident it can be done to our mutual advantage with minimal cash outlays and disruption to your routine.

I'll call you in a few days to begin working out the details.

Sincerely,

Workshop Presenter

Essentials Of An Introductory Letter To A Lecture Agent

- This letter should be coolly professional. Remember that lecture agents are inundated with letters from would-be speakers. You have to show you are an in-demand expert with realistic expectations.

- In the first paragraph, establish that you have experience and what kind it is.

- Cite recent clients and the kinds of presentations you made. It is not necessary in this letter to tell how much you were paid.

- Provide an indication of the length and format of your programs.

- Indicate that you have relevant support materials available including publicity, tapes and testimonials from prior performances. These materials should demonstrate that you are professionally expert and easy to work with. Give some indication that audiences warm to you.

- Cite some of your topics. An exhaustive list is not necessary just now.

- Seek a nonexclusive relationship so that many agents can market you simultaneously.

- Ask for information about the agent's firm. This is a joint ascertainment process. You need to make sure this firm is right for you.

- Indicate how you'll follow up.

SAMPLE INTRODUCTORY LETTER TO A LECTURE AGENT

Dear Lecture Agent:

I should like to explore with you the possibility of my securing representation with your firm. As you will notice from the enclosed materials, I have a good deal of experience addressing both professional associations and in giving all-day workshops at various colleges and universities. These are all fee arrangements.

In the last year alone, I have given 2 programs at the University of Minnesota, one at the University of Colorado and have addressed such professional associations as the Crafts Association, California Bar Association, American Llama Breeders Association, and the North Central Sugar Beet Conference. At the latter meeting I was the keynoter.

I give programs ranging in length from 45 minutes to 2 days, although most are two to three hour workshops. For your information, I enclose some of the publicity I have received. I have tapes and testimonial letters also available should you care to see them.

On the whole my programs deal with small business formation and development. Subjects include finding venture capital, marketing and public relations, profiting from trade shows, recruiting and retaining employees, and diversification and franchising. My newest program deals with developing overseas markets.

I can attest and have materials to demonstrate that audience reaction has always been particularly strong. Moreover, I am consistently asked back for follow-up meetings.

I am most interested in the possibility of non-exclusive representation but am willing to consider alternatives.

If you are interested in pursuing matters, kindly send me information on your firm and its clients after reviewing which I'll telephone to discuss matters further.

Sincerely,

Lecturer

Essentials Of An Invitation Letter To Clinic Prospects

- Your objective with this letter is to come across as the accessible expert. You want to be perceived as helpful, concerned and ready to be of further use to people who have already made an investment in you. The tone of this letter should be cordial and frank.

- Indicate that it would be useful to have a refresher. If people have urged you to have one, say so.

- Outline the program. Tell what you're going to present, how and why. A clinic is a superb opportunity not merely to impart but also to integrate significant information into the lives and habits of people who have a problem to be solved.

- If you can, invite participants to bring relevent materials for you to review and improve.

- Set the cost at ⅓ to ½ that of the original program. Let the prospects know what a bargain this is. (It is, by the way!)

- Since clinics are always best limited for optimum group interaction, tell prospects what the cap is for this program. Stick to it.

- Ask for an early decision.

Note: If necessary follow up this letter with a post card or second letter to secure the number of participants you need.

SAMPLE INVITATION LETTER TO CLINIC PROSPECTS

Dear Colleague:

It's time for us to get together again! As you will recall the last time we met was at my "Unabashed Promoters" Workshop at Alma Mater. That program has now been offered several times and some of the alumni have kindly suggested to me that a refresher clinic is very much in order.

I'm happy to oblige.

I have therefore scheduled Saturday, June 3 from 9 a.m. to 4 p.m. for a unique consultation and workshop session. The purpose of this clinic is simple: both to reprise some of my unabashed marketing and promotional techniques and to review your own efforts towards implementing them in your business and professional practice.

Here's how the day will be arranged:

- We'll begin with a two-hour review of material previously covered. In addition, I'll be bringing you up-to-date on my new public relations techniques and procedures.

- Thereafter we shall spend one hour on each of the following special topics:

    - formulating a Quintessential American Success Image

    - mastering appropriate media resources

    - dominating the print media with Problem Solving Process, Sentinel and White Knight articles

    - exploiting electronic media

    - benefiting from your own field specific promotional possibilities.

During each of these sections, I shall, as usual, be presenting information. However, you are also welcome and indeed requested to bring samples and cases from your own work. Bring any and all marketing materials including letters, articles, cards, brochures, &c., and I shall review them for you and use them as learning situations for the group.

The cost of this special clinic is just $100 for the day, a far cry from my regular $100 per hour consulting fee. It is absolutely limited to 12 people. To keep the cost down, lunch is on your own.

Please let me know as soon as you can if you're attending. Here are the specifics:

- day
- date
- time
- place
- cost

Looking forward to seeing you!

Sincerely,

Clinic Presenter

ABOUT THE AUTHOR

Over the last several years, Dr. Jeffrey Lant has emerged as one of America's most well-known business authorities. His provocative and information-packed articles on a wide variety of business development topics (under the title "Sure Fire Business Success") are now carried by over 95 publications nationwide. Major electronic databases like CompuServe (U.S. Entrepreneurs Network), GEnie (Ephote), Delphi, and Boston Citinet also carry his articles. Well over a million and a half people monthly get their business get-ahead information from Jeffrey. Unlike most such writers, Jeffrey's telephone number also runs along with these articles, so that his readers can call for additional information, hints, and the "kick where it helps" that all of us occasionally need.

A practicing management consultant for the last 9 years, Jeffrey is president of Jeffrey Lant Associates, Inc. Based in Cambridge, Massachusetts, he works nationally. Some of his work includes fund raising assistance to nonprofit organizations, public relations consultation, and expert copywriting for organizations of every kind. His practice is distinguished by his own distinctive brand of enthusiasm, excitement and positive problem-solving skills.

A well-known speaker on such topics as establishing a successful consulting practice, effective marketing, publishing profitable books, succeeding in your own mail order business, running a profitable home-based business, and many other topics, Jeffrey ranges the country giving speeches, workshops and conference presentations. An animated and often electrifying platform speaker, Jeffrey never merely talks to an audience, but also seeks to involve them in his presentation. Intellectually demanding of himself, Jeffrey demands no less of his audiences!

Over the past 8 years, Jeffrey has written a book each year. His titles include the five volumes in his well-known "Get Ahead" Series, including **THE CONSULTANT'S KIT: ESTABLISHING AND OPERATING YOUR SUCCESSFUL CONSULTING BUSINESS** (now in an 8th printing); **THE UNABASHED SELF-PROMOTER'S GUIDE: WHAT EVERY MAN, WOMAN, CHILD AND ORGANIZATION IN AMERICA NEEDS TO KNOW ABOUT GETTING AHEAD BY EXPLOITING THE MEDIA; MONEY TALKS: THE COMPLETE GUIDE TO CREATING A PROFITABLE WORKSHOP OR SEMINAR IN ANY FIELD**, and **TRICKS OF THE TRADE: THE COMPLETE GUIDE TO SUCCEEDING IN THE ADVICE BUSINESS**. His latest book is **MONEY MAKING MARKETING: FINDING THE PEOPLE WHO NEED WHAT YOU'RE SELLING AND MAKING SURE THEY BUY IT**. His other titles include **DEVELOPMENT TODAY: A FUND RAISING GUIDE FOR NONPROFIT ORGANIZATIONS; INSUBSTANTIAL PAGEANT: CEREMONY AND CONFUSION AT QUEEN VICTORIA'S COURT**; and (as Editor) **OUR HARVARD: REFLECTIONS ON COLLEGE LIFE BY TWENTY-TWO DISTINGUISHED GRADUATES**.

Jeffrey, his work, and innovative ideas are also featured in many books including *What Color Is Your Parachute?, The Harvard Guide To Careers, Create Your Own Career Opportunities, The Complete Guide To Self Publishing, Maverick: Succeeding As A Free-Lance Entrepreneur, Playing Hardball With Soft Skills, Cash In On Today's Educational Market, Win Them Over: A Survival Guide For Corporate Consultant Relations Programs; Marketing To The Fortune 500, How To Get Happily Published, Homemade Money, The Consultant's Guide To Winning Clients, The Do-It-Yourself Publicity Kit* and many others. His credentials and achievements are also featured in over 18 different biographical guides from *Who's Who In Finance & Industry* to *The International Who's Who Of Intellectuals*.

His achievements have been recognized by many organizations, including the Boston and Cambridge City Councils; twice by the House of Representatives of the State of Massachusetts, by two Governors of Massachusetts, by the State of Texas, and by the cities of Charleston, South Carolina; Cape May, New Jersey; and Eureka, California. In July, 1987, he received special recognition from the Governor of Massachusetts upon the completion of the first five volumes of his "Get Ahead" Series. The Learning Resources Network (LERN), an association of several hundred providers of adult continuing educators, named him. "Outstanding Writer—1985."

Jeffrey is a graduate of the University of California, Santa Barbara (B.A. *summa cum laude* '69); Northeastern University, Boston (Certificate of Advanced Graduate Studies in Higher Education Administration, '76); and Harvard University (M.A. '70 and Ph.D. '75). He has never had a business course in his entire career!

Jeffrey is 41 years old and currently lives in Cambridge, Massachusetts, surrounded by mountains of paper, an underused exercise machine, and a computer and telephone which connect him to millions of people striving to build strong businesses of every kind. You can reach him at 50 Follen St., Suite 507, Cambridge, MA 02138 or by calling (617) 547-6372.

Jeffrey Lant's
SURE-FIRE BUSINESS SUCCESS CATALOG

SUMMER, 1988

Dear Get-Ahead Friend,

If you're like me, you're always looking for new ways to make your business more profitable. And now you've found them. Right here . . .

You get exactly what you need to make more money . . . and make it faster! *And* premiums that ensure you're paying the least possible amount for the profit-making information you need.

And this time there's lots that's new, too.

Invest just $150 here before October 1, 1988, and I'll give you —free with my compliments—your choice of *any one* of my three new 60–minute audio cassettes. Use them to 1) create marketing documents that get your prospects to buy **NOW**; 2) get **FREE** time on radio and television to promote your products and services, and 3) find out what you have to do to master the art of profit-making marketing—and sell more! *And* if you order over $200 by October 1, 1988, you get all three of these 60-minute cassettes absolutely **FREE** . . . a $42 offer. You can't get this from anyone else in America, not from a single bookstore. **ONLY HERE**. Only if you act **NOW**!

Then you can get a **SPECIAL PRICE** on my new book **CASH COPY: HOW TO OFFER YOUR PRODUCTS AND SERVICES SO YOUR PROSPECTS BUY THEM . . . NOW!** You're going to spend thousands, even tens of thousands, of dollars on all your marketing materials. Don't you think you should know what it takes to get your prospects to respond to them . . . faster? Now you can — and save money, too. But only if you act by October 1, 1988. **WAIT AND YOU HAVE TO PAY FULL PRICE.** But if you act **NOW** you also get a **FREE** copy of the handy 64-page booklet *Connections: How to get more, pay less and phone free* as an extra premium.

And don't forget, if you want to make money giving talk programs, use them to get clients and publicity, my well-known book **MONEY TALKS: THE COMPLETE GUIDE TO CREATING A PROFITABLE WORKSHOP OR SEMINAR IN ANY FIELD** is *just out* in a **REVISED, SECOND EDITION**. To celebrate, when you get **MONEY TALKS**, you can *select any one of my 27 Special Reports with my compliments*. Absolutely free. But you have to act by October 1, 1988 when this Special Offer expires.

Sadly, you may be about to lose this great source of profit-making information. If there's a ** next to your name on page 308, this is your last catalog. You'll have to buy something to keep getting it. So do!

Your continuing profit generator,

Jeffrey

All prices include shipping!

Remember: different materials come from different producers and will not necessarily arrive at the same time!

Summer Selection #1

To order write this number on page 308 . . . along with everything else you want!

Get a deal on Jeffrey's newest book **CASH COPY: HOW TO OFFER YOUR PRODUCTS AND SERVICES SO YOUR PROSPECTS BUY THEM . . . NOW!**

While you're in business, you'll spend thousands — maybe tens of thousands of dollars — on your brochures, cover letters, ads, annual reports, flyers, response coupons — and all your other marketing communications. Don't you think you should find out what it takes to get the highest possible response to everything you're using?

Or are you happy just plodding along . . . wasting over 98% of your money on marketing materials that just don't get your prospects to buy?

Now Jeffrey Lant, one of America's top marketers, tells you exactly how to get more responses from **EVERYTHING** you produce to get buyers, whatever you're selling.

Learn his secrets for:
- creating offers your prospects find irresistible;
- getting your prospects to buy what you're selling **NOW**, not later;
- getting and using testimonials that make people want to buy what you're selling;
- making all your marketing communications client-centered so your prospects want to buy;
- transforming every feature of every one of your products and services into a buyer-centered benefit;
- making your copy interesting, not dull; ensuring that your prospects pay attention to what you're saying;

Helping make your business more profitable since 1979

- thinking like your prospects, so you'll create copy that motivates them to act;
- outpositioning your competitors, so that your prospects want to buy from you — and only from you!

Get specific tips on marketing communications like brochures, cover letters, flyers, fund raising proposals, classified and space ads, envelop teasers, workshop brochures, book announcements... and much, much more. Learn the key rules of what you need to write and how you need to write it.

Wonder no more about how to turn your prospects into buyers. What you need is right here. Ready to use. Easy to follow. Filled with the kind of specific, practical information that is the hallmark of everything Jeffrey creates.

And now you can get this crucial resource at the **SPECIAL PRE-PUBLICATION PRICE** of $16. But only until 10/1/88. Save $9. Your autographed first edition of **CASH COPY** (about 350 pages) will be sent in October. Don't try to create any marketing document until you master these key rules for getting your prospects to respond NOW! If you order after 10/1/88, send $25. No exceptions!

ADDITIONAL BONUS OFFER

Order CASH COPY before 10/1/88 and get — absolutely free! — your copy of the 64-page booklet *Connections: How to get more, pay less and phone free* (a $4 retail offer!). See full description on page 306. All you have to do is send your business card (or letterhead) with your order for **CASH COPY** and write 'SEND ME CONNECTIONS, PLEASE' on the back. *Connections* will be sent at once!

But, no business card, no free copy.

#2
MONEY TALKS: THE COMPLETE GUIDE TO CREATING A PROFITABLE WORKSHOP OR SEMINAR IN ANY FIELD. BRAND NEW EDITION!!! JUST OUT!!! If you want to make money with talk programs of any kind, find out how to use these programs to get clients and publicity, then you need the new Second Revised Edition of this well-known book. It's got everything you need to start making money — really big money — on the talk circuit with workshops, lectures, seminars — every kind of talk program. Find out how to get sponsors — or sponsor programs yourself; make money from "back of the room" sales, even when you don't have a product. And when you do. **THE MOST COMPLETE BOOK EVER WRITTEN ON THIS IMPORTANT SUBJECT**. *And to celebrate this New Edition, if you buy this book before 10/1/88, you may select any one of my 27 Special Reports with my compliments.* 308 pages. $34

All New. Now get three 60-minute audio cassettes with Jeffrey's unrelentingly detailed advice. Just $14 each. $35 for all three!

#3
HOW TO GET FREE TIME ON RADIO AND T.V. AND USE IT TO GET YOUR PROSPECTS TO BUY WHAT YOU'RE SELLING. Listen as Jeffrey gives you the secrets of getting valuable free time on radio and television so you can sell your products and services without spending any of your money. Getting on *just one* program could return your investment dozens of times! $14

Rent my mailing list. If you're selling anything like I am, now you can get access to a whole lot of eager beaver buyers. My list is managed by:
Worldata
500 N. Broadway
Jericho, NY 11753.
Or call:
(516) 931-2442

#4
HOW TO CREATE MARKETING DOCUMENTS THAT GET YOUR PROSPECTS TO BUY WHAT YOU'RE SELLING... NOW! Since you spend thousands of dollars on your marketing documents, don't you think you should know what will get people to respond to them faster ... to buy what you're selling **NOW**? Here's just what you need to know. $14

#5
ESSENTIALS OF MONEY MAKING MARKETING: WHAT YOU'VE REALLY GOT TO DO TO SELL YOUR PRODUCTS AND SERVICES, EVERY DAY! Jeffrey shares his secrets of successful marketing, what you've got to do, when and how you've got to do it to sell your products and services. $14.

#6
Get all three of Jeffrey's new 60-minute audio cassettes for just $35. Just like getting 30 minutes of Jeffrey's consultation free! Don't forget — if your order totals over $200, you get all three of these audio cassettes absolutely free! Until 10/1/88 only!

Here they are ... 27 fact-filled 2000-word Special Reports by Dr. Jeffrey Lant. Packed with information you read easily, put to work fast. Sent first-class the day you order ... Just four bucks each. $10 for any group of three!!!

#7
HOW TO USE WORKSHOPS AND OTHER TALK PROGRAMS TO GET CLIENTS. In honor of the publication of the new Second Edition of his well-known book MONEY TALKS: THE COMPLETE GUIDE TO CREATING A PROFITABLE WORKSHOP OR SEMINAR IN ANY FIELD, Jeffrey tells you how to use lectures and talk programs to get clients. $4

#8
THINKING ON YOUR FEET, ANSWERING QUESTIONS WELL WHETHER YOU KNOW THE ANSWER — OR NOT. People who can't deal effectively with questions present a poor self-image and can harm a company. Here Jeffrey interviews Marian Woodall, author of a new book on the subject, about how people can master the crucial "thinking on your feet" strategies. $4

#9
WHY YOU NEED SPECIAL REPORTS: HOW TO WRITE THEM, USE THEM TO GET PEOPLE TO BUY WHAT YOU'RE SELLING NOW, TO PUBLICIZE YOUR BUSINESS, AND MAKE MONEY! The secret to successful marketing is making people take action NOW to get what you're selling. Jeffrey shows you how to create inexpensive but powerful Special Reports and how to turn them into compelling marketing tools that get your prospects to respond **NOW**, and that you can also sell profitably. $4

#10
HOW TO SAVE THOUSANDS ON YOUR MORTGAGE: THE SECRET YOUR BANKER WON'T SHARE — BUT YOU MUST KNOW AND USE! Jeffrey tells you how paying back even small amounts on your mortgage loan offers you the possibility of saving literally tens of thousands of dollars — dollars you can put to better use in other ways. Mind boggling information every home owner should know and use. $4

#11
YOUR GRAND OPENING: HOW TO START YOUR MARKETING DOCUMENTS SO PEOPLE BUY WHAT YOU'RE SELLING. If your marketing documents don't draw people in immediately, you — and your next sale — are lost. Jeffrey tells you precisely what to do to begin documents so your prospects read what you have to say — and buy what you have to sell $4

#12
COPY FLAWS THAT DOOM YOUR EXPENSIVE MARKETING DOCUMENTS TO LINE BIRDCAGES IN SAINT LOUIS. Jeffrey tells you just what you need to know to write marketing copy that gets people to buy. Key rules of profit-making copy. $4

Check out your local bookstore to see books by Jeffrey Lant and Debra Ashton ... but remember, you only get the SPECIAL DEALS for them here.

#13
COMPUTER-ASSISTED MARKETING: HOW TO INCREASE YOUR PRODUCTIVITY AND MAKE EVERY PROSPECT AND CUSTOMER FEEL YOU'RE DELIVERING *EXACTLY* WHAT HE WANTS. People have computers but aren't using them effectively. Now learn to turn the computer into your best marketing tool. You'll read things here you've never seen before and increase your marketing productivity astonishingly. $4

#14
MONEY MAKING MAIL, OR HOW TO AVOID THE TEN BIGGEST MAIL ORDER MISTAKES. Every day I get deluged with mail order offers that make me weep for the trees that have died. What rubbish! There are rules to succeed in mail order. Here's what you should avoid — and what you should do. $4

#15
HOW TO CREATE AND USE OFFERS YOUR PROSPECTS FIND IRRESISTIBLE. The trick to marketing is to create and sell offers — not products and services. Here's what you need to know about offers, how to create them and use them so that your prospects will buy. (Example? Three of these reports for just $10). $4

#16
KNOWING WHAT TO DO WHEN PEOPLE OWE YOU MONEY, OR HOW TO GET PAYMENT IN FULL. Don't give way to the rage and frustration of being owed money by deadbeats. Get what you're owed. Here's what you need to do in practical detail. $4

#17
HOW TO USE THE YELLOW PAGES TO GET THE GREEN STUFF. If you're in the yellow pages now — and want to learn how to increase the return on your investment — or want to avoid the mistakes of yellow pages advertising before you make them, use the guidelines in this Special Report. $4

#18
HOW AUTHORS AND THEIR PUBLISHERS MUST WORK TOGETHER TO SELL MORE BOOKS. Here are precise steps for how to construct a profitable author-publisher partnership, what each must do to make money from books. $4

#19
YOUR IRA: WHY YOU *STILL* NEED IT, WHAT YOU NEED TO KNOW ABOUT INVESTING IT. If you've lost interest in the IRA, think again. Tax-free compounding of earning's no joke, and millions can still take their contribution off their taxes. Here's the low-down. $4

#20
TELESMARTS: EFFECTIVELY USING TELEMARKETING TO SELL YOUR PRODUCTS AND SERVICES. Most people are hideously ill-equipped to use the phone to sell anything. Here's the basics (and some advanced tips, too) on how you can turn the phone into a profitable business tool. Have I reached out and touched you? $4

#21
HOW TO OVERCOME SALES OBJECTIONS, INCLUDING THE BIGGEST ONE OF ALL: "YOUR PRICE IS TOO HIGH!" If you're in sales (and if you're reading this, you are), you've got to learn how to deal with objections. Here's what you need to know so that you can. But if you say "The price is too high" about this, I'll scream. $4

#22
HOW TO STOP BEING THE LOWLY ORDER-TAKER, BECOME THE CONSUMMATE MARKETER, AND GET MORE SALES FROM NEW BUYERS. The dumb marketer simply sells a prospect what that prospect wants to buy. The expert marketer learns the prospect's problem and persuades him to take an upgraded solution. Here's how to do that. $4

#23
TESTIMONIALS FOR YOUR PRODUCT OR SERVICE: WHY YOU NEED THEM, HOW TO GET THEM, HOW TO USE THEM. If you aren't using testimonials now, you are missing a prime marketing device. If you are, make sure you're doing it right! $4

#24
MAXIMIZING MEMORY POWER: NEVER FORGET GOOD OL' WHAT'S HIS NAME! Gives you specific guidelines to improve your memory. Don't miss out on opportunities because you forget crucial information. $4

#25
UNDERSTANDING AND PROFITING FROM THE RULE OF SEVEN: CONNECTING WITH YOUR BUYERS AND CONNECTING WITH THEM AGAIN UNTIL THEY BUY WHAT YOU'RE SELLING. Most marketing gambits don't work. In part this is because you don't hit your prospects sufficiently often to interest them in what you're selling. Now learn how you can. The Rule of Seven is the prime rule of marketing. $4

#26
MARKETING YOUR BOOK BEFORE IT'S PUBLISHED. Stupid authors and publishers wait to begin marketing and making money from their books until they are physically available. Don't you be one of them. Follow the detailed guidelines in this report and make money long before your book is even printed. $4

#27
SCANDALOUS SCHEMES, SCAMS, AND SKULDUGGERY: TIPS FROM THE COUNCIL OF BETTER BUSINESS BUREAUS ON HOW TO PROTECT YOUR BUSINESS. Tells you how to protect yourself from a whole series of scams, including credit card fraud, external and internal crimes. $4

#28
WHAT TO DO WHEN YOUR PROSPECT SAYS NO. We all get turned down. Now what? Tears? Rage? No! Use Jeffrey's step-by-step guidelines to get the sale after all — or do what it takes to get the next one! $4

Interested in making every marketing document you use get more people to buy what you're selling? You should be using Jeffrey's well-known copywriting talents. Ask for details!

The U.S. Small Business Administration only recommends one book to new and aspiring consultants. It's THE CONSULTANT'S KIT. Over 25,000 sold. Get one!

#29
ESSENTIALS OF MONEY MAKING MARKETING. Successful marketing is the key to business success. Now learn precisely what you have to do to improve your marketing. Follow these steps; sell more. $4

#30
SMARTER BARTER: (OCCASIONALLY) DOING QUITE WELL WITHOUT CASH. Jeffrey tells you how to barter your brains, products and services for what you want. $4

#31
WHY YOU NEED A BUSINESS PLAN, WHY YOU RESIST CREATING ONE. Makes a clear case for why you must have a business plan to succeed, how to overcome your resistance to creating one, and what should go in it. A must, particularly for new and struggling entrepreneurs. $4

#32
NUTS AND JOLTS OF ENTRY-LEVEL NON-CREDIT WORKSHOPS. Most people doing most talk programs don't make any money. This report tells you why and shows you what to do about it. If you really want to make money giving talk programs, get these suggestions and follow them! $4

#33
COSTLY MISTAKES (PARTICULARLY NONFICTION) PUBLISHERS MAKE AND HOW TO AVOID THEM. Most publishers are reasonably good at printing books. Most are lousy at selling them. Jeffrey deals with the mistakes nonfiction publishers make and shows you how to avoid them and make money from your book. Perfect for authors and publishers! $4

#34
Three Report Special. Get any **THREE** *of these Special Reports for just $10. Note: if you want this special price you must order in multiples of* **THREE**. *Three Special Reports cost $10. Six cost $20. If you order other amounts you pay full price!!!*

Profit From Jeffrey Lant's Remorselessly Thorough Get-Ahead Series.

MONEY TALKS is part of Jeffrey's five-volume Get Ahead Series. If you get all five books, you get a very special discount price... The other books in this series include:

#36
THE CONSULTANT'S KIT: ESTABLISHING AND OPERATING YOUR SUCCESSFUL CONSULTING BUSINESS. The one book specifically recommended by the U.S. Small Business Administration to new and aspiring consultants in *any* field tells you exactly what you need to know to make a success of your new consulting business. If you're thinking about consulting or have been in business under a year, this is the resource you need. It's the only resource on consulting recommended by *What Color Is Your Parachute?* (the best-selling career guide of all time) because it provides you with exactly what you need to launch a profitable consulting business. 203 pages $34

#37
THE UNABASHED SELF-PROMOTER'S GUIDE: WHAT EVERY MAN, WOMAN, CHILD AND ORGANIZATION IN AMERICA NEEDS TO KNOW ABOUT GETTING AHEAD BY EXPLOITING THE MEDIA. A recent review said this may be "the most important single book on promotion ever written." We agree! Stop paying money for paid ads. Find out how to get as much free publicity as you can, wherever you need it. This book is exhaustive. You'll use it for the rest of your business career whatever you're selling: product, service, organization or idea. Step-by-step guidelines for getting you and what you're promoting continuing media attention. The July, 1987 issue of *The Levison Letter* called this "The best business book ever written." If you're really interested in getting free media time and space, we think you'll agree. 366 pages. $34

#37
TRICKS OF THE TRADE: THE COMPLETE GUIDE TO SUCCEEDING IN THE ADVICE BUSINESS. Specifically designed for people who *really* want to squeeze the last drop of profit from their problem-solving information. Here's where you get complete details on the Mobile-Mini Conglomerate: 10 steps that you'll use to get the utmost benefit from your problem-solving information. Tells you how to get clients, how to work with clients, how to get the results you want, how to build long-term relationships, even how to work with Flatworms, people who say they want results, but really want to obstruct. It's all here. Herman Holtz, himself a master of the consulting genre, said this may be the most important book ever written on consulting. 315 pages $34

#38
MONEY MAKING MARKETING: FINDING THE PEOPLE WHO NEED WHAT YOU'RE SELLING AND MAKING SURE THEY BUY IT. With these 285 technique-stuffed pages, you can succeed in selling more of your products and services. Because you'll know how to:

- do marketing research — even when you hate it;
- use the Rule of Seven to create marketing plans that'll connect you to your prospects the right number of times so they'll buy what you're selling;
- write marketing documents that get people to read — and to buy. You'll know what you need to know about creating offers that get prospects to buy, about getting and using testimonials, about how to use prospect pain to get them to take action.
- get free publicity from every kind of media source. Stop paying for advertising. Get better promotional coverage for free!
- master small space ads and classifieds so that your ads will pull more responses;
- use the telephone profitably. You'll know who to call, when to call, how to call — all you need to know to profit from the phone.
- make money with mail. Learn how to write profit-making direct response copy, how to select responsive lists, and how to transform a prospect into a customer and a customer into a repeat buyer. Get what you need to know to create a profitable catalog.

And much, much more. **MONEY MAKING MARKETING**, 285 pages. $34

Quit fooling around with your marketing. Everything you need is right here.

Over 1,500,000 people monthly now rely on Jeffrey's Sure-Fire Business Success articles to help their businesses make money!

#39
SPECIAL FIVE-BOOK OFFER. Now get all five books in Jeffrey's Get-Ahead Series, including **MONEY MAKING MARKETING, THE CONSULTANT'S KIT, THE UNABASHED SELF-PROMOTER'S GUIDE, MONEY TALKS** and **TRICKS OF THE TRADE** for just $145. Save $25

#40
Missed Jeffrey's recent four-hour national video teleconference on "Money Making Marketing: Finding The People Who Need What You're Selling And Making Sure They Buy It"? Now get the complete 31-page transcript with Jeffrey's program notes. Learn what it really takes to market any product or service. Complete step-by-step instructions. Just $12.

If you want to break into the lucrative national video conference market, you won't want to miss this unprecedented opportunity to get a copy of this script — and learn how to sell it both to people attending the program, and others interested in the subject.

#41
Get Jeffrey's detailed, written critique of your marketing documents. Find out if you are doing all you can to get your prospects to respond **NOW. SEND ANY TWO** of the marketing documents you're now using and just $35. Stop wasting your money on unproductive marketing. Get help **NOW!**

Need Money For Your Nonprofit Organization? Here's Where You Start To Get It . . .

#42
DEVELOPMENT TODAY: A FUND RAISING GUIDE FOR NONPROFIT ORGANIZATIONS. This is your one essential resource for raising capital, project, and operating funds. Complete details on successful fund-raising planning, who to involve and what they do, how to get best results from your Board, how to target the right corporations and foundations, how to raise money in your community, how to profitably use direct mail — even what to do when your proposal gets turned down. Comes complete with a Samples Section of ready-to-use documents, just like all Jeffrey's books. 276 pages. $28.95

#43
THE COMPLETE GUIDE TO PLANNED GIVING: EVERYTHING YOU NEED TO KNOW TO COMPETE SUCCESSFULLY FOR MAJOR GIFTS. This new book by Debra Ashton is the most complete resource ever produced on planned giving. Planned giving is the fastest-growing area of fund raising. Here's what you need to know to profit from it. Based on the Tax Reform Act of 1986, **THE COMPLETE GUIDE TO PLANNED GIVING** contains step-by-step techniques so you can profit from every aspect of the subject. We have never seen a book with this much information on planned giving, so lucid and easy to use. That's why Attorney Lynda Moerschbaecher, Editor of *Charitable Gift Planning News* says, "I give this superb book my unqualified recommendation." 407 pages. $38.50

Write down these numbers on page 308 and complete details will be sent.

#44
Jeffrey can help you improve every marketing document you're using or want to create. Let him improve your cover letters, brochures, flyers, ads, annual reports — everything you're using to get buyers. Jeffrey is fast and inexpensive. Get the details!

#45
Get Lifetime Rights To Jeffrey's Very Lucrative Special Reports. Looking for new best-selling products, but don't have the time to create them? Now get Lifetime Rights to his Special Reports. Make thousands of dollars selling some of America's most well-known information products.

#46
Make money as a JLA book dealer. Make big money by selling Jeffrey's books. You get at least 50% off and can get 60% off the retail price if you buy by the case. We'll supply the sales copy.

#47
Sponsor a workshop or talk with Jeffrey. Jeffrey is one of America's top-rated platform speakers — informative, inspirational, intelligent. If you're an organization, use his talents to make your meetings better; if you're a promoter work with him to produce a profitable program. Get the low-down!

#48
Are you an aspiring author with a book or idea that could fit into this catalog? Jeffrey is looking for new books to publish. But they have to be **REALLY GOOD.** Ask for details. Jeffrey is glad to consider books originally published by others that are now out of print.

#49
Have your product featured in this catalog, Jeffrey's Sure-Fire-Business Success Column (now reaching over 1,500,000 people monthly) and/or a Special Report. You *can* be a part of this information empire.

#50
Distribute this catalog. Got a group that needs this information? Giving a program and want to include this catalog? You can. Just tell Jeffrey how many you need, why you need them, and where to send them. We're glad to be of service.

#51
Great business development and motivational tapes. We've got a new mini-catalog of 40 of the best business and motivational tapes now available. If you'd like a copy, request it.

#52 & #53
Nonprofit organizations. We can help you raise money through (#52) direct mail and with corporation and foundation fund raising and (#53) by getting major gifts through planned giving. Ask us.

Don't spend another dime on paid advertising until you find out how much FREE publicity you can get for what you're selling. Use THE UNABASHED SELF-PROMOTER'S GUIDE — and Jeffrey's brand-new audio program — to find out!

Developing And Protecting Ideas, Products And Your Creative Work

#54
THAT'S A GREAT IDEA: THE NEW PRODUCT HANDBOOK. This book's subtitle says it all: "How to get, evaluate, protect, develop and sell new product ideas." You learn precisely what you need to know about what to do with your brilliant ideas. This guide is thoughtful, thorough, insightful, and detailed. $13.45

#55
HOW TO ZIG IN A ZAGGING WORLD: UNLEASHING YOUR HIDDEN CREATIVITY. We all need to become more creative. That's why I'm recommending this new book by John Keil to you. This is a fun book about a serious subject. Use it to come up with great ideas and know what to do with them when you've got them. You'll find out how to handle criticism, deadlines, pressure and stress. How to use brainstorming and sell your ideas to people who must approve them. In short, you'll learn a little more about being creative. $16.95

#56
PATENT IT YOURSELF. This is the most breathtakingly thorough book ever written on how to patent your baby. It's written by an author (Patent Attorney David Pressman) who really understands precisely what you've got to do. Subtitled "A Complete Legal Guide For Inventors", you should have this volume on hand if you're even thinking of developing a new product. Cheap at $28.45

#57

Barely a day goes by that someone doesn't call to ask how to use copyright. Don't call me anymore! Now you can get exactly what you need in David Weinstein's *exhaustive* and straightforward **HOW TO PROTECT YOUR CREATIVE WORK: ALL YOU NEED TO KNOW ABOUT COPYRIGHT.** 343 pages tell you precisely what you need to know about what can be protected, what cannot, your rights as a copyright holder, fair use, limitations on your rights, copyright registration, and much, much more. If you're bright enough to create something needing copyright, don't be dumb enough not to use this resource! $21.45

Getting Organized

#58

Here it is, the book you've been waiting for to organize your personal and business lives. **ORGANIZE YOURSELF!** is replete with shrewd observations and guidelines on bringing order to desks, calendars, bookshelves, taxes, travel, investments, medical payments, personal inventory control, job searches, budgeting, filing systems and more. If you're the kind of person who will lose this catalog within moments of getting it, do yourself a favor. Send $11.45 now.

Getting Your Own Way And Negotiating Successfully

#59

THE ART OF GETTING YOUR OWN SWEET WAY. Expert Philip Crosby is now out with a new revised 2nd edition of this classic book on getting people to do what you want them to do. I don't care whether you're mom negotiating at dinner or an entrepreneur trying to get an important contract, you've got to figure out how to work with and through other people. That's where Crosby comes in. He tells you how to deal with problem situations ... so you get what you want. 230 pages. $25.50

#60

I'm including this entry for all my friends who cave in when negotiating — and call me later, regretting their spinelessness. With **NEGOTIATE THE DEAL YOU WANT: TALKING YOUR WAY TO SUCCESS IN BUSINESS, COMMUNITY AFFAIRS AND PERSONAL ENCOUNTERS,** you get the step-by-step guidelines you need to 200 negotiating situations. Winning at life means succeeding in negotiation. Whether you're a push-over or just want to become the complete master of persuasive skills, get this book. $13.45

Creating An Effective Business Plan And Getting Start-Up Money

#61

You know you need a *written* business plan, and you know you don't have one. That's why you need **THE BUSINESS PLANNING GUIDE.** It's not just a book. It's your basic business tool and roadmap. Packed with forms, checklists and immediately usable examples, this will give you exactly what you need: a specific, written business plan. In about 130 pages, you'll get your MBA in small business management. Over 150,000 businesses already have. Now it's your turn. $20.45

#62

START-UP MONEY: HOW TO CREATE A BUSINESS PLAN & LOAN PACKAGE TO FINANCE YOUR SMALL BUSINESS. So many people have asked me about how to get start-up money from banks that I went looking for a resource that *really* tells you. This is it. If you need to get a loan for your business, this is precisely what you need to get it. $16.45

Essential Marketing Books
(In addition to MONEY MAKING MARKETING, of course!)

Marketing books are a dime a dozen. Most are severely disappointing. These, I think, are worth paying close attention to not only because of the specific techniques they provide but also because of the mind-set towards successful marketing they'll help you create.

If you didn't request this catalog, you are not on our mailing list. We rented your name! Even if you're not buying anything today, fill out the coupon on page 307 to keep receiving this unique source of profit-making information.

Got a tape recorder? Want to get ahead? Use Jeffrey's new audio cassettes to turn your scrap time into profit.

#63
STREETFIGHTING: LOW-COST ADVERTISING/PROMOTION STRATEGIES FOR YOUR SMALL BUSINESS is an ingenious book. It needs to be read and thought about. Jeff Slutsky understands that small businesses need a different approach to marketing than big businesses and that this approach starts in the streetfighting mentality. Get it. $28.45

#64
The same is true for Conrad Levinson's book **GUERRILLA MARKETING: SECRETS FOR MAKING BIG PROFITS FROM YOUR SMALL BUSINESS**. It's got complete step-by-step guidelines on what to do and how to do it to get the biggest bang for the littlest buck. I know you hate marketing, but with these two books and **MONEY MAKING MARKETING**, you'll be a lot better off than you are now. $11.45

#65
Except for marketing consultants, I've never met anyone who actually *liked* market research. Yet if your business is to be a success, you have to do it. Now you can learn precisely what you need to do in Breen and Blankenship's **DO IT YOURSELF MARKETING RESEARCH**. It comes complete with all the questionnaires and forms you need. Businesses regularly fail because of a lack of knowledge of their markets. Don't let this happen to you! $40.45

#66
If you're going to succeed in business, you are going to have to master the ins and outs of creating effective brochures, catalogs, fliers, and pamphlets. Now you can with Robert Bly's superb book **CREATE THE PERFECT SALES PIECE**. It tells you precisely what to do to create sales marketing materials which others will read and use. $17.45

#67
If you can learn to write short, crisp, interesting, upbeat, benefit-rich, active copy, anything you write will be better. This is the kind of copy Robert Bly is the master of writing. Now in **THE COPYWRITER'S HANDBOOK: A STEP-BY-STEP GUIDE TO WRITING COPY THAT SELLS**, you'll get the lowdown on precisely what you need to do to write persuasive, downright compelling copy. You know, the kind of copy you're not writing (but are reading) now. $14.45

Setting Up A Partnership Or A Subchapter "S" Corporation

#68
THE PARTNERSHIP BOOK: HOW TO WRITE YOUR OWN SMALL BUSINESS PARTNERSHIP AGREEMENT. After a very long search, I'm quite prepared to dub this the best book now available on putting together a mutually-satisfying partnership agreement. A partnership is a business marriage and is subject to terrible consequences if it doesn't go right. With this book in hand, you'll minimize the chances for partnership failure. Exhaustively detailed. $21.45

#69
STARTING YOUR SUBCHAPTER "S" CORPORATION: HOW TO BUILD A BUSINESS THE RIGHT WAY. My friend Arnold Goldstein is one of America's most prolific — and sensible — business writers. Now he's right where he ought to be, right when he should be — telling you how to profit from the new tax laws when you start your business as a Subchapter "S" Corporation, as you surely will. Don't even think of incorporating without reading this detailed 182 page guide. $17.95

Selling On The Telephone, Overcoming Call Reluctance

#70
James Porterfield's **SELLING ON THE PHONE: A SELF-TEACHING GUIDE** is concise, detailed, and intelligent. Use it to find how a telemarketing sale works, how to project product knowledge over the phone, conceive your basic sales-call strategy, prospect, grab attention, analyze the needs of your prospects, answer objections, ask for the order, and close. Porterfield will help you create a positive mental attitude for phone work, use words that sell, listen effectively, and use your voice the right way. $17.45. Don't forget you can call in your order (617) 547-6372.

> *"Thanks for writing the best business help books I've read."*
>
> Attorney I. B. Mackey, Jr., San Antonio, TX

#71

Millions of people suffer from call reluctance. I got a vivid picture of just how bad this problem was when I ran an article about it and about this book's excellent suggestions on how to overcome it. My telephone rang for days. If you suffer from call reluctance and sometimes just cannot bring yourself to make that next important sales call, suffer no more. Get **THE PSYCHOLOGY OF CALL RELUCTANCE: HOW TO OVERCOME THE FEAR OF SELF-PROMOTION**. $22.45

Getting Your Message To Millions On The Radio, Profitably Advertising

#72

Today's advances in telecommunications make it possible for you to reach buyers across America without ever leaving your home or office. Radio stations call you. All you have to do is be good on the air to benefit from the exposure. (Need I say you will be, if you use my book **THE UNABASHED SELF-PROMOTER'S GUIDE**?) Now reserve a place in Bill Harrison's **RADIO INTERVIEW REPORT** which goes out monthly to thousands of radio program directors. I use this service myself with superb results. The cost is a most-reasonable $85 for a single insertion. Write this number and complete details will be sent or send $85 now and get the process under way quicker!

> "Following advice given in THE UNABASHED SELF-PROMOTER'S GUIDE, I succeeded in getting the producer of Cleveland's 'Morning Exchange' to make me a regular guest on their program *at their expense*."
>
> Howard Berg
> Brooklyn, NY

#73

Jane Maas is the brains behind the "I Love New York" advertising campaign, surely one of the most successful ever conceived. You can profit from what she knows by reading her short, intelligent book **HOW TO ADVERTISE: A PROFESSIONAL GUIDE FOR THE ADVERTISER. WHAT WORKS, WHAT DOESN'T AND WHY.** Spend $14.45 here and the next ads you place will be more profitable.

#74

ADVERTISING IN THE YELLOW PAGES: HOW TO BOOST PROFITS AND AVOID PITFALLS. If you're in the yellow pages now or even thinking of advertising there, get this new book by W.F. Wagner. It's got the exact information you need to cut your cost, deal with sales reps, get the right position, and write the right copy. With Wagner, if you're in the yellow (pages), you'll get the green. $16.45

Overcoming Every Conceivable Sales Objection You'll Ever Hear

#75

Face it. Your prospects are going to resist you and your offer. So you've got to learn how to overcome their objections. That's where **CLOSING THE SALE: SUCCESSFUL STRATEGIES THAT OVERCOME BUYER RESISTANCE** comes in. In precise no-nonsense fashion it offers every conceivable objection you'll hear — and tells you precisely what to do about them. Hesitating to take action now? "I'm sure the more you think about it, the more you will realize the value of my offer. Why not act now?" $8.95

> If you're a consultant who didn't earn at least $1,000 today you need **TRICKS OF THE TRADE**. Stop fooling around with your practice. Find out what you really need to do to make money — and help more people!

Collection Techniques For The Small Business

#76

You've got uncollected and uncollectible invoices sitting in your drawer right now. If you used the techniques in **PAYMENT IN FULL: A GUIDE TO SUCCESSFUL BILL COLLECTING**, some of them wouldn't be there. If you'd use it now, you can still collect on some of them. $27.95 is also a pretty fair price to pay to cut the anger you feel about the deadbeats who're ripping you off.

Key Business Problems And How To Solve Them

— The business law you need to know.

#77

THE LAW (IN PLAIN ENGLISH) FOR SMALL BUSINESSES. This easy-to-read, sensible book covers 23 crucial areas in which you need legal knowledge, including contracts, consignment, multi-level marketing, licensing, warranties, and zoning. All small business owners need basic legal information; here's where you find it. $13.45

— Cutting your business insurance costs.

#78
101 WAYS TO CUT YOUR BUSINESS INSURANCE COSTS WITHOUT SACRIFICING PROTECTION. Specialists McIntyre and Gibson provide what you need to know about how you can reduce your cost for property, liability and workers compensation insurance. Use this as your basic reference on *all* business insurance and as your handy desk-top advisor on saving money on insurance premiums. $23.45

— How to get more done in less time.

#79
WORKING SMART: HOW TO ACCOMPLISH MORE IN HALF THE TIME. Michael LeBoeuf knows what you've got to know: that time is your most important resource and until you make it work for you, you can't get everything else you want. Here you get many tips including 10 ways to make the telephone work for you; 14 things you can do to make meetings useful; 6 ways to strengthen your ability to concentrate and complete tasks; 20 suggestions for effective delegation . . . and much more. 232 pages. $11.95

— How to make things happen.

#80
RUNNING THINGS: THE ART OF MAKING THINGS HAPPEN. Are you the kind of person who makes things happen — or wonders what happened? If you want to know how to set objectives and achieve success (*whatever organization you're in*), get this superb 253 page book (*entertaining, too!*) by well-known master Philip Crosby. I was thinking the other day how many people talk about success and achievement and how few accomplish anything. Be one who does! Get this resource — and use it! $22.95

Giving Effective Speeches, Being Able To Answer Every Question Every Time

#81
Another poll just rated fear of public speaking as Americans' top anxiety. Now do something about it by using **HOW TO WRITE AND GIVE A SPEECH.** In this compelling little book, authority Joan Detz provides you with complete step-by-step guidelines on how to make effective speeches without falling apart. There are many other books on this subject, but I haven't seen one yet that compresses so much valuable information into so little space. $12.00

#82
THINKING ON YOUR FEET: ANSWERING QUESTIONS WELL WHETHER YOU KNOW THE ANSWER, OR NOT. This is exactly what you need if you know someone who can't 'think on their feet', can't answer questions appropriately, and is always embarrassing himself and your company. Or perhaps that's you. Either way, you need Marian Woodall's excellent little 100-page book. Stay poised and in control. And answer the question — the way you want it answered. Just $12.95.

Remember, if you order any book on page 307, you get one of my Special Reports FREE!

When Working For Or With Jerks

#83
KEEPING YOUR COOL UNDER FIRE. Theodora Wells has written the book for all of us who want to avoid a murder rap because we've bumped off an offensive flatworm, or other s.o.b. She shows you how to put your feelings to work for you, find out what's really happening in a situation, define the results that will gain something for you with others, and give you options for gaining the results you want. Don't burn any more. Master the art of non-defensive communication. $32.95

When You Want To Buy — Or Sell — A Business

#84
BUYING AND SELLING A BUSINESS: A STEP BY STEP GUIDE. Robert Klueger's just-published book gives you what you need to know about choosing the right business for you, find out why the seller's selling, get crucial information about the business' finances, negotiate the sale, close the deal — and know how to sell, when you want to. $17.95

Publishing Effective Newsletters

#85
Howard Penn Hudson is America's newsletter guru. If there's something to be known about newsletters, he knows it. That's why you should use **PUBLISHING NEWSLETTERS: A COMPLETE GUIDE TO MARKETS, EDITORIAL CONTENT, DESIGN, PRINTING, SUBSCRIPTIONS, AND MANAGEMENT.** Take my word for it: this is the best book on newsletters ever written. $23.45

On Writing Your Book, Or Booklet, And Profitably Self-Publishing Them

#86
Dan Poynter knows that *everyone* wants to write a book. Few people know how. That's why you need **IS THERE A BOOK INSIDE YOU?** It provides you with just the information you need to make writing your book easier. It also tells you how to find someone to help you, if you decide you need to collaborate. $13.45

#87
What Dan Poynter has done for books, Jay Barnes does for booklets. A good way of getting started in the publishing business is by writing and selling a booklet. This is *precisely* what Jay tells you how to do in **WRITING FOR FUN AND MONEY.** $18.50

If you are going to succeed in self-publishing, get the following books. Don't cavil. Just do it. They are the best in the nation and a trifling investment if you really want to succeed:

#88
John Kremer has written three of these books, including **BOOK MARKETING MADE EASIER.** This is a complete, step-by-step guide to everything you need to do in marketing your book. It's written in checklist format and comes complete with dates of when to do the task and a list of crucial marketing sources and their addresses. $18.45

#89
Then use Kremer's **101 WAYS FOR MARKETING YOUR BOOKS: FOR PUBLISHERS AND AUTHORS.** This is the book that separates the wannabees from people who are serious about making money with books. Kremer, the arch-realist of book marketing, tells you precisely what you've got to do and precisely how to do it to make money with your books. $18.45

#90
Go on to Kremer's **BOOK MARKETING OPPORTUNITIES: A DIRECTORY.** The essence of book marketing is two things: persistence and knowing the available marketing outlets. This amazing resource is packed with over 3000 book marketing outlets of every kind. If you don't get this resource, don't presume to think you're a book marketer. $28.50

#91
Then use Poynter's **SELF-PUBLISHING MANUAL.** If you're going to self-publish, you are going to have to get this book. It's that simple. It is stuffed with step-by-step details every self-publisher must master. I read it yearly. One tip from this book recently made me several thousand dollars. Oh, yes, I'm a believer! $18.45

#92
If you want your book to be used by schools (where really big money can be made with a single title), then get Simone Bibeau's **CASH IN ON TODAY'S EDUCATIONAL MARKET.** Simone has struck classroom gold several times, and tells you precisely how to do so, too. $18.45.

Designing Your Logo

#93
I get calls about this subject constantly. Here's what I tell them all: get **DESIGN YOUR OWN LOGO: A STEP-BY-STEP GUIDE FOR BUSINESSES, ORGANIZATIONS, AND INDIVIDUALS.** You know you need a logo. You know you want to cut your designer fees. So, I know you need this handy little guide. $13.45

Every Business Letter You Ever Need

#94
Instead of struggling to compose business letters, why not keep a pattern book near at hand? It'll save you a lot of time. One of the most complete and sensible now available is **HANDBOOK OF BUSINESS LETTERS.** If it's a business problem and can be dealt with in a letter, that letter is probably here. Save yourself a lot of time and creative juice. Use this. $47.45

Finding Out About Your Competitors

#95
Leonard Fuld is the reigning star of competitor intelligence. By that I mean how to gather information *legally* about your competitors. His book **COMPETITOR INTELLIGENCE** has got the basics as well as clever tricks of the trade for advanced competitor sleuths. Because you cannot afford James Bond, use Fuld. $29.45

"Jeffrey, thank you for the fantastic job you did for us in Charlotte. The response to your presentation at the Carolinas Chapter of the International Association for Financial Planning has been excellent!" — Daniel Taylor, President

> "Without your books, I would still be working away at some boring 9-5 job just waiting for a reorganization, a new boss who knows less than me, or job assignments fit for a fifth grader... Now I am working to death and getting paid a bunch and loving it. Thanks to you."
> — Lon Hosford
> Milford, NJ

Finding Facts And People Fast

#96
All of us are dependent on information, knowing where to find it and where to find it fast. That's why you need **FINDING FACTS FAST**, the best little book ever written on quick, economical information gathering. $7.45

#97
If you've lost touch with a loved one or friend or just want to track down the animal who's skipped town on your bill, use Eugene Ferraro's book **YOU CAN FIND ANYONE: A COMPLETE GUIDE ON HOW TO LOCATE MISSING PERSONS.** $15.45

Setting Fees

#98
One of the most perplexing problems business people have is how much to charge for their services. Wonder no more. Kate Kelly tells you **HOW TO SET YOUR FEES AND GET THEM.** Her guidebook is filled with information and examples of how to charge the right rates for your services. $18.50

Keeping Your Business Records Straight, Reducing Your Taxes To The Legal Minimum

#99
The best book ever written on keeping your small business records in order is **SMALL TIME OPERATOR** by Bernard Kamaroff. If you haven't gotten it yet, get it now. It provides everything you need to know about bookkeeping and accounting. $14

#100
If reducing taxes doesn't interest you, you're crazy. If it does, get David Kennedy's well-known annual **PERFECTLY LEGAL.** It's that simple. He's got 475 foolproof methods for paying less tax. Get it. $23.95

Making Money From Mail Order

#101
SELL IT BY MAIL: MAKING YOUR PRODUCT THE ONE THEY BUY. If you're selling a product by mail, you'd better get James Lumley's intelligent, step-by-step guide to direct marketing techniques. What's great about this book is that it's studded with Key Points and Caution Notes, the things you've got to know and keep in mind to sell your products by mail. $23.95

#102
Then get Julian Simon's superb book **HOW TO START AND OPERATE A MAIL-ORDER BUSINESS.** This is frankly the best book ever written on mail order, and wherever you are — beginner or guru — you are going to profit from it. It's exhaustively detailed. $41 New Edition!

> *If you're ordering materials produced by multiple publishers, they will come in multiple packages. So don't call if you only get a partial shipment. The rest is on its way...*

#103
THE DIRECT MARKETER'S LEGAL ADVISOR. If you're selling through the mail — or expect to — you're part of a regulated industry and had better know the law. Robert Posch gives it to you in 242 fact-filled pages. Get details on the 30-day rule; on comparative pricing methods; on how to use key words like "free", "new", even "sale". Find out how to run a sweepstakes... or how to run a simulated check promotion without getting a million dollar fine. Much more. *All* crucial. $36.95

Successfully Working At Home

There's a lot of nonsense written about working at home. It can be very, very tough. Only a fraction of the homebased businesses in existence even *gross* over $15,000 a year. Part of this problem would be solved if homebased business people really mastered **MONEY MAKING MARKETING.** If they're not smart enough to do this, they deserve the paltry money they get. But you'll do better, if you...

#104
Master this essential resource by Barbara Brabec, one of the brightest and most thorough experts in the business. Get her book **HOME MADE MONEY.** It's simply stuffed with useful information. I read every page and have profited mightily from the lady's insight. $17.95

#105

Finally, use Tyler Hicks' book **HOW TO START YOUR OWN BUSINESS ON A SHOESTRING AND MAKE UP TO $500,000 A YEAR.** Ty Hicks is one smart cookie. In addition to a lot of sensible advice about what it takes to start and run a business, he includes a list of over 1,000 businesses you can run from your home. $12.45

Winning Your Small Claims Cases

#106

If you are running a business, you are going to be the plaintiff in a small claims action. So you'd better plan for it. That's why you need **EVERYBODY'S GUIDE TO SMALL CLAIMS COURT: HOW TO WIN YOUR CASE, COLLECT YOUR MONEY, AND SMILE ALL THE WAY HOME.** It's the best book ever written on what it takes to win your action and get your money. $14.45

Being a Successful International Consultant

#107

THE INTERNATIONAL CONSULTANT. So many people have asked me about the nitty-gritty of functioning as an international consultant that I'm delighted Peter Guttmann's book on the subject has just come out in an updated edition. Find out from this well-known authority how to pursue foreign prospects, write proposals, negotiate contracts, administer overseas work, handle liability, and much, much more. Don't leave home without it. $25.95

A Key — and Really Cheap — Information Source

#108

CONNECTIONS: HOW TO GET MORE, PAY LESS AND PHONE FREE. This clever 64-page booklet by David Dewan gives you over 700 toll-free numbers, name-brand discounts, emergency hotlines, and free offers. Ridiculously cheap at $4. Useful for any age. Remember: you get it **FREE** if you buy my new book **CASH COPY** and send me your business card (or letterhead) marked "Send Connections, please!" Anyone looking for a clever product to produce should take a look at how this one is assembled. $4

Timely Investment Advise

#109

Make Big Bucks — Pay Down Your Mortgage Early! Marc Eisenson shows you the best place to invest in these uncertain days is your home sweet home by paying down your mortgage early. His 40 page booklet **A BANKER'S SECRET** explains why and shows you how much you'll save by paying just a little bit each month. Truly staggering amounts! And when you get it here, Marc will create a unique Mortgage Reduction Schedule for you. You get everything for just $21.45!

#110

IRA INVESTING MADE EASY. If you're one of the millions of American workers who can still get both tax-deductibility and tax-deferral from IRA compounding, but are not doing so, I BEG YOU TO USE THIS BOOK. Unless you think the world will end before you do, you need this benefit. And if you're one of the workers who has lost the tax-deductible contribution, this book will convince you you still need the benefits of tax-deferred compounding. Just $11.45.

How To Stop Procrastinating

#110

If you've read **TRICKS OF THE TRADE,** you know how I feel about Flatworms, the people who always talk about wanting to get something done, and never do it. If you suffer from this problem, or any of the other debilitating aspects of procrastination, then get Burka and Yuen's **PROCRASTINATION: WHY YOU DO IT, WHAT TO DO ABOUT IT.** It offers detailed techniques on how to overcome your procrastination. If you can't, resign yourself to being a Flatworm. $12.45

"What happened to my order?" Your order can be delayed by a number of factors, including the fact you sent a check with a post office box as return address. Unless these checks are guaranteed with a MC or Visa, we hold them until they clear. The post office is not always reliable . . . shipping clerks take orders in sequence . . . books sometimes go out of stock and have to be reprinted. People make mistakes. Give me the benefit of the doubt. Inquire before you scream. I'll work out your problem. But I'll also remember how you treat me . . .

Don't go yet. There's more...

Over the years, I've noticed that dramatically fewer numbers of people order from page 307 than pages 294 or 295. But I'd like to change all that and make catalog history. So... if you order any of the items on this page... page 307 ONLY... you may select any one of my Special Reports (items 7 to 33) with my compliments. Call it market research. Or a clever offer. But DO take advantage of it. Just let me know which Special Report you'd like. Remember: just one!

#111
THE INVENTOR'S NOTEBOOK. For those of you who long to create something new, here's the book you need. It's a real inventor's workbook... complete with information on how to record your conception, preserve information about its building and testing, distinctive design information and then the key facts you need about legal protection, trademarks, marketing and financing. Don't start your next invention without this crucial workbook. When you've completed it, you'll have just what you need to get your baby off to a good start. $22.95

#112
MAKE YOUR OWN CONTRACT: TEAR-OUT AGREEMENTS FOR EVERYDAY USE. Attorney Stephen Elias has written all the contractual agreements you need. All you have to do is have the good sense to acquire — and use — them: for borrowing or lending money, buying or selling property, releases to settle legal disputes, hiring people to do repairs, deposits to hold personal property for later purchase, contracts with independent contractors and much more. $15.95

#113
BANKRUPTCY: DO IT YOURSELF. If you haven't followed my advice — or if I didn't get to you quick enough, you may need some help with Chapter 7 (that's personal) bankruptcy. Or you may have a friend who needs what Attorney Janice Kosel has to say about how bankruptcy works, if you should file for it now, how to fill out the necessary papers and use the forms, meet with your creditors and what you need to do then. Why, she even has advice on the emotional side of this very emotional issue. Spare yourself even more grief. Get this very intelligent hands-on guide which includes information on the particulars in all the states. Just $20.95

#114
PERSUASIVE WRITING: GETTING YOUR MESSAGE ACROSS IN BUSINESS. Yes, it's Herman Holtz — again. And again, he's as intelligent as ever. This time he shows you how to write business communications that get results. You're going to use up reams of paper during your business career. How about learning how to write proposals, reports, speeches, sales letters, house organs, newsletter, magazine articles — and lots of other crucial communications? SO GET WHAT YOU WANT FROM THEM. Don't just write. Write to persuade. And let Herman, America's most prolific business writer, show you how. 238 pages. $17.95

#115
GETTING NEW CLIENTS. My friend Jeffrey Davidson is a fountainhead of superior information on this crucial subject. Use his new book to develop a market niche, establish and reach objectives for the number of new clients you want; get appointments with prospects; prepare yourself with what they want to know; properly open the discussion — and close it... so you get the business. When you're selling a service, you've got to master the information in this intelligent book. 305 pages. $25.95

Your books and information will be sent to the name and address on the mailing label on page 308, unless you fill out the coupon below.

Send items to: Name _____

Company _____

Street Address _____

City/Town _____ State _____ Zip _____

Day Telephone (___) _____

IF YOU HAVEN'T SEEN THIS CATALOG BEFORE AND DIDN'T REQUEST IT, YOU ARE NOT ON THE MAILING LIST. EVEN IF YOU'RE NOT BUYING ANYTHING NOW BUT WANT TO KEEP GETTING THE CATALOG, CHECK 'MAILING LIST' HERE ☐, COMPLETE COUPON ABOVE (OR MAKE SURE I HAVE YOUR MAILING LABEL). I'LL MAKE SURE YOU KEEP GETTING IT!

Order Form   *Complete 30-Day Money-Back Guarantee!*

Photocopy or return this page to: Dr. Jeffrey Lant, Jeffrey Lant Associates
50 Follen St., #507, Cambridge, MA 02138

CLEARLY write down the number(s) of the items you are ordering. Some items in the catalog involve information being sent you. Write these numbers down here, too.

___, ___, ___, ___, ___, ___, ___, ___, ___, ___, ___, ___, ___, ___, ___, ___, ___, ___, ___, ___,

Note: If you are ordering my Special Reports (see pages 295-297), write down the number(s) of the Reports you want here. ___, ___, ___, ___, ___, ___, ___, ___, ___. (Remember, you get any three for $10. If you don't order in multiples of three, each Special Report is $4. No exceptions.

If you are ordering books and Special Reports by Dr. Jeffrey Lant, they are sent the day you order (unless you are using a post office box address that is not guaranteed by a MC/Visa). Other books are sent to you direct from their publishers by fourth class/book rate shipping. Allow four-six weeks. If you want them faster, add $3 per item for first class or UPS shipping. Remember: to ship UPS, I must have a street address!

If you want your items sent to Canada, add $1 for *each* item ordered and $1 to the total for our bank's fees, even if you pay in U.S. dollars! If you want shipment to any other country, you must pay by credit card. I'll charge your account surface or air shipping. Tell me how you want them shipped. Check ☐ surface ☐ air.

Total your order:$_____ x 5% sales tax for Massachusetts residents = $_____.

Remember, if your order totals at least $150 you can select *any one* of my three new 60-minute audio cassettes as my gift to you. Put the number of the tape you want here _____. If *your order totals over $200, you get all three audio cassettes with my compliments*. And if you are getting the new edition of **MONEY TALKS**, just published, you get *any one* of my 27 Special Reports FREE. Have you ordered something from page 307 (item numbers 111–115)? You get a FREE Special Report, too. Either way, write down the number of the Report here. (You get two, of course, if you're ordering both **MONEY TALKS** *and* an item from page 307) _____.

Unless you are a government agency, college, library or other official organization (in which case, include your Purchase Order # here _____) complete payment must accompany your order. I cannot invoice individuals! If paying by check, make it payable to Jeffrey Lant Associates, Inc. If you are using a post office box number for shipment, I require a MasterCard/VISA number and expiration date to guarantee your check, or else I wait for your check to clear. Sadly, several rip-off artists use post office boxes to defraud reputable merchants like me. Hence this extra step. Needless to say, if the check is good, I don't use the credit card!
If paying by credit card (or using a post office box for shipment):

✓ ☐ MasterCard ☐ Visa. #_____
Expiration date_____   Signature_____

For faster service, place your order by telephone twenty-four hours a day at (617) 547-6372. (Yes, I really do answer my own phone). Before calling make sure your credit card is handy. The order tape doesn't last forever!

Your books and information will be sent to the name and address on the mailing label below, unless you fill out the coupon on page 307.

Jeffrey Lant Associates

Bulk Rate
U.S. Postage
PAID

50 FOLLEN STREET, SUITE 507
CAMBRIDGE, MASSACHUSETTS 02138